Mathematical Theory of Entropy

GIAN-CARLO ROTA, *Editor*
ENCYCLOPEDIA OF MATHEMATICS AND ITS APPLICATIONS

Volume		Section
1	LUIS A. SANTALÓ **Integral Geometry and Geometric Probability,** 1976	Probability
2	GEORGE E. ANDREWS **The Theory of Partitions,** 1976	Number Theory
3	ROBERT J. McELIECE **The Theory of Information and Coding** A Mathematical Framework for Communication, 1977	Probability
4	WILLARD MILLER, Jr. **Symmetry and Separation of Variables,** 1977	Special Functions
5	DAVID RUELLE **Thermodynamic Formalism** The Mathematical Structures of Classical Equilibrium Statistical Mechanics, 1978	Statistical Mechanics
6	HENRYK MINC **Permanents,** 1978	Linear Algebra
7	FRED S. ROBERTS **Measurement Theory** with Applications to Decisionmaking, Utility, and the Social Sciences, 1979	Mathematics and the Social Sciences
8	L. C. BIEDENHARN and J. D. LOUCK **Angular Momentum in Quantum Physics:** Theory and Application, 1981	Mathematics of Physics
9	L. C. BIEDENHARN and J. D. LOUCK **The Racah-Wigner Algebra in Quantum Theory**, 1981	Mathematics of Physics
10	JOHN D. DOLLARD and CHARLES N. FRIEDMAN **Product Integration** with Application to Differential Equations, 1979	Analysis

GIAN-CARLO ROTA, *Editor*
ENCYCLOPEDIA OF MATHEMATICS AND ITS APPLICATIONS

Volume		Section
11	WILLIAM B. JONES and W. J. THRON **Continued Fractions:** Analytic Theory and Applications, 1980	Analysis
12	NATHANIEL F. G. MARTIN and JAMES W. ENGLAND **Mathematical Theory of Entropy,** 1981	Real Variables
13	GEORGE A. BAKER, JR. and PETER GRAVES-MORRIS **Padé Approximants, Vol. I:** Basic Theory, 1981	Mathematics of Physics
14	GEORGE A. BAKER, JR. and PETER GRAVES-MORRIS **Padé Approximants, Vol. II:** Extensions and Applications, 1981	Mathematics of Physics

Other volumes in preparation

ENCYCLOPEDIA OF MATHEMATICS and Its Applications

GIAN-CARLO ROTA, Editor
Department of Mathematics
Massachusetts Institute of Technology
Cambridge, Massachusetts

GIAN-CARLO ROTA, *Editor*
ENCYCLOPEDIA OF MATHEMATICS AND ITS APPLICATIONS
Volume 12

Section: Real Variables
James K. Brooks, *Section Editor*

Mathematical Theory of Entropy

Nathaniel F. G. Martin
University of Virginia
Charlottesville, Virginia

James W. England
Swarthmore College
Swarthmore, Pennsylvania

Foreword by
James K. Brooks
University of Florida, Gainesville

1981

Addison-Wesley Publishing Company
Advanced Book Program
Reading, Massachusetts

London • Amsterdam • Don Mills, Ontario • Sydney • Tokyo

Library of Congress Cataloging in Publication Data

Martin, Nathaniel F. G.
Mathematical theory of entropy.

(Encyclopedia of mathematics and its applications; v. 12)
Bibliography: p.
Includes index.
1. Entropy (Information theory) 2. Ergodic theory.
3. Statistical mechanics. 4. Topological dynamics.
I. England, James W. II. Title. III. Series.
Q360.M316 519.2 81-834
ISBN 0-201-13511-6 AACR2

ABCDEFGHIJ-HA-8987654321

American Mathematical Society (MOS) Subject Classification Scheme (1980): 28-02, 28A65, 28D20, 94A17, 28D05, 54H20, 58F11, 60G10, 82A05, 94A15.

Manufactured in the United States of America

To Our Wives
Jo Martin *and* **Mary England**

CONTENTS

Editor's Statement

A large body of mathematics consists of facts that can be presented and described much like any other natural phenomenon. These facts, at times explicitly brought out as theorems, at other times concealed within a proof, make up most of the applications of mathematics, and are the most likely to survive changes of style and of interest.

This ENCYCLOPEDIA will attempt to present the factual body of all mathematics. Clarity of exposition, accessibility to the non-specialist, and a thorough bibliography are required of each author. Volumes will appear in no particular order, but will be organized into sections, each one comprising a recognizable branch of present-day mathematics. Numbers of volumes and sections will be reconsidered as times and needs change.

It is hoped that this enterprise will make mathematics more widely used where it is needed, and more accessible in fields in which it can be applied but where it has not yet penetrated because of insufficient information.

GIAN-CARLO ROTA

Foreword

Entropy is a subject which has played a central role in a number of areas such as statistical mechanics and information theory. The connections between the various applications of entropy have become clearer in recent years by the introduction of probability theory into its foundations. It is now possible to see a number of what were previously isolated results in various disciplines as part of a more general mathematical theory of entropy.

This volume presents a self-contained exposition of the mathematical theory of entropy. Those parts of probability theory which are necessary for an understanding of the central topics concerning entropy have been included. In addition, carefully chosen examples are given in order that the reader may omit proofs of some of the theorems and yet by studying these examples and discussion obtain insight into the theorems.

The last four chapters give a description of those parts of information theory, ergodic theory, statistical mechanics, and topological dynamics which are most affected by entropy. These chapters may be read independently of each other. The examples show how ideas originating in one area have influenced other areas. Chapter III contains a brief description of how entropy as a measure of information flow has affected information theory and complements the first part of *The Theory of Information and Coding* by R. J. McEliece (volume 3 of this ENCYCLOPEDIA). Recent applications of entropy to statistical mechanics and topological dynamics are given in chapters V and VI. These two chapters provide a good introduction to *Thermodynamic Formalism* by D. Ruelle (volume 5 of this ENCYCLOPEDIA). The chapter on ergodic theory describes the development of Kolmogorov's adoption of Shannon entropy to the study of automorphisms on a finite measure space. It contains the culmination of this work in the proof of the Isomorphism Theorem of Kolmogorov and Ornstein. The mathematical treatment presented here of the major properties of entropy and the various applications to other fields make this volume a valuable addition to the ENCYCLOPEDIA.

JAMES K. BROOKS
General Editor, Section on Real Variables

Preface

Thirty years ago, Claude Shannon published a paper with the title "A mathematical theory of communication". In this paper, he defined a quantity, which he called entropy, that measures the uncertainty associated with random phenomena. The effects of this paper on communications in both theory and practice are still being felt, and his entropy function has been applied very successfully to several areas of mathematics. In particular, an extension of it to dynamic situations by A. N. Kolmogorov and Ja. G. Sinai led to a complete solution of a long-unsolved problem in ergodic theory, to a new invariant for differentiable dynamic systems, and to more precision in certain concepts in classical statistical mechanics.

Our intent in this book is to give a rather complete and self-contained development of the entropy function and its extension that is understandable to a reader with a knowledge of abstract measure theory as it is taught in most first-year graduate courses and to indicate how it has been applied to the subjects of information theory, ergodic theory, and topological dynamics. We have made no attempt to give a comprehensive treatment of these subjects; rather we have restricted ourselves to just those parts of the subject which have been influenced by Shannon's entropy and the Kolmogorov-Sinai extension of it. Thus, our purpose is twofold: first, to give a self-contained treatment of all the major properties of entropy and its extension, with rather detailed proofs, and second, to give an exposition of its uses in those areas of mathematics where it has been applied with some success. Our most extensive treatment is given to ergodic theory, since this is where the most spectacular results have been obtained.

The word entropy was first used in 1864 by Rudolph Clausius, in his book *Abhandlungen über die Wärmetheorie*, to describe a quantity accompanying a change from thermal to mechanical energy, and it has continued to have this meaning in thermodynamics. The connection between entropy as a measure of uncertainty and thermodynamic entropy was unclear for a number of years. With the introduction of measures, called Gibbs states, on infinite systems, this connection has been made clear. In the last chapter, we discuss this connection in the context of classical lattice systems.

In this connection we cannot resist repeating a remark made by Claude Shannon to Myron Tribus that Tribus reports in his and Edward McIrvine's article "Energy and information" (*Scientific American*, 1971). Tribus was speaking to Shannon about his measure of uncertainty and

Shannon said, "My greatest concern was what to call it. I thought of calling it 'information,' but the word was overly used, so I decided to call it 'uncertainty.' When I discussed it with John von Neumann, he had a better idea. Von Neumann told me, You should call it entropy, for two reasons. In the first place, your uncertainty function has been used in statistical mechanics under that name, so it already has a name. In the second place, and more important, no one knows what entropy really is, so in a debate you will always have the advantage." We hope our reader will also have the advantage after reading this book.

The preparation of our manuscript would have been much more difficult without the generous support of the Mathematics Departments at the University of Virginia and Swarthmore College, and the careful and accurate typing of Beverley Watson, whose care and patience in typing the bulk of the manuscript and whose facility for accurately translating the first author's tiny, sometimes illegible, scrawl are most gratefully acknowledged. Our thanks also go to Janis Babbitt, Barbara Smith, and Jo Fields, who typed portions of the first chapter, and to Marie Brown, who typed the revisions. Finally, our thanks go to Alan Saleski for his careful reading of the first three chapters.

NATHANIEL F. G. MARTIN
JAMES W. ENGLAND

Special Symbols

Symbol	Description	Section
$(\Omega, \mathfrak{F}, P)$	Probability space	1.1
$(\Omega_\xi, \mathfrak{F}_\xi, P_\xi)$	Factor space of ξ	1.2
$(S, \mathbb{S}, u_f)$	Discrete probability space with distribution f	1.2
$(I, \mathfrak{L}, \lambda)$	Unit interval with Lebesgue measure	1.2
$\Sigma(S)$	Set of doubly infinite sequences of elements from S	1.2
$\Sigma'(S)$	Set of (one-sided) infinite sequences of elements from S	4.8
$\mathfrak{Z}$ or $\mathfrak{Z}(\mathfrak{U})$	Collection of all measurable partitions	1.3; 4.4
$\mathfrak{Z}_k(\Omega)$	Collection of all measurable partitions with no more than k atoms	4.4
$(\Omega, \mathfrak{F}, P, \mathbf{T})$	Dynamical system	1.7
$(\mathbf{T}, \xi)$	Stationary stochastic process determined by ξ	1.7
$(\mathbf{B}; p_1, \ldots, p_k)$	Bernoulli shift with distribution $(p_1, \ldots, p_k)$	4.3
Tail $(\mathbf{B}, \xi_0)$	Tail of the process $(\mathbf{B}, \xi_0)$	4.3
Ω_Λ	Configuration space of a lattice system in Λ	6.3
$[\Sigma(S), \mu]$	Information source	3.2
$[\Sigma(S), P(\omega, \ ), \Sigma(B)]$	Channel	3.4
$\hat{\xi}$	The σ-field of ξ-sets	1.3
$\xi, \eta, \zeta, \alpha, \beta$	Measurable partitions	1.2
ν	Trivial partition	1.2
ε	Point partition	1.2
$\pi(\mathbf{T})$ or π	Pinsker partition of $\mathbf{T}$	2.9
$\mathfrak{A}, \mathfrak{B}$	Open covers of a topological space	5.2
$\xi \leqslant \eta$	ξ is refined by η	1.3
$\xi \overset{c}{\leqslant} \eta$	ξ is c-refined by η	4.4
$\mathfrak{A} < \mathfrak{B}$	Open cover $\mathfrak{B}$ refines $\mathfrak{A}$	5.2

Symbol	Description	Section
$\xi \overset{c}{\copyright} \eta$	ξ is c-independent of η	4.3
$\xi \vee \eta$	Supremum or common refinement of ξ and η	1.3
$\bigvee_\alpha \xi_\alpha$	Supremum or common refinement of the family $\{\xi_\alpha\}$	1.3
$\mathcal{A} \vee \mathcal{B}$	Common refinement of open cover	5.2
$\xi \wedge \eta$	Infimum of partitions	1.3
$\bigwedge_\alpha \xi_\alpha$	Infimum of the family of partitions $\{\xi_\alpha\}$	1.3
ξ^n	Common refinement of $\{\mathbf{T}^j\xi : 0 \leqslant j \leqslant n-1\}$	4.3
ξ^+	Common refinement of $\{\mathbf{T}^j\xi : 0 \leqslant j < \infty\}$	4.3
ξ^{-n}	Common refinement of $\{\mathbf{T}^{-j}\xi : 1 \leqslant j \leqslant n\}$	4.3
${}^1\xi^{-n}$	Common refinement of $\{\mathbf{T}^{-j}\xi : 0 \leqslant j \leqslant n-1\}$	4.5
ξ^-	Common refinement of $\{\mathbf{T}^{-j}\xi : 1 \leqslant j < \infty\}$	4.3
ξ^∞	Common refinement of $\{\mathbf{T}^j\xi : -\infty < j < \infty\}$	4.3
$\lvert d(\xi) - d(\eta) \rvert$	Distribution distance between ξ and η	4.4
$\lvert \xi - \eta \rvert$	Partition distance between ξ and η	4.4
$R(\xi, \eta)$	Rohlin distance between ξ and η	4.4
$\bar{d}$	$\bar{d}$-metric	4.5
Ham	Hamming metric	4.5
$\mathbf{N}_\xi$	Projection onto the factor space of ξ	1.3
$\mathbf{N}_{\zeta,\xi}$	Projection of factor space of ζ onto factor space of ξ	1.3
$\mathbf{M}_{\xi^{-n}}(l)$	ξ n-name of l	4.5
p_Λ	Restriction of a configuration to Λ	6.4
$p_{\Lambda_1\Lambda_2}$	Restriction of a configuration Ω_{Λ_2} to Λ_1	6.4
$E(x)$	Expected value of the random variable x	1.4

Symbol	Description	Section
$P(\ \vert A)$	Conditional probability given the event A	1.5
$P^{\xi}(\ \vert c)$ or $P^{\xi}(\omega,\ )$	Canonical family of measures for ξ	1.5
$E^{\xi}(x\vert c)$ or $E^{\xi}(x)$	Conditional expectation of random variable x given ξ	1.6
$d(\xi)$	Discrete probability vector associated with an ordered partition	4.4
$\bar{I}(\xi)$	Information function of ξ	2.2
$H(\xi)$	Entropy of ξ	2.2
$I(\xi/\eta)$	Conditional information of ξ given η	2.4; 2.6
$H(\xi/\eta)$	Conditional entropy of ξ given η	2.4; 2.6
$I(\xi;\eta)$	Mutual information between ξ and η	2.5
$h(\mathbf{T},\xi)$	Entropy of $\mathbf{T}$ given ξ or rate of information generation	2.7
$h(\mathbf{T})$ or $h_{\mu}(\mathbf{T})$	Entropy of $\mathbf{T}$	2.8
$H(\mathscr{A})$	Entropy of open cover $\mathscr{A}$	5.2
$h(\mathbf{T},\mathscr{A})$	Topological entropy of $\mathbf{T}$ given $\mathscr{A}$	5.2
$h_d(\mathbf{T},K)$	Bowen topological entropy of $\mathbf{T}$ given a compact set K	5.4
$h_d(\mathbf{T})$	Bowen topological entropy of $\mathbf{T}$	5.4
$S(P)$	Entropy of the state P	6.3
$S(\mu)$	Mean entropy of a translation invariation state μ	6.5
$P(\mathbf{T},\ )$	Pressure of a continuous map $\mathbf{T}$	5.4
$P(\phi)$	Pressure of a translation invariant interaction ϕ	6.5
$\mu(\phi)$	Energy of the interaction ϕ for the state μ	6.5
U_{Λ}	Energy function	6.4
$W_{\Lambda_1\Lambda_2}$	Interaction between Λ_1 and Λ_2	6.4
$\mathfrak{Z}_{\Lambda}(\phi)$	Partition function	6.4
$C(P)$	Capacity of a channel	3.4
$R(\mu,P)$	Rate of transmission of a channel	3.4

Mathematical Theory of Entropy

CHAPTER 1

Topics from Probability Theory

In this preliminary chapter we shall give an exposition of certain topics in probability theory which are necessary to understand and interpret the definition and properties of entropy. We have tried to write the chapter in such a way that a reader with a knowledge of measure theory as given in Ash [15], Halmos [55], or any other basic measure theory text can follow the arguments and understand the examples. We introduce just those parts of probability theory which are necessary for the subsequent chapters and attempt to make them meaningful by use of very simple examples. We also restrict the discussion to "nice" probability spaces, so that conditional expectation and conditional probability are more intuitive and hopefully easier to understand. These "nice" spaces also make it possible to use partitions as models for random experiments, even those experiments which are limits of sequences of experiments.

1.1 Probability Spaces

Entropy is a quantitative measurement of uncertainty associated with random phenomena. In order to define this quantity precisely, it is necessary to have a mathematical model for random phenomena which is general enough to include many different physical situations and which has enough structure to allow us to use mathematical reasoning to answer questions about the phenomena.

Such a model is given by a mathematical structure called a probability space, which is nothing more than a measure space in which the measure of the universe set is 1. Thus, a probability space is a triple $(\Omega, \mathfrak{F}, P)$ where Ω is a set, $\mathfrak{F}$ is a collection of subsets of Ω, and P is a nonnegative real valued function defined on $\mathfrak{F}$ such that

ENCYCLOPEDIA OF MATHEMATICS and Its Applications, Gian-Carlo Rota (ed.).
Vol. 12: Nathaniel F. Martin and James W. England, Mathematical Theory of Entropy.
ISBN 0-201-13511-6

C1. $\mathcal{F}$ is a σ-field, i.e., it is closed under countable unions, complements, and contains Ω;

C2. P is a measure, i.e., if $\{E_n\}$ is a countable pairwise disjoint collection of sets from $\mathcal{F}$, then

$$P\left(\bigcup E_n\right)=\sum P(E_n);$$

3.C $$P(\Omega)=1.$$

In the triple $(\Omega, \mathcal{F}, P)$, Ω is called the *sample* space, or *outcome* space; the points of Ω are *outcomes*, sets in $\mathcal{F}$ are *events*, and P is the probability.

A random experiment such as tossing a coin or drawing a ball from an urn can be represented mathematically as a probability space. For example, consider the experiment which consists of drawing a ball from an urn which contains 3 red balls, 2 white balls, and 5 blue balls, where the only distinguishing feature of the balls is their color. The only possible outcomes of the experiment will be a ball of a certain color, so the outcomes can be represented by the set $\Omega=\{r, w, b\}$ where r will stand for "a red ball was drawn" and similarly for w and b.

If we actually perform this experiment a great many times, each time replacing the ball after noting its color, the ratio of the number of times a ball of a given color is drawn to the total number of draws will seem to approach a certain limiting value. This value is taken to be the probability or likelihood of obtaining a ball of that color on any draw. In the experiment described in the previous paragraph these values will be .3 for red, .2 for white, and .5 for blue. What is being demonstrated is that in the long run, one will get a red ball 30% of the time, a white ball 20% of the time, and a blue ball 50% of the time. This should be expected, since 30% of the balls in the urn are red, etc.

Using these numbers, we get a function f, called the distribution, on the space $\Omega=\{r, w, b\}$, which we use to obtain the probability of events.

The probability measure is to be defined on subsets of the outcome space Ω, and these subsets are to represent events associated with the experiment. In this example, an event is any meaningful statement which can be made concerning the occurrence or nonoccurrence of red, white, or blue balls. Such a statement can be represented by a subset of Ω. For example, the statement "either a red or a blue ball is drawn" is represented by the set $\{r, b\}$. An event $E\subset\Omega$ will occur provided the outcome of the draw is a member of this set. In this finite case the collection of events will be the collection of all unions of outcomes. This is the collection of all subsets of Ω. Thus, $\mathcal{F}=\{\{r\}, \{w\}, \{b\}, \{r,w\}, \{r, b\}, \{w, b\}, \Omega,\varnothing\}$.

To obtain a probability measure of an event $E\in\mathcal{F}$ from the distribution function f given by $f(r)=.3$, $f(w)=.2$, $f(b)=.5$, all we need to do is sum the values of f over the outcomes in the event. Thus $P(\{r,b\})=f(r)+f(b)=.8$. The value of $P(\{r,b\})$ should represent the relative frequency of obtaining either a red or a blue ball in many independent repetitions of the experiment. In actual experiments this relative frequency does come close to .8. We should expect this, since 80% of the balls in the urn are either red or blue.

This same random experiment can be represented by another measure space in which the outcomes are not points but sets themselves. Consider the space $(I, \mathfrak{L}, \lambda)$, where I is the unit interval $[0,1]$, $\mathfrak{L}$ is the collection of Lebesgue measurable subsets of I, and λ is Lebesgue measure. Let R, W, B be any three measurable subsets of $[0,1]$ which are pairwise disjoint and such that $\lambda(R)=.3$, $\lambda(W)=.2$, $\lambda(B)=.5$. The experiment can be modeled by the probability space $(\Omega', \mathfrak{F}', P')$ where Ω' is the set $\{R,W,B\}$, $\mathfrak{F}'$ is the collection of subsets of $\mathfrak{L}$ which are unions of elements from Ω', and P' is the restriction of λ to $\mathfrak{F}'$.

It is easy to see that the two measure spaces $(\Omega, \mathfrak{F}, P)$ and $(\Omega', \mathfrak{F}', P')$ are the same in the sense that there is a bijection ϕ of Ω to Ω' with the property that $\phi(\mathfrak{F})=\mathfrak{F}'$ and for any set $F\in\mathfrak{F}$, $P'(\phi(F))=P(F)$. The second representation of the experiment has some advantages over the first because it is embedded in a space with a rich mathematical structure which is well understood. This second characterization is a *factor space* of a Lebesgue space, as we shall see in the next section.

1.2 Measurable Partitions and Lebesgue Spaces

A partition of a probability space $(\Omega, \mathfrak{F}, P)$ is a collection of subsets of Ω which are disjoint and whose union is Ω. The sets in the partition are called *atoms* of the partition. There are two partitions which we will use quite often. They are the point partition ε whose atoms are the singleton sets of Ω, i.e.,

$$\varepsilon=\{\{\omega\}:\omega\in\Omega\}$$

and the trivial partition ν whose atoms are the empty set and Ω.

If ξ is a partition of $(\Omega, \mathfrak{F}, P)$, any subset of Ω which is a union of atoms of ξ is called a *ξ-set*. For example, the collection of ε-sets of Ω is the collection of all subsets of Ω and the collection of ν-sets consists of $\varnothing$ and Ω. A partition ξ is *measurable* if there exists a countable family $\{B_n: n=1,2,\ldots\}$ of ξ-sets which are $\mathfrak{F}$-measurable (i.e., members of $\mathfrak{F}$) and have the following separation property:

S1. *For any pair C_1, C_2 of atoms from ξ with C_1 not equal to C_2, there exists a set B_n such that either $C_1\subset B_n$ and $C_2\subset\Omega-B_n$ or vice versa.*

It can be shown that the atoms of a measurable partition are measurable, but it is not necessarily true that any partition of an arbitrary measure space into measurable sets is a measurable partition.

Measurable partitions are also models of random experiments, as we saw in the example $(\Omega', \mathscr{F}', P')$ in the last section. In this example, the Lebesgue space being partitioned is the unit interval, and the atoms of the partition $\{R, W, B\}$ represent the outcomes of the experiment.

As another example consider the experiments of tossing a fair coin and drawing a ball from an urn which contains red, white, and blue balls in the proportion 3:2:5. The latter experiment is modeled as the space $(\Omega_1, \mathscr{F}_1, P_1)$ where $\Omega_1 = \{r, w, b\}$ and $\mathscr{F}_1$ and P_1 are as described in Section 1.1. The coin tossing experiment can be modeled as the space $(\Omega_2, \mathscr{F}_2, P_2)$ where $\Omega_2 = \{h, t\}$, $\mathscr{F}_2 = \{\{h\}, \{t\}, \Omega_2, \varnothing\}$, and P_2 is obtained from a distribution on Ω_2 which assigns $\frac{1}{2}$ to h and $\frac{1}{2}$ to t. All of the probablistic structure in the coin tossing experiment can be obtained as a measurable partition ζ of the urn space as follows.

Take $\zeta = \{\{r, w\}, \{b\}\}$ and identify $\{r, w\}$ with h and $\{b\}$ with t. Since $P_1\{r, w\} = P_2\{h\}$ and $P_1\{b\} = P_2\{t\}$, it is very easy to see that if we define an outcome space to be the atoms of ζ, the field of events to be the $\mathscr{F}_1$-measurable ζ-sets, and the probability to be P_1 restricted to these ζ-sets, the resulting space is the coin tossing space. This construction makes the coin tossing experiment a *factor space* associated with the partition ζ of the urn experiment.

Let $(\Omega, \mathscr{F}, P)$ be a probability space and ξ a measurable partition of Ω. The factor space of Ω associated with the partition ξ is the probability space $(\Omega_\xi, \mathscr{F}_\xi, P_\xi)$ where Ω_ξ consists of the atoms of ξ, $\mathscr{F}_\xi$ consists of $\mathscr{F}$-measurable ξ-sets and P_ξ is the restriction of P to $\mathscr{F}_\xi$.

The representation $(\Omega_2, \mathscr{F}_2, P_2)$ of the coin tossing experiment given above is not strictly the factor space of $(\Omega_1, \mathscr{F}_1, P_1)$ associated with the partition $\{\{r, w\}, \{h\}\}$. However, it is *isomorphic* to this factor space. Isomorphism is a way of identifying different mathematical models of the same observed phenomenon. Two probability spaces $(\Omega_1, \mathscr{F}_1, P_1)$ and $(\Omega_2, \mathscr{F}_2, P_2)$ are isomorphic if there exists a bijection $\mathbf{T}$ of Ω_1 onto Ω_2 such that both $\mathbf{T}$ and $\mathbf{T}^{-1}$ are measurable and $P_2(\mathbf{T}E_1) = P_1(E_1)$ for all $E_1 \in \mathscr{F}_1$ and $P_1(\mathbf{T}^{-1}E_2) = P_2(E_2)$ for all $E_2 \in \mathscr{F}_2$. The bijection $\mathbf{T}$ is called an isomorphism between the spaces.

The definition of isomorphism just given is accurate enough for the urn space and coin tossing spaces, since the only set of measure zero in either space is the empty set. In more complex spaces, which are needed for more complex phenomena such as the action of a particle under Brownian motion, there are many sets of probability zero which are not empty. Since these events do not affect the probabilities, the definition of isomorphism between probability spaces should only require that the function $\mathbf{T}$ be a bijection after a set of probability zero is removed from both Ω_1 and Ω_2.

Sometimes this is called isomorphism (mod 0) or isomorphism almost everywhere. In this book, an isomorphism will be an isomorphism (mod 0).

Returning to the example of the coin tossing and urn experiments, it is easy to check that $(\Omega_2, \mathcal{F}_2, P_2)$ is isomorphic to $(\Omega_{1\zeta}, \mathcal{F}_{1\zeta}, P_{1\zeta})$ and the urn experiment $(\Omega_1, \mathcal{F}_1, P_1)$ is isomorphic to the factor space $(I_\xi, \mathcal{F}_\xi, \lambda_\xi)$ of $(I, \mathcal{L}, \lambda)$ defined in Section 1.1, where $\xi = \{R, W, B\}$.

There is a class of probability spaces which is well understood mathematically and is such that most interesting random phenomena can be modeled as a factor space of them. Such a space, called a *Lebesgue space*, is a measure space which is isomorphic to a segment of the unit interval with Lebesgue measure together with a countable number of point masses such that the total measure of the segment and the point masses is one. Thus a nonatomic Lebesgue space is isomorphic to $(I, \mathcal{L}, \lambda)$ described in Section 1.1. A totally atomic Lebesgue space is isomorphic to a countable collection of point masses. (Countable includes finite as well as countably infinite sets.)

The axiomatic definition of a Lebesgue space is rather complicated, but it is worth giving, since it will allow us to identify many common probability spaces as Lebesgue spaces with a minimum of effort.

The first objects we must define in order to understand a Lebesgue space are basis and complete basis for a measure space. (Keep in mind that we have the uniform assumption that all measure spaces are complete in the measure theory sense, i.e., all subsets of sets of measure zero are measurable. Unfortunately, the word complete associated with basis has a different meaning.)

A countable collection $\Gamma = \{B_n\}$ of measurable sets is said to be a *basis* for the probability space $(\Omega, \mathcal{F}, P)$ if it satisfies the following two conditions:

B1. Γ *separates points of* Ω, *i.e., for any two points* ω, ω' *of* Ω *there exists a set* $B \in \Gamma$ *such that either* $\omega \in B$ *and* $\omega' \notin B$ *or vice versa.*

B2. *The (measure theoretic) completion of the* σ*-field generated by* Γ *is* $\mathcal{F}$.

Notice that if a space $(\Omega, \mathcal{F}, \mathrm{P})$ has a basis, then the point partition in this space is a measurable partition.

Now suppose that $\Gamma = \{B_n : n \in N\}$ is a basis for $(\Omega, \mathcal{F}, P)$, where N is either Z^+ or $\{1, 2, \ldots, N\}$. For the moment let B^0 denote B, and B^1 denote $\Omega - B$ for any set $B \in \Gamma$. Suppose that a is a member of $\{0,1\}^N$, the set of all functions from N to $\{0,1\}$. Consider the set

$$A = \bigcap_{n \in N} B_n^{a(n)}.$$

[For example, if $N = Z^+$ and $a = \{1, 0, 0, \ldots\}$, then $A = (\Omega - B_1) \cap B_2 \cap B_3 \cap \cdots$.] Because Γ is a basis, property B1 implies that A contains at most one point. Using this procedure we can associate with each sequence $a \in \{0,1\}^N$ a set A which is either the empty set or a set containing one point. It is also true that if a_1 and a_2 are distinct functions with associated sets A_1 and A_2, then $A_1 \cap A_2 = \varnothing$. Therefore the collection γ of all sets A obtained from the sequences in $\{0,1\}^N$ is a partition of Ω. Even more is true. This partition is a measurable partition (since the sets in Γ are measurable γ-sets which separate atoms of γ) and is either the point partition $\varepsilon = \{\{\omega\} : \omega \in \Omega\}$ or the point partition with the empty set adjoined.

The basis Γ is said to be *complete* if the associated partition γ just described is the point partition, or equivalently if each sequence $a \in \{0,1\}^N$ gives a nonempty set $\bigcap B_n^{a(n)}$. Notice that a basis is complete if and only if the map which sends $\omega \in \Omega$ to the sequence $a \in \{0,1\}^N$, where $\bigcap_{n \in N} B_n^{a(n)} = \{\omega\}$, is a bijection.

As an example of a space with a complete basis, take the unit interval with Lebesgue measure, $(I, \mathcal{L}, \lambda)$, and define B_n by

$$B_n = \bigcup \left[\frac{2j}{2^n}, \frac{2j+1}{2^n} \right],$$

where the union is extended over all j between 0 and $2^{n-1}-1$. Then $\Gamma = \{B_n : n \in Z^+\}$ is a complete basis.

Since we are usually concerned just with the measure on the space, and sets of measure zero can be neglected, a weaker form of completeness is adequate. Essentially, this type of completeness for a basis means that the space of the basis can be embedded in another space with a basis in such a way that the universe sets have the same measure and the basis elements in the space are the restrictions of the basis elements of the larger space to the original set. More precisely, a measure space $(\Omega, \mathcal{F}, \mu)$ is *complete* (mod 0) with respect to a basis $\{B_n\}$ [or the basis is complete (mod 0)] if and only if there exists a measure space $(\Omega', \mathcal{F}', \mu')$ with a complete basis $\{B_n'\}$ and an injection $\mathbf{T}$ of Ω into Ω' such that the image of Ω in Ω' is measurable, $\mu'(\Omega' - \mathbf{T}\Omega) = 0$, and $B_n = \mathbf{T}^{-1} B_n'$. It is clear that $(\mathbf{T}\Omega, \mathcal{F}' \cap \mathbf{T}\Omega, \mu')$ is (strictly) isomorphic to $(\Omega, \mathcal{F}, \mu)$ and $\{B_n' \cap \mathbf{T}\Omega\}$ is a basis for the space $(\mathbf{T}\Omega, \mathcal{F}' \cap \mathbf{T}\Omega, \mu')$ which corresponds to $\{B_n\}$. The isomorphism is given by $\mathbf{T}$.

The ideas in the above paragraphs are due to Rohlin, and in his development [122] of them he shows that if a space is complete (mod 0) with respect to one basis, then it is complete (mod 0) with respect to every basis. A *Lebesgue space* is defined to be any totally finite measure space which is complete (mod 0) with respect to some basis. We shall always assume that our Lebesgue spaces are probability spaces. Thus a Lebesgue space for the remainder of this book will mean a probability space with a basis which is complete (mod 0) with respect to this basis.

In the next few paragraphs, we list several examples of Lebesgue spaces which arise from natural phenomena. Some of these models are associated with various stochastic processes which we will discuss more fully in Section 1.7.

Example 1.1 (*Discrete Lebesgue space* $(S, \mathcal{S}, \mu_f)$). Let S denote a finite or countably infinite set, and let f denote a distribution on S. (Recall that a distribution is any function on S such that $f(s) \geq 0$ and $\Sigma_{s \in S} f(s) = 1$.) Let $\mathcal{S}$ denote the collection of all subsets of S, and define μ_f on $\mathcal{S}$ by $\mu_f(E) = \Sigma_{s \in E} f(s)$. The resulting space is a totally atomic probability space which is a Lebesgue space.

A complete (mod 0) basis for $(S, \mathcal{S}, \mu_f)$ may be constructed as follows: If S is finite, enlarge it to a set S' whose cardinality is 2^k, where k is the integer such that $2^{k-1} < |S| \leq 2^k$. ($|S|$ denotes the cardinality of S.) Without loss of generality we may assume $S = \{1, 2, \ldots, |S|\}$. Extend f to f' on S' by defining $f(j) = 0$ for $|S| < j \leq 2^k$. A complete basis for $(S', \mathcal{S}', \mu_{f'})$ can be obtained by taking B_1' to be the odd integers; B_2' is obtained by taking the first two integers, skipping the next two, taking the next two, etc; B_3' is obtained by taking the first four integers, skipping the next four, etc. In general B_n' is obtained by taking the first 2^{n-1} integers, skipping the next 2^{n-1}, etc. It is not difficult to see that $(S, \mathcal{S}, \mu_f)$ can be embedded in $(S', \mathcal{S}', \mu_{f'})$ in such a way that the basis $\{B_n'\}$ gives a complete (mod 0) basis.

In case S is countably infinite, the same construction will work directly on S to obtain a complete (mod 0) basis.

Example 1.2 (*The unit interval* $(I, \mathcal{L}, \lambda)$). Let I denote the closed unit interval $[0, 1]$, and $\mathcal{L}$ the collection of all Lebesgue measurable subsets of I. (Recall that the Lebesgue sets are the completion of the Borel sets with respect to Lebesgue measure.) The measure λ denotes Lebesgue measure on $\mathcal{L}$.

A complete basis for $(I, \mathcal{L}, \lambda)$ is given by $\{B_n\}$ for $B_n = \bigcup_j [j/2^n, (j+1)/2^n]$, where $j = 1, 3, 5, \ldots, 2^n - 1$. Since $(I, \mathcal{L}, \lambda)$ has a complete basis, every basis is complete (mod 0), and hence a basis such as the set of open intervals with rational end points is also a complete (mod 0) basis.

Example 1.3 (*A product sequence space over* S, $(\Sigma(S), \mathcal{F}, \mu)$). This space consists of all doubly infinite sequences of elements from a discrete space $(S, \mathcal{S}, \mu_f)$ with product measure.

The construction of this space is obtained as follows: The set $\Sigma(S)$ consists of all functions on the integers Z to S. For any finite set $G \subset Z$ and collection $\{s_i : i \in G\}$ let

$$C\{s_i : i \in G\} = \{\omega \in \Sigma(S) : \omega(i) = s_i, i \in G\}.$$

This set is called a cylinder set with base G. Define a set function μ on the collection of all cylinder sets by the equation

$$\mu=(C\{s_i: i\in G\})=\prod_{i\in G}\mu_f(\{s_i\})$$

$$=\prod_{i\in G}f(s_i).$$

The collection of all finite pairwise disjoint unions of cylinder sets forms a field, and the usual extension of μ to this field is countably additive. By the Caratheodory extension theorem there exists a unique extension, also denoted by μ, to the σ-field generated by this field. Let $\mathfrak{F}$ denote the completion of this σ-field with respect to μ.

A complete (mod 0) basis for the sequence space is given by the collection of all cylinder sets based on a single integer. That is, the basis consists of sets of the form $\{\omega\in\Sigma(S): \omega(i)=s\}$ where s is selected from S, and i ranges over the integers.

Example 1.4 (*A product sequence space over I*, $(\Sigma(I),\mathfrak{F},\mu)$). This space consists of all doubly infinite sequences of elements from the unit interval with product measure. The construction is similar to Example 1.3 and is as follows:

The set $\Sigma(I)$ consists of all functions from Z to I. For any finite set $G\subset Z$ and collection $\{E_i: i\in G\}$ of sets E_i from $\mathfrak{L}$, the set

$$C\{E_i: i\in G\}=\{\omega\in\Sigma(I): \omega(i)\in E_i \text{ for all } i\in G\}$$

is a cylinder set based on G. Define a set function μ on the cylinder sets by

$$\mu(C\{E_i: i\in G\})=\prod_{i\in G}\lambda(E_i)$$

and extend in the same way as was done in Example 1.3 to obtain a unique measure μ on the completion $\mathfrak{F}$ of the σ-field generated by the field of all finite disjoint unions of cylinder sets.

A complete (mod 0) basis for the space $(\Sigma(I),\mathfrak{F},\mu)$ is given by the collection of all cylinder sets of the form

$$\{\omega\in\Sigma(I): \omega(i)\in B_n\}$$

where $i\in Z$ and $B_n=\cup_j[j/2^n, (j+1)/2^n]$, for $j=1,3,\ldots,2^n-1$.

Example 1.5 (*A general sequence space over S*, $(\Sigma(S),\mathfrak{F},m)$). This example is similar to Example 1.3 except the measure m is not a product measure.

Let $\Sigma(S)$ be as defined in Example 1.3, and let $\mathfrak{F}'$ denote the σ-field generated by the field of finite disjoint unions of cylinder sets. Assume that for each finite subset G of Z we have a probability measure P_G on the σ-field $\mathfrak{F}_G$ generated by the collection of all cylinder sets based on G. Further assume that the collection of measures $\{P_G: G \text{ a finite subset of } Z\}$ has the property that if $G_1 \subset G_2$, then P_{G_2} restricted to $\mathfrak{F}_{G_1}$ is P_{G_1}. This condition is called the Kolmogoroff consistency condition, and such a family of measures is called a consistent family of measures.

The σ-field $\mathfrak{F}'$ is generated by $\bigcup \mathfrak{F}_G$, where the union is taken over all finite subsets G of Z. For any set $E \in \bigcup \mathfrak{F}_G$, define $m(E) = P_{G'}(E)$, where G' is any finite set such that $E \in \mathfrak{F}_{G'}$. The collection $\bigcup \mathfrak{F}_G$ is a field, and m is countably additive on this field. It follows that m extends to a unique measure on $\mathfrak{F}'$, also denoted by m, called the Kolmogoroff extension of the consistent family P_G. The space $(\Sigma(S), \mathfrak{F}, m)$ is a Lebesgue space, where $\mathfrak{F}$ is the m completion of $\mathfrak{F}'$.

A complete (mod 0) basis for $(\Sigma(S), \mathfrak{F}, m)$ is given by the family of all sets of the form

$$\{\omega \in \Sigma(S) : \omega(i) = s\}$$

for $i \in Z$ and $s \in S$.

Example 1.6 (*A general sequence space over I*, $(\Sigma(I), \mathfrak{F}, m)$). This space is constructed in exactly the same way as Example 1.5 from a consistent family $\{P_G: G \text{ a finite subset of } Z\}$ of probability measures on $\mathfrak{F}_G$, where $\mathfrak{F}_G$ is again the σ-field generated by all cylinder sets contained in $\Sigma(I)$ based on G. This space is also a Lebesgue space with the same basis as that given for Example 1.4.

Example 1.7 (*Sequence space over a general Lebesgue space* Ω, $(\Sigma(\Omega), \mathfrak{F}, m)$). If a construction such as that used in Example 1.3, 1.4, 1.5, or 1.6 is used, but $(S, \mathbb{S}, \mu_f)$ or $(I, \mathfrak{L}, \lambda)$ is replaced by an arbitrary Lebesgue space, the resulting space is also a Lebesgue space.

Example 1.8 (*A space which is not a Lebesgue space*, $(Y^R, \mathfrak{F}, P)$). Let $(Y, \mathfrak{Y})$ be either $(I, \mathfrak{L})$, $(S, \mathbb{S})$, or the reals with the Borel sets. Let R denote the set of real numbers, and Y^R the set of all functions on R to Y. For each finite subset $G \subset R$, let $\mathfrak{F}_G$ denote the σ-field generated by the cylinder sets based on G. Assume that $\{P_G: G \text{ a finite subset of } R\}$ is a consistent family of probability measures on $\mathfrak{F}_G$. The Kolmogoroff extension theorem implies there exists a unique probability measure P on the σ-field $\mathfrak{F}'$ generated by the sets in the union of the σ-fields $\mathfrak{F}_G$. If $\mathfrak{F}$ denotes the completion of $\mathfrak{F}'$ with respect to P, it is not the case that $(Y^R, \mathfrak{F}, P)$ is a Lebesgue space. Intuitively, it is not a Lebesgue space because there are too many points in Y^R for the number of separating sets available in $\mathfrak{F}$. Certain restrictions on the functions allowed in Y^R, or a hypothesis of regularity such as those given by Doob [36], will make it into a Lebesgue space.

Example 1.9 (*Polish spaces*, $(X, \mathcal{B}^-, \mu)$). Let X be a metrizable topological space complete with respect to some metric (such spaces are called Polish spaces), and let μ be a regular Borel measure on X with $\mu(X)=1$. If $\mathcal{B}^-$ denotes the μ-completion of the Borel sets, then $(X, \mathcal{B}^-, \mu)$ is a Lebesgue space. (See Section 2 of Chapter V in Parathasarathy [109].)

1.3 The Lattice of Measurable Partitions

In the last section we introduced the notion of a measurable partition of a probability space and the factor space associated with a partition. Rohlin proved that if ξ is a measurable partition of a Lebesgue space $(\Omega, \mathcal{F}, P)$, then the factor space $(\Omega_\xi, \mathcal{F}_\xi, P_\xi)$ is also a Lebesgue space. This factor space can be a model for a specific random experiment, and if $(\Omega_\eta, \mathcal{F}_\eta, P_\eta)$ is the factor space associated with another partition η, it may be the model of another random experiment. The probabilistic relationship between the two experiments can be given by knowing how the partitions ξ and η are related in the Lebesgue space $(\Omega, \mathcal{F}, P)$.

Let $\mathcal{Z}$ denote the collection of all measurable partitions of a fixed Lebesgue space $(\Omega, \mathcal{F}, P)$. If ξ and η are in $\mathcal{Z}$, we say ξ is refined by η and write $\xi \leqslant \eta$ if and only if each atom of ξ is an η-set, i.e., a union of atoms from η. It is easy to check that this defines a partial order on $\mathcal{Z}$. A more useful partial order is obtained if we neglect sets of measure zero. We say ξ is refined by η (mod 0), and write $\xi \leqslant \eta$ (mod 0), provided there exists a set Z of measure zero such that $\xi' \leqslant \eta'$ on $\Omega - Z$, where ξ' and η' denote the partitions ξ and η with the points of Z removed from their atoms. In the sequel $\xi \leqslant \eta$ will always denote that ξ is refined by η (mod 0).

There is a very close relationship between measurable partitions of a Lebesgue space $(\Omega, \mathcal{F}, P)$ and sub-σ-fields of $\mathcal{F}$. For $\xi \in \mathcal{Z}$ let $\xi\hat{}$ denote the collection of all $\mathcal{F}$-measurable ξ-sets. It is easy to check that $\xi\hat{}$ is a σ-field, and clearly $\xi\hat{} \subset \mathcal{F}$. Conversely, suppose $\mathcal{F}'$ is a sub-σ-field of $\mathcal{F}$. Since $(\Omega, \mathcal{F}, P)$ is a Lebesgue space, there exists a basis $\{B_n\}$ for Ω which is complete (mod 0). Since $\mathcal{F}$ is generated by the countable collection $\{B_n\}$ (i.e., it is countably generated) and since $\mathcal{F}' \subset \mathcal{F}$, $\mathcal{F}'$ must be countably generated. Let $\{B_n'\}$ be such a countable generating family, and ξ the partition of Ω whose atoms are of the form $\bigcap \hat{B}_n'$ where $\hat{B}_n'$ is either B_n' or $\Omega - B_n'$. Then ξ is a measurable partition of $(\Omega, \mathcal{F}, P)$ and $\xi\hat{} = \mathcal{F}'$.

This technique defines a map of $\mathcal{Z}$ to the collection of all sub-σ-fields of $\mathcal{F}$ which will be one to one if we identify partitions which are equal (mod 0), i.e. such that $\xi \leqslant \eta$ (mod 0) and $\eta \leqslant \xi$ (mod 0). This will be denoted by $\xi = \eta$ (mod 0). It is easy to see that in this case the two partitions contain the same atoms if a set of measure zero is removed from Ω.

The order relationship of refinement in $\mathfrak{Z}$ is carried by this map into containment in the collection of sub-σ-fields of $\mathfrak{F}$, so that $\xi \leqslant \eta$ (mod 0) if and only if $\xi\hat{} \subset \eta\hat{}$. Using the correspondence it is easy to see that $(\mathfrak{Z}, \leqslant)$ is a complete lattice. For if $\{\xi_\alpha : \alpha \in A\}$ is any collection of measurable partitions of $(\Omega, \mathfrak{F}, P)$ and $\bigvee_\alpha \xi_\alpha$ denotes the measurable partition associated with the σ-field generated by $\{\xi_\alpha\hat{} : \alpha \in A\}$, then $\xi_\beta \leqslant \bigvee_\alpha \xi_\alpha$ (mod 0) for all $\beta \in A$, and if $\xi_\alpha \leqslant \eta$ (mod 0) for all $\alpha \in A$, then $\bigvee_\alpha \xi_\alpha \leqslant \eta$ (mod 0) and $\bigvee_\alpha \xi_\alpha$ is the supremum of the collection. Dually, let $\bigwedge_\alpha \xi_\alpha$ denote the measurable partition associated with the sub-σ-field $\bigcap_\alpha \xi_\alpha\hat{}$. Then $\bigwedge_\alpha \xi_\alpha$ is the infimum of the collection. The point partition ε and the trivial partition are such that $\nu \leqslant \xi \leqslant \varepsilon$ for any $\xi \in \mathfrak{Z}$. Moreover, $\varepsilon\hat{} = \mathfrak{F}$, and $\nu\hat{}$ is the collection of sets from $\mathfrak{F}$ with probability either zero or one. [Recall that ν is now denoting the (mod 0) equivalence class of the trivial partition consisting of $\varnothing$ and Ω.]

Let $\{\xi_n\}$ be an increasing sequence of partitions. The limit of this sequence is defined to be $\bigvee_n \xi_n$ and we write $\xi_n \uparrow \bigvee_n \xi_n$. In particular, $\xi_n \uparrow \xi$ will mean $\xi_n \leqslant \xi_{n+1}$ (mod 0) and $\xi = \bigvee_n \xi_n$. Likewise, $\xi_n \downarrow \xi$ will mean $\xi_n \geqslant \xi_{n+1}$ and $\xi = \bigwedge_n \xi_n$.

In case $\{\mathfrak{F}_n\}$ is a sequence of σ-fields we write $\mathfrak{F}_n \uparrow \mathfrak{F}$, provided $\mathfrak{F}_n \subset \mathfrak{F}_{n+1}$ and $\mathfrak{F}$ is the completion of the σ-field generated by $\bigcup_n \mathfrak{F}_n$. Using the map associating measurable partitions with sub-σ-fields of $\mathfrak{F}$, it is easy to see that $\xi_n \uparrow \xi$ if and only if $\xi_n\hat{} \uparrow \xi\hat{}$. From this observation we obtain the following lemma.

Lemma 1.10. *If ζ_n is a sequence of measurable partitions such that $\zeta_n \uparrow \zeta$ and if $\varepsilon > 0$, $B \in \zeta\hat{}$ are given, then there exists a set $B' \in \bigcup_{n=1}^{\infty} \zeta_n\hat{}$ such that $P(B \triangle B') < \varepsilon$.*

Basically this lemma says that the ζ_n-sets as n ranges over the integers are dense in the metric space of the measure algebra $(\bigvee \zeta_n)\hat{}$.

It can be easily checked that if $\{\zeta_n : n = 1, 2, \ldots\}$ is a countable family of measurable partitions, then $\bigvee_{n=1}^{\infty} \xi_n$ is (mod 0) the collection of all sets of the form $\bigcap_{n=1}^{\infty} A_n^{j_n}$ where $A_n^{j_n}$ is an arbitrary atom of ξ_n. For example consider the Lebesgue space $(I, \mathfrak{L}, \lambda)$, where I is $[0,1)$. If $\xi_1 = \{[0, \frac{1}{2}), [\frac{1}{2}, 1)\}$ and $\xi_2 = \{[0, \frac{3}{4}), [\frac{3}{4}, 1)\}$, then

$$\xi_1 \vee \xi_2 = \left\{ \left[0, \tfrac{1}{2}\right), \left[\tfrac{1}{2}, \tfrac{3}{4}\right), \left[\tfrac{3}{4}, 1\right) \right\}.$$

We call the supremum $\bigvee_\alpha \xi_\alpha$ the *common refinement* of the partitions ξ_α. In case ξ is the common refinement of the sequence of partitions $\{\xi_n : n = 1, 2, \ldots\}$, then there exists a sequence $\{\zeta_n\}$ such that $\zeta_n \uparrow \zeta$, namely $\zeta_n = \bigvee_{j=1}^{n} \xi_j$.

As an example, suppose ξ_n is the partition of $(I, \mathfrak{L}, \lambda)$ into intervals of the form $[j/2^n, (j+1)/2^n)$. Then $\xi_n \leqslant \xi_{n+1}$ and $\xi_n \uparrow \varepsilon$ (mod 0). In case ξ_n is the partition of $(I, \mathfrak{L}, \lambda)$ into intervals of the form $[j/n, (j+1)/n)$, then ξ_n is not refined by ξ_{n+1} for all n, but if $\zeta_n = \bigvee_{k=1}^{n} \xi_k$, then $\zeta_n \leqslant \zeta_{n+1}$ and $\zeta_n \uparrow \varepsilon$ (mod 0).

In case ξ and η are measurable partitions, they have associated factor spaces $(\Omega_\xi, \mathcal{F}_\xi, P_\xi)$ and $(\Omega_\eta, \mathcal{F}_\eta, P_\eta)$, which we think of as models of two random experiments. In case $\xi \leqslant \eta$, each atom of η is contained in a unique atom of ξ. Interpreting this in terms of the outcomes of the experiments modeled by the factor spaces, each outcome of Ω_η uniquely determines an outcome in Ω_ξ. Thus knowing outcomes of the experiment modeled by Ω_ξ gives complete knowledge concerning the outcome of the experiment modeled by Ω_ξ. From this point of view the order relationship in $\mathfrak{Z}$ gives a mathematical model for dependence between experiments.

What we will do now is show by way of certain maps how the order relationship in $\mathfrak{Z}$ and factor spaces are connected. These maps are defined as follows: Let ξ be a measurable partition of the Lebesgue space $(\Omega, \mathcal{F}, P)$. For each $\omega \in \Omega$, let $\mathbf{N}_\xi(\omega)$ denote the atom of ξ which contains ω. The map $\mathbf{N}_\xi$ is called the projection associated with ξ and $\mathbf{N}_\xi$ maps Ω onto Ω_ξ. By definition of $(\Omega_\xi, \mathcal{F}_\xi, P_\xi)$ the projection associated with ξ has the following properties:

P1. It is a Boolean σ-isomorphism of $\xi^\wedge$ onto $\mathcal{F}_\xi$, i.e., for any countable collection of sets $E_n \in \xi^\wedge$, $\mathbf{N}_\xi(\cup E_n) = \cup \mathbf{N}_\xi(E_n)$ and $\mathbf{N}_\xi(\Omega - E) = \Omega_\xi - \mathbf{N}_\xi(E)$ for $E \in \xi^\wedge$.
P2. $P(\mathbf{N}_\xi^{-1}(F)) = P_\xi(F)$ *for all* $F \in \mathcal{F}_\xi$.
P3. $P_\xi(\mathbf{N}_\xi(E)) = P(E)$ for all $E \in \xi^\wedge$.

In case $\xi \leqslant \zeta$, given any atom $D \in \zeta$ there is a unique atom $C \in \xi$ such that $C \supset D$. Let $\mathbf{N}_{\zeta,\xi}$ be the map on Ω_ζ onto Ω_ξ which sends d to c provided $\mathbf{N}_\zeta^{-1}(d) \subset \mathbf{N}_\xi^{-1}(c)$. That is $\mathbf{N}_\zeta^{-1}(d) \subset \mathbf{N}_\xi^{-1}(\mathbf{N}_{\zeta,\xi}(d))$. From this point of view $\mathbf{N}_{\varepsilon,\xi} = \mathbf{N}_\xi$. It is a routine calculation to show that $\mathbf{N}_{\zeta,\xi}$ satisfies P1, P2, and P3 with the obvious modifications.

Take any atom $C \in \xi$, and let c denote the element $\mathbf{N}_\xi(C)$ of Ω_ξ. Since we are assuming that $\xi \leqslant \zeta$, the set $\mathbf{N}_{\zeta,\xi}^{-1}(c)$ is a certain subset of Ω_ζ. For each $d \in \mathbf{N}_{\zeta,\xi}^{-1}(c)$, $\mathbf{N}_\zeta^{-1}(d)$ is a subset of C and $\{\mathbf{N}_\zeta^{-1}(d) : d \in \mathbf{N}_{\zeta,\xi}^{-1}(c)\}$ is a partition of C. As c ranges over Ω_ξ, $\{\mathbf{N}_\zeta^{-1}(d) : d \in \mathbf{N}_{\zeta,\xi}^{-1}(c)\}$ is ζ.

As an example let $\xi = \{(0, \frac{1}{2}], (\frac{1}{2}, 1]\}$ and $\zeta = \{(0, \frac{1}{4}], (\frac{1}{4}, \frac{1}{2}], (\frac{1}{2}, 1]\}$. Then

$$\mathbf{N}_{\zeta,\xi}\left(0, \tfrac{1}{4}\right] = \left(0, \tfrac{1}{2}\right],$$

$$\mathbf{N}_{\zeta,\xi}\left(\tfrac{1}{4}, \tfrac{1}{2}\right] = \left(0, \tfrac{1}{2}\right].$$

$$\mathbf{N}_{\zeta,\xi}\left(\tfrac{1}{2}, 1\right] = \left(\tfrac{1}{2}, 1\right].$$

The map can be illustrated as follows:

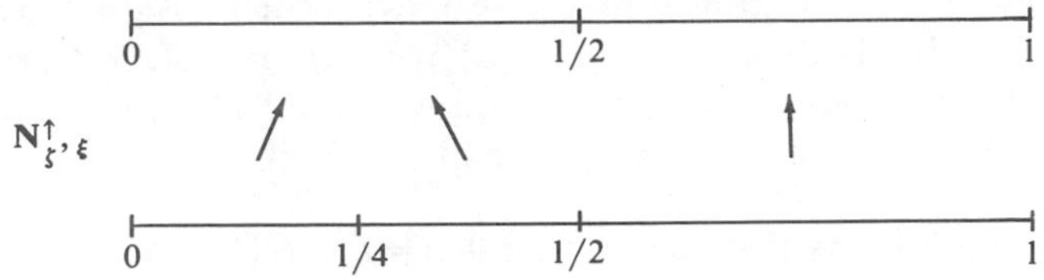

Thus $\mathrm{N}_{\zeta,\xi}^{-1}(0,\frac{1}{2}]$ is the two intervals $(0,\frac{1}{4}]$ and $(\frac{1}{4},\frac{1}{2}]$.

Example 1.11. Consider the Lebesgue space $(\Sigma(S), \mathfrak{F}, \mu)$ defined in Example 1.3 and let ξ denote the partition whose atoms are the sets $\{\omega \in \Sigma(S) : \omega(0) = s\}$ for each $s \in S$. The factor space associated with ξ is isomorphic to the space $(S, \mathbb{S}, \mu_f)$. If η denotes the partition of $\Sigma(S)$ whose atoms are of the form $\{\omega \in \Sigma(S) : \omega(1) = t\}$ for each $t \in S$, then

$$\xi \vee \eta = (\{\omega \in \Sigma(S) : \omega(0) = s, \omega(1) = t\})$$

as s, t range over S. It is easy to see that $(\Omega_{\xi\vee\eta}, \mathfrak{F}_{\xi\vee\eta}, P_{\xi\vee\eta})$ is isomorphic to the product of two copies of $(\Sigma(S), \mathbb{S}, \mu_f)$. The minimum $\xi \wedge \eta$ of ξ and η is the trivial partition ν.

Example 1.12. Consider $(\Sigma(I), \mathfrak{F}, \mu)$ as defined in Example 1.4. The partition $\xi = (\{\omega \in \Sigma(I) : \omega(0) = x\} : x \in I)$ is a measurable partition, and $(\Sigma(I)_\xi, \mathfrak{F}_\xi, \mu_\xi)$ is isomorphic to $(I, \mathfrak{L}, \lambda)$.

Example 1.13. In the Lebesgue space $(I, \mathfrak{L}, \lambda)$ of Example 1.2 the partition $\{[0, 0.3), [0.3, 0.5), [0.5, 1)\}$ gives a factor space isomorphic to the Lebesgue space described in the first section as a model for the urn experiment.

1.4 Random Variables

Intuitively a random variable is a quantity, usually a numerical quantity, obtained from a random experiment whose value depends upon the outcome of the experiment. If a probability space $(\Omega, \mathfrak{F}, P)$ represents the experiment, with the points in Ω corresponding to outcomes, then we can see how a random variable is represented mathematically as a function on Ω to the reals. Clearly the probability structure must come into play, and this is accomplished by requiring the function to be $\mathfrak{F}$-measurable.

As an example suppose you are playing the following game. A ball is drawn from the urn described in Section 1.1. If it is red or white you win one dollar, and if it is blue you lose one dollar. Your winnings after one play is a random variable in that its value depends upon the probability distribution of the outcomes in the urn experiment. As a function this random variable is defined on $\{r,w,b\}$ with $x(r)=+1$, $x(w)=+1$, and $x(b)=-1$. The probability that you will win a dollar is the probability of the event that either a red or a white ball is drawn. Thus

$$\text{Probability that you win a dollar} = P\{\omega\in\Omega : x(\omega)=1\}$$
$$= P\{r,w\} = .5.$$

The probability that you lose a dollar is given by

$$P\{\omega\in\Omega : x(\omega)=-1\} = P\{b\} = .5.$$

Let $(S,\mathbb{S})$ denote a measurable space where $S=\{+1,-1\}$ and $\mathbb{S}$ is the collection of all subsets of S. Let $(\Omega,\mathcal{F},P)$ be the probability space associated with the urn experiment. That is, $\Omega=\{r,\omega,b\}$, $\mathcal{F}$ is the collection of subsets of Ω, and P is the probability obtained from the distribution function $f\{r\}=.3$, $f\{\omega\}=.2$, $f\{b\}=.5$. The random variable x which models your fortune after one play of the game is defined on Ω to S.

If ε denotes the point partition in S, then the collection $x^{-1}(\varepsilon)=\{x^{-1}(1), x^{-1}(-1)\}=\{\{r,w\},\{b\}\}=\xi$ is a measurable partition of $(\Omega,\mathcal{F},P)$, and the factor space $(\Omega_\xi,\mathcal{F}_\xi,P_\xi)$ is isomorphic to the coin tossing experiment. From this example it is clear how a random variable on a Lebesgue space gives rise to a measurable partition of the space. If the range space of the random variable x is a measurable space whose point partition ε is measurable, then $x^{-1}(\varepsilon)$ is a measurable partition and gives rise to a factor space which is a Lebesgue space. In particular, if the range of this random variable is a Lebesgue space, then $x^{-1}(\varepsilon)$ is a measurable partition. The "natural" domain of a random variable is this factor space, since these are the only outcomes of the experiment which can actually be detected by the random variable. For example, in the game of drawing colored balls from an urn, if you play the game and the person drawing hands you a dollar after a draw, all you know is that either a red or a white ball was drawn, and there is no possible way to determine which one. As far as the random variable is concerned, the outcome was $\{r,w\}$, which is a point in the factor space.

To reiterate, if x is a random variable on a Lebesgue space $(\Omega,\mathcal{F},P)$ to a space whose point partition is measurable, then $x^{-1}(\varepsilon)$ is a measurable partition, which we shall call the partition induced by x. The associated factor space we shall denote by $(\Omega_x,\mathcal{F}_x,P_x)$.

The expected value or expectation, $E(x)$, of a real (or complex) random variable x is the integral of this random variable with respect to the probability measure. To indicate why this integral is called the expected value, consider the random variable x defined above which represents your winnings after one play of the urn game. Then

$$E(x)=\int_{\Omega} P(dw)x(w)=(1)P\{r,w\}+(-1)P\{b\}$$

$$=.5-.5=0.$$

Now consider playing the game many times, where the ball is returned and mixed after each play, and determine what your average winnings per game is after a large number of plays. If you play N times, then about $P\{r,w\}=.5$ of these times you will win one dollar and about $P\{b\}=.5$ of these times you will lose one dollar. Thus your fortune after N plays is about

$$(+1)NP\{r,w\}+(-1)NP\{b\},$$

and the average winnings per game is

$$\frac{1}{N}[(+1)NP\{r,w\}+(-1)NP\{b\}]=E(x).$$

Let us think about this from another point of view. If you play the game N times, let N_1 represent the number of times you win one dollar and N_{-1} represent the number of times you lose one dollar. Then your fortune is $(+1)N_1+(-1)N_{-1}$, and your average winnings per game is given by

$$\frac{1}{N}[(+1)N_1+(-1)N_{-1}]=(+1)\frac{N_1}{N}+(-1)\frac{N_{-1}}{N}.$$

Since $N_1/N \to P\{r,w\}$ and $N_{-1}/N \to P\{b\}$ by the definition of P, the average winnings per game is asymptotic to $E(x)=(1)P\{r,w\}+(-1)P\{b\}$.

1.5 Conditional Probability and Independence

An experiment represented by a Lebesgue space $(\Omega, \mathfrak{F}, P)$ is performed and results in an outcome $\omega \in \Omega$. Let E and F denote events from $\mathfrak{F}$, and suppose we know that the outcome ω results in the event E, i.e., $\omega \in E$. What is the probability that F occurred? It is clear that this probability is no longer $P(F)$, because if E and F are disjoint, then $\omega \in E$ implies that $\omega \notin F$, and we are certain that F did not occur.

We will define a function $P(\ |E)$ on the σ-field $\mathfrak{F}$ so that only those events which have nonempty intersection with E have positive probability, and the function gives the probability of an event knowing that an outcome resulted in E. Then $(E, E\cap\mathfrak{F}, P(\ |E))$, where $E\cap\mathfrak{F}$ denotes those subsets of E which are in $\mathcal{F}$, will be a probability space which contains all the uncertainty after we know the event E has occurred.

In case $P(E)>0$ it is easy to obtain a definition for $P(\ |E)$. To motivate this definition consider the urn experiment of Section 1.1. Suppose we known the event $\{r,w\}$ has occurred because a red ball was drawn. We know that red and white balls are distributed in the ratio of 3:2, so that the probability that a red ball was selected should be $\frac{3}{5}$. Likewise the probability that the event $\{r,w\}$ occurred because a white ball was drawn should be $\frac{2}{5}$. Clearly, the probability that $\{r,w\}$ occurred because a blue ball was drawn is zero. Thus,

$$P(\{r\}|\{r,w\})=\frac{3}{5}=\frac{P(\{r\}\cap\{r,w\})}{P(\{r,w\})}$$

and in general

$$P(E|\{r,w\})=\frac{P(E\cap\{r,w\})}{P(\{r,w\})}.$$

Using this example as a model, if C is an event in a Lebesgue space $(\Omega,\mathcal{F},P)$ and if $P(C)>0$, we define the *conditional probability* given the event C to be the probability measure $P(\ |C)$ defined for any event $E\in\mathcal{F}$ by the equation

$$P(E|C)=\frac{P(E\cap C)}{P(C)}. \tag{1.1}$$

It is not difficult to see that if $P(C)>0$, then $P(\ |C)$ is a probability on $\mathcal{F}$ which is supported by C [i.e., $P(\Omega-C|C)=0$] and that $(C,\mathcal{F}(C),P(\ |C))$ is a probability space, where $\mathcal{F}(C)$ denotes $\{F\cap C: F\in\mathcal{F}\}$.

Using Equation (1.1), we see that if $P(E)>0$ and F is some event, then the probability that both E and F result from the outcome Ω, $P(E\cap F)$, is given by the equation

$$P(E\cap F)=P(E)P(F|E), \tag{1.2}$$

and the probability that an outcome results in both E and F is the product of the probability that the outcome results in E with the probability that the outcome results in F knowing that the outcome resulted in E.

An event F is *independent* of an event E if the probability of F is unaffected by the knowledge that an outcome resulted in the event E. Thus F is independent of E if and only if $P(F|E)=P(F)$, and Equation (1.2) implies that F is independent of E if and only if $P(E\cap F)=P(E)P(F)$.

Let $\xi=\{C_1,C_2,\ldots,C_j,\ldots\}$ be a countable (mod 0) partition of a Lebesgue space $(\Omega,\mathfrak{F},P)$, and assume $P(C_j)>0$ for each j. For each $C\in\xi$, we have the spaces $(C,\mathfrak{F}(C),P(\ |C))$, and these are also Lebesgue spaces. The original space is a *direct integral* of these spaces in the following sense. The set Ω is the disjoint union of the C from ξ, $\mathfrak{F}$ is the disjoint union of $\mathfrak{F}(C)$, and for any $F\in\mathfrak{F}$,

$$P(F)=\Sigma P(F\cap C|C)P(C),$$

where the sum is over all $C\in\xi$. This last equation can be written as

$$P(F)=\int_{\Omega_\xi}P_\xi(dC)P(F|C) \tag{1.3}$$

where we are identifying the atom $C\in\xi$ with a point of Ω_ξ. The collection of spaces

$$\{(C,\mathfrak{F}(C),P(\ |C)):C\in\xi\},$$

or just the measures $P(\ |C))$, is called a *canonical family of measures* for the partition ξ.

The technique just outlined allows us to decompose a complicated random experiment $(\Omega,\mathfrak{F},P)$ into a family of random experiments $(C,\mathfrak{F}(C),P(\ |C))$ associated with a countable partition ξ, whose atoms are thought of as the outcome of some subexperiment of $(\Omega,\mathfrak{F},P)$. It would be desirable to have such a decomposition associated with any measurable partition of a Lebesgue space. The definition of $P(\ |C)$ given above will not be applicable, since if ξ is a nondenumerable partition it is easily possible for $P(C)=0$ for each atom C of ξ. The following theorem gives the existence of such measures.

THEOREM 1.14. *Let ξ be a measurable partition of the Lebesgue space $(\Omega,\mathfrak{F},P)$ and $\mathbf{N}_\xi$ the projection associated with ξ. For P_ξ-almost all $c\in\Omega_\xi$ there exists a probability measure $P^\xi(\ |c)$ on $\mathfrak{F}$ such that:*

1.14.1 $P^\xi(\Omega-\mathbf{N}_\xi^{-1}(c)|c)=0.$

1.14.2 *For any $F\in\mathfrak{F}$, $P^\xi(F|\ )$ is an $\mathfrak{F}_\xi$-measurable function defined P_ξ-almost everywhere on Ω_ξ [hence $P^\xi(F|\mathbf{N}_\xi(\ ))$ is a $\xi^\wedge$-measurable function defined P-a.e. on Ω].*

1.14.3 *For any $F\in\mathfrak{F}$*

$$P(F)=\int_{\Omega_\xi}P_\xi(dc)P^\xi(F|c)$$

$$=\int_\Omega P(d\omega)P^\xi(F|\mathbf{N}_\xi(\omega)).$$

Proof. Since $(\Omega, \mathfrak{F}, P)$ is a Lebesgue space, it is isomorphic to a segment (the nonatomic part) together with a finite or countable collection of atoms. It is enough to construct the measures for the nonatomic part, so we shall assume $(\Omega, \mathfrak{F}, P)$ is isomorphic to $[0,1]$.

Let $\mathfrak{B}$ denote the field of subsets of $\mathfrak{F}$ which is the image under the isomorphism of the field of finite disjoint unions of intervals in $[0,1]$ with rational end points. A rational simple function is a $\mathfrak{B}$-measurable function on Ω to the rationals with a finite range. Let $\mathfrak{S}$ denote the rational simple functions. It is easy to see that if $f=\Sigma_{j=1}^{n} f_j 1_{F_j}$, where f_j are distinct rationals and $\{F_j\}$ is a partition of Ω, then $f \in \mathfrak{S}$ and all functions in $\mathfrak{S}$ are of this form. The collection $\mathfrak{S}$ is a countable, dense subspace of $\mathfrak{L}^1(\Omega, \mathfrak{F}, P)$, the pseudonormed linear space of all integrable functions on $(\Omega, \mathfrak{F}, P)$. We shall need to distinguish between functions of Ω and a.e. equivalence classes of functions. For this purpose in this proof $\mathfrak{L}^1$ and $\mathfrak{L}^\infty$ will denote the pseudonormed spaces of functions and L^1, L^∞ will denote the normed spaces of a.e. equivalence classes of functions.

For each $F \in \mathfrak{F}$, define the measure μ_F on $\mathfrak{F}_\xi$ by the equation

$$\mu_F(A) = P_\xi(A \cap \mathbf{N}_\xi(F)).$$

Since μ_F is a finite measure absolutely continuous with respect to P_ξ, the Radon-Nikodym theorem implies the existence of a unique class P_F in $L^1(\Omega_\xi, \mathfrak{F}_\xi, P_\xi)$ such that

$$\mu_F(A) = \int_A P_\xi(dc)\hat{P}_F(c) \tag{1.4}$$

for any representative $\hat{P}_F$ of P_F. Notice this implies that if p is any $\mathfrak{F}_\xi$-measurable function such that $\mu_F(A) = \int_A P_\xi(dc)p(c)$, then $p \in P_F$.

Now suppose F_1 and F_2 are disjoint sets in $\mathfrak{F}$. Then for any A

$$P_\xi(A \cap \mathbf{N}_\xi(F_1 \cup F_2)) = P_\xi(A \cap \mathbf{N}_\xi(F_1)) + P_\xi(A \cap \mathbf{N}_\xi(F_2)),$$

so that

$$\int_A P_\xi(dc) P_{F_1 \cup F_2} = \int_A P_\xi(dc)\left[P_{F_1} + P_{F_2}\right],$$

and by uniqueness $P_{F_1 \cup F_2} = P_{F_1} + P_{F_2}$. Thus the equation

$$\mathbf{P}\left(\sum_{j=1}^{n} q_j 1_{c_j}\right) = \sum_{j=1}^{n} q_j P_{c_j}$$

defines a bounded linear operator on $\mathbb{S}$ to $L^1(\Omega_\xi, \mathcal{F}_\xi, P_\xi)$. Since $\mathbb{S}$ is a subspace of $\mathcal{L}^\infty$ and $\|\mathbf{P}(f)\|_\infty \leqslant \|f\|_\infty$, we may pick for each $f \in \mathbb{S}$ a representative of $\mathbf{P}(f)$, say $\hat{\mathbf{P}}(f)$, which is in $\mathcal{L}^\infty(\Omega_\xi, \mathcal{F}_\xi, P_\xi)$.

For rational numbers α, β and functions f, g in $\mathbb{S}$ let

$$D(\alpha,\beta; f,g) = \{c \in \Omega_\xi : \alpha\hat{\mathbf{P}}(f)(c) + \beta\hat{\mathbf{P}}(g)(c) \neq \hat{\mathbf{P}}(\alpha f + \beta g)(c)\}.$$

Suppose $f = \Sigma_i f_i 1_{F_i}$ and $g = \Sigma_j g_j 1_{G_j}$. Then

$$\begin{aligned}\hat{\mathbf{P}}(\alpha f + \beta g) &= \mathbf{P}(\alpha f + \beta g) \qquad P_\xi\text{-a.e.}\\ &= \alpha\mathbf{P}(f) + \beta\mathbf{P}(g)\\ &= \alpha\hat{\mathbf{P}}(f) + \beta\hat{\mathbf{P}}(g) \qquad P_\xi\text{-a.e.,}\end{aligned}$$

so that $P_\xi(D(\alpha,\beta; f,g)) = 0$, and if D is the union of all $D(\alpha,\beta; f,g)$ it is also a set of P_ξ-measure zero.

Now for each $c \in \Omega_\xi - D$, $\hat{\mathbf{P}}(\cdot)(c)$ is a bounded linear functional on $\mathbb{S}$ which extends to a bounded linear functional on $\mathcal{L}^1(\Omega, \mathcal{F}, P)$. By the Riez representation theorem there is a unique $\phi_c \in L^\infty(\Omega, \mathcal{F}, P)$ such that $\|\phi_c\|_\infty = \|\hat{\mathbf{P}}(\cdot)(c)\|_1$ and

$$\hat{\mathbf{P}}(f)(c) = \int_\Omega P(d\omega)\phi_c(\omega) f(\omega).$$

For each $c \in \Omega_\xi - D$ define $P^\xi(\ |c)$ on $\mathcal{F}$ by

$$\begin{aligned}P^\xi(F|c) &= \int_\Omega P(d\omega)\phi_c(\omega) 1_F(\omega)\\ &= \int_F P(d\omega)\phi_c(\omega).\end{aligned}$$

It is clear that $P^\xi(\ |c)$ is a probability on $\mathcal{F}$ and for each $F \in \mathcal{F}$, $P^\xi(F|\cdot)$ is $\mathcal{F}_\xi$-measurable. Moreover

$$P^\xi(F|c) = \hat{\mathbf{P}}(1_F)(c) = \hat{P}_F(c) \qquad P_\xi\text{-a.e.,}$$

and by (1.4)

$$P(F) = P_\xi(\mathbf{N}_\xi(F)) = \int_{\Omega_\xi} P_\xi(dc) P^\xi(F|c).$$

To complete the proof we only need to show that $P^{\xi}(\ |c)$ is supported on $\mathbf{N}^{-1}(c)$. Equation (1.4) gives us that for any $A\in\Omega_{\xi}$, $F\in\mathfrak{F}$,

$$\int_A P_{\xi}(dc)P^{\xi}(F|c)=P_{\xi}(A\cap\mathbf{N}_{\xi}(F))$$

so in particular

$$\int_A P_{\xi}(dc)P^{\xi}(\Omega-\mathbf{N}_{\xi}^{-1}(A)|c)=0.$$

Let $N_A=\{c\in A: P^{\xi}(\Omega-\mathbf{N}^{-1}(A)|c)>0\}$. By the previous equation $P_{\xi}(N_A)=0$. Since $(\Omega_{\xi},\mathfrak{F}_{\xi},P_{\xi})$ is a Lebesgue space, this is a countable basis $\{A_n\}$ which is complete mod 0. Hence for almost all $c\in\Omega_{\xi}$ we have $c=\bigcap A_n^{c(n)}$, where $c(n)$ is zero or one and $A_n^0=A_n$, $A_n^1=\Omega_{\xi}-A_n$.

Let $N=\bigcup_{n=1}^{\infty}N_{A_n}\cup\bigcup_{n=1}^{\infty}N_{\Omega_{\xi}-A_n}$. Then $P_{\xi}(N)=0$, and if $c\notin N$, then $P^{\xi}(\Omega-\mathbf{N}_{\xi}^{-1}A_n^{c(n)}|c)=0$ and we have

$$\begin{aligned}P^{\xi}(\Omega-\mathbf{N}_{\xi}^{-1}(c)|c)&\leqslant\sum_{n=1}^{\infty}P^{\xi}(\Omega-\mathbf{N}_{\xi}^{-1}(A_n^{c(n)})|c)\\&=0.\end{aligned}$$

The collection of measures $\{P^{\xi}(\ |c): c\in\Omega'_{\xi}\}$ where $\Omega'_{\xi}=\Omega_{\xi}-N$ and $P_{\xi}(N)=0$ is called a canonical family of measures for ξ, and the a.e. defined functions $P^{\xi}(\ |\mathbf{N}_{\xi}(\omega))$ are called regular conditional probabilities given $\hat{\xi}$.

The canonical family of measures decomposes the space $(\Omega,\mathfrak{F},P)$ into subspaces $(C,\mathfrak{F}(C),P^{\xi}(\ |c))$, where $C=\mathbf{N}_{\xi}^{-1}(c)$, which are also Lebesgue spaces. The original space is a direct integral of these subspaces in the same way as was described for a countable partition, with Theorem 1.14.3 analogous to (1.3).

One can see from the proof of Theorem 1.14 that the canonical family of measures is unique in the sense that if $\{\bar{P}^{\zeta}(\ |c)\}$ is another canonical family for ζ, then $\bar{P}^{\zeta}(\ |c)=P^{\zeta}(\ |c)$ for P_{ζ}-almost all $c\in\Omega_{\zeta}$. This uniqueness gives the following fundamental property (which Rohlin calls the transitivity property) of canonical families of measures.

Suppose ξ and ζ are measurable partitions of $(\Omega,\mathfrak{F},P)$ and $\xi\leqslant\zeta$ (mod 0). Let $\{P^{\xi}(\ |c)\}$ and $\{P^{\zeta}(\ |d)\}$ denote the canonical families of measures associated with ξ and ζ respectively. If $\zeta(C)$ denotes the partition $\mathbf{N}_{\zeta}^{-1}(\mathbf{N}_{\zeta\xi}^{-1}(c))$ of $C=\mathbf{N}_{\xi}^{-1}(c)$, where $\mathbf{N}_{\zeta}$ and $\mathbf{N}_{\zeta\xi}$ are the associated projections, then $\zeta(C)$ is a measurable partition of the Lebesgue space $(C,\mathfrak{F}(C),P^{\xi}(\ |c))$ and has a canonical family of measures $\{P^{\zeta(C)}(\ |d):\mathbf{N}_{\zeta}^{-1}(d)\in\zeta(C)\}$. If C is allowed to vary over the atoms of ζ, then $\{P^{\zeta(C)}(\ |d):\mathbf{N}_{\zeta}^{-1}(d)\in\zeta(C),\ C\in\zeta\}$ is a canonical family of measures for ζ, and consequently by the uniqueness property $P^{\zeta(C)}(\ |d)=P^{\zeta}(\ |d)$ for P_ζ-almost all d such that $N_\zeta^{-1}(d)\in\zeta(C)$.

If $P^{\zeta}(\ |c)$ is a canonical family of measures for ζ, the functions $P^{\zeta}(\ |N_\zeta(\omega))$ defined almost everywhere on Ω to the collection of measures on $(\Omega,\mathfrak{F})$ will be denoted by $P^{\zeta}(\omega,\ )$. Since $P^{\zeta}(\ |c)$ is supported by $N_\zeta^{-1}(c)$, if E is any $\zeta^{\wedge}$-measurable set and $F\in\mathfrak{F}$, then

$$P(F\cap E)=\int_E P(d\omega)P^{\zeta}(\omega,F), \tag{1.5}$$

and we can interpret this as saying the probability of both E and F is the sum of the product of the probability that F occurs given an outcome in E with the probability of this outcome.

Suppose ξ and η are partitions of $(\Omega,\mathfrak{F},P)$. We shall think of the atoms of ξ and η as being outcomes of two subexperiments of Ω. The Lebesgue spaces $(A,\mathfrak{F}(A),P^{\xi}(\ |a))$ represent the probabilities of events given the outcome $A\in\xi$, or $N_\zeta(A)=a\in\Omega_\zeta$. In particular, for each set $D\in\eta^{\wedge}$ (an event from the subexperiment η), $P^{\xi}(D|a)$ is the probability that D occurs given the outcome a of the experiment Ω_ξ, or ξ. The experiment η is said to be *independent* of the experiment ξ if

$$P^{\xi}(D|a)=P_\eta(N_\eta(D))$$

for P_ξ-almost all $a\in\Omega_\xi$ and all $D\in\eta^{\wedge}$. This can be rewritten as

$$P^{\xi}(\omega,D)=P(D), \qquad \omega\in\Omega, \quad D\in\eta^{\wedge}. \tag{1.6}$$

Suppose η is independent of ξ and $C\in\xi^{\wedge}$, $D\in\eta^{\wedge}$. Then using Equations (1.5) and (1.6), we have

$$\begin{aligned}P(D\cap C)&=\int_C P(d\omega)P^{\xi}(\omega,D)\\&=P(D)P(C),\end{aligned}$$

and since $P(D\cap C)$ is also equal to $\int_D P(d\omega)P^{\eta}(\omega,C)$, we have that

$$\int_D P(d\omega)P^{\eta}(\omega,C)=P(D)P(C)$$

for all $D\in\eta^{\wedge}$ and $C\in\xi^{\wedge}$. This equation then implies that $P^{\eta}(\omega,C)=P(C)$ for almost all $\omega\in\Omega$. Thus ξ is independent of η if and only if η is independent of ξ, and we shall say ξ and η are independent. This argument also indicates that ξ and η are independent if and only if

$$P(C\cap D)=P(C)P(D)$$

for all $C\in\xi^{\wedge}$ and $D\in\eta^{\wedge}$.

The following generalization of Fubini's theorem is very useful in probability theory and is closely associated with canonical families of measures.

THEOREM 1.15. *Let* $(\Omega_1, \mathcal{F}_1, \mu_1)$ *be a probability space, and* $(\Omega_2, \mathcal{F}_2)$ *be a measurable space. Assume that for each* $\omega_1 \in \Omega_1$ *there is a probability measure* $\mu(\omega_1, \cdot)$ *on* $\mathcal{F}_2$ *such that for fixed* $E \in \mathcal{F}_2$, $\mu(\cdot, E)$ *is a measurable function on* $(\Omega_1, \mathcal{F}_1, \mu_1)$. *Then there exists a unique measure* $\bar{\mu}$ *on* $(\Omega_1 \times \Omega_2, \mathcal{F}_1 \times \mathcal{F}_2)$ *such that if* $A_1 \in \mathcal{F}_1$ *and* $A_2 \in \mathcal{F}_2$, *then*

$$\bar{\mu}(A_1 \times A_2) = \int_{A_1} \mu_1(d\omega_1)\mu(\omega_1, A_2).$$

Moreover, if f either is a nonnegative measurable function on $(\Omega_1 \times \Omega_2, \mathcal{F}_1 \times \mathcal{F}_2)$ *or is* $\bar{\mu}$*-integrable, then*

$$F(\omega_1) = \int_{\Omega_2} \mu(\omega_1, d\omega_2) f(\omega_1, \omega_2)$$

either is a nonnegative and measurable function on $(\Omega_1, \mathcal{F}_1)$ *or is* μ_1 *integrable, respectively, and*

$$\int_{\Omega_1} \mu_1(d\omega_1) F(\omega_1) = \int_{\Omega_1 \times \Omega_2} \bar{\mu}(d\omega_1, d\omega_2) f(\omega_1, \omega_2).$$

Proof. For $C \in \mathcal{F}_1 \times \mathcal{F}_2$ and $\omega_1 \in \Omega_1$, let $C(\omega_1)$ denote the ω_1 section of C, i.e., the set $\{\omega_2 \in \Omega_2 : (\omega_1, \omega_2) \in C\}$. By showing that the collection of sets $\mathcal{C} = \{C \in \mathcal{F}_1 \times \mathcal{F}_2 : C(\omega_1) \in \mathcal{F}_2\}$ is a σ-field which contains the measurable rectangles $A \times B$, $A \in \mathcal{F}_1$, $B \in \mathcal{F}_2$, one obtains that $\mathcal{C} = \mathcal{F}_1 \times \mathcal{F}_2$ and hence $C(\omega_1) \in \mathcal{F}_2$ for every set $C \in \mathcal{F}_1 \times \mathcal{F}_2$ and $\omega_1 \in \Omega_1$. Therefore for each $C \in \mathcal{F}_1 \times \mathcal{F}_2$, $\mu(\ , C(\ ))$ is a function on Ω_1.

By showing that $\mathcal{D} = \{C \in \mathcal{F}_1 \times \mathcal{F}_2 : \mu(\ , C(\ ))$ is $\mathcal{F}_1$-measurable$\}$ is a monotone class which contains the field of finite disjoint unions of measurable rectangles, one obtains that this $\mathcal{D} = \mathcal{F}_1 \times \mathcal{F}_2$ and hence $\mu(\ , C(\ ))$ is $\mathcal{F}_1$-measurable for each $C \in \mathcal{F}_1 \times \mathcal{F}_2$.

Define $\bar{\mu}$ on $\mathcal{F}_1 \times \mathcal{F}_2$ by

$$\bar{\mu}(C) = \int_{\Omega_1} \mu_1(d\omega_1)\mu(\omega_1, C(\omega_1)). \tag{1.7}$$

To show $\bar{\mu}$ is a measure it is enough to prove that it is countably additive. To this end let $\{C_n\}$ be a countable disjoint collection of sets from $\mathcal{F}_1 \times \mathcal{F}_2$.

For each $\omega_1 \in \Omega_1$, $(\cup_{n=1}^{\infty} C_n)(\omega_1) = \cup_{n=1}^{\infty} C_n(\omega_1)$ and the sections $C_n(\omega_1)$ are disjoint. Since $\mu(\omega_1, \ )$ is a measure,

$$\mu\left(\omega_1, \left(\bigcup_{n=1}^{\infty} C_n\right)(\omega_1)\right) = \sum_{n=1}^{\infty} \mu(\omega_1, C_n(\omega_1))$$

and all terms are nonnegative. By the monotone convergence theorem we have

$$\bar{\mu}\left(\bigcup_{n=1}^{\infty} C_n\right) = \int_{\Omega_1} \mu_1(d\omega_1)\mu\left(\omega_1, \left(\bigcup_{n=1}^{\infty} C_n\right)(\omega_1)\right)$$

$$= \sum_{n=1}^{\infty} \int_{\Omega_1} \mu_1(d\omega_1)\mu(\omega_1, C_n(\omega_1))$$

$$= \sum_{n=1}^{\infty} \bar{\mu}(C_n).$$

It is clear that $\bar{\mu}$ is a probability, and it is unique by the Caratheodory extension theorem. Since $(A_1 \times A_2)(\omega_1) = A_2$, we have $\bar{\mu}(A_1 \times A_2) = \int_{\Omega_1} \mu_1(d\omega_1)\mu(\omega_1, A_2)$.

To complete the proof, notice that if $C \in \mathcal{F}_1 \times \mathcal{F}_2$,

$$\int_{\Omega_2} \mu(\omega_1, d\omega_2) 1_C(\omega_1, \omega_2) = \mu(\omega_1, C(\omega_1)),$$

and we have already shown this is a $\mathcal{F}_1$-measurable function. Thus,

$$\int_{\Omega_1} \mu_1(d\omega_1) \int_{\Omega_2} \mu(\omega_1, d\omega_2) 1_C(\omega_1, \omega_2) = \bar{\mu}(C)$$

$$= \int_{\Omega_1 \times \Omega_2} \bar{\mu}(d(\omega_1, \omega_2)) 1_C(\omega_1, \omega_2).$$

The proof is completed by approximating $\bar{\mu}$-integrable and nonnegative functions by simple functions.

Now suppose ξ and ζ are measurable partitions of the Lebesgue space $(\Omega, \mathcal{F}, P)$. Neglecting a subset of measure zero, we may apply Theorem 1.15 to the spaces $(\Omega, \xi\hat{\ }, P), (\Omega, \zeta\hat{\ })$ and the measures $P^{\xi}(\omega, \ )$ to obtain a unique probability $\bar{\mu}$ on the space $(\Omega \times \Omega, \xi\hat{\ } \times \zeta\hat{\ })$ such that

$$\bar{\mu}(C \times D) = \int_C P(d\omega) P^{\xi}(\omega, D)$$

for all $C \in \xi^\wedge$ and $D \in \zeta^\wedge$. From Equation (1.5) and the definition of $\bar{\mu}$, we have that $P(C \cap D) = \bar{\mu}(C \times D)$, and it follows that $(\Omega, \xi^\wedge \cap \zeta^\wedge, P)$ is isomorphic to $(\Omega \times \Omega, \xi^\wedge \times \zeta^\wedge, \bar{\mu})$. Reversing the roles of ξ and ζ, we see that the measure

$$\bar{\nu}(D \times C) = \int_D P(d\omega) P^{\zeta}(\omega, C)$$

satisfies $P(D \cap C) = \bar{\nu}(D \times C)$, and the measure spaces $(\Omega, \xi^\wedge \cap \zeta^\wedge, P)$, $(\Omega \times \Omega, \xi^\wedge \times \zeta^\wedge, \bar{\mu})$, and $(\Omega \times \Omega, \zeta^\wedge \times \xi^\wedge, \bar{\nu})$ are all isomorphic.

Suppose that ξ and ζ are independent partitions, so that $P(C \cap D) = P(C)P(D)$ for all $C \in \xi^\wedge$, $D \in \zeta^\wedge$. Then the measures $\bar{\mu}$ and $\bar{\nu}$ are ordinary product measures. That is, $\bar{\mu}(C \times D) = P(C)P(D) = \bar{\nu}(D \times C)$. This shows that two partitions ξ and ζ are independent if and only if the measure space $(\Omega \times \Omega, \xi^\wedge \times \zeta^\wedge, \bar{\mu})$ is the product of the two measure spaces $(\Omega, \xi^\wedge, P)$ and $(\Omega, \zeta^\wedge, P)$.

Suppose f is a measurable function on $(\Omega \times \Omega, \xi^\wedge \times \zeta^\wedge)$ which is $\bar{\mu}$-integrable. By Theorem 1.15 we have

$$\int_{\Omega \times \Omega} \bar{\mu}(d\omega_1, d\omega_2) f(\omega_1, \omega_2) = \int_{\Omega} P(d\omega_1) \int_{\Omega} P^{\xi}(\omega_1, d\omega_2) f(\omega_1, \omega_2)$$

and

$$\int_{\Omega \times \Omega} \bar{\nu}(d\omega_2, d\omega_1) f(\omega_1, \omega_2) = \int_{\Omega} P(d\omega_2) \int_{\Omega} P^{\zeta}(\omega_2, d\omega_1) f(\omega_1, \omega_2),$$

and since $\bar{\mu}$ and $\bar{\nu}$ are isomorphic measures, it follows that

$$\int_{\Omega} P(d\omega_1) \int_{\Omega} P^{\xi}(\omega_1, d\omega_2) f(\omega_1, \omega_2) = \int_{\Omega} P(d\omega_2) \int_{\Omega} P^{\zeta}(\omega_2, d\omega_1) f(\omega_1, \omega_2). \tag{1.8}$$

It is not difficult to see that the canonical family of measures associated with the point partition ε of a Lebesgue space is given by the indicator functions of the measurable sets. Thus,

$$P^{\varepsilon}(\omega, A) = 1_A(\omega) \qquad \text{a.e.} \tag{1.9}$$

Also, the canonical family of measures for the trivial partition ν is the measure P, so that

$$P^{\nu}(\omega, A) = P(A) \qquad \text{a.e.} \tag{1.10}$$

Using the first of these equations and Equation (1.8), we have that if x is an integrable random variable on $(\Omega, \mathfrak{F}, P)$ and ξ is a measurable partition, then for $A \in \mathfrak{F}$

$$\int_A P(d\omega_1)\int_\Omega P^{\xi}(\omega_1, d\omega_2)x(\omega_2) = \int_\Omega P(d\omega_1)\int_\Omega P^{\xi}(\omega_1, d\omega_2)1_A(\omega_1)x(\omega_2)$$

$$= \int_\Omega P(d\omega_2)\int_\Omega P^{\varepsilon}(\omega_2, d\omega_1)1_A(\omega_1)x(\omega_2)$$

$$= \int_\Omega P(d\omega_2)x(\omega_2)P^{\varepsilon}(\omega_2, A)$$

$$= \int_A P(d\omega_2)x(\omega_2). \qquad (1.11)$$

To illustrate these ideas, consider the following experiment. We have two urns labeled H and T. In the urn labeled H are three red balls and two white balls, and in the urn labeled T are five blue balls. An unbiased coin is tossed. If the outcome is heads, a ball is drawn from the urn marked H; if tails, from the urn marked T. This compound experiment may be modeled in the space $(S, \mathbb{S}, \mu_f)$ where S is the finite set consisting of the symbols r, w, b; $\mathbb{S}$ is the collection of subsets of S, and the distribution f is given by $f(r)=.3, f(w)=.2, f(b)=.5$. (This example is the first example we gave of a probability space in Section 1.) The coin tossing part of the compound experiment is modeled by the partition $\xi=(H, T)$, where $H=\{r, w\}$ and $T=\{b\}$, of the space $(S, \mathbb{S}, \mu_f)$. Then $S_\xi = \{H, T\}$ with $P_\xi(H)=.5$ and $P_\xi(T)=.5$. The compound experiment can be modeled by the point partition $\varepsilon=(\{r\},\{w\},\{b\})$. The canonical family of measures for ξ is given by

$$P^{\xi}(\{r\}|H)=.6, \qquad P^{\xi}(\{w\}|H)=.4, \qquad P^{\xi}(\{b\}|H)=0,$$

$$P^{\xi}(\{r\}|T)=0, \qquad P^{\xi}(\{w\}|T)=0, \qquad P^{\xi}(\{\mathrm{b}\}|T)=1.$$

The probability of obtaining a white ball from this compound experiment is the same as that of drawing a white ball from an urn with 3 red balls, 2 white balls, and 5 blue balls, because

$$\text{Prob}\{w\} = \int_{S_\xi} P_\xi(d\mathrm{s})P^{\xi}(\{w\}|\mathrm{s})$$

$$= P_\xi(\{H\})P^{\xi}(\{w\}|H) + P_\xi(\{T\})P^{\xi}(\{w\}|T)$$

$$= (.5)(.4) + (.5)(0) = .2.$$

The experiments represented by ξ and ε are clearly not independent.

As another example consider the experiment of drawing a ball from the urn which contains 3 red balls, 2 white balls, and 5 blue balls. We draw a ball, note its color, return the ball to the urn, mix the balls, and draw another ball. The outcome of the experiment will be a pair of labels, for example (r,w), which will denote that a red ball was drawn the first time and a white ball the second. Intuitively, this experiment represents two independent trials of the original urn experiment which is represented by the Lebesgue space $(S,\mathbb{S},\mu_f)$ described above. Let $S^2=S\times S$ and $\mathbb{S}^2=\mathbb{S}\times\mathbb{S}$. The element (s_1,s_2) in S^2 represents an outcome of the experiment, and $E\in\mathbb{S}^2$ an event. In particular consider an event of the form $E_1\times E_2$. The probability of this event is given by

$$\int_{E_1}\mu_f(ds_1)P(s_1,E_2) \tag{1.12}$$

where $P(s_1,E_2)$ is the probability that E_2 occurs given that s_1 was drawn the first time. In this simple case (since we have discrete spaces) we can just consider points. The probability that a red ball, say, was the outcome of the second draw is .3 regardless of the outcome of the first draw because 30% of the balls in the urn are still colored red. Thus $P(s_1,\{r\})=P\{r\}=.3$ for any $s_1\in S$. Continuing for white and blue balls and using Equation (1.12), we see that

$$P(\{s_1,s_2\})=\mu_f\{s_1\}\mu_f\{s_2\},\qquad (s_1,s_2)\in S^2,$$

and the probability measure is the product of the measure μ_f with itself. This compound experiment consisting of two independent trials of the experiment represented by $(S,\mathbb{S},\mu_f)$ is given by $(S^2,\mathbb{S}^2,\mu_f\times\mu_f)$, the product measure space. If ξ and ζ denote the partitions

$$\xi=(\{(s_1,s_2):s_1=r\},\{(s_1,s_2):s_1=w\},\{(s_1,s_2):s_1=b\}),$$

$$\zeta=(\{(s_1,s_2):s_2=r\},\ \{(s_1,s_2):s_2=w\},\{(s_1,s_2):s_2=b\}),$$

then ξ represents the first trial and ζ the second trial as subexperiments of the space $(S^2,\mathbb{S}^2,\mu_f\times\mu_f)$. It is clear that ξ and ζ are independent.

Now consider drawing two balls from the urn without replacement. Again the experiment may be modeled as a set of pairs of elements, but the probability will not be given by the product measure. Let $(S^2,\mathbb{S}^2)$ be the same measurable space as above, with the pair (s_1,s_2) representing the outcome "a ball of color s_1 on the first draw and a ball of color s_2 on the second." The partition ξ described above represents the part of the experiment which consists of drawing the first ball. Thus $(S^2_\xi,\mathbb{S}^2_\xi,P^2_\xi)$ is to be isomorphic to $(S,\mathbb{S},\mu_f)$, where P^2 is the (as yet unknown) probability in

S^2. The isomorphism can be given by associating $s \in S$ with $\{(s_1, s_2) : s_1 = s\}$ in S_ξ^2. Then

$$P^2(\{(s_1,s_2):s_1=s\})=\mu_f(\{s\})=\begin{cases} .3 & \text{if} \quad s=r, \\ .2 & \text{if} \quad s=w, \\ .5 & \text{if} \quad s=b. \end{cases}$$

The canonical family of measures $P^\xi(\ |s)$ may be computed by observing the distributions in the urn after a ball has been selected. Thus

$$P^\xi(\{(r,r)\}|r)=\tfrac{2}{9}, \qquad P^\xi(\{(r,w)\}|r)=\tfrac{2}{9}, \qquad P^\xi(\{r,b\}|r)=\tfrac{5}{9},$$

and

$$P^\xi(\{(s_1,s_2)\}|r)=0 \qquad \text{if} \quad s_1 \neq r.$$

Similar values may be calculated for $P^\xi(\ |w)$ and $P^\xi(\ |b)$. From these values and Equation (1.12), we can calculate $P^2(A)$ for any $A \in \mathcal{S}^2$. For example, suppose $A = \{(r,w),(w,w),(b,w)\}$. Then

$$P^2(A)=\int_{S_{\xi 2}} P_\xi(ds)P^\xi(A|s)$$

$$-\sum_{s\in S} \mu_f(s)P^\xi(A|s)$$

$$=\tfrac{18}{90}.$$

With the probability space $(S^2, \mathcal{S}^2, P^2)$ representing the compound experiment of drawing without replacement, the partition ζ described above represents the subexperiment consisting of the second draw. The partitions ξ and ζ are not independent, because the set A defined above is a set in $\xi\hat{}$ with $P^\xi(A|r)=\frac{2}{9}$ while $P_\zeta(A)=P^2(A)=\frac{2}{10}$.

1.6 Conditional Expectation of Random Variables

In Section 1.4, the expected value of a real valued random variable x was defined to be the integral of x over the probability space on which it is defined, and its interpretation as the value one expects on the average in many independent trials was given. In this section, we shall give a definition and interpretation of the value we should expect on the average if we know the outcome of some experiment. This will be called the conditional expectation of x.

Suppose the random variable x is defined on the Lebesgue space $(\Omega, \mathcal{F}, P)$, and E is an event from $\mathcal{F}$ with $P(E)>0$. If we are told that an experiment has resulted in the event E, then the probabilities of events need to be modified to make use of this information. This modification was obtained in the last section by using the probability space $(E, \mathcal{F}(E), P(\ |E))$ in place of $(\Omega, \mathcal{F}, P)$. The expected value of our random variable must also be changed to take into account the knowledge that event E has occurred. The value we now expect for the random variable x should be the integral of x restricted to the probability space $(E, \mathcal{F}(E), P(\ |E))$, or since $P(\ |E)$ is supported by E, the integral of x with respect to the conditional probability $P(\ |E)$.

As we did in Section 1.5, we now extend these ideas to measurable partitions. If ξ is a measurable partition of $(\Omega, \mathcal{F}, P)$, then for almost all $a \in \Omega_\xi$ the Lebesgue space $(A, \mathcal{F}(A), P^\xi(\ |a))$, where $A = \mathrm{N}_\xi^{-1}(a)$ and $P^\xi(\ |a)$ is a member of the canonical family of measures associated with ξ, carries the information that outcome $a \in \Omega_\xi$ or event $A \in \mathcal{F}$ has occurred. The integral of the random variable x over this space is the value we expect for x if we know A has occurred. The function $E^\xi(x|\ )$ defined almost everywhere on $(\Omega_\xi, \mathcal{F}_\xi, P_\xi)$ by the equation

$$E^\xi(x|a) = \int_\Omega P^\xi(d\omega|a)x(\omega) \tag{1.13}$$

is called the *conditional expectation* of x given the partition ξ. Notice that $E^\xi(x|a)$ is only defined for those $a \in \Omega_\xi$ for which $P^\xi(\ |a)$ exists, and its value at any such a is the average of x over the space $(A, \mathcal{F}(A), P^\xi(\ |a))$, since $P^\xi(\Omega - A|a) = 0$ implies that

$$\int_\Omega P^\xi(d\omega|a)x(\omega) = \int_A P^\xi(d\omega|a)x(\omega).$$

It is usually more convenient to have the conditional expectation as a function on the original Lebesgue space $(\Omega, \mathcal{F}, P)$ than on the factor space $(\Omega_\xi, \mathcal{F}_\xi, P_\xi)$. To accomplish this, all we need to do is compose $E^\xi(x|\ )$ with the projection N_ξ associated with ξ which sends a point ω to the atom of ξ which contains it. This composition will be denoted by $E^\xi(x|\omega)$, that is, if x is a real valued random variable on $(\Omega, \mathcal{F}, P)$ which is integrable and ξ is a measurable partition of Ω, then

$$E^\xi(x|\omega) = \int_\Omega P^\xi(d\bar{\omega}|\mathrm{N}_\xi(\omega))x(\bar{\omega})$$

$$= \int_\Omega P^\xi(\omega, d\bar{\omega})x(\bar{\omega}),$$

and we shall usually suppress the variable ω and write $E^{\xi}(x)$. It is not difficult to see that $E^{\xi}(x)$ is an almost everywhere defined $\xi^{\wedge}$-measurable function on Ω which is constant on the atoms of ξ.

As an example, consider a countable partition ξ with atoms $A_j, j=1,2,\ldots$, such that $P(A_j)>0$ for at least one j. For all such j,

$$P^{\xi}(E|a_j)=\frac{P(E\cap A_j)}{P(A_j)},$$

where $N_{\xi}^{-1}(a_j)=A_j$. If x is a given integrable random variable on $(\Omega,\mathcal{F},P)$, its average over $(A_j,\mathcal{F}(A_j),P^{\xi}(\ |a_j))$, is

$$\int_{A_j} x(\omega)\frac{P(d\omega)}{P(A_j)}=\frac{1}{P(A_j)}\int_{A_j} P(d\omega)x(\omega).$$

Thus,

$$E^{\xi}(x|\omega)=\sum\left[\frac{1}{P(A_j)}\int_{A_j} P(d\omega)x(\omega)\right]1_{A_j}(\omega) \tag{1.14}$$

where the sum is taken over all j such that $P(A_j)>0$. In particular, if F is any measurable set in Ω,

$$E^{\xi}(1_F|\omega)=\sum\frac{P(F\cap A_j)}{P(A_j)}1_{A_j}(\omega). \tag{1.15}$$

Suppose ζ is an arbitrary measurable partition on $(\Omega,\mathcal{F},P)$ and $F\in\mathcal{F}$. Then

$$\begin{aligned} E^{\zeta}(1_F|\omega) &= \int_{\Omega} P^{\zeta}(d\omega|N_{\xi}(\omega))1_F(\omega) \\ &= P^{\zeta}(F|N_{\xi}(\omega)) \\ &= P^{\zeta}(\omega,F). \end{aligned} \tag{1.16}$$

The properties of E^{ζ} will be used extensively in the sequel, and we will now derive them.

PROPOSITION 1.16. *If x is an integrable random variable on $(\Omega,\mathcal{F},P)$ and ε, ν denote respectively the point partition and the trivial partition, then*

$$E^{\varepsilon}(x)=x \quad a.e. \quad \text{and} \quad E^{\nu}(x)=E(x) \quad a.e.$$

Proof. This follows immediately from the definition and the values of $P^{\varepsilon}(\ |a)$ and $P^{\nu}(\ |a)$ given by Equations (1.9) and (1.10).

THEOREM 1.17. *Let ξ be a measurable partition of the Lebesgue space $(\Omega, \mathfrak{F}, P)$.*

1.17.1. *If x is almost everywhere equal to a constant K on Ω, then $E^{\xi}(x) = K$ almost everywhere on Ω.*

1.17.2. *If x and y are integrable random variables such that $x \leqslant y$ a.e., then $E^{\xi}(x) \leqslant E^{\xi}(y)$ a.e.*

1.17.3. *If x is an integrable random variable, then $|E^{\xi}(x)|$ is less than or equal to $E^{\xi}(|x|)$ a.e.*

1.17.4. *If x and y are integrable random variables and c_1, c_2 are real numbers, then*

$$E^{\xi}(c_1x + c_2y) = c_1E^{\xi}(x) + c_2E^{\xi}(y) \qquad a.e.$$

1.17.5. *If $\{x_n\}$ is a sequence of real valued random variables such that $\lim_{n\to\infty} x_n = x$ a.e. and there exists an integrable random variable y such that $|x_n| \leqslant y$ a.e. for all n, then*

$$\lim_{n\to\infty} E^{\xi}(x_n) = E^{\xi}(x) \qquad a.e.$$

Proof. All of the statements follow immediately from the definition, since for fixed ω outside a set of measure zero $E^{\xi}(\ |\omega)$ is an integral, and these are classical properties of the integral.

Another property of conditional expectation which follows immediately from its definition as an integral is Jensen's inequality.

THEOREM 1.18. *Let ϕ be a real valued continuous convex function defined on the reals, and let x be an integrable random variable defined on the Lebesgue space $(\Omega, \mathfrak{F}, P)$. If ζ is any measurable partition of Ω, then*

$$E^{\zeta}(\phi(x)) \geqslant \phi(E^{\zeta}(x)) \qquad \text{a.e}$$

In most discussions, the conditional expectation is defined as the Radon-Nikodym derivative of a certain measure. We shall show now that $E^{\zeta}(x)$ is a version of a Radon-Nikodym derivative and then use the uniqueness of these derivatives to obtain other important properties of the conditional expectation.

Let $\mathfrak{F}'$ be a given sub-σ-field of $\mathfrak{F}$, and x an integrable random variable on $(\Omega, \mathfrak{F}, P)$. Define the signed measure m on $\mathfrak{F}$ by

$$m(A) = \int_A P(d\omega)x(\omega).$$

Then m is absolutely continuous with respect to P restricted to $\mathcal{F}'$, and by the Radon-Nikodym theorem there exists a unique $\mathcal{F}'$-measurable function f such that $m(A)=\int_A P(d\omega)f(\omega)$ for all $A\in\mathcal{F}'$. The key fact to note here is that f is $\mathcal{F}'$-measurable. The uniqueness means that if g is any other $\mathcal{F}'$-measurable function such that $m(A)=\int_A P(d\omega)g(\omega)$ for all $A\in\mathcal{F}'$, then $g=f$ a.e.

Let ζ be a measurable partition of Ω such that $\zeta^{\wedge}=\mathcal{F}'$. By Theorem 1.15 and the definition of $E^{\zeta}(x|\omega)$ is $\zeta^{\wedge}$-measurable and if $A\in\zeta^{\wedge}$ we have from Equation (1.11) that

$$\int_A P(d\omega)E^{\zeta}(x|\omega)=\int_A P(d\omega)x(\omega).$$

It now follows from the uniqueness of f that $f=E^{\zeta}(x)$ a.e. and $E^{\zeta}(x)$ is a version of the Radon-Nikodym derivative.

THEOREM 1.19. *If x and y are integrable random variables on $(\Omega,\mathcal{F},P)$ and ξ is a measurable partition such that x is $\xi^{\wedge}$-measurable, then*

$$E^{\xi}(xy)=xE^{\xi}(y) \qquad \text{a.e.}$$

Proof. Let A be any ξ-set. Then

$$\int_A P(d\omega)\left[x(\omega)E^{\xi}(y|\omega)\right]=\int_A P(d\omega)x(\omega)\int_\Omega P^{\xi}(\omega,d\omega_1)y(\omega_1).$$

However, using Fubini's Theorem 1.15 applied to $x(\omega)y(\omega_1)1_A(\omega)$ gives

$$\begin{aligned}\int_A P(d\omega)\left[x(\omega)E^{\xi}(y|\omega)\right]&=\int_\Omega P(d\omega)\int_\Omega P^{\xi}(\omega,d\omega_1)1_A(\omega)x(\omega)y(\omega_1)\\&=\int_\Omega P(d\omega_1)\int_\Omega P^{\xi}(\omega_1,d\omega)1_A(\omega)x(\omega)y(\omega_1)\\&=\int_\Omega P(d\omega_1)E^{\xi}(1_Ax|\omega_1)y(\omega_1)\\&=\int_\Omega P(d\omega_1)1_A(\omega_1)x(\omega_1)y(\omega_1)\\&=\int_A P(d\omega_1)x(\omega_1)y(\omega_1),\end{aligned}$$

since $1_A x$ is $\xi^\wedge$-measurable and we have

$$\int_A P(d\omega)\left[x(\omega)E^\xi(y|\omega)\right]=\int_A P(d\omega)E^\xi(xy|\omega)$$

for all $A\in\xi^\wedge$. Since both $xE^\xi(y)$ and $E^\xi(xy)$ are $\xi^\wedge$-measurable we have that

$$E^\xi(xy)=xE^\xi(y) \qquad \text{a.e.}$$

The next theorem should be intuitively clear. Let $\xi\leqslant\zeta$, so that ξ is a subexperiment of ζ. Averaging a function over atoms in ζ and then averaging these averages over the atoms in ξ should give the same result as averaging over the atoms in ξ.

THEOREM 1.20. *If x is an integrable random variable on $(\Omega,\mathcal{F},P)$, and ξ and ζ are measurable partitions of Ω such that $\xi\leqslant\zeta$, then*

$$E^\xi(E^\zeta(x))=E^\xi(x).$$

Proof. Let $A\in\xi^\wedge$. Then

$$\int_A P(d\omega)E^\xi(E^\zeta(x|\omega))=\int_A P(d\omega)\int_\Omega P^\xi(\omega,d\omega_1)E^\zeta(x|\omega_1)$$

$$=\int_A P(d\omega)\int_{\Omega_\xi} P^\xi(d\omega_1|\mathbf{N}_\xi(\omega))E^\zeta(x|\omega_1).$$

By using the transitive property of canonical families of measures we have

$$\int_{\Omega_\xi} P^\xi(d\omega_1|\mathbf{N}_\xi(\omega))E^\zeta(x|\omega_1)=\int_{\Omega_\zeta} P^\zeta(d\omega_1|\mathbf{N}_\zeta(\omega))E^\zeta(x|\omega_1)$$

and thus

$$\int_A P(d\omega)E^\xi(E^\zeta(x|\omega))=\int_A P(d\omega)\int_\Omega P^\zeta(\omega,d\omega_1)E^\zeta(x|\omega_1)$$

$$=\int_A P(d\omega)E^\zeta(x|\omega)$$

$$=\int_A P(d\omega)x(\omega),$$

since $A \in \zeta^{\hat{}}$. Thus for each $A \in \xi^{\hat{}}$

$$\int_A P(d\omega) E^{\xi}(E^{\zeta}(x|\omega)) = \int_A P(d\omega) E^{\xi}(x|\omega),$$

and it follows from uniqueness that

$$E^{\xi}(E^{\zeta}(x)) = E^{\xi}(x) \qquad \text{a.e.}$$

1.7 Stochastic Processes and Dynamical Systems

A stochastic process is a mathematical abstraction of random phenomena which develops according to a parameter, usually time, and whose development is governed by probabilistic laws. For example, the repeated draws of a ball from an urn can be represented by a stochastic process. Other examples of situations or phenomena which can be represented by stochastic processes are the repeated tosses of a coin, the position of the oil drop in Millikan's oil drop experiment, the winnings of a gambler playing a series of games of roulette, the number of people waiting in line at a movie theater, etc.

For our purposes, stochastic sequences will usually be adequate. These are processes in which the parameter set is countable and therefore may be taken to be the integers or some subset of the integers.

DEFINITION 1.21. A stochastic sequence in a measurable space $(\Gamma, \mathcal{G})$ is a collection of random variables defined on some Lebesgue space with ranges in Γ which is indexed by a subset of the integers.

For example, consider repeated drawings with replacement from an urn which contains red, white, and blue balls in the ratio of 3:2:5, and put no restriction on the number of draws that are to be made. This experiment can be represented by the Lebesgue space $(\Sigma(S), \mathcal{F}, \mu)$ described in Example 1.3 with $S = \{r, w, b\}$. For each positive integer n, define x_n on $\Sigma(S)$ by

$$x_n(\omega) = \omega(n),$$

where $\omega(n)$ denotes the nth coordinate of the sequence ω. The collection $\{x_n : n \in Z\}$ is a stochastic sequence whose nth term represents the outcome of the nth draw.

Now suppose that you are playing the following gambling game with the above urn. If a red or white ball is drawn, you win one dollar; if a blue ball is drawn, you lose one dollar. We assume you have an unlimited supply of money and the game never ends. The drawing of balls from the urn is represented by the Lebesgue space $(\Sigma(S), \mathcal{F}, \mu)$, and if we define g on S by

$$g(s)=\begin{cases} +1 & \text{if} \quad s=r, \\ +1 & \text{if} \quad s=w, \\ -1 & \text{if} \quad s=b, \end{cases}$$

then $g \circ x_n$ is a random variable on $\Sigma(S)$. Its value will depend on the outcome of the nth draw and represents what you win (or lose) as a consequence of this draw. Thus $\{g \circ x_n : n=1,2,\dots\}$ is a stochastic sequence which represents the game.

The probabilistic law governing the development of a stochastic process is given by the *joint probability distributions* of the random variables that determine the process. If x is a random variable on a Lebesgue space $(\Omega, \mathcal{F}, P)$, then the *distribution space* of x is the factor space associated with the partition $x^{-1}(\varepsilon)$ of Ω, where ε denotes the point partition in the range space of x. In all the cases that we will consider this range space will itself be a Lebesgue space (or at least countably generated), so that $x^{-1}(\varepsilon)$ is a measurable partition. In Section 1.4 we denoted this factor space by $(\Omega_x, \mathcal{F}_x, P_x)$. The probability P_x is called the *distribution* of x. As we pointed out in Section 1.4, the outcomes in the distribution space of x are exactly those events from $\mathcal{F}$ which can be determined by knowing the values attained by x.

Suppose now that $\{x_n : n \in I\}$ is some finite set of random variables on $(\Omega, \mathcal{F}, P)$ to a space $(\Gamma, \mathcal{G})$, where $\mathcal{G}$ is generated by a countable collection of sets. The *joint distribution space* of this collection is defined to be the factor space associated with the common refinement of the partitions $x_n^{-1}(\varepsilon)$ for $n \in I$. The *joint probability distribution* or *joint distribution* for the collection $\{x_n : n \in I\}$ is P_ζ, where $\zeta = \bigvee_{n \in I} x_n^{-1}(\varepsilon)$. This measure is uniquely determined by the values

$$P\{\omega \in \Omega : x_n(\omega) \in B_n, n \in I\}, \tag{1.17}$$

where $\{B_n\}$ are selected from a countable generating family for $\mathcal{F}$. The numbers given in (1.17) as $\{B_n : n \in I\}$ varies over subsets in a countable generating family are what are most often referred to as the joint probability distributions of the random variables $\{x_n : n \in I\}$.

In most applications it is just the joint probability distributions that are known, and a stochastic process is classified according to the properties of the distributions of all finite collections of random variables selected from the process. For example, if $\{x_n : n \in Z\}$ is a stochastic sequence such that for every finite subset I of Z the partitions $\{x_t^{-1}(\varepsilon) : t \in I\}$ are independent, then $\{x_n\}$ is called an independent process. The example given above of drawing balls from an urn with replacement is an independent process. For another example, a stochastic sequence $\{x_n : n \in Z^+\}$ is called a Gaussian process if the joint distribution for each finite subset of Z^+ is normal.

Two stochastic processes are *equivalent*, or the same process, if they have the same parameter set T and isomorphic finite joint distribution spaces for each finite subset of T.

For example, consider the two stochastic process $\{g_n : n \in Z^+\}$ and $\{y_n : n \in Z^+\}$, where $g_n = g \circ x_n$ with x_n and g defined as above. Let y_n be defined as follows: Set $S_1 = \{+1, -1\}$ and $f_1(+1) = \frac{1}{2}$, $f_1(-1) = \frac{1}{2}$. Construct the Lebesgue space $(\Sigma(S_1), \mathcal{F}_1, \mu_1)$ as was described in Example 1.3 and take

$$y_n(\omega) = \omega(n)$$

for any sequence $\omega \in \Sigma(S_1)$. It is easy to check that these two stochastic sequences are *equivalent*. Notice that the second sequence is a model of a sequence of coin tossing games with one dollar won if a head turns up, say, and one dollar lost if a tail turns up.

Suppose we have a stochastic sequence in $(\Gamma, \mathcal{G})$ with parameter set T, and we only know the joint probability distributions of the sequence. It is usually possible to construct a canonical Lebesgue space and random variables on this space which represents the process. This is done by taking Ω to be the Cartesian product of as many copies of Γ as there are elements in T, and $\mathcal{F}$ to be the product σ-field of the same number of copies of $\mathcal{G}$. The probability P is constructed using Kolmogoroff's extension theorem, as was done in obtaining Examples 1.3–1.7. In these examples the given consistent families of measures are the joint probability distributions of the sequence. The sequence of random variables is obtained as above by taking the nth random variable to be the projection onto the nth coordinate. The space $(\Omega, \mathcal{F}, P)$ obtained this way is sometimes called the realization space or path space of the process. Notice that a point $\omega \in \Omega$ is a possible sequence of elements of Γ obtained as the process develops in time.

Because the realization space of a process contains all the pertinent information about the process, some people consider a stochastic process to be a probability measure on the Cartesian product of some family $\{(\Gamma_t, \mathcal{G}_t) : t \in T\}$ of measurable spaces. We do not choose to do this, however, and will usually consider a stochastic process as an indexed set of random variables on a Lebesgue space.

Now consider the Lebesgue space $(\Sigma(S), \mathcal{F}, \mu)$ defined in Example 1.3, and define a map $\mathbf{T}$ on $\Sigma(S)$ to itself by

$$(\mathbf{T}\omega)(n) = \omega(n+1)$$

Thus $\mathbf{T}$ sends the sequence $(\ldots, \omega_{-1}, \omega_0, \omega_1, \ldots)$ to the sequence $(\ldots, \omega_0, \omega_1, \omega_2, \ldots)$. One can check without too much difficulty that if C is a cylinder set, then $\mathbf{T}^{-1}(C)$ is also, and since the cylinder sets generate $\mathcal{F}$, $\mathbf{T}$ is a measurable function on $(\Sigma(S), \mathcal{F})$ to itself. Also, it is true that if $F \in \mathcal{F}$, then $\mu(\mathbf{T}^{-1}F) = \mu(F)$, and $\mathbf{T}$ is a transformation which preserves the measure μ.

The map defined above is called the shift transformation and is an example of a *metric endomorphism*.

DEFINITION 1.22. A metric endomorphism of a Lebesgue space $(\Omega, \mathcal{F}, P)$ is a measurable transformation $\mathbf{T}$ on Ω to Ω such that for any $F \in \mathcal{F}$ we have $\mathbf{T}^{-1}F \in \mathcal{F}$ and $P(\mathbf{T}^{-1}F) = P(F)$. If the range of $\mathbf{T}$ is almost all of Ω, and the restriction of $\mathbf{T}$ to a subset of Ω of measure 1 is invertible, and this inverse map is a metric endomorphism, then $\mathbf{T}$ is a *metric automorphism*.

Notice that what we called an isomorphism (mod 0) between $(\Omega, \mathcal{F}, P)$ and itself in Section 1.2 is a metric automorphism.

A dynamical system is a quadruple $(\Omega, \mathcal{F}, P, \mathbf{T})$ where $(\Omega, \mathcal{F}, P)$ is a Lebesgue space and $\mathbf{T}$ is a metric endomorphism on Ω. In case $\mathbf{T}$ is a metric automorphism, the dynamical system will be said to be invertible.

Let $(\Omega, \mathcal{F}, P, \mathbf{T})$ be a dynamical system, and x be a random variable on $(\Omega, \mathcal{F}, P)$. Since $\mathbf{T}$ is a metric endomorphism, $x \circ \mathbf{T}^n$ is a random variable for each $n \in Z^+$, and consequently if we define

$$x_n(\omega) = x(\mathbf{T}^n(\omega)),$$

then $\{x_n : n \in Z^+\}$ is a stochastic process. In case the dynamical system is invertible (i.e., $\mathbf{T}$ is a metric automorphism), then $x \circ \mathbf{T}^{-n}$ is also a random variable and $\{x_n : n \in Z\}$ is a stochastic process.

Because $P(\mathbf{T}^{-1}E) = P(E)$, the stochastic processes described in the previous paragraph have stationary joint distributions and are examples of *stationary* stochastic processes. This type of stochastic process is defined as follows. Suppose $\{B_1, B_2, \ldots, B_n\}$ is a collection of sets from a generating family for $\mathcal{G}$ where x takes values in $(\Gamma, \mathcal{G})$. Then

$$x^{-1}(B_1) \cap \mathbf{T}^{-1}(x^{-1}B_2) \cap \cdots \cap \mathbf{T}^{-n}(x^{-1}B_n) \in \mathcal{F},$$

and since $\mathbf{T}$ is measure preserving,

$$P\left[x^{-1}(B_1) \cap \cdots \cap \mathbf{T}^{-n}(x^{-1}(B_n))\right]$$

$$= P\left[\mathbf{T}^{-1}x^{-1}(B_1) \cap \cdots \cap \mathbf{T}^{-n-1}x^{-1}(B_n)\right].$$

This last equation states that the joint probability distribution of $\{x_1, \ldots, x_{n+1}\}$ is the same as the joint probability distribution of $\{x_0, x_1, \ldots, x_n\}$. It is easy to show that this implies that if I is any finite subset of integers, the joint probability distribution of $\{x_n : n \in I\}$ is the same as that of

$$\{x_{n+k} : n \in I\} \text{ for any } k \in Z^+.$$

The physical interpretation of a stochastic process $\{x_t : t \in Z\}$, as we indicated at the beginning of this section, is that of a phenomenon developing with the parameter t, which we shall think of as time. The stationarity of a stochastic process insures that the probability structure is unchanged by the passage of time. Consequently such processes represent a "steady state" phenomenon, i.e., a dynamic structure that is independent of time.

Let $(\Omega, \mathcal{F}, P, \mathbf{T})$ be an invertible dynamical system and ξ a measurable partition of Ω. Suppose the random variable x on Ω to the factor space Ω_ξ is the canonical projection $\mathbf{N}_\xi$ which sends ω to the atom of ξ that contains ω. Then $\{x \circ \mathbf{T}^n : n \in Z\}$ is a stationary stochastic process, and we see how every measurable partition on a dynamical system can give rise to a stationary stochastic sequence.

Conversely, if $\{x_n : n \in Z\}$ is a stationary stochastic sequence, let ξ_n denote the measurable partition $x_n^{-1}(\varepsilon)$, where ε is the point partition in the range of the random variables, and let ξ denote $\bigvee_{-\infty}^{+\infty} \xi_n$. Each point $\bar{\omega}$ in the factor space, $(\Omega_\xi, \mathcal{F}_\xi, P_\xi)$ has a representation of the form

$$\bar{\omega} = \bigcap_{n=-\infty}^{+\infty} x_n^{-1}(r_n),$$

where $(\ldots, r_{-1}, r_0, r_1, \ldots)$ is a doubly infinite sequence of elements from the range of the x's. Define the transformation $\mathbf{T}$ on Ω_ξ by

$$\mathbf{T}(\bar{\omega}) = \bigcap_{n=-\infty}^{+\infty} x_{n+1}^{-1}(r_n).$$

Since the process is stationary, $\mathbf{T}$ is measure preserving and $(\Omega_\xi, \mathcal{F}_\xi, P_\xi, \mathbf{T})$ is an invertible dynamical system. The stationary stochastic process $\{y_n : n \in Z\}$, where $y_0 = \mathbf{N}_{\xi\xi_0}$ is the canonical projection of Ω_ξ onto Ω_{ξ_0} and $y_n = y_0 \circ \mathbf{T}^n$, is equivalent to the process $\{x_n : n \in Z\}$.

In view of the last two paragraphs, stationary stochastic sequences are equivalent to measurable partitions of a dynamical system, and stationary stochastic processes can be represented as $(\mathbf{T}, \xi)$, where $\mathbf{T}$ is a metric automorphism (or endomorphism) and ξ is a measurable partition of the Lebesgue space on which $\mathbf{T}$ is defined. The type of the process is determined by the joint distribution of the random variables, and these in turn are given by the factor spaces associated with the partition $\bigvee_{j \in S} \mathbf{T}^{-j}\xi$.

For example, the process $(\mathbf{T}, \xi)$ is an *independent* process, or ξ is an independent partition, if and only if the collection $\{\mathbf{T}^{-j}\xi : j \in Z\}$ of partitions is independent. (Here we assume $\mathbf{T}$ is a metric automorphism, so that $\mathbf{T}\xi \equiv \{\mathbf{T}C : C \in \xi\}$ is also a measurable partition.) The process $(\mathbf{T}, \xi)$ is a *Markov process*, or ξ is a *Markov partition*, if for every $n > 1$ the conditional probability of ξ given $\bigvee_{j=1}^{n} \mathbf{T}^{-j}\xi$ is equal to the conditional probability of ξ given $\mathbf{T}^{-1}\xi$.

Consider a dynamical system $(\Omega, \mathfrak{F}, P, \mathbf{T})$ as a mathematical model of a universe with a mechanism (given by $\mathbf{T}$) which depicts development in time. The measurable partitions of Ω correspond to random experiments, so that if ξ is a given experiment, $\mathbf{T}^{-1}\xi$ represents the same experiment conducted one time unit later. The fact that $\mathbf{T}$ is probability preserving insures that the probability structure of the experiment does not change with the passage of time. Atoms of $\bigvee_{j=0}^{n} \mathbf{T}^{-j}\xi$ are the outcomes of $n+1$ repetitions of the experiment. From this point of view it is interesting to know whether or not all possible events can be obtained from repetitions of the experiment, and in particular if there exists a finite experiment whose repetitions give every event. A partition ξ is said to be a *generating* partition for $(\Omega, \mathfrak{F}, P, \mathbf{T})$ if $\bigvee_{j=-\infty}^{+\infty} \mathbf{T}^{j}\xi = \varepsilon$ (mod 0), or equivalently if and only if $(\bigvee_{-n}^{n} T^{j}\xi)^{\hat{}} \uparrow \mathfrak{F}$. Rohlin [126, 127], Parry [112–116], and Krieger [71] have made major contributions to the problem of giving conditions on $\mathbf{T}$ which insure the existence of finite or countable generating partitions.

If ξ is any measurable partition of a space $(\Omega, \mathfrak{F}, P)$ and $\mathbf{T}$ is a metric automorphism of Ω, then ξ is a generating partition for $(\Omega_{\xi^\infty}, \mathfrak{F}_{\xi^\infty}, P_{\xi^\infty}, \mathbf{T}_{\xi^\infty})$, where $\xi^\infty = \bigvee_{-\infty}^{+\infty} \mathbf{T}^{j}\xi$. The transformation $\mathbf{T}_{\xi^\infty}$ is defined by

$$\bigcap_{j=-\infty}^{\infty} \mathbf{T}^{j}(A_j) \rightarrow \bigcap_{j=-\infty}^{\infty} \mathbf{T}^{j+1}(A_j),$$

where $\bigcap_{j=-\infty}^{+\infty} \mathbf{T}^{j}(A_j)$ is a representative of an atom of Ω_{ξ^∞} and the sequence $(A_j)_{j=-\infty}^{+\infty}$ is selected arbitrarily from ξ.

1.8 The Ergodic Theorem and the Martingale Convergence Theorem

Suppose x is a given real valued random variable on $(\Omega, \mathfrak{F}, P)$, and $\mathbf{T}$ is a metric endomorphism of Ω. As we saw in the previous section, $x_n = x \circ \mathbf{T}^n$ is a stationary stochastic sequence, and if $\omega \in \Omega$ is selected, the sequence $x_0(\omega), x_1(\omega), \ldots, x_n(\omega), \ldots$ is a representation of the values the random variable x takes on as time passes. After N time units have passed, the time average of x is $(1/N)\Sigma_{j=0}^{N-1} x_j(\omega) = (1/N)\Sigma_{j=0}^{N-1} x(\mathbf{T}^{j}\omega)$. If the limit of the sequence

$$\left\{\frac{1}{N}\sum_{0}^{N-1} x(\mathbf{T}^j\omega)\right\}_{N>1}$$

exists, this limit represents the value we would expect x to assume on the average. In particular, suppose $x(\omega)=1_A(\omega)$, where A is an event in $\mathcal{F}$. Then

$$\frac{1}{N}\sum_{0}^{N-1} x(\mathbf{T}^j\omega)=\frac{1}{N}\sum_{0}^{N-1} 1_{\mathbf{T}^{-j}A}(\omega)$$

represents the average number of occurrences of A in N repetitions of the experiment represented by the partition $\{A,\Omega-A\}$. To see this, recall that A occurs if and only if $\omega\in A$. If ω is the outcome at time 0, then $\mathbf{T}\omega$ is the outcome at time 1, and in general $\mathbf{T}^n\omega$ is the outcome at time n. Thus $\omega\in\mathbf{T}^{-j}A$ if and only if $\mathbf{T}^j\omega\in A$, so $1_{\mathbf{T}^{-j}A}(\omega)=1$ if and only if A occurs at time j.

In case $\{A,\Omega-A\}=\xi$ is an independent partition (i.e., $\{\mathbf{T}^{-j}\xi: j\in Z\}$ is an independent family of partitions), then these partitions represent independent trials of a two outcome experiment. In this case, from our intuitive idea of probability, we should have this average number of occurrences of A converging to $P(A)$. As a matter of fact, the strong law of large numbers is just the statement that

$$\lim_{N\to\infty}\frac{1}{N}\sum_{0}^{N-1} 1_A(\mathbf{T}^j\omega)=P(A) \qquad P\text{-a.e.}$$

provided $\{A,\Omega-A\}$ is an independent partition for $\mathbf{T}$.

Suppose $(\Omega,\mathcal{F},P)$ is the unit interval with Lebesgue measure, and $\mathbf{T}$ is the transformation that sends $(0,\frac{1}{2}]$ linearly onto $(\frac{1}{2},1]$ and sends $(\frac{1}{2},1]$ linearly onto $(0,\frac{1}{2}]$. Let $A=(\frac{1}{4},\frac{1}{2}]\cup(\frac{3}{4},1]$. By an easy computation you can see that

$$\lim_{N\to\infty}\frac{1}{N}\sum_{1}^{N-1} 1_A(\mathbf{T}^j\omega)=\begin{cases}1 & \text{if} \quad \omega\in A,\\ 0 & \text{if} \quad \omega\notin A,\end{cases}$$

and it is not the case that this limit is almost everywhere the constant $P(A)$. It is clear that if there are any sets which are invariant under T, the same thing will happen for these sets.

Suppose however that there are no nontrivial (i.e. not probability 0 or 1) T-invariant sets. In this case a very important theorem, the ergodic theorem, states that essentially the same thing happens for this $\mathbf{T}$ as in the case where $\{A,\Omega-A\}$ was an independent partition under $\mathbf{T}$. Such metric endomorphisms are called *ergodic*.

DEFINITION 1.23. A dynamical system $(\Omega, \mathcal{F}, P, \mathbf{T})$, or a metric endomorphism $\mathbf{T}$ is *ergodic* if $P(\mathbf{T}^{-1}A \triangle A)=0$ implies that either $P(A)=0$ or $P(A)=1$.

Before stating the ergodic theorem, we state and prove a lemma which is central in the proof. The proof of the lemma that we give here is due to Garsia.

MAXIMAL ERGODIC LEMMA. *If $(\Omega, \mathcal{F}, P, \mathbf{T})$ is a dynamical system, x is an integrable random variable on Ω, and*

$$A=\left\{\omega\in\Omega:\ \sup_n \frac{1}{n}\sum_{j=0}^{n-1} x\circ\mathbf{T}^j(\omega)>0\right\},$$

then

$$\int_A P(d\omega)x(\omega)\geqslant 0.$$

Proof. Define the operators S_n and S_n^+ on the integrable random variables, i.e., on $L^1(\Omega, \mathcal{F}, P)$, as follows:

$$(S_n x)(\omega)=\begin{cases} 0 & \text{if} \quad n=0,\\ \sum_{j=0}^{n-1} x\circ\mathbf{T}^j(\omega) & \text{if} \quad n=1,2,3,\ldots,\end{cases}$$

$$(S_n^+ x)(\omega)=\max\{S_k(\omega): k=0,1,2,\ldots,n\}.$$

Notice that $S_n^+ x\geqslant 0$ and if $A_n=\{\omega: S_n^+ x(\omega)>0\}$, then A_n is an increasing sequence of measurable sets whose union is A.

For $k=0,1,\ldots,n$, we have $S_n^+ x\geqslant S_k x$, so that $S_n^+ x\circ\mathbf{T}\geqslant S_k x\circ\mathbf{T}$. Thus

$$x+S_n^+ x\circ\mathbf{T}\geqslant x+S_k x\circ\mathbf{T}=S_{k+1}x, \qquad k=0,1,\ldots,n$$

or

$$x+S_n^+ x\circ\mathbf{T}\geqslant S_k x, \qquad k=1,2,\ldots,n+1,$$

and we have that

$$x+S_n^+ x\circ\mathbf{T}\geqslant \max\{S_k x: 1\leqslant k\leqslant n\}.$$

Since $S_n^+ x>0$ on A_n and $S_0 x=0$,

$$\max\{S_k x: 1\leqslant k\leqslant n\}=S_n^+ x \qquad \text{on } A_n.$$

Thus

$$\int_{A_n} P(d\omega)[x+S_n^+ x\circ \mathbf{T}] \geqslant \int_{A_n} P(d\omega)S_n^+ x,$$

and since $S_n^+ x\circ \mathbf{T}$ is nonnegative and $S_n^+ x=0$ on $\Omega - A_n$,

$$\int_{A_n} P(d\omega)x \geqslant \int_{\Omega} P(d\omega)S_n^+ x - \int_{\Omega} P(d\omega)S_n^+ x\circ \mathbf{T}.$$

Since $\mathbf{T}$ is measure preserving, the right hand side is zero, and the lemma follows, since A_n increases to A.

THEOREM 1.24 (Ergodic theorem). *If* $(\Omega, \mathfrak{F}, P, \mathbf{T})$ *is an ergodic dynamical system and* x *is an integrable real random variable, then*

$$\lim_{n\to\infty} \frac{1}{n}\sum_{j=0}^{n-1} x\circ \mathbf{T}^j(\omega) = \int_{\Omega} P(d\omega)x(\omega)$$

both a.e. *and in* L^1 *norm.*

Proof. Let $a<b$ be real numbers, and define $\Omega(a,b)$ by

$$\Omega(a,b)=\{\omega\in\Omega : \underline{L}(\omega)<a<b<\bar{L}(\omega)\}$$

where $\underline{L}(\omega)=\liminf(1/n)\Sigma_{j=0}^{n-1}x\circ \mathbf{T}^j(\omega)$ and $\bar{L}(\omega)$ is the lim sup of the same expression. Since $\underline{L}\circ \mathbf{T}=\underline{L}$ and $\bar{L}\circ\mathbf{T}=\bar{L}$, it is clear that $\Omega(a,b)$ is $\mathbf{T}$-invariant. Thus we may apply the maximal ergodic lemma to the function $x(\omega)-b$ restricted to $\Omega(a,b)$ to get

$$\int_A P(d\omega)x \geqslant bP(A)$$

where

$$A=\left\{\omega\in\Omega(a,b) : \sup_n \frac{1}{n}\sum_{j=0}^{n-1}(x-b1_{\Omega})\circ \mathbf{T}^j(\omega)>0\right\}.$$

Since $\limsup_{n\to\infty}(1/n)\Sigma_{j=0}^{n-1}x\circ\mathbf{T}^j(\omega)>b$ for all $\omega\in\Omega(a,b)$, we have that $\Omega(a,b)\subset A$; hence $\Omega(a,b)=A$ and

$$\int_{\Omega(a,b)} P(d\omega)x \geqslant bP(\Omega(a,b)).$$

Applying the same argument to $a-x(\omega)$ restricted to $\Omega(a,b)$ gives

$$\int_{\Omega(a,b)} P(d\omega)x \leqslant aP(\Omega(a,b)).$$

Thus

$$(b-a)P(\Omega(a,b)) \leqslant 0.$$

Since $b-a>0$, we have that $P(\Omega(a,b))=0$.

Now the set of points where $(1/n)\Sigma_{j=0}^{n-1} x\circ \mathbf{T}^j$ fails to converge is the set where $\underline{L}(\omega)<\overline{L}(\omega)$, and this set is obtained by taking the union of the sets $\Omega(r_1,r_2)$ over all pairs (r_1,r_2) of rational numbers with $r_1<r_2$. Since we have shown each of these sets has measure zero, we have that

$$\lim_{n\to\infty} \frac{1}{n} \sum_{j=0}^{n-1} x\circ \mathbf{T}^j(\omega) = \hat{x}(\omega) \qquad \text{a.e.}$$

It is immediate that $\hat{x}\circ\mathbf{T}=\hat{x}$, and Fatou's lemma implies that $\hat{x}$ is integrable.

We next show that x and $\hat{x}$ have the same expected value, i.e., $\int_\Omega P(d\omega)x(\omega)=\int_\Omega P(d\omega)\hat{x}(\omega)$. This follows immediately from the dominated convergence theorem provided x is bounded. For the general case it is enough to prove it for x a nonnegative function.

In this case, Fatou's lemma implies that $\int_\Omega P(d\omega)\hat{x}(\omega) \leqslant \int_\Omega P(d\omega)x(\omega)$. Suppose then that equality does not occur. Then $\int_\Omega P(d\omega)\hat{x}(\omega) < \int_\Omega P(d\omega)x(\omega)$. Since $\int_\Omega P(d\omega)x(\omega) = \sup\{\int_\Omega P(d\omega)g(\omega) : 0 \leqslant g \leqslant x,\ g$ bounded$\}$ there exists a bounded function $0\leqslant g\leqslant x$ such that $\int_\Omega P(d\omega)\hat{x}(\omega) < \int_\Omega P(d\omega)g(\omega) = \int_\Omega P(d\omega)\hat{g}(\omega)$. However since $g\leqslant x$, we have $\hat{g}\leqslant\hat{x}$ and therefore a contradiction, and equality must occur.

Now $\hat{x}\circ\mathbf{T}=\hat{x}$ implies that $\hat{x}$ must be measurable with respect to the σ-field of $\mathbf{T}$-invariant sets. But $\mathbf{T}$ is ergodic, so this σ-field is a.e. trivial, i.e., consists only of sets of measure zero or one, and hence any function measurable with respect to this σ-field must be a.e. constant. Thus $\hat{x}= \int_\Omega P(d\omega)\hat{x}(\omega)=\int_\Omega P(d\omega)x(\omega)$.

It is immediate from the dominated convergence theorem that the convergence is also in L^1 norm provided x is a bounded function. The general case can be obtained by approximation with bounded functions.

More general versions of the ergodic theorem are true, but this version is sufficient for our uses. The ergodic theorem was proven for mean convergence by von Neumann and for a.e. convergence by Birkhoff. Consequently if one is referring to mean convergence the theorem is called the mean or von Neumann ergodic theorem, and if one is referring to pointwise a.e. convergence the theorem is called the pointwise or Birkhoff ergodic theorem.

Now we will consider another type of stochastic sequence, called a martingale. Suppose $\{x_n : n \in Z\}$ is a given stochastic sequence in Γ, and ξ^t denotes the partition $\bigvee_{n=-\infty}^{t} x_n^{-1}(\varepsilon)$, where ε is the point partition in Γ. If we think of x_n as being the result of some random experiment at time n, then $(\xi^t)^\wedge$ denotes the collection of events which can be determined by the process from the infinite past to time t. If $\xi^\infty = \bigvee_{t=0}^{\infty} \xi^t$ and $\xi_{-\infty} = \bigwedge_{t=0}^{-\infty} \xi^t$, these partitions represent respectively outcomes determined by the process if it is allowed to run for all time and outcomes predetermined for the process.

In case the random variables in the process have finite expected values, i.e., x_n has a finite integral, then calculating the conditional expectation of x_{n+1} given the partition ξ^n incorporates the information obtained up to time n in predicting values for the outcome of the experiment the next time. In case the conditional expectation of x_{n+1} given the partition ξ^n is the same as the random variable x_n, then knowing the past will not change what one expects to get in the future. For example, suppose x_n represents the fortune at time n of a gambler who is playing a game. If he has played the game n times he knows his fortune, namely x_n. The conditional expectation of x_{n+1} given ξ^n represents what he expects his fortune to be at the completion of the next play, using all the information he can obtain from plays up to now. If this conditional expectation is the same as his current fortune, then the game can be considered to be "fair" since knowledge of the past will not increase or decrease what he expects to win in the future. Such processes are called martingales.

Definition 1.25. Let $\{x_n : n \in Z^+\}$ be a sequence of real valued random variables, and $\{\xi_n\}$ a sequence of measurable partitions such that x_n is $\hat{\xi}_n$-measurable for each n. The sequence of random variables is a *martingale* sequence adapted to ξ_n if $\xi_n \leqslant \xi_{n+1}$ for each $n \in Z^+$ and

$$E^{\xi_n}(x_m) = x_n \qquad \text{for all} \quad m > n.$$

It is said to be a *reversed martingale* sequence adapted to ξ_n if $\xi_n \geqslant \xi_{n+1}$ and

$$E^{\xi_m}(x_n) = x_m \qquad \text{for all} \quad m > n.$$

There is a theorem due to Doob which insures that martingales and reversed martingales converge. The proof of this theorem, like the proof of the ergodic theorem, is based on a lemma which we state and prove before stating the martingale theorem. In order to understand the lemma we introduce some notation.

Suppose x is a function on $N=\{1,2,\dots,n\}$ to the real numbers and $[a,b]$ is a nondegenerate interval of reals. Think of $x_j=x(j)$ as the position of a moving particle at time j, and let h denote the number of times this particle crosses the interval $[a,b]$ from left to right during the time interval N. We will now derive an inequality involving the integer h.

Let

$$k_1=\min\{k\in N: x_k\leqslant a\},$$

$$k_2=\min\{k\in N: x_k\geqslant b, k>k_1\},$$

and in general

$$k_{2j+1}=\min\{k\in N: x_k\leqslant a, k>k_{2j}\},$$

$$k_{2j+2}=\min\{k\in N: x_k\geqslant b, k>k_{2n+1}\}.$$

If the set in the defining relation for k_l, $1\leqslant l\leqslant n$, is empty, take $k_l=n+1$. In this way we have defined a function k on $\{1,2,\dots,n\}$ to $\{1,2,\dots,n,n+1\}$ such that $k_2>n$ if and only if $h=0$, and if $k_2\leqslant n$, then h is the largest integer such that $k_{2h}\leqslant n$.

Define a function i on $\{1,2,\dots,n+1\}$ by

$$i(k)=\begin{cases}0 & \text{if} \quad k\leqslant k_1,\\ 1 & \text{if} \quad k_{2j}<k\leqslant k_{2j+1},\\ 0 & \text{if} \quad k_{2j+1}<k\leqslant k_{2j+2}.\end{cases}$$

In case $h>0$, if $k_{2h+1}\leqslant n$,

$$\begin{aligned}\sum_{k=2}^{n} i(k)[x(k)-x(k-1)] &= [x(k_3)-x(k_2)]+[x(k_5)-x(k_4)]\\ &\quad+\cdots+[x(2h+1)-x(2h)]\\ &\leqslant (a-b)h,\end{aligned}$$

and if $k_{2h+1}>n$,

$$\begin{aligned}\sum_{k=2}^{n} i(k)[x(k)-x(k-1)] &= [x(k_3)-x(k_2)]+\cdots+[x(n)-x(2h)]\\ &= [x(k_3)-x(k_2)]+\cdots\\ &\quad+[a-x(2h)]+[x(n)-a]\\ &\leqslant (a-b)h+[x(n)-a].\end{aligned}$$

In case $h=0$, the first inequality is trivially true, since $i(k)=0$ for all k. Thus in all cases

$$\sum_{k=2}^{n} i(k)[x_k - x_{k-1}] \leqslant (a-b)h + [x(n)-a]^+.$$

If one runs through the same arguments, with obvious modifications, for a position function x defined on $N=\{-n,-n+1,\ldots,-1\}$ and lets h denote the number of crossings of $[a,b]$, one obtains

$$\sum_{k=2}^{n} i(k)[x_k - x_{k-1}] \leqslant (a-b)h + [x(-1)-a]^+.$$

CROSSINGS LEMMA (Doob). *Let* $\{x_1, x_2, \ldots, x_n\}$ *be a martingale or reversed martingale adapted to* $\{\xi_k : k=1,2,\ldots,n\}$, *and* $[a,b]$ *a nondegenerate interval. For each* $\omega \in \Omega$, *let* $H(\omega)$ *denote the number of crossings of* $[a,b]$ *by the sequence* $\{x_1(\omega),\ldots,x_n(\omega)\}$ *if one has a martingale, or by the sequence* $\{y_{-n}(\omega),\ldots,y_{-1}(\omega)\}$, *where* $y_{-i}(\omega)=x_i(\omega)$, *if one has a reversed martingale. Then*

$$(b-a)\int_\Omega P(d\omega)H(\omega) \leqslant \sup_{1\leqslant k\leqslant n} \int_\Omega P(d\omega)[x_k(\omega)-a]^+.$$

Proof. We will give the proof for a martingale. The proof for a reversed martingale is similar.

Let $I(k)(\omega)$ denote $i(k)$ in the inequality derived before the statement of the lemma for the sequence $\{x_1(\omega),\ldots,x_n(\omega)\}$. Then for each ω,

$$\sum_{k=2}^{n} I(k)(\omega)[x_k(\omega)-x_{k-1}(\omega)] \leqslant (a-b)H(\omega) + [x_n(\omega)-a]^+.$$

The functions $I(k)$ and H are easily seen to be measurable and nonnegative, so we may integrate this inequality to obtain

$$\sum_{k=2}^{n} \int_{A_k} P(d\omega)[x_k(\omega)-x_{k-1}(\omega)]$$

$$\leqslant (a-b)\int_\Omega P(d\omega)H(\omega) + \int_\Omega P(d\omega)[x_n(\omega)-a]^+,$$

where $A_k=\{\omega : I(k)(\omega)=1\}$.

Since $\{x_k\}$ is a martingale,

$$\int_{A_k} P(d\omega)[x_k - x_{k-1}] = \int_\Omega P(d\omega)[x_{k_{2j+1}} - x_{k_{2j}}]$$

$$= \int_\Omega P(d\omega) E^{\xi_{k_{2j}}}(x_{k_{2j+1}} - x_{k_{2j}})$$

$$= 0.$$

Thus

$$(b-a)\int_\Omega P(d\omega) H(\omega) \leqslant \int_\Omega P(d\omega)[x_n(\omega) - a]^+.$$

Using the properties of conditional expectation derived in Section 1.6 and the fact that $\{x_k\}$ is a martingale adapted to $\{\xi_k\}$, we have that for $k \leqslant n$,

$$E^{\xi_k}[x_n - a]^+ \geqslant E^{\xi_k}[x_n - a] = x_k - a.$$

Since $E^{\xi_k}[x_n - a]^+ \geqslant 0$, we have that

$$E^{\xi_k}[x_n - a]^+ \geqslant [x_k - a]^+$$

for all $k \leqslant n$. Therefore

$$\int_\Omega P(d\omega)[x_n(\omega) - a]^+ = \int_\Omega P(d\omega) E^{\xi_k}[x_n - a]^+$$

$$\geqslant \int_\Omega P(d\omega)[x_k - a]^+$$

for all $k \leqslant n$, so that

$$(b-a)\int_\Omega P(d\omega) H(\omega) \leqslant \sup_{1 \leqslant k \leqslant n} \int_\Omega P(d\omega)[x_k(\omega) - a]^+$$

and the lemma is proven.

THEOREM 1.26 (Martingale convergence theorem). *If $\{x_n : n \in Z^+\}$ is either a martingale or a reversed martingale adapted to $\{\xi_n\}$ and $\sup_n E(|x_n|) < \infty$, then*

$$\lim_{n\to\infty} x_n = x \qquad \text{a.e.}$$

If $\{x_n\}$ is a martingale, then x is $\bigvee_{n=0}^\infty \xi_n\hat{\ }$-measurable and if $\{x_n\}$ is a reversed martingale x is $\bigwedge_{n=0}^\infty \xi_n\hat{\ }$-measurable.

Proof. For real numbers $a<b$, define $\Omega(a,b)$ by

$$\Omega(a,b)=\left\{\omega:\ \liminf_{n\to\infty} x_n(\omega)<a<b<\limsup_{n\to\infty} x_n(\omega)\right\}.$$

As in the proof of the ergodic theorem, if we show that $P(\Omega(a,b))=0$, then $x(\omega)=\lim_{n\to\infty}x_n(\omega)$ exists a.e.

Let $H_n(\omega)$ denote the number of crossings of $[a,b]$ by $\{x_1(\omega),\dots,x_n(\omega)\}$ if $\{x_k\}$ is a martingale, or by $\{x_n(\omega),\dots,x_1(\omega)\}$ if $\{x_k\}$ is a reversed martingale. For any $\omega\in\Omega(a,b)$, $H_n(\omega)$ is an increasing sequence and $H(\omega)=\lim_{n\to\infty}H_n(\omega)=\infty$.
By the crossings lemma

$$\int_{\Omega(a,b)}P(d\omega)H_n(\omega)\leqslant(b-a)^{-1}\sup_{1\leqslant k\leqslant n}\int_\Omega P(d\omega)[x_k(\omega)-a]^+$$

$$\leqslant(b-a)^{-1}\left[\sup_{1\leqslant k\leqslant n}E(|x_k|)+|a|\right].$$

Thus

$$\int_{\Omega(a,b)}P(d\omega)H(\omega)\leqslant(b-a)^{-1}[\sup E(|x_n|)+|a|]<\infty,$$

and $P(\Omega(a,b))=0$.

Since x is a limit of functions x_n, each measurable with respect to $\xi_n\hat{}$, x is measurable with respect to the limit of the $\xi_n\hat{}$, which is $\bigvee_{n=0}^\infty\xi_n\hat{}$ if $\{x_n\}$ is a martingale and is $\bigwedge_{n=0}^\infty\xi_n\hat{}$ if it is a reversed martingale.

COROLLARY 1.27. *If $\{\xi_n\}$ is a montone sequence of measurable partitions with limit ξ, and x is a bounded random variable, then*

$$\lim_{n\to\infty}E^{\xi_n}(x)=E^{\xi}(x)$$

a.e. *and in L^1-norm.*

Proof. Assume first that $\xi_n\downarrow\xi$. It follows from Theorem 1.20 that $y_n=E^{\xi_n}(x)$ is a reversed martingale, so by the martingale theorem $y=\lim_{n\to\infty}y_n$ exists a.e. By Theorem 1.17, $|y_n|=|E^{\xi_n}(x)|\leqslant E^{\xi}(|x|)\leqslant\|x\|_\infty<\infty$, since x is bounded, and the dominated convergence theorem implies that $y_n\to y$ in L_1 norm. Using Theorem 1.17 again, we have that $E^{\xi}(y_n)\to E^{\xi}(y)=y$, since y is $\xi\hat{}$-measurable. However, $\xi\leqslant\xi_n$ for every n, so

$$E^{\xi}(y_n)=E^{\xi}(E^{\xi_n}(x))=E^{\xi}(x)\quad\text{and}\quad y=E^{\xi}(x).$$

Next assume that $\xi_n \uparrow \xi$. In this case $y_n = E^{\xi_n}(x)$ is a martingale, and again we have $y = \lim y_n$ exists a.e., and since $\{y_n\}$ is bounded, the limit is also in L_1-norm. Let $\varepsilon > 0$, and $A \in \xi^{\wedge}$ be given. Since $y_n \to y$ in L_1, there is N_1 such that for $n \geqslant N_1$

$$\int_{\Omega} P(d\omega)|y_n - y| < \varepsilon/3,$$

and since $\xi_n \uparrow \xi$, there is N_2 such that for $n \geqslant N_2$ there is $B_n \in \xi_n^{\wedge}$ such that $P(A \triangle B_n) < (\varepsilon/3)\|x\|_\infty$. Take $n \geqslant \max\{N_1, N_2\}$. Then

$$\begin{aligned}
&\left|\int_A P(d\omega)x(\omega) - \int_A P(d\omega)y(\omega)\right| \\
&\quad \leqslant \left|\int_A P(d\omega)x - \int_{B_n} P(d\omega)x\right| + \left|\int_{B_n} P(d\omega)x - \int_{B_n} P(d\omega)y\right| \\
&\quad\quad + \left|\int_{B_n} P(d\omega)y - \int_A P(d\omega)y\right| \\
&\quad \leqslant 2\|x\|_\infty P(A \triangle B_n) + \left|\int_{B_n} P(d\omega)E^{\xi_n}(x) - \int_{B_n} P(d\omega)y\right| \\
&\quad < \frac{2\varepsilon}{3} + \frac{\varepsilon}{3} = \varepsilon.
\end{aligned}$$

Since ε is arbitrary,

$$\int_A P(d\omega)y(\omega) = \int_A P(d\omega)x(\omega) = \int_A P(d\omega)E^{\xi}(x)$$

for all $A \in \xi^{\wedge}$. By the uniqueness of conditional expectation, $y = E^{\xi}(x)$ a.e.

The following example is of considerable importance. Suppose $(\Omega, \mathfrak{F}, P, \mathbf{T})$ is an invertible dynamical system and ξ is a finite measurable partition of Ω. If $\xi_n = \bigvee_{j=n}^{\infty} \mathbf{T}^{-j}\xi$, then $\mathbf{T}^{-1}\xi_n = \xi_{n+1}$ and $\xi_n \geqslant \xi_{n+1}$. The sequence $\{\xi_n\}_{n=0}^{\infty}$ is decreasing, and $P^{\xi_n}(\omega, E) = E^{\xi_n}(1_E)$ is a reversed martingale, so by Corollary 1.27 $\lim_{n\to\infty} P^{\xi_n}(\omega, E) = P^{\xi_\infty}(\omega, E)$, where $\xi_\infty = \bigwedge_{n=1}^{\infty} \bigvee_{j=n}^{\infty} \mathbf{T}^{-j}\xi$. This partition, or the σ-field it generates, is called the *tail* of the stochastic process $(\mathbf{T}, \xi)$. The events in the tail of a process are those events which depend only on the infinitely distant future. For example, the event

$$\left\{\omega : \limsup_{n\to\infty} \frac{1}{n} \sum_{n=1}^{\infty} 1_A \circ \mathbf{T}^j(\omega) < \alpha\right\}$$

is a tail event.

Since **T** is invertible, there is also another σ-field which can be associated with **T** that represents events in the far distant past. Remember that x is in $\mathbf{T}^{-1}E$ if and only if $\mathbf{T}x \in E$. Since $\mathbf{T}x$ corresponds to the outcome of an experiment performed tomorrow, $\mathbf{T}x \in E$ indicates that E occurs tomorrow. Thus $\mathbf{T}^{-1}E$ is an event in tomorrow's experiment. From the same argument $\mathbf{T}E$ corresponds to an event in yesterday's experiment. The tail of the process $(\mathbf{T}^{-1}, \xi)$ corresponds to the infinite past of the process $(\mathbf{T}, \xi)$. From the definition of tail of a process we can easily see that the infinite past of the process $(\mathbf{T}, \xi)$ is given by $\bigwedge_{n=1}^{\infty} \bigvee_{j=n}^{\infty} \mathbf{T}^j \xi$. Again using Corollary 1.27, the conditional probability given the infinite past is $\lim_{n\to\infty} P^{\bigvee_{j=n}^{\infty} \mathbf{T}^j \xi}(\omega, \cdot)$.

CHAPTER 2

Entropy and Information

In this chapter we shall give a mathematical definition of the information in a random event and the entropy of experiments with a countable number of outcomes. We shall also indicate how the entropy is a measure of uncertainty and then give the main properties satisfied by both information and entropy. Then the definition of entropy will be extended to include experiments with an arbitrary number of outcomes, and the properties of entropy will be proven for this case. Finally we give the definitions of the rate of information generation and the entropy of a dynamical system and derive their most important properties. We conclude with several examples and a brief discussion of two useful extensions of these definitions.

2.1 Information and Uncertainty of Events

Let $(\Omega, \mathfrak{F}, P)$ be a Lebesgue space and E an event in $\mathfrak{F}$. Thinking of the Lebesgue space as being a mathematical model of some random experiment, suppose an outcome of this experiment results in the event E. We have gained some information because we know that E occurred. The purpose of this first section is to define a function I on the events in a Lebesgue space so that $I(E)$ will give a quantitative measure of the information gained if the event E results from the outcome of the experiment.

Before the experiment is performed, the uncertainty of its outcome resulting in the event E should equal the information we have gained if the outcome does result in E. Therefore the information in an event will also be a quantitative measure of the amount of uncertainty in this event.

ENCYCLOPEDIA OF MATHEMATICS and Its Applications, Gian-Carlo Rota (ed.).
Vol. 12: Nathaniel F. Martin and James W. England, Mathematical Theory of Entropy.
ISBN 0-201-13511-6

DEFINITION 2.1. The *information*, or *uncertainty*, is a real valued function of events which depends only on the probabilities of the events and satisfies the following:

2.1.1. An event with probability one of occurring has zero uncertainty.

2.1.2. If one event has smaller probability of occurring than another, then the first event has more uncertainty than the second.

2.1.3. The uncertainty of the simultaneous occurrence of two independent events is the sum of their individual uncertainties.

Our first task is to obtain an expression in terms of known functions, if possible, for the quantity of uncertainty. Since I is to depend only on the probabilities of events, we look for a real valued function Λ defined on $[0,1]$ such that if $I(E)$ is taken to be $\Lambda(P(E))$, then I will satisfy Definition 2.1.1, 2.1.2, and 2.1.3. It is easy to see that if Λ is a monotone decreasing function on $[0,1]$ which vanishes at 1, then the resulting information will satisfy Definition 2.1.1 and 2.1.2. The only remaining requirement is to determine the condition on Λ which will insure 2.1.3.

Suppose E and F are independent. Then Definition 2.1.3 means that $I(E\cap F)=I(E)+I(F)$, and since $P(E\cap F)=P(E)P(F)$, 2.1.3 is equivalent to $\Lambda(P(E)P(F))=\Lambda(P(E))+\Lambda(P(F))$. Thus the function Λ must satisfy the functional equation

$$\Lambda(xy)=\Lambda(x)+\Lambda(y). \tag{2.1}$$

It is a classical result that the only measurable solution to Equation (2.1) is given by a constant multiple of the natural logarithm, and therefore we must take $\Lambda(t)=C\log t$. This function does vanish at 1 for any value of the constant C, but will be monotone decreasing only if C is negative. Therefore if we define Λ by the equation

$$\Lambda(t)=\begin{cases} -b\log t, & 0<t\leqslant 1, \\ \infty, & t=0, \end{cases} \tag{2.2}$$

where b is any positive real number, then the function I defined for any event $E\in\mathcal{F}$ by

$$I(E)=\Lambda(P(E)) \tag{2.3}$$

satisfies the properties of an uncertainty. In addition, if we require that the uncertainty depend measurably on the probabilities of events, this is the only function which will have the required properties of Definition 2.1.

2.2 The Information Function of an Experiment and Entropy

In the first chapter we saw how the measurable partitions of a fixed Lebesgue space are mathematical models of random experiments. We now define an information function on the set of partitions which will give the information contained in the random experiments represented by these partitions.

Let ζ be a given countable measurable partition of $(\Omega, \mathfrak{F}, P)$. The information function of the partition ζ, denoted by $I(\zeta)$, is a function defined on Ω whose value at any outcome $\omega \in \Omega$ is the information obtained from the occurrence of that atom A of ζ which contains ω. Thus

$$I(\zeta)(\omega) = -b \sum_{A \in \zeta} 1_A(\omega) \log P(A), \tag{2.4}$$

where 1_A denotes the indicator function of the set A. From the point of view of ζ as an experiment, it has outcomes which are the atoms of ζ, and $I(\zeta)$ has constant value on each of these outcomes. This value is the information obtained from the outcome or the uncertainty concerning this outcome. In terms of factor spaces, $I(\zeta)$ is a function on the factor space $(\Omega_\zeta, \mathfrak{F}_\zeta, P_\zeta)$, and gives a quantitative measure of the uncertainty of each outcome in this space.

It is clear that $I(\zeta)$ is defined and finite almost everywhere on Ω and that it is $\zeta^\wedge$-measurable. Thus it is a random variable on $(\Omega, \mathfrak{F}, P)$, and since it is nonnegative, has an integral (which may be infinite).

Definition 2.2. The *entropy* of a countable measurable partition ζ of a Lebesgue space $(\Omega, \mathfrak{F}, P)$ is the expected value of the information function of the partition. The entropy of ζ is denoted by $H(\zeta)$, and we have

$$H(\zeta) = \int_\Omega P(d\omega) I(\zeta)(\omega)$$

$$= -b \sum_{A \in \zeta} P(A) \log P(A).$$

(We assume $t \log t = 0$ for $t = 0$.)

The entropy of a countable partition is then the average amount of uncertainty, or average amount of information, contained in the experiment represented by the partition.

Theorem 2.3. If ζ is a partition with k atoms, then

$$0 \leqslant H(\zeta) \leqslant b \log k.$$

Moreover, $H(\zeta)=0$ if and only if ζ contains an atom of probability one and $H(\zeta)=b\log k$ if and only if ζ is an equipartition, i.e., $P(A)=k^{-1}$ for each $A\in\zeta$.

Proof. It is clear from the definition that $H(\zeta)\geqslant 0$ with equality if and only if ζ has an atom of probability one. To obtain the other inequality consider that

$$b\log k-H(\zeta)=b\sum_{A}P(A)[\log kP(A)]$$

and since $\log t\geqslant 1-t^{-1}$, with equality if and only if $t=1$, $P(A)\log kP(A)\geqslant P(A)\{1-[kP(A)]^{-1}\}$. Thus

$$b\log k-H(\zeta)\geqslant 0,$$

with equality if and only if $kP(A)=1$ for all $A\in\zeta$.

This theorem illustrates the fact that the entropy of an experiment measures the degree of "randomness" of the experiment. The most "random" experiment with k outcomes would be one in which any outcome was as likely to occur as any other outcome. Such an experiment is modeled by a equipartition with k atoms, and the entropy of such partitions is maximum. The least random experiment would be one in which a particular event is sure to occur.

This theorem also allows us to give an interpretation of the constant b. If a particular experiment with k outcomes is considered, the uncertainty for this experiment is no greater than $b\log k$. If b is taken to be $(\log k)^{-1}$, then the uncertainty for this particular experiment is no greater than 1, and this value is assumed by the most random distribution on the k outcomes. Thus we say that for k outcome experiments one unit of uncertainty is obtained with the most random distribution. In view of this, the value that we take for b will determine the units of uncertainty. Notice that $(\log k)^{-1}\log t=\log_k t$, so if the information of events is taken to be defined in terms of logarithms to the base k, i.e. $I(E)=-\log_k P(E)$, then the unit of uncertainty is based on k-outcome experiments. Since the smallest nontrivial outcome space, or partition, must contain two elements, information and entropy is quite often defined in terms of logarithms to the base 2, and the unit of information associated with this base are called bits.

For example, consider the experiment of drawing colored balls from the urn with three red, two white, and five blue balls. If this experiment is modeled by the partitions of the unit interval into three intervals of length

.3, .2, and .5 respectively, then in terms of bits

$$I(\zeta)(\omega)=\begin{cases}-\log_2 .3, & \omega\in[0,.3],\\ -\log_2 .2, & \omega\in(.3,.5],\\ -\log_2 .5, & \omega\in(.5,1].\end{cases}$$

and

$$\begin{aligned}H(\zeta)&=-.3\log_2 .3-.2\log_2 .2-.5\log_2 .5\\ &=1.49 \text{ bits}.\end{aligned}$$

In most of the discussions in this book the units of information will be unimportant and we will take the constant b to equal one. Sometimes the units associated with this value are called "nats," since the natural logarithm is used. To change units from nats to units based on a k-outcome experiment it is only necessary to multiply by $(\log k)^{-1}$, so that, for example, to go from nats to bits we multiply by $(\log 2)^{-1}$.

In summary, the information function of a countable partition ζ of a Lebesgue space $(\Omega, \mathfrak{F}, P)$ is denoted by $I(\zeta)$ and is defined by the equation

$$I(\zeta)(\omega)=-\sum_{A\in\zeta} 1_A(\omega)\log P(A). \tag{2.5}$$

The entropy is denoted by $H(\zeta)$ and has the value

$$H(\zeta)=-\sum_{A\in\zeta} P(A)\log P(A). \tag{2.6}$$

2.3 An Example

In this example we shall illustrate how entropy measured in bits gives a lower bound to the expected number of yes-no questions which must be asked in any scheme designed to determine the outcome of an experiment with a finite number of outcomes. This interpretation of entropy is made rigorous by the "noiseless coding theorem" which is the first half of Theorem 3.5. In fact, the discussion we give here with minor changes constitutes a proof of the noiseless coding theorem.

We will also show how entropy can be used to devise a yes-no questioning scheme. This scheme, while not optimal, in terms of requiring the least possible expected number of questions illustrates our interpretation of entropy as a measure of uncertainty. At each step we shall ask a yes-no question based on a partition with the maximum available entropy. In this way we ask questions whose answers remove the largest possible uncertainty about the outcome at each stage. For an expanded discussion of possible questioning schemes the interested reader should consult Aczél and Dorоćzy [4].

Suppose we have an experiment with n outcomes and we want to devise a scheme of questioning so that the expected number of questions necessary to determine the outcome of the experiment is as small as possible. Our questions will receive only two answers, yes or no. The first thing we do is divide the outcomes of the experiment into two sets, E_1 and E_2, and ask the first question: "Is the outcome in E_1?" We should choose E_1 and E_2 in such a way that their probabilities are as close to $\frac{1}{2}$ as possible. Among all two set partitions of the outcomes, this would make the entropy of the partition $\{E_1, E_2\}$ as large as possible. The answer to the first question will then remove the maximum uncertainty possible, with a yes-no question, about the outcome of the experiment.

If the answer to the question, "Is the outcome in E_1?" is yes then we repeat the process of the last paragraph using just the outcomes in E_1 and the conditional probabilities given that E_1 occurred. That is, divide E_1 into two sets E_{11} and E_{12} in such a way that the entropy of the partition (E_{11}, E_{12}) of the space $(E_1, P(\ |E_1))$ is a maximum. The second question should be: "Is the outcome in E_{11}?"

In case the answer to the first question was no, we know that E_2 occurred and we must ask our second question about outcomes which give rise to E_2. Thus the second question in this case is obtained by partitioning the space $(E_2, P(\ |E_2))$ into two sets E_{21}, E_{22} such that the entropy of the partition is a maximum.

Continuing in this way, we eventually arrive at partitions which contain single outcomes and a question about this single outcome will determine that it occurred.

We shall now show that the entropy in bits of an experiment with a finite number of outcomes is a lower bound to the expected number of yes-no questions needed to determine an outcome using any yes-no questioning scheme. Such a questioning scheme is based on an increasing sequence of partitions of the outcome spaces such that each partition contains no more than twice as many atoms as the previous partition, and the last partition consists of singleton sets (i.e. the point partition). In order to make the notation clear we describe a questioning scheme (without probabilities) for an experiment with four outcomes $\{x_1, x_2, x_3, x_4\}$. (See Figure 2.1.)

The sequence of partitions giving rise to this scheme is,

$$\xi_1 = \{E_1 = \{x_1, x_2, x_3\}, E_2 = \{x_4\}\}$$

$$\xi_2 = \{E_{11} = \{x_1\}, E_{12} = \{x_2, x_3\}, E_2\}$$

$$\xi_3 = \{E_{11}, E_{121} = \{x_2\}, E_{122} = \{x_3\}, E_2\}.$$

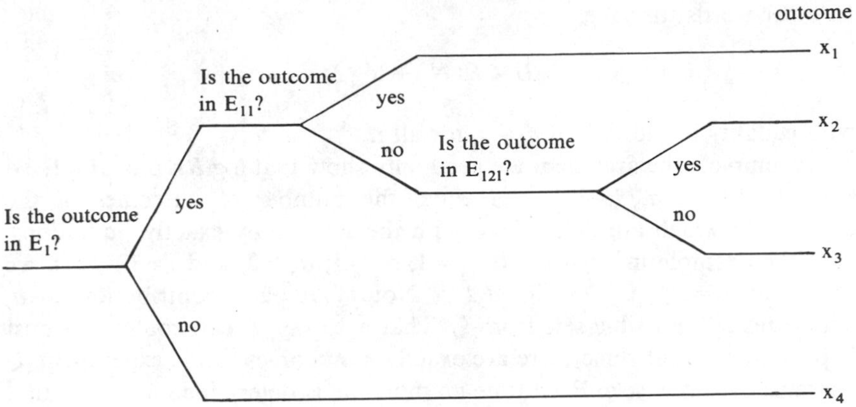

Figure 2.1

With this notation we consider an experiment, with n possible outcomes $\{x_1, x_2, \ldots, x_n\}$. Let l be the maximum number of questions needed by some scheme to determine the outcome of the experiment and as above let $\xi_1, \xi_2, \xi_3, \ldots, \xi_l$ denote the increasing sequence of partitions which determines the scheme. Note that if $E_{i_1, i_2, \ldots, i_k}$ consists of only one outcome, say x_j, for some k, then the scheme requires k questions to determine this outcome. For each $j = 1, 2, \ldots, n$ we let N_j denote the number of questions required with this scheme to determine that the outcome is x_j. (For the example in Figure 2.1, we have $N_1 = 2$, $N_2 = N_3 = 3$ and $N_4 = 1$.) For $i = 1, 2, \ldots, n$, let p_i be the probability of x_i so that $E(N) = \sum_{i=1}^n p_i N_i$ is the expected number of questions needed to determine the outcome of the experiment. In these terms we wish to show that $H = -\sum p_i \log_2 p_i \leqslant E(N) = \sum p_i N_i$. To do this note first that $N_i = -\log_2 2^{-N_i}$ and let $B = \sum_{i=1}^n 2^{-N_i}$. If we let $q_i = \dfrac{2^{-N_i}}{B}$ for $i = 1, 2, \ldots, n$ then $\sum_{i=1}^n q_i = 1$ and we can apply Lemma 2.8 to obtain

$$
\begin{aligned}
-\sum_{i=1}^{n} p_i \log_2 p_i &\leqslant -\sum_{i=1}^{n} p_i \log_2 q_i \\
&= -\sum_{i=1}^{n} p_i \log_2 2^{-N_i}/B \\
&= -\sum_{i=1}^{n} p_i \log_2 2^{-N_i} + \left(\sum_{i=1}^{n} p_i\right) \log_2 B.
\end{aligned}
$$

In other words we have,

$$H \leqslant E(N) + \log B$$

with equality if and only if $p_i = q_i$ for all i.

To complete the argument we need only show that $\log B \leqslant 0$ or $B \leqslant 1$. To see this we let a_i, $i = 1,2,\ldots,l$ equal the number of outcomes of the experiment which are determined with the scheme by exactly i questions. (For the example in Figure 2.1, $a_1 = 1$, $a_2 = 1$, $a_3 = 2$, and $l = 3$.) Then we note that $B = \Sigma_{i=1}^{n} 2^{-N_i} = \Sigma_{i=1}^{p} a_i 2^{-i}$. Note that each contribution to a_i eliminates 2^{l-i} possible sets from ξ_l. That is to say, ξ_l can contain at most 2^l possible sets but since there are exactly n outcomes to the experiment, ξ_l contains exactly n sets. Each time an outcome is determined in i steps that removes 2^{l-i} possible sets from ξ_l. Thus a_l, the number of outcomes determined by l questions satisfies the inequality

$$a^l \leqslant 2^l - \sum_{i=1}^{l-1} a_i 2^{l-i}.$$

In other words, $a_l 2^{-l} \leqslant 1 - \Sigma_{i=1}^{l-1} a_i 2^{-i}$ or $\Sigma_{i=1}^{l} a_i 2^{-i} \leqslant 1$, which completes the argument. In case we have $H = E(N)$ then $B = 1$ and $p_i = q_i = 2^{-N_i}$ for all i.

As a specific example consider the experiment ζ of drawing a ball from the urn of Chapter 1. There are three outcomes of the experiment with probabilities $P(R) = .3$, $P(W) = .2$ and $P(B) = .5$. In the last section we calculated $H(\zeta) = 1.49$ bits. Our best questioning scheme is based on the sequence of partitions $\xi_1 = \{\{B\},\{R,W\}\}$, $\xi_2 = \{\{B\},\{R\},\{W\}\}$. If N denotes the number of questions necessary to determine the outcome then $E(N) = .5 + 2(.3) + 2(.2) = 1.5$. By direct calculation it would be easy to show that this is the smallest expected value for any questioning scheme.

2.4 Conditional Information and Conditional Entropy

In the example discussed in Section 2.3 it was necessary to consider the information of events under the assumption that a given event had occurred. This happened when we received the answer to the first question, thereby knowing that event E_1 occurred. The entropy was then considered only for the space $(E_1, P(\ |E_1))$. In this section we use this idea to define the conditional information, $I(\xi/\zeta)$, of a measurable partition ξ given the partition ζ and the conditional entropy $H(\xi/\zeta)$ of ξ given ζ.

Let ξ be a countable measurable partition of a Lebesgue space $(\Omega, \mathcal{F}, P)$ and ζ any measurable partition of the same space. For P_ζ-almost all atoms $C \in \zeta$, the space $(C, \mathcal{F}(C), P^\zeta(\omega,\ ))$ where ω is any point in C, is a Lebesgue space and corresponds to the space which we should use if we know event C has occurred (cf. Section 1.5). The partition ξ induces a partition $\xi \cap C = \{A \cap C: A \in \xi\}$ of this space. The conditional information of ξ given ζ is the information function whose value at ω gives the information of the event $A \cap C$ as a event in the space $(C, \mathfrak{F}(C), P^{\zeta}(\omega, \ ))$, where $A \cap C$ is the unique atom of $\xi \vee \zeta$ which contains ω. Thus the conditional information of ξ given ζ, denoted by $I(\xi/\zeta)$, is a function on $(\Omega, \mathfrak{F}, P)$ defined by

$$I(\xi/\zeta)(\omega) = -\sum_{A \in \xi} 1_A(\omega) \log P^{\zeta}(\omega, A) \qquad \text{a.e.} \tag{2.7}$$

The conditional information is a real valued random valuable, and the expected value of this random variable is the conditional entropy of ξ given ζ. This quantity is denoted by $H(\xi/\zeta)$ and using (2.7) we have

$$H(\xi/\zeta) = E\left[-\sum_{A \in \xi} 1_A(\omega) \log P^{\zeta}(\omega, A)\right]. \tag{2.8}$$

Since $P^{\xi}(\omega, A)$ is $\xi^{\wedge}$-measurable,

$$E^{\zeta}\left[-1_A(\omega) \log P^{\zeta}(\omega, A)\right] = -P^{\zeta}(\omega, A) \log P^{\zeta}(\omega, A) \qquad \text{a.e.,}$$

using Theorem 1.19 and the result that $E^{\zeta}(1_A) = P^{\zeta}(\ , A)$ a.e. Since for any integrable random variable x we have $E(E^{\zeta}(x)) = E(x)$, Equation (2.8) can be written as

$$\begin{aligned} H(\xi/\zeta) &= \sum_{A \in \xi} E\left[E^{\zeta}(1_A(\omega) \log P^{\zeta}(\omega, A)\right] \\ &= E\left\{-\sum_{A \in \xi} P^{\zeta}(\omega, A) \log P^{\zeta}(\omega, A)\right\}. \end{aligned} \tag{2.9}$$

(Recall that $t \log t$ is zero if t is equal to zero.) Therefore, since $P^{\zeta}(\omega, A)$ is zero off of the atom $\mathbf{N}_{\zeta}^{-1}(\mathbf{N}_{\zeta}(\omega))$ of ζ, for any $\bar{\omega} \in \mathbf{N}_{\zeta}^{-1}(\mathbf{N}_{\zeta}(\omega)) = C$

$$-\sum_{A \in \xi} P^{\zeta}(\bar{\omega}, A) \log P^{\zeta}(\bar{\omega}, A) \tag{2.10}$$

is a constant and is the entropy of the partition $\xi \cap C$ in the Lebesgue space $(C, \mathfrak{F}(C), P^{\zeta}(\bar{\omega}, \ ))$. Since (2.10) is $\zeta^{\wedge}$-measurable, (2.9) can be written as

$$H(\xi/\zeta) = \int_{\Omega_{\zeta}} P_{\zeta}(dC) H(\xi \cap C) \tag{2.11}$$

where $H(\xi \cap C) = -\sum_{A \in \xi} P^{\zeta}(\omega, A) \log P^{\zeta}(\omega, A)$ for $\omega \in C$, and we have that $H(\xi/\zeta)$ is the average over the factor space $(\Omega_{\zeta}, \mathfrak{F}_{\zeta}, P_{\zeta})$ of the entropies of the induced partition $\xi \cap C$ in each atom (outcome) C of ζ.

2.5 Properties of Entropy and Conditional Entropy

In this section we prove three basic properties of entropy and information of countable partitions which are central in the theory and are also easily interpreted. Later we will extend the definition of entropy to arbitrary measurable partitions.

The first property concerns how both the information function I and the entropy H of compound experiments can be expressed in terms of the information or entropy of the factor experiments. For example, the entropy of the experiment of drawing two balls without replacement from an urn can be calculated in terms of the entropy of the experiment which consists of drawing the first ball and the entropy of the experiment which consists of drawing the second ball knowing the outcome of the first draw.

THEOREM 2.4. *If ξ and η are countable measurable partitions and ζ is a measurable partition of the Lebesgue space $(\Omega, \mathfrak{F}, P)$, then*

$$I(\xi\vee\eta/\zeta)=I(\xi/\zeta)+I(\eta/\xi\vee\zeta) \qquad P\text{-a.e.} \tag{2.12}$$

Proof. Using the definition of the conditional information function, we have for P-almost all $\omega\in\Omega$,

$$I(\xi/\zeta)(\omega)+I(\eta/\xi\vee\zeta)(\omega)$$

$$=-\sum_{A\in\xi} 1_A(\omega)\log P^{\zeta}(\omega, A)-\sum_{B\in\eta} 1_B(\omega)P^{\xi\vee\zeta}(\omega, B)$$

$$=-\sum_{A\in\xi}\sum_{B\in\eta} 1_{A\cap B}(\omega)\log P^{\zeta}(\omega, A)P^{\xi\vee\zeta}(\omega, B). \tag{2.13}$$

Let C be any atom of ζ such that $(C, \mathfrak{F}(C), P^{\zeta})$ is a nontrivial Lebesgue space, and let A and B be atoms of ξ and η respectively. In the space $(C, \mathfrak{F}(C), P^{\zeta})$, $\xi\cap C=\{A'\cap C: A'\in\xi\}$ is a measurable partition, and the transitivity property of canonical families of measures implies that the canonical family associated with this partition is $P^{\xi\vee\zeta}$. Apply Equation (1.5), we have

$$P^{\zeta}(\omega, A\cap B\cap C)=\int_{A\cap C} P^{\zeta}(\omega, d\overline{\omega})P^{\xi\vee\zeta}(\overline{\omega}, B\cap C) \qquad P-\text{a.e. on } C,$$

since $A\cap C\in\xi\cap C$ and $B\cap C\in\mathfrak{F}(C)$. However, $P^{\xi\vee\zeta}$ is a constant almost everywhere on $A\cap C$, since this set is an atom of $\xi\vee\zeta$. Therefore

$$P^{\zeta}(\omega, A\cap B\cap C)=P^{\zeta}(\omega, A\cap C)P^{\xi\vee\zeta}(\omega, B\cap C)$$

for almost all ω in C. But P^{ζ} is supported by atoms of ζ, so

$$P^{\zeta}(\omega, A\cap B)=P^{\zeta}(\omega, A)P^{\xi\vee\zeta}(\omega, B) \qquad P\text{-a.e. on } \Omega. \tag{2.14}$$

Since

$$I(\xi\vee\eta/\zeta)(\omega)=-\sum_{A\in\xi}\sum_{B\in\eta} 1_{A\cap B}(\omega)\log P^{\zeta}(\omega, A\cap B) \qquad \text{a.e.,}$$

the theorem follows from (2.13) and (2.14).

COROLLARY 2.5. *Let ξ, η be countable measurable partitions and ζ an arbitrary measurable partition. Then*

$$I(\xi/\nu)=I(\xi) \qquad P\text{-a.e.,} \tag{2.15}$$

$$H(\xi/\nu)=H(\xi), \tag{2.16}$$

$$H(\xi\vee\eta/\zeta)=H(\xi/\zeta)+H(\eta/\xi\vee\zeta), \tag{2.17}$$

$$I(\xi\vee\eta)=I(\xi)+I(\eta/\xi) \qquad P\text{-a.e.,} \tag{2.18}$$

$$H(\xi\vee\eta)=H(\xi)+H(\eta/\xi). \tag{2.19}$$

Proof. Equations (2.15) and (2.16) follow immediately from the fact that $P^{\nu}(\omega, E)=P(E)$ and the definitions. Equation (2.18) follows from (2.12) and (2.15), since $\xi\vee\nu=\xi$, and Equation (2.19) follows in the same way from (2.17). Finally, (2.17) is obtained by integrating (2.12).

COROLLARY 2.6. *If ξ and η are countable partitions with $\xi\leqslant\eta$, then*

$$I(\xi/\zeta)\leqslant I(\eta/\zeta) \qquad P\text{-a.e.,} \tag{2.20}$$

$$H(\xi/\zeta)\leqslant H(\eta/\zeta), \tag{2.21}$$

$$I(\xi)\leqslant I(\eta) \qquad P\text{-a.e.,} \tag{2.22}$$

$$H(\xi)\leqslant H(\eta), \tag{2.23}$$

Proof. The inequality (2.20) follows from (2.12) and the nonnegativity of the information function. The remaining inequalities follow from (2.20).

The second basic property relates the order relationship of mod 0 refinement between measurable partitions to the entropy and the information function. Recall that the interpretation of $\xi\leqslant\zeta$ was that every outcome of ζ uniquely determined an outcome of ξ. Thus if $\xi\leqslant\zeta$ there should be no uncertainty about ξ after ζ has been performed.

Theorem 2.7. *Let ξ be a countable partition and ζ an arbitrary measurable partition of $(\Omega, \mathfrak{F}, P)$. Then $H(\xi/\zeta)=0$ if and only if $\xi \leqslant \zeta$ (mod 0), and $I(\xi/\zeta)=0$ if and only if $H(\xi/\zeta)=0$.*

Proof. Suppose $\xi \leqslant \zeta$. For any $A \in \xi$ we have $P^{\zeta}(\ , A)=E^{\zeta}(1_A)$, and since A is a ζ-set, 1_A is $\zeta^{\wedge}$-measurable, so that $P^{\zeta}(\omega, A)=1_A(\omega)$ a.e. Thus

$$I(\xi/\zeta)(\omega) = -\sum_A 1_A(\omega)\log 1_A(\omega) = 0 \qquad \text{a.e.}$$

Since

$$H(\xi/\zeta) = \int_{\Omega} P(d\omega) I(\xi/\zeta)(\omega),$$

$H(\xi/\zeta)=0$.

Suppose $H(\xi/\zeta)=0$. Using Equation (2.9),

$$\int_{\Omega} P(d\omega)\left[-\sum_A P^{\zeta}(\omega, A)\log P^{\zeta}(\omega, A)\right] = 0,$$

and since the integrand is nonnegative

$$\sum_A P^{\zeta}(\omega, A)\log P^{\zeta}(\omega, A) = 0. \qquad \text{a.e.}$$

Thus $P^{\zeta}(\omega, A)$ is equal almost everywhere to either zero or one, and since it is a $\zeta^{\wedge}$-measurable function, there is a set $F \in \zeta^{\wedge}$ such that $P^{\zeta}(\omega, A) = 1_F(\omega)$ a.e.

However, for any set $E \in \zeta^{\wedge}$

$$P(A\cap E) = \int_E P(d\omega) P^{\zeta}(\omega, A) = P(E \cap F),$$

so that using F and F^c (where F^c denotes $\Omega - F$) successively for E, we have $P(A\cap F)=P(F)$ and $P(A\cap F^c)=0$. Thus $P(A \triangle F)=0$ and $F=A$ P-a.e., so that $A \in \zeta^{\wedge}$. (Recall that $\zeta^{\wedge}$ is the completion of the collection of all ζ-sets.) Thus $\xi^{\wedge} \subset \zeta^{\wedge}$, and it follows that $\xi \leqslant \zeta$ (mod 0).

Finally, since the information function is nonnegative, Equation (2.8) shows that $H(\xi/\zeta)=0$ implies that $I(\xi/\zeta)=0$ almost everywhere.

Lemma 2.8. *Let x_i and y_i, $i=1,2,\ldots$ be nonnegative real numbers such that $1=\Sigma x_i \geqslant \Sigma y_i$. Then*

2.8.1. $\Sigma_i x_i \log x_i y_i^{-1} \geqslant 0$,
2.8.2 $\Sigma_i x_i \log x_i y_i^{-1} = 0$ if and only if $x_i = y_i$ for all i.

Proof. Observe that $\log t \leqslant t-1$ for all $t>0$, with equality only if $t=1$. Thus taking $t=y_i x_i^{-1}$ gives

$$\log\frac{y_i}{x_i}=\frac{y_i}{x_i}-1-P_i \qquad \text{for} \quad P_i \geqslant 0,$$

and $P_i=0$ if and only if $x_i=y_i$. Therefore

$$\sum x_i \log\frac{x_i}{y_i}=\sum_i x_i-\sum_i y_i+\sum_i x_i P_i$$

and Statement 2.8.1 follows, since $\Sigma x_i \geqslant \Sigma y_i$. Statement 2.8.2 follows from this equation, since the right hand side is zero only if $P_i=0$ for all i. This implies that $x_i=y_i$ for all i.

THEOREM 2.9. *Let ξ be a countable measurable partition such that $H(\xi)<\infty$, and ζ a measurable partition. Then $H(\xi/\zeta)=H(\xi)$ if and only if ξ and ζ are independent.*

Proof. Suppose that ξ and ζ are independent. Then $P^{\zeta}(\omega, A)=P(A)$ P-almost everywhere, and $H(\xi/\zeta)=H(\xi)$ follows immediately from (2.9) and (2.6).

Next assume $H(\xi/\zeta)=H(\xi)$. Using Equation (2.8) we have

$$\int_{\Omega} P(d\omega)\Big\{-\sum_A 1_A(\omega)\log P^{\zeta}(\omega, A)\Big\}=\int_{\Omega} P(d\omega)\Big\{-\sum_A 1_A(\omega)\log P(A)\Big\}$$

and

$$\int_{\Omega} P(d\omega)\Big\{\sum_A 1_A(\omega)\log P^{\zeta}(\omega, A)P(A)^{-1}\Big\}=0.$$

Since $\log P^{\zeta}(\omega, A)P(A)^{-1}$ is $\zeta\hat{}$-measurable, we may apply Theorem 1.19 and Equation (1.16) to obtain

$$\int_{\Omega} P(d\omega)\Big\{\sum_A P^{\zeta}(\omega, A)\log P^{\zeta}(\omega, A)P(A)^{-1}\Big\}=0.$$

Apply Lemma 2.8 to observe that the integrand is almost everywhere nonnegative. Thus

$$\sum_{A\in\xi} P^{\zeta}(\omega, A)\log P^{\zeta}(\omega, A)P(A)^{-1}=0 \qquad P\text{-a.e.},$$

and a second application of Lemma 2.8 gives that

$$P^{\zeta}(\omega, A)=P(A) \qquad P\text{-a.e.}$$

for each $A \in \xi$ with positive measure, and the theorem follows.

COROLLARY 2.10. *If $H(\eta)<\infty$ and $H(\xi)<\infty$ and ξ and η are countable partitions, then $H(\xi \vee \eta)=H(\xi)+H(\eta)$ if and only if ξ and η are independent.*

Proof. Use (2.19).

The third property specifies how the order relationship between partitions affects the conditional entropy if the conditioning partitions are related by the order. If $\zeta_1 \leqslant \zeta_2$ and ξ is a finite experiment, $H(\xi/\zeta_i)$ represents the uncertainty of ξ if ζ_i is assumed known. Since the outcome of ζ_1 is uniquely determined by ζ_2, there is more "information" in ζ_2 than in ζ_1, and consequently there can't be less uncertainty about ξ after knowing the outcome of ζ_1 than there is after knowing the outcome of ζ_2.

THEOREM 2.11. *If ξ is a countable measurable partition and ζ_1 and ζ_2 are arbitrary measurable partitions with $\zeta_1 \leqslant \zeta_2$, then $H(\xi/\zeta_1) \geqslant H(\xi/\zeta_2)$.*

Proof. Let $\Lambda(t)=-t\log t$. Using the convexity of $-\Lambda$, Theorem 1.18, and Theorem 1.20 we have

$$\begin{aligned} H(\xi/\zeta_1) &= E\Big\{-\sum_{A\in\xi} P^{\zeta_1}(\omega, A)\log P^{\zeta_1}(\omega, A)\Big\} \\ &= E\Big\{\sum_{A} \Lambda\big(E^{\zeta_1}(1_A)\big)\Big\} \\ &= E\Big\{\sum_{A} \Lambda\big(E^{\zeta_1}\big(E^{\zeta_2}(1_A)\big)\big)\Big\} \\ &\geqslant E\Big\{\sum_{A} E^{\zeta_1}\big\{\Lambda\big(E^{\zeta_2}(1_A)\big)\big\}\Big\} \\ &= E\Big\{-\sum_{A} P^{\zeta_2}(\omega, A)\log P^{\zeta_2}(\omega, A)\Big\} \\ &= H(\xi/\zeta_2). \end{aligned}$$

COROLLARY 2.12. *If ξ and η are countable measurable partitions and ζ is an arbitrary measurable partition, then*

$$H(\eta/\zeta) \leqslant H(\eta),$$
$$H(\xi\vee\eta/\zeta) \leqslant H(\xi/\zeta)+H(\eta/\zeta).$$

Proof. The first inequality follows from Equation (2.16) and Theorem 2.11, since $\nu \leq \zeta$ for any ζ. The second follows from Equation (2.17) and the theorem.

In information theory another combination of the conditional entropy is used which measures the amount of information gained about an experiment ξ if we know another experiment η. This quantity is called by Osteyee and Good [107] the mutual information between ξ and η and is denoted by $I(\xi;\eta)$. Recall that the uncertainty concerning ξ is measured by $H(\xi)$, and the uncertainty remaining about ξ if we know the outcome of η is measured by the conditional entropy $H(\xi/\eta)$. The difference $H(\xi)-H(\xi/\eta)$ is then a measure of the amount of uncertainty removed by knowing η. Thus if ξ and η are countable partitions with finite entropy, $I(\xi;\eta)$ is defined by the equation

$$I(\xi;\eta)=H(\xi)-H(\xi/\eta). \tag{2.24}$$

By applying Equation (2.19) we may write

$$I(\xi;\eta)=H(\xi)+H(\eta)-H(\xi\vee\eta), \tag{2.25}$$

and it is clear that $I(\xi;\eta)=I(\eta;\xi)$. It follows from Corollary 2.12 that $I(\xi;\eta)\geq 0$ and from Corollary 2.10 that $I(\xi;\eta)=0$ if and only if ξ and η are independent.

As a final set of relationships for entropy and information, we show how they behave with respect to metric endomorphisms.

THEOREM 2.13. *If $(\Omega,\mathfrak{F},P,\mathbf{T})$ is a dynamical system and ξ is a countable measurable partition of Ω, then*

$$I(\mathbf{T}^{-1}\xi/\mathbf{T}^{-1}\zeta)=I(\xi/\zeta)\circ\mathbf{T} \quad \text{a.e.}, \tag{2.26}$$

$$H(\mathbf{T}^{-1}\xi/\mathbf{T}^{-1}\zeta)=H(\xi/\zeta). \tag{2.27}$$

Proof. Since $\mathbf{T}$ preserves the measure P, we have $P\mathbf{T}^{-1}=P$, where $P\mathbf{T}^{-1}$ denotes the measure on $\mathfrak{F}$ whose value at $E\in\mathfrak{F}$ is given by $P(\mathbf{T}^{-1}(E))$. Therefore the change of variable formula gives

$$\int_{\mathbf{T}^{-1}A}P(d\omega)(P^{\zeta}(\ ,C)\circ\mathbf{T}(\omega))=\int_A P(d\omega)P^{\zeta}(\omega,C)$$

for any $C\in\xi^{\wedge}$ and $A\in\zeta^{\wedge}$. By the definition of $P^{\zeta}(\omega,C)$ we have that

$$\int_{\mathbf{T}^{-1}A}P(d\omega)(P^{\zeta}(\ ,C)\circ\mathbf{T}(\omega))=P(A\cap C).$$

It is immediate from the definitions that

$$\int_{\mathrm{T}^{-1}A} P(d\omega)P^{\mathrm{T}^{-1}\zeta}(\omega,\mathrm{T}^{-1}C)=P(A\cap C),$$

and since both $P^{\zeta}(\ ,C)\circ\mathrm{T}$ and $P^{\mathrm{T}^{-1}\zeta}(\ ,\mathrm{T}^{-1}C)$ are $\mathrm{T}^{-1}\zeta^{\wedge}$-measurable, we have that these two functions are equal almost everywhere. Equations (2.26) and (2.27) now follow from the definitions.

2.6 Entropy of Arbitrary Measurable Partitions and Limit Theorems

So far we have only defined the entropy associated with experiments that have a countable number of outcomes. It is useful to extend the definitions of entropy and conditional entropy to arbitrary measurable partitions. This is particularly true in the case of limit theorems, since in most cases of interest a sequence $\{\xi_n\}$ of finite partitions is obtained whose limit is not countable.

In this section we extend our definitions and state a theorem of Rohlin which is basic to showing that the extended entropy satisfies most of the properties of the previous section. In addition we will prove the basic limit theorems for information of countable partitions and entropy of arbitrary partitions.

Definition 2.14. If ξ is a measurable partition of the Lebesgue space $(\Omega,\mathfrak{F},P)$, then the *entropy* $H(\xi)$ of ξ is defined by

$$H(\xi)=\begin{cases} -\sum\limits_{C\in\xi} P(C)\log P(C) & \text{if } \xi \text{ is countable,}\\ \infty & \text{otherwise.}\end{cases}$$

The *conditional entropy* of ξ given a measurable partition ζ, $H(\xi/\zeta)$, is defined by

$$H(\xi/\zeta)=\int_{\Omega_\zeta} P_\zeta(dC)H(\xi\cap C).$$

In the definition of $H(\xi/\zeta)$, $H(\xi\cap D)$ denotes the entropy of the measurable partition $\xi\cap D=\{C\cap D: C\in\xi\}$ of the Lebesgue space $(D,\mathfrak{F}(D),P^{\zeta}(\omega,\ ))$. This is an $\mathfrak{F}_\zeta$-measurable, nonnegative, almost everywhere defined function on $(\Omega_\zeta,\mathfrak{F}_\zeta,P_\zeta)$.

It is not difficult to see that $H(\ )$ and $H(\ /\zeta)$ defined above on the collection of all measurable partitions of $(\Omega,\mathfrak{F},P)$ are actually extensions of the similarly named functions of Sections 2.2 and 2.4.

Notice that in case $H(\xi/\zeta)$ is finite, then the function $H(\xi\cap D)$ is finite for P_ζ-almost all $D\in\zeta$. Thus $\xi\cap D$ is equal ($P^\zeta(\ ,D)$-mod 0) to a countable partition for P_ζ-almost all $D\in\zeta$.

We should remark at this point that if ξ and ζ are countable measurable partitions, then (2.17) and Theorem 2.7 imply that $H(\xi\vee\eta/\eta)=H(\xi/\eta)$. This same result holds if ξ and η are arbitrary measurable partitions, because for P_η-almost all $D\in\eta$, $(\xi\vee\eta)\cap D=\xi\cap D$.

The following theorem is the basic tool for extending the previous results on entropy to arbitrary measurable partitions. The proof we give is from Parry [116].

THEOREM 2.15 (Rohlin's fundamental cross section theorem). *Suppose α and β are measurable partitions of $(\Omega,\mathfrak{F},P)$, and for P_β-almost all atoms $B\in\beta$, the partition $\alpha\cap B$ of the space $(B,\mathfrak{F}(B),P^\beta(\ |b))$ is countable* mod 0. *Then there exists a countable measurable partition of γ of $(\Omega,\mathfrak{F},P)$ such that*

$$\alpha\vee\beta=\gamma\vee\beta \qquad (P\text{-mod } 0).$$

If $H(\alpha/\beta)<\infty$, then γ can be chosen so that $H(\gamma)<\infty$, and if $H(\alpha/\beta)<1$, then it can be chosen so that $H(\gamma)<6\sqrt{H(\alpha/\beta)}$.

Proof. Since we may replace α with $\alpha\vee\beta$, there is no loss in generality in assuming that $\alpha\geqslant\beta$, and by replacing Ω with Ω_α we may also assume $\alpha=\varepsilon$. With these assumptions we need to construct a countable γ such that $\gamma\vee\beta=\varepsilon$.

By the assumptions and hypothesis, P_β-almost all B in β consist of a countable number of points with positive measure together with a set of $P^\beta(\ |b)$-measure zero. Suppose

$$B=\{B_1,B_2,\ldots,B_k,\ldots\}\cup B_0,$$

where $P^\beta(B_j|b)\geqslant P^\beta(B_{j+1}|b)>0$ for $j=1,2,\ldots$ and $P^\beta(B_0|b)=0$.

Rohlin [126] shows that for each such $B\in\beta$ one can select one of the points of maximal measure, say B_1, such that $C_1=\bigcup_{B\in\beta}B_1$ is $\mathfrak{F}$-measurable. The set C_1 is called a maximum measurable cross section of β. Consider $\Omega-C_1$ in place of Ω, and let $C_2=\bigcup_{B\in\beta}B_2$ be a maximum measurable cross section for $\beta\cap(\Omega-C_2)$. Continue by induction to obtain disjoint $\mathfrak{F}$-measurable sets $C_1,C_2,\ldots,C_n,\ldots$ with $C_n=\bigcup_{B\in\beta}B_n$. Take $\gamma=\{C_1,C_2,\ldots,C_n,\ldots\}$. Then

$$P\left(\bigcup_{k=1}^{\infty}C_k\right)=\sum_{k=1}^{\infty}P(C_k)=\sum_{k=1}^{\infty}\int_{\Omega_\beta}P_\beta(db)P^\beta(C_k|b)$$

$$=\int_{\Omega_\beta}P_\beta(db)\sum_{k=1}^{\infty}P^\beta(B_k|b)=1$$

and γ is a (mod 0) partition such that $\gamma \vee \beta = \varepsilon$ (mod 0).

We shall show that $H(\gamma)$ is finite provided $H(\alpha/\beta)$ is finite. Suppose $H(\alpha/\beta) = \delta^2 < \infty$. Since $\gamma \vee \beta = \beta \vee \alpha$, $H(\gamma/\beta) = \delta^2$.

Choose $s \geq 2$, and let $L = \{k : k \geq 2,\ P(C_k) \geq k^{-s}\}$ and $K = \{k : k \geq 2,\ P(C_k) < k^{-s}\}$. Then

$$H(\gamma) = -P(C_1)\log P(C_1) - \sum_L P(C_k)\log P(C_k) - \sum_k P(C_k)\log P(C_k). \tag{2.28}$$

We now estimate each of the three terms on the right hand side of this equation.

Since $P^\beta(C_j|b) = P^\beta(B_j|b) \geq P^\beta(B_{j+1}|b) = P^\beta(C_{j+1}|b)$ P_β-almost everywhere, $P^\beta(C_1|b) \geq P^\beta(C_k|b)$ P_β-a.e., and hence using Jensen's inequality on the convex function log, we have

$$\begin{aligned}
\delta^2 &= \int_{\Omega_\beta} P_\beta(db)\left[-\sum_{j=1}^{\infty} P^\beta(C_k|b)\log P^\beta(C_k|b)\right] \\
&\geq \int_{\Omega_\beta} P_\beta(db)\left[-\log P^\beta(C_1|b)\sum_{j=1}^{\infty} P^\beta(B_k|b)\right] \\
&= \int_{\Omega_\beta} P_\beta(db)\left[-\log P^\beta(C_1|b)\right] \\
&\geq -\log P(C_1),
\end{aligned}$$

and hence

$$-P(C_1)\log P(C_1) \leq \delta^2. \tag{2.29}$$

Again using the monotonicity of $P^\beta(C_j|b)$,

$$1 \geq \sum_{j=1}^{n} P^\beta(C_j|b) \geq nP^\beta(C_n|b) \qquad P_\beta\text{-a.e.,}$$

so $-\log P^\beta(C_n|b) \geq \log n$. Thus

$$\begin{aligned}
\delta^2 &= \int_{\Omega_\beta} P_\beta(db)\left[-\sum_{k=1}^{\infty} P^\beta(C_k|b)\log P^\beta(C_k|b)\right] \\
&\geq \int_{\Omega_\beta} P_\beta(db)\left[\sum_{k=1}^{\infty} P^\beta(C_k|b)\log k\right] \\
&= \sum_{k=1}^{\infty} P(C_k)\log k
\end{aligned}$$

and since $k \in L$ implies $P(C_k) \geqslant 1/k^s$,

$$-\sum_L P(C_k)\log P(C_k) \leqslant \sum_L P(C_k)[s \log k]$$
$$\leqslant s\delta^2. \tag{2.30}$$

To obtain the final estimate notice that since $s \geqslant 2$ and $k \geqslant 2$, we have $k^{-s} \leqslant e^{-1}$, and that $-t\log t$ is increasing on $[0, e^{-1})$. Thus for $k \in K$, $P(C_k) < k^{-s}$ and

$$-\sum_K P(C_k)\log P(C_k) \leqslant \sum_K sk^{-s}\log k$$
$$\leqslant \int_1^\infty st^{-s}\log t\,dt + s2^{-s}\log 2$$
$$\leqslant s(1-s)^{-2} + s^{-1} < 5s^{-1}. \tag{2.31}$$

Substituting (2.29), (2.30), and (2.31) into (2.28) gives

$$H(\gamma) \leqslant \delta^2 + s\delta^2 + 5s^{-1} < \infty.$$

If $\delta^2 = H(\alpha/\beta) < 1$, take $s = \delta^{-1}\sqrt{5}$. Then

$$H(\gamma) \leqslant \delta + \delta\sqrt{5} + \delta\sqrt{5} < 6\sqrt{H(\alpha/\beta)}.$$

LEMMA 2.16. *If* ξ, η, *and* ζ *are measurable partitions of* $(\Omega, \mathfrak{F}, P)$ *and* $\xi \leqslant \eta$ (mod 0), *then*

$$H(\xi/\zeta) \leqslant H(\eta/\zeta) \tag{2.32}$$

and

$$H(\zeta/\xi) \geqslant H(\zeta/\eta). \tag{2.33}$$

Proof. From the inequality (2.23) and Definition 2.14, $H(\xi \cap D) \leqslant H(\eta \cap D)$ for P_ζ-almost all $D \in \zeta$, and (2.32) follows by integration.

To prove (2.33) we assume $H(\zeta/\xi) < \infty$. Then by Theorem 2.15 there is a countable partition γ of $(\Omega, \mathfrak{F}, P)$ such that $H(\gamma) < \infty$ and $\gamma \vee \xi = \zeta \vee \xi$. Thus $\gamma \vee \xi \vee \eta = \zeta \vee \xi \vee \eta$, and since $\xi \leqslant \eta$, we also have $\gamma \vee \eta = \zeta \vee \eta$. Making use of the remark preceding the statement of Theorem 2.15, we have

$$H(\zeta/\xi) = H(\zeta \vee \xi/\xi) = H(\gamma \vee \xi/\xi) = H(\gamma/\xi),$$

and similarly

$$H(\zeta/\eta) = H(\gamma/\eta).$$

Since $H(\gamma) < \infty$, $H(\gamma/\xi) \geq H(\gamma/\eta)$ by Theorem 2.11.

In order to continue our extensions of the results in Section 2.5 we will need to approximate by finite partitions. Approximations always necessitate limit (or continuity) theorems, so we shall now prove some limit theorems for entropy and information. These theorems will also be used in subsequent sections and are basic to the use of entropy in ergodic theory and information theory.

The first result is a technical one due to Neveu [92] and Chung [31]. The proof given here follows Parry [116].

LEMMA 2.17. *Let ξ be a measurable partition with $H(\xi) < \infty$. If $\{\zeta_n\}$ is an increasing sequence of measurable partitions of $(\Omega, \mathfrak{F}, P)$, then*

$$\int_\Omega P(d\omega)\Big\{ \sup_n I(\xi/\zeta_n) \Big\} \leq H(\xi) + 1.$$

Proof. Let $f(\omega) = \sup_n I(\xi/\zeta_n)(\omega)$, and define

$$F(y) = P\{\omega \in \Omega : f(\omega) > y\}.$$

Then from elementary measure theory

$$\int_\Omega f\, dP = \int_0^\infty F(y)\, dy,$$

and the result is obtained by calculating an upper bound for $F(y)$.

For any $y > 0$,

$$\begin{aligned} F(y) &= P\Big\{x : \sup_n \Big[-\sum_A 1_A(x) \log P^{\zeta_n}(x, A) \Big] > y \Big\} \\ &= \sum_{A \in \xi} P\Big\{ x \in A : \sup_n (-\log P^{\zeta_n}(x, A)) > y \Big\} \\ &= \sum_{A \in \xi} P\Big[A \cap \Big\{ x : \inf_n P^{\zeta_n}(x, A) < e^{-y} \Big\} \Big]. \end{aligned} \tag{2.34}$$

For fixed $y > 0$ and $A \in \xi$, define

$$A_n = \{x : P^{\zeta_n}(x, A) < e^{-y},\ P^{\zeta_k}(x, A) \geq e^{-y},\ 0 < k < n\}$$

for $n=1,2,3,\ldots$. Since $\zeta_k \leqslant \zeta_n$ for $k<n$, we have $A_n \in \zeta_n\hat{}$, and by the properties of conditional probability

$$P(A\cap A_n)=\int_{A_n} P(d\omega)P^{\zeta_n}(\omega, A)$$
$$\leqslant e^{-y}P(A_n).$$

Therefore, since

$$P\Big\{x\in A:\inf_n P^{\zeta_n}(x,A)<e^{-y}\Big\}=\sum_{n=1}^{\infty} P(A\cap A_n),$$

we have

$$\sum_{n=1}^{\infty} P(A\cap A_n)\leqslant e^{-y}P\Big(\bigcup A_n\Big)\leqslant e^{-y}.$$

Applying this bound in Equation (2.34) we have

$$F(y)\leqslant \sum_{A\in\xi} \min\{P(A),e^{-y}\}.$$

Therefore

$$\int_\Omega P(d\omega)\sup_n I(\xi/\zeta_n)(\omega)\leqslant \sum_{A\in\xi}\int_0^\infty \min\{P(A),e^{-y}\}\,dy$$
$$=\sum_{A\in\xi}\left[\int_0^{-\log P(A)} P(A)\,dy+\int_{-\log P(A)}^{\infty} e^{-y}\,dy\right]$$
$$=-\sum_{A\in\xi} P(A)\log P(A)+\sum_{A\in\xi} P(A)$$
$$=H(\xi)+1.$$

THEOREM 2.18. *Let ξ be a measurable partition of $(\Omega,\mathfrak{F},P)$ such that $H(\xi)<\infty$, and $\{\zeta_n\}$ be a sequence of measurable partitions such that $\zeta_n\uparrow\zeta$. Then*

$$I(\xi/\zeta_n)\to I(\xi/\zeta) \qquad P\text{-a.e. and } L_1. \tag{2.35}$$

If ξ is an arbitrary measurable partition and there exists k such that $H(\xi/\zeta_k)<\infty$, then

$$H(\xi/\zeta_n)\downarrow H(\xi/\zeta). \tag{2.36}$$

Proof. Suppose first that $H(\xi)<\infty$. Then ξ is countable, so that $I(\xi/\zeta_n)(\omega)=-\Sigma_{A\in\xi}1_A(\omega)\log P^{\zeta_n}(\omega, A)$. For each $A\in\xi$ Corollary 1.27 gives us that $P^{\zeta_n}(\omega, A)\rightarrow P^{\zeta}(\omega, A)$ a.e. with respect to P. Since $-\log t$ is continuous, $-\log P^{\zeta_n}(\omega, A)$ converges P-a.e. on A and the a.e. convergence in (2.35) follows. The L_1 convergence follows from Lemma 2.17 and the Lebesgue dominated convergence theorem.

In case $H(\xi)<\infty$, Equation (2.36) follows from (2.35) by integration. Assume $H(\xi/\zeta_k)<\infty$ for some k. By Theorem 2.15 there exists a measurable partition γ such that $H(\gamma)<\infty$ and $\xi\vee\zeta_k=\gamma\vee\zeta_k$. Since $\zeta_n\uparrow\zeta$ we have $\xi\vee\zeta_n=\gamma\vee\zeta_n$ for all $n\geqslant k$ and $\xi\vee\zeta=\gamma\vee\zeta$. As in the proof of Lemma 2.16, $H(\xi/\zeta_n)=H(\gamma/\zeta_n)$ for $n\geqslant k$ and $H(\xi/\zeta)=H(\gamma/\zeta)$. Since $H(\gamma)<\infty$, $H(\gamma/\zeta_n)\uparrow H(\gamma/\zeta)$ and the result follows.

THEOREM 2.19. *If $\{\xi_n\}$ is a sequence of countable measurable partitions such that $\xi_n\uparrow\xi$ and ξ is a countable partition, then*

$$I(\xi_n/\zeta)\uparrow I(\xi/\zeta) \qquad \text{a.e.} \tag{2.37}$$

If $\{\xi_n\}$ is a sequence of arbitrary measurable partitions and $\xi_n\uparrow\xi$, then

$$H(\xi_n/\zeta)\uparrow H(\xi/\zeta). \tag{2.38}$$

Proof. Assume that ξ_n and ξ are countable. Since $\xi_n\uparrow\xi$, for each atom $A\in\xi$ there exists a sequence $\{A_n\}$ of atoms such that $A_n\in\xi_n$, $A_n\supset A_{n+1}$, and $\bigcap_{n=1}^{\infty}A_n=A$. For almost all $\omega\in A$, $I(\xi_n/\zeta)(\omega)=-\log P^{\zeta}(\omega, A_n)$, and since $P^{\zeta}(\omega,\ )$ is a probability measure for almost all $\omega\in A$ and the logarithm is continuous, $I(\xi_n/\zeta)\rightarrow I(\xi/\zeta)$ a.e. on A. Since ξ is countable, (2.37) follows.

Now suppose ξ_n are arbitrarily measurable partitions and $\xi_n\uparrow\xi$. In case $H(\xi_n/\zeta)=\infty$ for some n, Equation (2.38) is true because of Lemma 2.16. Therefore, we may assume that $H(\xi_n/\zeta)<\infty$ for all $n\geqslant 1$, and it follows that for P_ζ almost all $D\in\zeta$, $\xi_n\cap D$ is equal ($P^{\zeta}-$mod 0) to a countable partition ξ_n' of the fiber space $(D, \mathcal{F}(D), P^{\zeta})$. Since $H(\xi_n/\zeta)=\int_{\Omega_\zeta}P_\zeta(dD)$ $H(\xi_n\cap D)$, if we can show that for $\{\xi_n'\}$ a sequence of countable partitions such that $\xi_n'\uparrow\xi'$ we have $H(\xi_n')\uparrow H(\xi')$, then the result will follow from the monotone convergence theorem. By passing to the factor space associated with ξ' we may also assume that $\xi'=\varepsilon$.

Thus suppose $\{\xi_n'\}$ is a sequence of countable measurable partitions of $(\Omega', \mathcal{F}', P')$ such that $\xi_n'\uparrow\varepsilon$. In case ε is countable, Equation (2.37) implies that $I(\xi_n)\uparrow I(\varepsilon)$ and the monotone convergence theorem gives the result.

In case ε is not countable, $H(\varepsilon)=\infty$. Since $(\Omega', \mathcal{F}', P')$ is a Lebesgue space, it is isomorphic to a space $(X, \mathcal{Q}, \mu)$ where X consists of a segment J of the unit interval with Lebesgue measure together with an at most countable number of point masses. Since ε is not countable, the segment J

must have positive measure and its image B in Ω must have positive P'-measure. Moreover, for each $\omega \in B$, $P'\{\omega\}=0$.

Let N be given. For k sufficiently large those atoms of ξ'_k which intersect B must have measure less than or equal to $1/N$. For if not, there exists a subsequence $C_{k'}$ of atoms with $C_{k'} \in \xi_{k'}$ such that $C_{k'} \cap B \neq \varnothing$ and $P'(C_{k'}) > 1/N$. Since the sets $C_{k'}$ are atoms from an increasing sequence of partitions and $\Sigma P'(C_{k'})=\infty$, there is a subsequence $C_{k'_j}$ such that $C_{k'_j}\downarrow$. Since $\xi'_k \cap B \uparrow \varepsilon \cap B$, there can be at most one point in $\bigcap_j C_{k'_j}$, and hence $P(C_{k'_j})\downarrow 0$. This is a contradiction, since $P(C_{k'_j}) > 1/N$ for all j.

Thus there exists a subsequence $\xi'_{k'}$ such that each atom of $\xi'_{k'}$ which intersects B has measure less than or equal to $1/N$. Let

$$\mathfrak{B}_N = \{C \in \xi'_{k'} : C \cap B \neq \varnothing\}$$

and

$$B_N = \bigcup_{C \in \mathfrak{B}_N} C.$$

Since $\xi'_n \uparrow \varepsilon$, we have $B_N \downarrow B$ and $P(B_N) \geqslant P(B) > 0$ for all N. Then

$$\begin{aligned} H(\xi_{k'}) &= -\sum_{C \in \xi_{k'}} P(C)\log P(C) \\ &\geqslant \sum_{C \in \mathfrak{B}_N} P(C)\log P(C) \\ &\geqslant P(B)\log N, \end{aligned}$$

and it follows that $H(\xi_n)\uparrow\infty$.

THEOREM 2.20. *If ξ is a measurable partition and $\{\zeta_n\}$ is a sequence of measurable partitions such that $\zeta_n \downarrow \zeta$, then*

$$H(\xi/\zeta_n)\uparrow H(\xi/\zeta).$$

Proof. First we assume that ξ is a finite measurable partition. By Corollary 1.27 and the continuity of $-t\log t$ we have for each $A \in \xi$ that

$$-P^{\zeta_n}(\omega, A)\log P^{\zeta_n}(\omega, A) \to -P^{\zeta}(\omega, A)\log P^{\zeta}(\omega, A) \qquad \text{a.e.}$$

Since $|P^{\zeta_n}(\omega, A)\log P^{\zeta_n}(\omega, A)| \leqslant e^{-1}$ for all n, the convergence is also L_1. Since there are only a finite number of atoms in ξ,

$$-\sum_{A \in \xi} P^{\zeta_n}(\omega, A)\log P^{\zeta_n}(\omega, A) \to -\sum_{A \in \xi} P^{\zeta}(\omega, A)\log P^{\zeta}(\omega, A)$$

in L_1, and integration gives the result.

Next suppose that ξ is a countably infinite partition with $H(\xi)<\infty$. If $\xi=\{C_1, C_2, C_3,\dots\}$ let $\xi_n=\{C_1, C_2,\dots, C_{n-1}, B_n\}$ where $B_n=\bigcup_{j=n}^{\infty}C_j$. Then $\xi_n\uparrow\xi$ and the ξ_n are finite. Let $\delta>0$ be given. By Theorem 2.19, there exists K so that

$$H(\xi/\zeta)-H(\xi_K/\zeta)<\delta/2.$$

Since ξ_K is finite, from the first part of the proof there exists N sufficiently large so that

$$H(\xi_K/\zeta)-H(\xi_K/\zeta_n)<\delta/2.$$

for all $n\geqslant N$. Then

$$0\leqslant H(\xi/\zeta)-H(\xi/\zeta_n)=\left[H(\xi/\zeta)-H(\xi_K/\zeta)\right] \\ +\left[H(\xi_K/\zeta)-H(\xi_K/\zeta_n)\right]<\delta/2+\delta/2,$$

and the result follows for all ξ with finite entropy.

Next suppose ξ is an arbitrary measurable partition with $H(\xi/\zeta)<\infty$. By Theorem 2.15 there exists a countable partition γ with $H(\gamma)<\infty$ and $\xi\vee\zeta=\gamma\vee\zeta$. As before, we have $\xi\vee\zeta_n=\gamma\vee\zeta_n$ for all n, so that $H(\xi/\zeta_n)=H(\gamma/\zeta_n)$ and $H(\xi/\zeta)=H(\gamma/\zeta)$. The second part of the proof gives that $H(\gamma/\zeta_n)\uparrow H(\gamma/\zeta)$, and the result follows.

Finally assume that $H(\xi/\zeta)=\infty$ but $H(\xi/\zeta_n)<\infty$ for all n. Since ξ is a measurable partition, there exists a countable family $\{A_n\}$ of measurable ξ-sets which separate atoms of ξ. For each n, define η_n to be the partition $\{A_n, A_n^c\}$ and take $\xi_m=\eta_1\vee\eta_2\vee\cdots\vee\eta_m$. Then $\xi_m\uparrow\xi$, and Theorem 2.19 implies that if K is given there exists an M such that $H(\xi_M/\zeta)>K+1$.

Since ξ_M is finite, $H(\xi_M)<\infty$ and the first part of the proof gives us that $H(\xi_M/\zeta_n)\uparrow H(\xi_M/\zeta)$. Since $H(\xi_M/\zeta)$ is finite there exists N such that if $n\geqslant N$

$$1>H(\xi_M/\zeta)-H(\xi_M/\zeta_n) \\ =\left[H(\xi_M/\zeta)-H(\xi/\zeta_n)\right]+\left[H(\xi/\zeta_n)-H(\xi_M/\zeta_n)\right].$$

Since $\xi_M\leqslant\xi$, $H(\xi/\zeta_n)-H(\xi_M/\zeta_n)\geqslant 0$, so that

$$H(\xi/\zeta_n)>H(\xi_M/\zeta)-1>K$$

and we have $\lim_{n\to\infty}H(\xi/\zeta_n)=\infty$.

As a first application of these limit theorems suppose that $(\Omega, \mathfrak{F}, P, \mathbf{T})$ is a dynamical system (cf. Section 1.7) and ξ is a finite measurable partition of Ω. Let us interpret partitions as experiments and $\mathbf{T}$ as the mechanism which models the passage of time. Now if ζ is an arbitrary measurable partition of Ω, then $H(\xi/\bigvee_{j=1}^{n}\mathbf{T}^{-j}\zeta)$ represents the average uncertainty about the experiment ξ given the outcomes of experiment ζ performed n times. Theorem 2.18 implies that

$$\lim_{n\to\infty} H\left(\xi/\bigvee_{j=1}^{n}\mathbf{T}^{-j}\zeta\right)=H\left(\xi/\bigvee_{j=1}^{\infty}\mathbf{T}^{-j}\zeta\right), \tag{2.39}$$

and we have that the average uncertainty about ξ given knowledge of all future outcomes of ζ can be calculated by the limit of these uncertainties. In case $\mathbf{T}$ is a metric automorphism, the past history of the experiment to n time units in the past can be given by $\bigvee_{j=-\infty}^{-n}\mathbf{T}^{-j}\zeta$. Then $H(\xi/\bigvee_{j=-\infty}^{-n}\mathbf{T}^{-1}\zeta)$ is the average uncertainty about ξ if we known this past history of ζ. Theorem 2.20 implies that

$$\lim_{n\to\infty} H\left(\xi/\bigvee_{n=-\infty}^{-n}\mathbf{T}^{-j}\zeta\right)=H\left(\xi/\bigvee_{j=-\infty}^{\infty}\ \bigvee_{j=-\infty}^{-n}\mathbf{T}^{-j}\zeta\right), \tag{2.40}$$

and we have a way of calculating the average uncertainty about ξ knowing the predetermined events for the process $\{\mathbf{T}^{j}\zeta\}_{j=-\infty}^{+\infty}$.

Finally notice that in case $\mathbf{T}$ is an automorphism,

$$\lim_{n\to\infty} H\left(\xi/\bigvee_{j=-\infty}^{n}\mathbf{T}^{-j}\zeta\right)=H\left(\xi/\bigvee_{j=-\infty}^{\infty}\mathbf{T}^{-j}\zeta\right) \tag{2.41}$$

and this limit is the uncertainty about ξ given the total history, both past and future, of the experiment ζ.

We shall now apply the limit theorems just proven to extend some of the other results proven in Section 2.5 to entropy and conditional entropy for arbitrary measurable partitions. We shall also prove a result (Lemma 2.25) for invertible dynamical systems which we shall use in the next section. This lemma will also be used in Chapter 4 in discussing tails of processes.

THEOREM 2.21. *If ξ,η, and ζ are measurable partitions of $(\Omega,\mathcal{F},P)$, then*

$$H(\xi\vee\eta/\zeta)=H(\xi/\zeta)+H(\eta/\xi\vee\zeta).$$

Proof. Since ξ and η are measurable partitions, there exist sequences $\{\xi_n\}$ and $\{\eta_n\}$ of finite measurable partitions such that $\xi_n\uparrow\xi$ and $\eta_n\uparrow\eta$. Since η_m is finite for each m, we have $H(\eta_m/\xi_n\vee\zeta)<\infty$ for all $n\geqslant 1$ and Theorem 2.18 implies that $H(\eta_m/\xi_n\vee\zeta)\downarrow H(\eta_m/\xi\vee\zeta)$ as $n\to\infty$. Since ξ_n and η_m are finite,

$$H(\xi_n\vee\eta_m/\zeta)=H(\xi_n/\zeta)+H(\eta_m/\xi_n\vee\zeta).$$

If we take the limit of this equation as first $n\to\infty$ and then $m\to\infty$, the result follows from Theorem 2.18 and (2.19).

COROLLARY 2.22. *If ξ, η, ζ are measurable partitions, then*

$$H(\xi\vee\eta/\zeta)\leqslant H(\xi/\zeta)+H(\eta/\zeta).$$

THEOREM 2.23. *If ξ and ζ are measurable partitions, then*

$$H(\xi/\nu)=H(\xi), \tag{2.42}$$

$$H(\xi/\zeta)=0 \quad \textit{iff } \xi\leqslant\zeta. \tag{2.43}$$

Proof. Equation (2.42) is immediate from the definition. If $\xi\leqslant\zeta$, then $H(\xi/\zeta)=H(\xi\vee\zeta/\zeta)=H(\zeta/\zeta)$, and since $\zeta\cap D$ is the trivial partition on each atom $D\in\zeta$, $H(\zeta\cap D)=0$. Thus $H(\xi/\zeta)=0$. Suppose next that $H(\xi/\zeta)=0$. Since $H(\xi/\zeta)<\infty$, there exists γ with $H(\gamma)<\infty$ and $\xi\vee\zeta=\gamma\vee\zeta$ such that $H(\gamma/\zeta)=0$. By Theorem 2.7 $\gamma\leqslant\zeta$, so that $\xi\vee\zeta=\zeta$ and $\xi\leqslant\zeta$.

THEOREM 2.24. *If $(\Omega, \mathfrak{F}, P, \mathbf{T})$ is a dynamical system and ξ and η are measurable partitions of Ω, then $H(\mathbf{T}^{-1}\xi/\mathbf{T}^{-1}\eta)=H(\xi/\eta)$.*

Proof. Since ξ is a measurable partition, there exists a sequence $\{\xi_n\}$ of finite partitions such that $\xi_n\uparrow\xi$. Then $\mathbf{T}^{-1}\xi_n\uparrow\mathbf{T}^{-1}\xi$, and Theorem 2.13 gives us that $H(\xi_n/\eta)=H(\mathbf{T}^{-1}\xi_n/\mathbf{T}^{-1}\eta)$. The result follows now from Theorem 2.19.

LEMMA 2.25. *If $(\Omega, \mathfrak{F}, P, \mathbf{T})$ is an invertible dynamical system and α, β are measurable partitions such that either $\alpha\geqslant\beta$ and $H(\alpha/\bigvee_{j=1}^{\infty}\mathbf{T}^{-j}\beta)<\infty$ or $\alpha\leqslant\beta$ and $H(\beta/\bigvee_{j=1}^{\infty}\mathbf{T}^{-j}\alpha)<\infty$, then*

$$\lim_{n\to\infty}\frac{1}{n}H\left[\bigvee_{j=0}^{n-1}\mathbf{T}^{j}\alpha/\bigvee_{j=1}^{\infty}\mathbf{T}^{-j}\beta\right]=H\left(\alpha/\bigvee_{j=1}^{\infty}\mathbf{T}^{-j}\alpha\right).$$

Proof. For any partition ξ let ξ^n denote $\bigvee_{j=0}^{n-1}\mathbf{T}^{j}\xi$ and $\xi^{-}=\bigvee_{j=1}^{\infty}\mathbf{T}^{-j}\xi$. Suppose first that $\alpha\geqslant\beta$ and $H(\alpha/\beta^{-})<\infty$. By repeated application of Theorem 2.21 and use of Theorem 2.24 we have

$$\frac{1}{n}H(\alpha^n/\beta^{-})=\frac{1}{n}H(\alpha/\beta^{-})+\frac{1}{n}\sum_{k=1}^{n-1}H\big(\alpha/\mathbf{T}^{-k}(\alpha^k\vee\beta^{-})\big). \tag{2.44}$$

For any $k>0$,

$$\bigvee_{j=1}^{k}\mathbf{T}^{-j}\alpha\leqslant\bigvee_{j=1}^{k}\mathbf{T}^{-j}\alpha\vee\bigvee_{j=k+1}^{\infty}\mathbf{T}^{-j}\beta=\mathbf{T}^{-k}(\alpha^k\vee\beta^{-}).$$

Since $\alpha \geqslant \beta$, $\mathbf{T}^{-k}(\alpha^k \vee \beta^-)$ increases and for all k, $\mathbf{T}^{-k}(\alpha^k \vee \beta^-) \leqslant \alpha^-$. Thus $\mathbf{T}^{-k}(\alpha^k \vee \beta^-) \uparrow \alpha^-$. Also $\alpha \geqslant \beta$ implies that $\mathbf{T}^{-1}(\alpha \vee \beta^-) = \mathbf{T}^{-1}\alpha \vee \bigvee_{j=2}^{\infty} \mathbf{T}^{-j}\beta \geqslant \beta^-$. Thus $H(\alpha/\mathbf{T}^{-1}(\alpha \vee \beta^-)) \leqslant H(\alpha/\beta^-) < \infty$, and Theorem 2.18 implies that

$$H(\alpha/\mathbf{T}^{-k}(\alpha^k \vee \beta^-)) \downarrow H(\alpha/\alpha^-).$$

Since convergence implies Cesaro convergence, this result applied to (2.44) gives

$$\lim_{n\to\infty} \frac{1}{n} H(\alpha^n/\beta^-) = H(\alpha/\alpha^-).$$

Now assume that $\alpha \leqslant \beta$ and $H(\beta/\alpha^-) < \infty$. By Equation (2.44)

$$\frac{1}{n} H(\alpha^n/\alpha^-) = H(\alpha/\alpha^-),$$

and since $\beta^- \geqslant \alpha^-$, we have $(1/n)H(\alpha^n/\beta^-) \leqslant (1/n)H(\alpha^n/\alpha^-)$, so that

$$\limsup_{n\to\infty} \frac{1}{n} H(\alpha^n/\beta^-) \leqslant H(\alpha/\alpha^-).$$

Since $\alpha^n \leqslant \beta^n$, we have $\alpha^n \vee \beta^n = \beta^n$ and Theorem 2.21 gives

$$\frac{1}{n} H(\alpha^n/\beta^-) = \frac{1}{n} H(\beta^n/\beta^-) - \frac{1}{n} H(\beta^n/\alpha^n \vee \beta^-).$$

$$\geqslant H(\beta/\beta^-) - \frac{1}{n} H(\beta^n/\alpha^n \vee \alpha^-).$$

Using the first part of the proof we have $\lim_{n\to\infty} \frac{1}{n} H(\beta^n/\alpha^-) = H(\beta/\beta^-)$, so for $\varepsilon > 0$ given, there exist N such that for all $n \geqslant N$, $H(\beta/\beta^-) \geqslant \frac{1}{n} H(\beta^n/\alpha^-)$. Thus for all such n,

$$\frac{1}{n} H(\alpha^n/\beta^-) \geqslant \frac{1}{n} H(\beta^n/\alpha^-) - \frac{1}{n} H(\beta^n/\alpha^n \vee \alpha^-) - \varepsilon$$

$$= \frac{1}{n} H(\alpha^n/\alpha^-) - \varepsilon$$

$$= H(\alpha/\alpha^-) - \varepsilon$$

and $\liminf_{n\to\infty} \frac{1}{n} H(\alpha^n/\beta^-) \geqslant H(\alpha/\alpha^-)$. The second half of the lemma is proven.

2.7 Rate of Information Generation

Let $(\Omega, \mathfrak{F}, P, \mathbf{T})$ be a dynamical system, and ξ a measurable partition of Ω such that $H(\xi)<\infty$. The partition $\bigvee_{j=0}^{n-1}\mathbf{T}^{-j}\xi$ is a measurable partition which represents n repetitions of the experiment ξ. (The repetitions are not necessarily independent. The type of dependence is built into the transformation $\mathbf{T}$.) Thus $(1/n)H(\bigvee_{j=0}^{n-1}\mathbf{T}^{-j}\xi)$ is the average amount of uncertainty per trial.

If H_n denotes for the time being $H(\bigvee_{j=0}^{n-1}\mathbf{T}^{-j}\xi)$, Corollary 2.22 and Theorem 2.24 imply that $H_{n+m} \leqslant H_n + H_m$. This subadditivity, together with the fact that $\{H_n\}$ is a non-negative sequence, is enough to prove that $\lim n_{n\to\infty}(1/n)H_n = \inf_{n>0}\{(1/n)H_n\}$. The proof is as follows:

Let $n>m$ be given non-negative integers. There exist integers q, r with $0 \leqslant r < m$ such that $n = mq + r$. By subadditivity

$$H_n \leqslant H_{mq} + H_r \leqslant qH_m + rH_1.$$

Since $mq \leqslant n$ and $rm \leqslant m^2$ we have

$$mH_n \leqslant nH_m + m^2 H_1$$

and division by mn gives

$$\frac{1}{n}H_n \leqslant \frac{1}{m}H_m + \frac{m}{n}H_1.$$

Thus

$$\lim_{n\to\infty} \sup \frac{1}{n}H_n \leqslant \inf_{m>0}\left\{\frac{1}{m}H_m\right\} \leqslant \lim_{n\to\infty} \inf \frac{1}{n}H_n$$

and the result follows:

This limit is denoted by $h(\mathbf{T}, \xi)$ and represents the average amount of uncertainty in ξ per trial, or the rate at which information about ξ is generated by repeating the experiment ξ many times by the mechanism $\mathbf{T}$.

Definition 2.26. The *rate of information* about ξ generated by $\mathbf{T}$, or the *entropy of* $\mathbf{T}$ *given* ξ, is denoted $h(\mathbf{T}, \xi)$ and is defined by the equation

$$h(\mathbf{T}, \xi) = \lim_{n\to\infty} \frac{1}{n} H\left[\bigvee_{j=0}^{n-1} \mathbf{T}^{-j}\xi\right]. \tag{2.45}$$

THEOREM 2.27. *If* ξ *is a measurable partition of* $(\Omega, \mathcal{F}, P)$ *with* $H(\xi)<\infty$ *and* $\mathbf{T}$ *is a metric endomorphism on* Ω, *then*

$$h(\mathbf{T}, \xi)=H\left(\xi / \bigvee_{j=1}^{\infty} \mathbf{T}^{-j} \xi\right).$$

Proof. By repeated application of Theorem 2.21

$$\begin{aligned} H\left[\bigvee_{j=0}^{n-1} \mathbf{T}^{-j} \xi\right] = & H(\mathbf{T}^{-n+1}\xi)+H(\mathbf{T}^{-n+2}\xi/\mathbf{T}^{-n+1}\xi) \\ & +H(\mathbf{T}^{-n+3}\xi/\mathbf{T}^{-n+2}\xi \vee \mathbf{T}^{-n+1}\xi) \\ & +\cdots+H(\xi/\mathbf{T}^{-1}\xi \vee \cdots \vee \mathbf{T}^{-n+1}\xi). \end{aligned}$$

Using Theorem 2.24 on the terms on the right hand side of this equation gives

$$\frac{1}{n} H\left[\bigvee_{j=0}^{n-1} \mathbf{T}^{-j} \xi\right]=\frac{1}{n} H(\xi)+\frac{1}{n} \sum_{k=2}^{n} H\left[\xi / \bigvee_{j=1}^{k-1} \mathbf{T}^{-j} \xi\right].$$

Since $H(\xi)<\infty$, $(1/n)H(\xi)\to 0$. Moreover, $H(\xi/\bigvee_{j=1}^{k-1}\mathbf{T}^{-j}\xi)<\infty$ for all k, so that Theorem 2.18 implies that

$$\frac{1}{n} \sum_{k=2}^{n} H\left[\xi / \bigvee_{j=1}^{k} \mathbf{T}^{-j} \xi\right] \rightarrow H\left(\xi / \bigvee_{j=1}^{\infty} \mathbf{T}^{-j} \xi\right),$$

and the theorem follows.

If the hypothesis $H(\xi)<\infty$ is removed in the preceding theorem, the resulting statement is false, as the following example shows. Let $(\Omega, \mathcal{F}, P)$ be the unit interval with Lebesgue measure, and define $\mathbf{T}$ on Ω by $\mathbf{T}\omega=\omega+\omega_0 \pmod 1$, where ω_0 is an irrational number in Ω. Let $\xi_n=\{(j/2^n,(j+1)/2^n]: j=0,1,\ldots,2^n-1\}$ and define $\xi=\bigvee_{n=1}^{\infty}\xi_n$. The partition ξ is countable, but

$$H(\xi) \geqslant H(\xi_n)=2^n \log 2^n$$

for all n, so $H(\xi)=\infty$. Since ω_0 is irrational, $\bigvee_{j=1}^{\infty}\mathbf{T}^{-j}\xi_1=\varepsilon$, and since $\xi_1 \leqslant \xi$, $\bigvee_{j=1}^{\infty}\mathbf{T}^{-1}\xi=\varepsilon$. Thus $H(\xi/\bigvee_{j=1}^{\infty}\mathbf{T}^{-j}\xi)=0$, whereas $h(\mathbf{T},\xi)=\infty$.

Notice that this theorem tells us that if the average uncertainty in an experiment is finite, the rate at which $\mathbf{T}$ generates information about ξ is the same as the uncertainty in ξ given knowledge of all future outcomes of trials of ξ by using the mechanism $\mathbf{T}$.

Corollary 2.28. *If ξ is a measurable partition of $(\Omega, \mathfrak{F}, P, \mathbf{T})$ with $H(\xi)<\infty$, then ξ is an independent partition if and only if $h(\mathbf{T},\xi)=H(\xi)$ [i.e., $(\mathbf{T},\xi)$ is an independent process if and only if $h(\mathbf{T},\xi)=H(\xi)$].*

Proof. In case ξ is an independent partition, ξ is independent of $\bigvee_{j=1}^{n-1}\mathbf{T}^{-j}\xi$ for all n, so Theorem 2.9 implies that $H(\xi/\bigvee_{j=1}^{n-1}\mathbf{T}^{-j}\xi)=H(\xi)$. It now follows from the theorem that $h(\mathbf{T},\xi)=H(\xi)$.

Next suppose that $h(\mathbf{T},\xi)=H(\xi)$. Since $\nu\leqslant\bigvee_{j=1}^{n}\mathbf{T}^{-1}\xi\leqslant\bigvee_{j=1}^{\infty}\mathbf{T}^{-j}\xi$ for all n,

$$H(\xi)\geqslant H\left(\xi/\bigvee_{j=1}^{n}\mathbf{T}^{-j}\xi\right)\geqslant H\left(\xi/\bigvee_{j=1}^{\infty}\mathbf{T}^{-j}\xi\right),$$

and since $h(\mathbf{T},\xi)=H(\xi/\bigvee_{j=1}^{\infty}\mathbf{T}^{-j}\xi)$, we have that

$$H\left(\xi/\bigvee_{j=1}^{n}\mathbf{T}^{-j}\xi\right)=H(\xi)$$

for all n. Theorem 2.9 implies that ξ and $\bigvee_{j=1}^{n}\mathbf{T}^{-j}\xi$ are independent for all n. Thus ξ is independent of $\mathbf{T}^{-1}\xi$. Since $H(\xi/\mathbf{T}^{-1}\xi)=H(\mathbf{T}^{-1}\xi/\mathbf{T}^{-2}\xi)$, we have $\mathbf{T}^{-1}\xi$ independent $\mathbf{T}^{-2}\xi$. But ξ independent of $\mathbf{T}^{-1}\xi\vee\mathbf{T}^{-2}\xi$ and $\mathbf{T}^{-1}\xi$ independent of $\mathbf{T}^{-2}\xi$ implies that ξ is independent of $\mathbf{T}^{-2}\xi$. Thus $\{\xi,\mathbf{T}^{-1}\xi,\mathbf{T}^{-2}\xi\}$ are independent. Proceeding in this manner, it can be shown that for any n, $\{\xi,\mathbf{T}^{-1}\xi,\ldots,\mathbf{T}^{-n}\xi\}$ is an independent family of partitions and the theorem follows.

The fact that an independent partition gives a rate of information generation by $\mathbf{T}$ equal to its own uncertainty is not surprising, since the action of $\mathbf{T}$ on the partition corresponds to independent repetitions of the experiment. Thus knowledge of future outcomes of the experiment should not change the uncertainty about the experiment.

Note also that both $h(\mathbf{T},\xi)$ and $H(\xi/\bigvee_{j=1}^{\infty}\mathbf{T}^{-j}\xi)$ do not exceed $H(\xi)$. This is to be expected, since the average information obtained per trial about an experiment cannot exceed the total amount of uncertainty about the experiment. In addition, if $H(\xi)<\infty$, this maximum is attained if and only if the experiment is repeated independently, that is, ξ is an independent partition for $\mathbf{T}$. Thus applying Theorem 2.3, we have that if ξ is any partition with K atoms, then

$$h(\mathbf{T},\xi)\leqslant\log K, \tag{2.46}$$

with $h(\mathbf{T},\xi)=\log K$ if and only if ξ is an independent partition with each atom having probability $1/K$.

In Section 1.7 we showed how stationary stochastic sequences can be represented by measurable partitions of a dynamical system $(\Omega, \mathcal{F}, P, \mathbf{T})$. In case the parameter set of the process is infinite, $\mathbf{T}^n$ is defined for all n and the rate of information about the partition representing the process generated by $\mathbf{T}$ may be calculated. From this point of view we have a quantity associated with stochastic sequences. For example, if $\{x_n : n \in Z\}$ is a stationary stochastic sequence in a finite set Γ, the rate of information generated by the process is given by either $\lim(1/n)H(\bigvee_{j=0}^{n-1} x_j^{-1}(\varepsilon))$ or $H(x_0^{-1}(\varepsilon)/\bigvee_{j=1}^{\infty} x_j^{-1}(\varepsilon))$, where ε represents the point partition in Γ.

Notice that this quantity depends only on the joint distribution of the random variables and can be used, as we shall see later, to distinguish between non isomorphic stochastic sequences.

The following theorems are basic properties of the rate of information generation.

Lemma 2.29. *If ξ and η are measurable partitions of $(\Omega, \mathcal{F}, P)$ and $\mathbf{T}$ is a metric endomorphism, then*

$$h(\mathbf{T}, \xi) \leqslant h(\mathbf{T}, \eta) + H(\xi/\eta).$$

Proof. Since $\bigvee_{j=0}^{N-1} \mathbf{T}^{-j}\xi \leqslant \bigvee_{j=0}^{N-1} \mathbf{T}^{-j}\eta \vee \bigvee_{j=0}^{N-1} \mathbf{T}^{-j}\xi$, Lemma 2.16 and Theorems 2.21 and 2.23 imply that

$$H\left[\bigvee_{j=0}^{N-1} \mathbf{T}^{-j}\xi\right] \leqslant H\left[\bigvee_{j=0}^{N-1} \mathbf{T}^{-j}\eta\right] + H\left[\bigvee_{j=0}^{N-1} \mathbf{T}^{-j}\xi \Big/ \bigvee_{j=0}^{N-1} \mathbf{T}^{-j}\eta\right].$$

Corollary 2.22 gives us that

$$H\left[\bigvee_{j=0}^{N-1} \mathbf{T}^{-j}\xi \Big/ \bigvee_{j=0}^{N-1} \mathbf{T}^{-i}\eta\right] \leqslant \sum_{i=0}^{N-1} H\left[\mathbf{T}^{-i}\xi \Big/ \bigvee_{j=0}^{N-1} \mathbf{T}^{-j}\eta\right].$$

Since $\mathbf{T}^{-i}\eta \leqslant \bigvee_{j=0}^{N-1} \mathbf{T}^{-j}\eta$ for $0 \leqslant i < N$, the last two inequalities and Lemma 2.16 give

$$H\left[\bigvee_{j=0}^{N-1} \mathbf{T}^{-j}\xi\right] \leqslant H\left[\bigvee_{j=0}^{N-1} \mathbf{T}^{-j}\eta\right] + \sum_{i=0}^{N-1} H(\mathbf{T}^{-i}\xi/\mathbf{T}^{-i}\eta).$$

Applying Theorem 2.24 to the terms in the sum, we obtain

$$H\left[\bigvee_{j=0}^{N-1} \mathbf{T}^{-j}\xi\right] \leqslant H\left[\bigvee_{j=0}^{N-1} \mathbf{T}^{-j}\eta\right] + NH(\xi/\eta),$$

and the lemma follows by taking the limit of the inequality after dividing by N.

COROLLARY 2.30. *If* ξ *and* η *are measurable partitions and* $\xi \leqslant \eta$, *then* $h(\mathbf{T}, \xi) \leqslant h(\mathbf{T}, \eta)$.

THEOREM 2.31. *If* $\{\xi_n\}$ *is a sequence of measurable partitions such that* $\xi_n \uparrow \xi$ *and* $H(\xi/\xi_n) < \infty$ *for some* n, *then* $h(\mathbf{T}, \xi_n) \uparrow h(\mathbf{T}, \xi)$.

Proof. By Lemma 2.29 and its Corollary we have

$$h(\mathbf{T}, \xi_n) \leqslant h(\mathbf{T}, \xi) \leqslant h(\mathbf{T}, \xi_n) + H(\xi/\xi_n)$$

for all n. Since $H(\xi/\xi_n) < \infty$ for some n, Theorem 2.18 tells us that $H(\xi/\xi_n)$ converges to $H(\xi/\xi)$ as $n \to \infty$, and since $H(\xi/\xi) = 0$, the result follows.

Corollary 2.30 states that $h(\mathbf{T}, \ )$ is a monotone increasing function of partitions. The following theorem gives a much stronger order property of $h(\mathbf{T}, \ )$ as a function of partitions with finite entropy. It was discovered by Sinai [142] and is the key for using entropy in ergodic theory. As we shall see in Chapter 4, the use of entropy has been very effective in this field.

THEOREM 2.32 (Kolmogoroff–Sinai). *Let* ξ *and* η *be measurable partitions of the dynamical system* $(\Omega, \mathfrak{F}, P, \mathbf{T})$ *such that* $H(\xi) < \infty$. *If* $\xi \leqslant \bigvee_{j=0}^{\infty} \mathbf{T}^{-j}\eta$ *then* $h(\mathbf{T}, \xi) \leqslant h(\mathbf{T}, \eta)$. *In case* $\mathbf{T}$ *is a metric automorphism and* $\xi \leqslant \bigvee_{j=-\infty}^{+\infty} \mathbf{T}^{-j}\eta$ *then* $h(\mathbf{T}, \xi) \leqslant h(\mathbf{T}, \eta)$.

Proof. We will prove the theorem for $\mathbf{T}$ an endomorphism. The proof for an automorphism is similar.

Since $\xi \leqslant \bigvee_{j=0}^{\infty} \mathbf{T}^{-j}\eta$ and $\bigvee_{j=0}^{m} \mathbf{T}^{-j}\eta \uparrow \bigvee_{j=0}^{\infty} \mathbf{T}^{-j}\eta$, Theorem 2.18 implies that $H(\xi/\bigvee_{j=0}^{m} \mathbf{T}^{-j}\eta) \downarrow 0$. Let $\delta > 0$ be given, and choose M so that $H(\xi/\bigvee_{j=0}^{M} \mathbf{T}^{-j}\eta) < \delta$. Lemma 2.29 now gives that

$$h(\mathbf{T}, \xi) \leqslant h(\mathbf{T}, \zeta) + \delta,$$

where $\zeta = \bigvee_{j=0}^{M} \mathbf{T}^{-j}\eta$.

However,

$$\begin{aligned} h(\mathbf{T}, \zeta) &= \lim_{n \to \infty} \frac{1}{n} H\left[\bigvee_{k=0}^{n-1} \mathbf{T}^{-k}\left[\bigvee_{j=0}^{M} \mathbf{T}^{-j}\eta\right]\right] \\ &= \lim_{n \to \infty} \frac{M+n}{n} \frac{1}{M+n} H\left(\bigvee_{j=0}^{M+n-1} \mathbf{T}^{-j}\eta\right) \\ &= h(\mathbf{T}, \eta), \end{aligned}$$

and we have that $h(\mathbf{T},\xi)\leqslant h(\mathbf{T},\eta)+\delta$. The theorem follows, since δ is arbitrary.

Notice that this theorem is false if the hypothesis $H(\xi)<\infty$ is removed. To see this take $(\Omega,\mathcal{F},P,\mathbf{T})$ to be the same system as in the example following Theorem 2.27. Let $\eta=\{(0,\frac{1}{2}],(\frac{1}{2},1]\}$, and ξ to be the same partition as in that example. Since $\bigvee_{j=0}^{\infty}\mathbf{T}^{-j}\eta=\varepsilon$, we have $\xi\leqslant\bigvee_{j=0}^{\infty}\mathbf{T}^{-j}\eta$. Since $H(\eta)<\infty$, $h(\mathbf{T},\eta)=H(\eta/\bigvee_{j=1}^{\infty}\mathbf{T}^{-j}\eta)=H(\mathbf{T}\eta/\bigvee_{j=0}^{\infty}\mathbf{T}^{-j}\eta)=0$, but $h(\mathbf{T},\xi)=\infty$.

In case $\mathbf{T}$ is an automorphism, the next theorem gives a connection between the rate of generation of information about $\alpha\bigvee\beta$ and the rate of information generation about β.

THEOREM 2.33. *Let $(\Omega,\mathcal{F},P,\mathbf{T})$ be an invertible dynamical system and ξ and η measurable partitions of Ω. If $H(\xi\bigvee\eta/\eta^{-})<\infty$, then*

$$H\left(\xi\bigvee\eta/\bigvee_{j=1}^{\infty}\mathbf{T}^{-j}(\xi\bigvee\eta)\right)$$

$$=H\left(\eta/\bigvee_{j=1}^{\infty}\mathbf{T}^{-j}\eta\right)+H\left(\xi/\bigvee_{j=1}^{\infty}\mathbf{T}^{-j}\xi\vee\bigvee_{j=-\infty}^{+\infty}\mathbf{T}^{j}\eta\right).$$

Proof. For any partition α denote $\bigvee_{j=1}^{n}\mathbf{T}^{-j}\alpha$, $\bigvee_{j=0}^{n-1}\mathbf{T}^{j}\alpha$, $\bigvee_{j=1}^{\infty}\mathbf{T}^{-j}\alpha$, and $\bigvee_{j=-\infty}^{+\infty}\mathbf{T}^{j}\alpha$ by α^{-n}, α^{n}, α^{-}, and α^{∞}, respectively. We wish to prove

$$H(\xi\bigvee\eta/\xi^{-}\bigvee\eta^{-})=H(\eta/\eta^{-})+H(\xi/\xi^{-}\bigvee\eta^{\infty}).$$

By repeated application of Theorem 2.21 and use of Theorem 2.24 we have

$$\frac{1}{n}H(\xi^{n}/\xi^{-}\bigvee\eta^{-}\bigvee\eta^{n})=\frac{1}{n}\sum_{k=0}^{n-1}H(\xi/\xi^{-}\bigvee\mathbf{T}^{-k}(\eta^{-}\bigvee\eta^{n})).$$

However, it is easy to check that $\mathbf{T}^{-k}(\eta^{-}\bigvee\eta^{n})=\eta^{-}\bigvee\eta^{n-k}$, so

$$\frac{1}{n}H(\xi^{n}/\xi^{-}\bigvee\eta^{-}\bigvee\eta^{n})=\frac{1}{n}\sum_{k=1}^{n}H(\xi/\xi^{-}\bigvee\eta^{-}\bigvee\eta^{k}). \qquad (2.47)$$

Now $\eta^{-}\bigvee\eta^{k}\uparrow\eta^{\infty}$, and since $H(\xi/\xi^{-}\bigvee\eta^{-}\bigvee\eta^{k})\leqslant H(\xi/\eta^{-})<\infty$, Theorem 2.18 implies that $H(\xi/\xi^{-}\bigvee\eta^{-}\eta^{k})\rightarrow H(\xi/\xi^{-}\bigvee\eta^{\infty})$. Since convergence implies Cesaro convergence, taking the limit in Equation (2.47) gives

$$\lim_{n\to\infty}\frac{1}{n}H(\xi^{n}/\xi^{-}\bigvee\eta^{-}\bigvee\eta^{n})=H(\xi/\xi^{-}\bigvee\eta^{\infty}). \qquad (2.48)$$

Again using Theorem 2.21 we have

$$\frac{1}{n}H(\xi^n\vee\eta^n/\xi^-\vee\eta^-)=\frac{1}{n}H(\eta^n/\xi^-\vee\eta^-)+\frac{1}{n}H(\xi^n/\xi^-\vee\eta^-\vee\eta^n). \tag{2.49}$$

Since $(1/n)H(\xi^n\vee\eta^n/\xi^-\vee\eta^-)=H(\xi\vee\eta/\xi^-\vee\eta^-)$, Equation (2.49) can be written as

$$H(\xi\vee\eta/\xi^-\vee\eta^-)=\frac{1}{n}H(\eta^n/\xi^-\vee\eta^-)+\frac{1}{n}H(\xi^n/\xi^-\vee\eta^-\vee\eta^n), \tag{2.50}$$

and since $\eta\leqslant\xi\vee\eta$ and $H(\xi\vee\eta/\eta^-)\leqslant H(\xi/\eta^-)<\infty$, the second part of Lemma 2.25 gives us that

$$\lim_{n\to\infty}\frac{1}{n}H(\eta^n/\xi^-\vee\eta^-)=H(\eta/\eta^-). \tag{2.51}$$

Using Equations (2.48), and (2.51) in Equation (2.50) gives

$$H(\xi\vee\eta/\xi^-\vee\eta^-)=H(\eta/\eta^-)+H(\xi/\xi^-\vee\eta^\infty).$$

COROLLARY 2.34. *If* $H(\xi\vee\eta)<\infty$ *and* $\mathbf{T}$ *is an automorphism, then*

$$h(\mathbf{T},\xi\vee\eta)=h(\mathbf{T},\eta)+H(\xi/\xi^-\vee\eta^\infty),$$

and in particular

$$h(\mathbf{T},\xi\vee\eta)\leqslant h(\mathbf{T},\eta)+h(\mathbf{T},\xi).$$

2.8 Entropy of Dynamical Systems

As we indicated in Section 1.7, a dynamical system can be considered as a mathematical model of a random universe with a mechanism (the automorphism $\mathbf{T}$) that depicts development in time.

For example, consider a machine which produces letters from a finite alphabet S. Suppose one letter is produced in each time unit, and the probability that a letter in S is produced at time n does not depend on n and is given by the probability distribution $\{f(s):s\in S\}$. The structure of this machine can be modeled by the dynamical system $(\Sigma(S),\mathfrak{F},\mu,\mathbf{T})$, where $\mathbf{T}$ is the shift transformation defined in Section 1.7. In this model, for $\omega\in\Sigma(S)$, $\omega(n)$ represents the output of the machine at time n, and since $(\mathbf{T}\omega)(n)=\omega(n+1)$, $\mathbf{T}$ represents the passage of time.

Notice that the dynamical system given in the last paragraph is the realization space of an independent stochastic sequence in S. This particular system and related ones are known in information theory as discrete sources. More details are given in Chapter 3 on Information Theory.

Another example of a dynamical system arises in the study of the properties of gases. Suppose that a container contains a certain volume of gas and that microscopically the gas is considered to consist of molecules which are represented mathematically as point masses. Those macroscopic properties of the gas which can be measured, such as volume, temperature, and pressure, are determined by the dynamics of these molecules. In theory, if we knew the position and momentum of each molecule in the gas, we would know everything about the gas.

The state of the gas in this model is defined to be a point $(x_1, x_2, \ldots, x_{6N})$ in $6N$-dimensional space, whose components represent the 3 components of position of each of the N molecules and the 3 components of momentum of each of the N molecules. Suppose that x_j for $j=1,2,\ldots,3N$ represent position components and x_{3N+j} for $j=1,2,\ldots,3N$ represent momentum components of the corresponding molecules.

Let H be a function on $6N+1$-space which at the point $(x_1, x_2, \ldots, x_{6N}, t)$ gives the value of the total energy in the gas if it is in state $(x_1, \ldots, x_{6N})$ at time t. This function is called the Hamiltonian of the system, and the evolution of the system in time is governed by the Hamiltonian equations of motion,

$$\left.\begin{aligned} \dot{x}_j &= -\frac{\partial H}{\partial x_{3N+j}} \\ \dot{x}_{3N+j} &= \frac{\partial H}{\partial x_j} \end{aligned}\right\} \quad j=1,2,\ldots,3N. \tag{2.52}$$

Suppose we know that the system at time zero is in state $(a_1, a_2, \ldots, a_{6N})$ and the Hamiltonian is sufficiently smooth so that the system (2.52) has a unique solution $x_j = f_j(t)$ for $-\infty < t < \infty$, $j=1,2,\ldots,6N$, and all initial conditions $f_j(0) = a_j$. Since the functions f_j depend on the initial point, let us indicate this by writing the solution of the system with initial conditions $x_j = a_j$ by $f_j(t; a)$, where $a = (a_1, \ldots, a_{6N})$. In this way, for each a we get a function F_a from the reals R into $6N$-space,

$$F_a(t) = (f_1(t; a), \ldots, f_{6N}(t; a)),$$

and the value of this function gives the state of the gas at any time t.

Using this function we can define a transformation $\mathbf{T}$ of $6N$-space to itself by sending a to $F_a(1)$. Thus $\mathbf{T}(a)$ tells us the state of the gas one time unit after it was in state a.

Now suppose the container of gas is such that there is no change in the total energy with time. In this case the system is said to be conservative and the Hamiltonian is independent of t. Let E_0 be the total energy at time 0, so that any state $a=(a_1,\ldots,a_{6N})$ such that $H(a_1,\ldots,a_{6N})=E_0$ is a possible initial state for the system. In addition, since the energy of the system remains constant, $H\circ\mathbf{T}(a)$ is in E_0, and $\mathbf{T}(a)$ is in $H^{-1}(E_0)$ for any a in $H^{-1}(E_0)$. Thus $\mathbf{T}$ maps each surface of constant energy into itself.

In this conservative case, a fundamental theorem proven by Liouville states that $\mathbf{T}$ as a map of $6N$-space to itself preserves Lebesgue measure, so that as a map of $H^{-1}(E_0)$ to itself it preserves the surface measure of this space induced by Lebesgue meaure on $6N$-space. Since in applications H is usually not pathological (see, for example, Section 6.2), $H^{-1}(E_0)$ will be a bounded surface with finite area. Thus we have a dynamical system $(H^{-1}(E_0),\mathfrak{F}(E_0),P,\mathbf{T})$, where P denotes the normalized surface measure and $\mathfrak{F}(E_0)$ the completion of the Borel subsets of $H^{-1}(E_0)$. The study of dynamical systems of this type by G. D. Birkhoff and others led to the development of ergodic theory, which will be considered in Chapter 4.

A problem of considerable interest is to determine techniques for deciding when two dynamical systems are the "same," and for that matter what "same" should mean. A reasonable definition would have the probability spaces of the two dynamical systems isomorphic (mod 0) and to have this isomorphism connect points is such a way that connected points are always moved by the respective maps into connected points. This leads to the following definition.

Definition 2.35. Two dynamical systems $(\Omega_1,\mathfrak{F}_1,P_1,\mathbf{T}_1)$ and $(\Omega_2,\mathfrak{F}_2,P_2,\mathbf{T}_2)$ are *isomorphic* if there exists a metric isomorphism $\mathbf{S}$ of Ω_1 to Ω_2 such that $\mathbf{S}\circ\mathbf{T}_1=\mathbf{T}_2\circ\mathbf{S}$.

The rate of information generation by $\mathbf{T}$ on a partition ξ can be used to give a very effective method for proving that two dynamical systems are not isomorphic or—in one very important case—that they are. This method consists of calculating a number associated with the system which is the same for isomorphic systems. This number is called the entropy of the system, or the entropy of the transformation in the system, or the Kolmogoroff–Sinai invariant. If $(\Omega,\mathfrak{F},P,\mathbf{T})$ is a dynamical system, its entropy is denoted by $h(\mathbf{T})$, and sometimes by $h_P(\mathbf{T})$ to indicate the dependence of the invariant on the probability as well as the transformation.

The entropy as an isomorphism invariant was discovered and developed by Kolmogoroff, Sinai, and Rohlin in several fundamental papers [69, 142, 143, 123] and has revolutionized the field of ergodic theory, as we shall describe in Chapter 4. For the rest of this section we shall content ourselves with defining this invariant and proving its basic properties as well as some theorems useful in computation.

DEFINITION 2.36. The *entropy* or *Kolmogoroff–Sinai invariant* of the dynamical system $(\Omega, \mathfrak{F}, P, \mathbf{T})$ is denoted by $h(\mathbf{T})$ and is defined by the equation

$$h(\mathbf{T}) = \sup\{h(\mathbf{T},\xi) : \xi \text{ a finite measurable partition}\}.$$

As a guide to the meaning of $h(\mathbf{T})$ we can think of it as the greatest rate of generating information by the time mechanism $\mathbf{T}$ using all possible finite experiments from the universe. In many cases this quantity is actually a maximum, as we shall show. Before we do that, however, we prove that $h(\mathbf{T})$ is an isomorphism invariant.

THEOREM 2.37. *Let $(\Omega_1, \mathfrak{F}_1, P_1, \mathbf{T}_1)$ and $(\Omega_2, \mathfrak{F}_2, P_2, \mathbf{T}_2)$ be two dynamical systems, and suppose there exists a measure preserving transformation $\mathbf{S}$ from $(\Omega_1, \mathfrak{F}_1, P_1)$ to $(\Omega_2, \mathfrak{F}_2, P_2)$ such that $\mathbf{S}\circ\mathbf{T}_1 = \mathbf{T}_2\circ\mathbf{S}$. Then $h(\mathbf{T}_2) \leqslant h(\mathbf{T}_1)$.*

Proof. Let ξ_2 be a finite measurable partition of Ω_2. Making use of Theorem 2.13, we have

$$\begin{aligned} h(\mathbf{T}_2,\xi_2) &= \lim_{n\to\infty}\frac{1}{n}H\left[\bigvee_{j=0}^{n-1}\mathbf{T}_2^{-j}\xi_2\right] \\ &= \lim_{n\to\infty}\frac{1}{n}H\left[\bigvee_{j=0}^{n-1}\mathbf{S}^{-1}\mathbf{T}_2^{-j}\xi_2\right] \\ &= \lim_{n\to\infty}\frac{1}{n}H\left[\bigvee_{j=0}^{n-1}\mathbf{T}_1^{-j}\mathbf{S}^{-1}\xi_1\right] = h(\mathbf{T}_1,\mathbf{S}^{-1}\xi_1) \\ &\leqslant h(\mathbf{T}_1), \end{aligned}$$

and the theorem follows.

A dynamical system $(\Omega_2, \mathfrak{F}_2, P_2, \mathbf{T}_2)$ is said to be the homomorphic image of another system $(\Omega_1, \mathfrak{F}_1, P_1, T_1)$ if there exists a measure preserving transformation from Ω_1 to Ω_2 which satisfies the properties of the transformation $\mathbf{S}$ in Theorem 2.37. Two systems are said to be weakly isomorphic if each is the homomorphic image of the other. It is easily seen that isomorphism implies weak isomorphism.

Corollary 2.38. *If two dynamical systems are weakly isomorphic they have the same entropy.*

We now show that in many important cases the entropy of a dynamical system is actually a maximum of the set of rates of information generation and hence in these cases can be easily calculated.

Theorem 2.39. *If $(\Omega, \mathcal{F}, P, \mathbf{T})$ is a invertible dynamical system, and η is a measurable partition with $H(\eta) < \infty$ and $\bigvee_{j=-\infty}^{+\infty} \mathbf{T}^{-j}\eta = \varepsilon$, [i.e. η is a generating partition for $\mathbf{T}$] then $h(\mathbf{T}) = h(\mathbf{T}, \eta)$. If the system is not invertible and $\bigvee_{j=0}^{\infty} \mathbf{T}^{-j}\eta = \varepsilon$, the same conclusion is obtained.*

Proof. If ξ is a finite measurable partition, then since $\xi \leqslant \varepsilon$ and $\bigvee_{j=-\infty}^{\infty} \mathbf{T}^{-j}\eta = \varepsilon$, Theorem 2.32 implies that $h(\mathbf{T}, \xi) \leqslant h(\mathbf{T}, \eta)$ and we have that $h(\mathbf{T}) \leqslant h(\mathbf{T}, \eta)$. The reverse inequality is always satisfied.

Example 2.40. Consider the system $(\Sigma(S), \mathcal{F}, \mu, \mathbf{T})$ where $(\Sigma(S), \mathcal{F}, \mu)$ is the Lebesgue space described in Example 1.3 and $\mathbf{T}$ is the shift. Recall that μ is the product measure generated by a distribution function f on the finite set S. It is easy to see that if η is the "time zero" partition [i.e., the atoms of η are sets of the form $\{\omega \in \Sigma(S) : \omega(0) = s\}$ for $s \in S$], then η is an independent partition for $\mathbf{T}$ and $\bigvee_{-\infty}^{+\infty} \mathbf{T}^{-j}\eta = \varepsilon$. Therefore $h(\mathbf{T}) = h(\mathbf{T}, \eta)$ and

$$h(\mathbf{T}, \eta) = \lim_{n \to \infty} \frac{1}{n} H\left[\bigvee_{j=0}^{n-1} \mathbf{T}^{-j}\eta\right] = -\sum_{s \in S} f(s) \log f(s).$$

In particular if $S_1 = \{0, 1\}$ with $f(0) = f(1) = \frac{1}{2}$, then $h(\mathbf{T}_1) = \log 2$. The entropy of a shift based on a set $S = \{0, 1, 2\}$ with distribution $f(0) = f(1) = f(2) = \frac{1}{3}$ is $\log 3$ and it follows that these two systems are not isomorphic.

Corollary 2.41. *If $(\Omega, \mathcal{F}, P, \mathbf{T})$ is an invertible dynamical system and there exists a partition ξ with $H(\xi) < \infty$ such that $\bigvee_{j=0}^{\infty} \mathbf{T}^{j}\xi = \varepsilon$, then $h(\mathbf{T}) = 0$.*

Proof. Since $\mathbf{T}$ is invertible and $\bigvee_{j=-\infty}^{+\infty} \mathbf{T}^{-j}\xi \geqslant \bigvee_{j=0}^{\infty} \mathbf{T}^{-j}\xi$, Theorem 2.39 implies $h(\mathbf{T}) = h(\mathbf{T}, \xi)$. However, since $H(\xi) < \infty$,

$$h(\mathbf{T}, \xi) = H\left(\xi / \bigvee_{j=1}^{\infty} \mathbf{T}^{-j}\xi\right) = H\left(\mathbf{T}\xi / \bigvee_{j=0}^{\infty} \mathbf{T}^{-j}\xi\right) = 0.$$

Theorem 2.42. *A necessary and sufficient condition for $h(\mathbf{T}) = 0$ is that each finite partition ξ is refined by $\bigvee_{j=1}^{\infty} \mathbf{T}^{-j}\xi$.*

Proof. Since $H(\xi)<\infty$, $h(\mathbf{T},\xi)=H(\xi/\bigvee_{j=1}^{\infty}\mathbf{T}^{-j}\xi)$, which is zero if and only if $\xi \leqslant \bigvee_{j=1}^{\infty}\mathbf{T}^{-j}\xi$. The result now follows from the definition of $h(\mathbf{T})$.

Recall that in Section 1.3 we explained how $\xi \leqslant \eta$ indicated that outcomes of the experiment modeled by Ω_η determined all outcomes in the experiment modeled by Ω_ξ. If ξ is a measurable partition and $\mathbf{T}$ is invertible, then for any positive integer $n, \mathbf{T}^n\xi$ is a measurable partition. The atoms of this partition may be considered as outcomes of the experiment ξ obtained in the *past*, since $\omega \in \mathbf{T}^n A$ if and only if $\mathbf{T}^{-n}\omega \in A$, i.e., A occurred n time units in the past. From this point of view $\bigvee_{n=1}^{\infty}\mathbf{T}^n\xi$ represents the complete past of the experiment. Since $h(\mathbf{T}^{-1})=h(\mathbf{T})$, Theorem 8.9 implies that $h(\mathbf{T})=0$ if and only if every finite experiment ξ is determined by its past, i.e., $\xi \leqslant \bigvee_{n=1}^{\infty}\mathbf{T}^n\xi$. Thus invertible dynamical systems with zero entropy are said to be deterministic.

THEOREM 2.43. *If $(\Omega, \mathfrak{F}, P, \mathbf{T})$ is a dynamical system, then*

$$h(\mathbf{T}^k)=|k|h(\mathbf{T}) \qquad \textit{for} \quad k=0,1,2,\ldots, \tag{2.53}$$

and in case $\mathbf{T}$ *is invertible the same equation holds for negative values of* k. [*Here* $\mathbf{T}^k$ *denotes the composition of* $\mathbf{T}$ *with itself* k *times if* k *is positive,* $\mathbf{T}^0=$ identity, *and* $\mathbf{T}^k=(\mathbf{T}^{-1})^{-k}$ *if* k *is negative.*]

Proof. It follows easily from the definition that $h(\mathbf{T}^0)=0$ and $h(\mathbf{T}^{-1})=h(\mathbf{T})$ for invertible $\mathbf{T}$. Thus it is only necessary to prove (2.53) for positive values of k.

Let ξ be a finite measurable partition. For any positive integer n,

$$\frac{1}{kn}H\left[\bigvee_{j=0}^{kn-1}\mathbf{T}^{-j}\xi\right]=\frac{1}{kn}H\left(\bigvee_{l=0}^{n-1}(\mathbf{T}^k)^{-l}\eta\right),$$

where $\eta=\bigvee_{j=0}^{k-1}\mathbf{T}^{-j}\xi$. Therefore

$$h(\mathbf{T},\xi)=\frac{1}{k}h(\mathbf{T}^k,\eta)\geqslant\frac{1}{k}h(\mathbf{T}^k,\xi). \tag{2.54}$$

Since $\xi \leqslant \eta$, and we have $k \cdot h(\mathbf{T}) \geqslant h(\mathbf{T}^k)$.

Using the equality in (2.54), we have

$$h(\mathbf{T})=\frac{1}{k}\sup\left\{h\left[\mathbf{T}^k,\bigvee_{j=0}^{k-1}\mathbf{T}^{-j}\xi\right]:\xi \text{ a finite partition}\right\}$$

$$\leqslant\frac{1}{k}h(\mathbf{T}^k),$$

and the theorem is proven.

2.9 Factor Automorphisms and Factor Systems

Let $(\Omega, \mathfrak{F}, P, \mathbf{T})$ be an invertible dynamical system. We indicated in Section 1.7 how measurable partitions ξ of this system give rise to stationary stochastic processes which could then be represented by $(\mathbf{T}, \xi)$. Recall that if $\xi^\infty = \bigvee_{j=-\infty}^{+\infty} \mathbf{T}^{-j}\xi$, then the factor space $(\Omega_{\xi^\infty}, \mathfrak{F}_{\xi^\infty}, P_{\xi^\infty})$ is the "proper" space for studying the process, since it contains all the joint probability distributions of the process. We also showed how a map $\mathbf{T}$ can be used to define a map $\mathbf{T}_{\xi^\infty}$ on Ω_{ξ^∞} so that $(\Omega_{\xi^\infty}, \mathfrak{F}_{\xi^\infty}, P_{\xi^\infty}, \mathbf{T}_{\xi^\infty})$ is a dynamical system. This system is a *factor system* of the original system. We now show how factor systems can be defined in more general situations.

Notice that $\mathbf{T}^{-1}\xi^\infty \leqslant \xi^\infty$. This is the only requirement on a measurable partition that is necessary to define a factor system.

Definition 2.44. If ζ is a measurable partition of the system $(\Omega, \mathfrak{F}, P, \mathbf{T})$ such that $\mathbf{T}^{-1}\zeta \leqslant \zeta$, then the *factor endomorphism* $\mathbf{T}_\zeta$ induced by ζ is the metric endomorphism defined on the factor space $(\Omega_\zeta, \mathfrak{F}_\zeta, P_\zeta)$ by

$$\mathbf{T}_\zeta(c) = d$$

if and only if $\mathbf{T}^{-1}(\mathbf{N}_\zeta^{-1}(d))$ is the unique atom of $\mathbf{T}^{-1}\zeta$ which contains $\mathbf{N}_\zeta^{-1}(c)$.

It is not difficult to see that $\mathbf{T}_\zeta$ is a metric automorphism if and only if $\mathbf{T}^{-1}\zeta = \zeta$. The dynamical system $(\Omega_\zeta, \mathfrak{F}_\zeta, P_\zeta, \mathbf{T}_\zeta)$ is called the factor system associated with ζ. Notice that the partition ξ^∞ defined in the first paragraph satisfies the condition $\mathbf{T}^{-1}\xi^\infty = \xi^\infty$, so that $\mathbf{T}_{\xi^\infty}$ is a metric automorphism. Then the factor system $(\Omega_{\xi^\infty}, \mathfrak{F}_{\xi^\infty}, P_{\xi^\infty}, \mathbf{T}_{\xi^\infty})$ represents the complete stochastic process.

Suppose that ζ is a measurable partition of the system $(\Omega, \mathfrak{F}, P, \mathbf{T})$ such that $\mathbf{T}^{-1}\zeta \leqslant \zeta$. It is easy to see that the factor system $(\Omega_\zeta, \mathfrak{F}_\zeta, P_\zeta, \mathbf{T}_\zeta)$ is a homomorphic image of $(\Omega, \mathfrak{F}, P, \mathbf{T})$ under the canonical projection $\mathbf{N}_\zeta$. Conversely, if $(\Omega', \mathfrak{F}', P', \mathbf{T}')$ is a homomorphic image of $(\Omega, \mathfrak{F}, P, \mathbf{T})$, there exists a measurable partition ζ such that $\mathbf{T}^{-1}\zeta \leqslant \zeta$ and $(\Omega_\zeta, \mathfrak{F}_\zeta, P_\zeta, \mathbf{T}_\zeta)$ is isomorphic to $(\Omega', \mathfrak{F}', P', \mathbf{T}')$. Just take ζ to be $\mathbf{S}^{-1}(\varepsilon')$, where $\mathbf{S}$ is a metric homomorphism of Ω onto Ω' and ε' is the point partition in Ω'.

Since factor systems are homomorphic images of the original system, Theorem 2.37 implies that $h(\mathbf{T}_\zeta) \leqslant h(\mathbf{T})$ for any measurable partition ζ such that $\mathbf{T}^{-1}\zeta \leqslant \zeta$.

Lemma 2.45. *If ζ is a measurable partition of $(\Omega, \mathfrak{F}, P, \mathbf{T})$ and $\mathbf{T}^{-1}\zeta \leqslant \zeta$, then*

$$h(\mathbf{T}_\zeta, \xi') = h(\mathbf{T}, \mathbf{N}_\zeta^{-1}\xi')$$

for any measurable partition ξ' of Ω_ζ.

Proof. Since $\mathbf{N}_\zeta \circ \mathbf{T} = \mathbf{T}_\zeta \circ \mathbf{N}_\zeta$

$$H\left[\bigvee_{j=0}^{n-1} \mathbf{T}^{-j}\mathbf{N}_\zeta^{-1}\xi'\right] = H\left[\bigvee_{j=0}^{n-1} \mathbf{N}_\zeta^{-1}\mathbf{T}_\zeta^{-j}\xi'\right]$$
$$= H\left[\bigvee_{j=0}^{n-1} \mathbf{T}_\zeta^{-j}\xi'\right]$$

using Theorem 2.13. The lemma follows by applying the definition of rate of information generation.

THEOREM 2.46. *If ζ is a measurable partition of* $(\Omega, \mathfrak{F}, P, \mathbf{T})$ *and* $\mathbf{T}^{-1}\zeta \leqslant \zeta$, *then*

$$h(\mathbf{T}_\zeta) = \sup\{h(\mathbf{T}, \xi) : \xi \text{ finite}, \xi \leqslant \zeta\}.$$

Proof. First notice that if ξ is any measurable partition of Ω and $\xi \leqslant \zeta$, then $\mathbf{N}_\zeta^{-1}(\mathbf{N}_\zeta C) = C$ a.e. for each atom $C \in \xi$. Thus

$$\begin{aligned} h(\mathbf{T}_\zeta) &= \sup\{h(\mathbf{T}_\zeta, \xi') : \xi' \text{ a finite partition of } \Omega_\zeta\} \\ &= \sup\{h(\mathbf{T}, \mathbf{N}_\zeta^{-1}(\xi')) : \mathbf{N}_\zeta^{-1}(\xi') \text{ finite}\} \\ &= \sup\{h(\mathbf{T}, \xi) : \xi \text{ finite and } \xi \leqslant \zeta\}, \end{aligned}$$

and the theorem is proven.

Now suppose that ξ is a finite partition of an invertible dynamical system $(\Omega, \mathfrak{F}, P, \mathbf{T})$, and let $\zeta = \bigvee_{-\infty}^{+\infty} \mathbf{T}^{-j}\xi$. Then $\mathbf{N}_\zeta(\xi)$ is a generating partition for $(\Omega_\zeta, \mathfrak{F}_\zeta, P_\zeta, \mathbf{T}_\zeta)$, and the Kolmogoroff–Sinai theorem together with Lemma 2.45 implies that $h(\mathbf{T}_\zeta) = h(\mathbf{T}, \xi)$.

If ξ and η are finite partitions of the space $(\Omega, \mathfrak{F}, P, \mathbf{T})$, then the stochastic processes they represent are modeled respectively by the factor spaces $(\Omega_{\xi^\infty}, \mathfrak{F}_{\xi^\infty}, P_{\xi^\infty}, \mathbf{T}_{\xi^\infty})$ and $(\Omega_{\eta^\infty}, \mathfrak{F}_{\eta^\infty}, P_{\eta^\infty}, \mathbf{T}_{\eta^\infty})$. If these two factor spaces are isomorphic, then the processes they represent are equivalent in the sense defined in Section 2.7. (The converse of this statement is not true.) The entropy of these factor systems then gives a way to distinguish between nonisomorphic stationary process, but not between nonequivalent processes in general.

We will now prove some limit theorems concerning the entropy of factor automorphisms and use them to calculate the entropy of the product of two automorphisms.

THEOREM 2.47. *If ζ_n and ζ are measurable partitions of* $(\Omega, \mathfrak{F}, P, \mathbf{T})$ *with* $\zeta_n \uparrow \zeta$ *and* $\mathbf{T}^{-1}\zeta_n \leqslant \zeta_n$ *for all n, then*

$$h(\mathbf{T}_{\zeta_n}) \uparrow h(\mathbf{T}_\zeta).$$

Proof. By changing to the factor space $(\Omega_\zeta, \mathcal{F}_\zeta, P_\zeta)$ we may assume that ζ is the point partition. Then since $\zeta_n \uparrow \varepsilon$, for any finite partition ξ we have $H(\xi/\zeta_n) \downarrow 0$.

Let $\delta > 0$ be given, and select N so large that $H(\xi/\zeta_n) < \delta$ for all $n \geq N$. Since for fixed $n \geq N$, ζ_n is measurable, there exists a sequence of finite measurable partitions $\xi_m \uparrow \zeta_n$ that $H(\xi/\xi_m) \downarrow H(\xi/\zeta_n)$, and there is an M such that $H(\xi/\xi_M) < \delta$.

By Lemma 2.29,

$$\begin{aligned} h(\mathbf{T}, \xi) &\leq h(\mathbf{T}, \xi_M) + H(\xi/\xi_M) \\ &\leq h(\mathbf{T}, \xi_M) + \delta. \end{aligned}$$

However, $\xi_M \leq \zeta_n$ so by Theorem 2.46 $h(\mathbf{T}, \xi_M) \leq h(\mathbf{T}_{\zeta_n})$ and we have

$$h(\mathbf{T}, \xi) \leq h(\mathbf{T}_{\zeta_n}) + \delta.$$

It follows that $h(\mathbf{T}) \leq h(\mathbf{T}_{\zeta_n}) + \delta$ for all $n \geq N$. Since $h(\mathbf{T}_{\zeta_n}) \leq h(\mathbf{T})$, the theorem follows.

COROLLARY 2.48. *If $\xi_1 \leq \xi_2 \leq \cdots$ are measurable partitions of an invertible system $(\Omega, \mathcal{F}, P, \mathbf{T})$ such that $H(\xi_n) < \infty$ and $\bigvee_{n=1}^{\infty} \bigvee_{j=-\infty}^{+\infty} \mathbf{T}^{-j}\xi_n = \varepsilon$ then*

$$h(\mathbf{T}, \xi_n) \to h(\mathbf{T}).$$

In case $\mathbf{T}$ *is not invertible, then* $\bigvee_{n=1}^{\infty}(\bigvee_{j=0}^{\infty} \mathbf{T}^{-j}\xi_n) = \varepsilon$ *gives the same conclusion.*

Proof. Let ξ_n^∞ denote $\bigvee_{j=-\infty}^{+\infty} \mathbf{T}^{-j}\xi_n$ if $\mathbf{T}$ is invertible and $\bigvee_{j=0}^{\infty} \mathbf{T}^{-j}\xi_n$ if not. Then the Theorem 2.39 implies that

$$h(\mathbf{T}_{\xi_n^\infty}) = h(\mathbf{T}, \xi_n),$$

and the corollary follows from Theorem 2.47.

COROLLARY 2.49. *If $\xi_1 \leq \xi_2 \leq \cdots$ are measurable partitions with finite entropy and $\xi_n \uparrow \varepsilon$, then $h(\mathbf{T}, \xi_n) \to h(\mathbf{T})$.*

As an application of this last corollary, we shall calculate the entropy of the product of two metric automorphisms.

Suppose $(\Omega_1, \mathcal{F}_1, P_1, \mathbf{T}_1)$ and $(\Omega_2, \mathcal{F}_2, P_2, \mathbf{T}_2)$ are two dynamical systems. The product system is the system $(\Omega_1 \times \Omega_2, \mathcal{F}_1 \times \mathcal{F}_2, P_1 \times P_2, \mathbf{T}_1 \times \mathbf{T}_2)$ where the space of the system is the usual product of measure spaces and $\mathbf{T}_1 \times \mathbf{T}_2$ is defined by

$$\mathbf{T}_1 \times \mathbf{T}_2(\omega_1, \omega_2) = (\mathbf{T}_1(\omega_1), \mathbf{T}_2(\omega_2)).$$

THEOREM 2.50. *If* $(\Omega_1, \mathcal{F}_1, P_1, \mathbf{T}_1)$ *and* $(\Omega_2, \mathcal{F}_2, P_2, \mathbf{T}_2)$ *are dynamical systems, then*

$$h(\mathbf{T}_1 \times \mathbf{T}_2) = h(\mathbf{T}_1) + h(\mathbf{T}_2).$$

Proof. If ξ_1 and ξ_2 are partitions of Ω_1 and Ω_2 respectively, let $\xi_1 \times \xi_2$ denote the partition $\{C_1 \times C_2 : C_1 \in \xi_1, C_2 \in \xi_2\}$ of $\Omega_1 \times \Omega_2$. An easy calculation shows that if ξ_1 and ξ_2 are finite,

$$h(\mathbf{T}_1 \times \mathbf{T}_2, \xi_1 \times \xi_2) = h(\mathbf{T}_1, \xi_1) + h(\mathbf{T}_2, \xi_2). \tag{2.55}$$

Now let $\{\xi_1^n\}$ and $\{\xi_2^n\}$ be sequences of finite measurable partitions of Ω_1 and Ω_2 respectively such that $\xi_1^n \uparrow \varepsilon_1$ and $\xi_2^n \uparrow \varepsilon_2$, where ε_1 and ε_2 are the point partitions in the respective spaces. Then $\xi_1^n \times \xi_2^n \uparrow \varepsilon$, and we have from Corollary 2.49 that

$$h(\mathbf{T}_1 \times \mathbf{T}_2, \xi_1^n \times \xi_2^n) \to h(\mathbf{T}_1 \times \mathbf{T}_2).$$

Using Equation (2.55) and Corollary 2.49 again, we have the desired equation.

Our next result gives an upper bound on the entropy independent of the probability provided there is a finite generating partition.

THEOREM 2.51. *If* ξ *is a generating partition for* $(\Omega, \mathcal{F}, P, \mathbf{T})$, *and* ξ *consists of* K *atoms of positive probability, then*

$$h(\mathbf{T}) \leqslant \log K.$$

Proof. Since ξ is a finite generating partition, Theorem 2.39 gives that $h(\mathbf{T}) = h(\mathbf{T}, \xi)$. However, it follows immediately from the definition, Corollary 2.12, and Theorem 2.13 that $h(\mathbf{T}, \xi) \leqslant H(\xi)$. An application of Theorem 2.3 now shows that $H(\xi) \leqslant \log K$, and the theorem follows.

The final result of this section concerns factor automorphisms which have zero entropy. We shall show that there is a maximal such deterministic factor automorphism for each dynamical system. This result was obtained by Pinsker [117].

THEOREM 2.52 (Pinsker). *If* $(\Omega, \mathcal{F}, P, \mathbf{T})$ *is an invertible dynamical system, there exists an invariant measurable partition* π *such that* $h(\mathbf{T}_\pi) = 0$, *and if* ζ *is an invariant measurable partition, then* $h(\mathbf{T}_\zeta) = 0$ *if and only if* $\zeta \leqslant \pi$.

Proof. Let Z_0 denote the collection of all finite measurable partitions ξ of Ω such that $h(\mathbf{T}, \xi) = 0$. Let $\mathcal{P}$ be the collection of sets defined by

$$\mathcal{P} = \left\{A \in \mathcal{F} : A \in \xi^{\wedge} \text{ for some } \xi \in Z_0\right\}.$$

We shall show that $\mathcal{P}$ is a σ-field, and π will be the associated partition.

First notice that

$$\mathcal{P}=\{A\in\mathcal{F}\colon h(\mathbf{T},\alpha)=0;\ \alpha=\{A,\Omega-A\}\}.$$

From this characterization of $\mathcal{P}$ it follows immediately that $\mathcal{P}$ is closed under complementation. Suppose $A, B\in\mathcal{P}$. Let $\alpha=\{A,\Omega-A\}$, $\beta=\{B,\Omega-B\}$, $\gamma=\{A\cup B,\Omega-A\cup B\}$. Then since $\alpha\vee\beta\geqslant\gamma$, using Corollary 2.34 we have

$$h(\mathbf{T},\gamma)\leqslant h(\mathbf{T},\alpha\vee\beta)\leqslant h(\mathbf{T},\alpha)+h(\mathbf{T},\beta)=0$$

and $\mathcal{P}$ is closed under finite unions and hence is a field of sets.

Let $\{A_n\}$ be a sequence of sets from $\mathcal{P}$ such that $A_n\uparrow A$, and let $\alpha_n=\{A_n,\Omega-A_n\}$, $\alpha=\{A,\Omega-A\}$. Since $P[A_n\cap(\Omega-A)]=0$ and $P[(\Omega-A_n)\cap(\Omega-A)]=P(\Omega-A)$, we have

$$H(\alpha_n/\alpha)=-\left\{P(A\cap A_n)\log\frac{P(A\cap A_n)}{P(A)}\right.$$
$$\left.+P(A-A_n)\log\frac{P(A-A_n)}{P(A)}\right\}.$$

Since $P(A_n\cap A)\to P(A)$ and $P(A-A_n)\to 0$, we have that $H(\alpha_n/\alpha)\to 0$. Since

$$h(\mathbf{T},\alpha)\leqslant h(\mathbf{T},\alpha_n)+H(\alpha_n/\alpha),$$

we have that $h(\mathbf{T},\alpha)=0$, so that $A\in\mathcal{P}$ and $\mathcal{P}$ is a σ-field of sets.

We now show that $\mathcal{P}$ is invariant under $\mathbf{T}$, so that if $\pi\hat{}=\mathcal{P}$ then $\mathbf{T}^{-1}\pi\leqslant\pi$. Let $A\in\mathcal{P}$ and $\alpha=\{A,\Omega-A\}$. Then

$$0=h(\mathbf{T},\alpha)=H\left(\alpha/\bigvee_{j=1}^{\infty}\mathbf{T}^{-j}\alpha\right)=H\left(\mathbf{T}^{-1}\alpha/\bigvee_{j=1}^{\infty}\mathbf{T}^{-j}(\mathbf{T}^{-1}\alpha)\right),$$

so that $h(\mathbf{T},\mathbf{T}^{-1}\alpha)=0$. Since $\mathbf{T}^{-1}\alpha=\{\mathbf{T}^{-1}A,\Omega-\mathbf{T}^{-1}A\}$, it follows that $\mathbf{T}^{-1}A\in\mathcal{P}$.

Let ξ be a finite measurable partition of Ω, and suppose $\xi\leqslant\pi$. Since $A\in\mathcal{P}$ for each $A\in\xi$, we have $h(\mathbf{T},\alpha)=0$, where $\alpha=\{A,\Omega-A\}$. Moreover $\xi=\bigvee_{A\in\xi}\alpha$ and $h(\mathbf{T},\xi)\leqslant\sum_{A\in\xi}h(\mathbf{T},\alpha)=0$. Thus by Theorem 2.46, $h(\mathbf{T}_\pi)=0$.

Finally let ζ be an invariant measurable partition of Ω which is refined by π. Since every finite measurable partition which is refined by ζ is also refined by π, Theorem 2.46 implies that $h(\mathbf{T}_\zeta)=0$. Conversely, if $h(\mathbf{T}_\zeta)=0$ and ξ is any finite partition which is refined by ζ, then $h(\mathbf{T},\xi)=0$. In particular, if $A\in\zeta\hat{}$, then $\alpha=\{A,\Omega-A\}\leqslant\zeta$, so that $h(\mathbf{T},\alpha)=0$. But this implies that $A\in\mathcal{P}$. Hence $\zeta\hat{}\subseteq\mathcal{P}$ and we have $\zeta\leqslant\pi$.

2.10 Shannon's Theorem and the Equipartition Property

In this section we shall prove the Shannon–McMillan–Breiman theorem which was originally formulated by Shannon in his classical paper [138] on information theory and was proven for various types of convergence by McMillan [87] and Breiman [26].

To motivate this theorem, consider the example of the dynamical system $(\Sigma(S), \mathfrak{F}, \mu, \mathbf{T})$, where $\mathbf{T}$ is the shift and μ is product measure obtained from a distribution f on the finite set S (cf. Example 1.3 and Section 1.7). This corresponds to a stochastic sequence in $(S, \mathbb{S})$ of independent random variables with distribution f.

Let $z: \Sigma(S) \to S$ be the function defined by $z(\omega) = \omega(0)$, and notice that $(z \circ \mathbf{T}^j)(\omega) = \omega(j)$, so that the random variables in the sequence can be represented by $\{z \circ \mathbf{T}^j\}_{j=-\infty}^{+\infty}$. If $\xi = z^{-1}(\varepsilon)$, where ε is the point partition in S, then ξ is a generating partition for the dynamical system and $h(\mathbf{T}) = h(\mathbf{T}, \xi) = H(\xi)$ by Corollary 2.28.

The quantity $h(\mathbf{T}, \xi)$ was called the rate of information generation, yet it was actually a rate of *average* information rather than information, since

$$\lim_{n\to\infty} \frac{1}{n} H\left[\bigvee_{j=0}^{n-1} \mathbf{T}^{-j}\xi\right] = \lim_{n\to\infty} \frac{1}{n} E\left\{I\left[\bigvee_{j=0}^{n-1} \mathbf{T}^{-1}\xi\right]\right\}$$

where E denotes expected value. Suppose we try to calculate the actual rate of information generation, i.e.,

$$\lim_{n\to\infty} \frac{1}{n} I\left[\bigvee_{j=0}^{n-1} \mathbf{T}^{-j}\xi\right](\omega)$$

for $\omega \in \Sigma(S)$.

From the definition of the information function [Equation (2.5)] we have that

$$\begin{aligned} I\left[\bigvee_{j=0}^{n-1} \mathbf{T}^{-j}\xi\right](\omega) &= -\log \mu\{\bar\omega \in \Sigma(S) : \bar\omega(j) = \omega(j), 0 \leqslant j < n\} \\ &= -\log\left\{\prod_{j=0}^{n-1} \mu\{\bar\omega \in \Sigma(S) : \bar\omega(j) = \omega(j)\}\right\} \\ &= -\sum_{j=0}^{n-1} \log f(\omega(j)) \\ &= -\sum_{j=0}^{n-1} (\log f \circ z) \circ \mathbf{T}^j(\omega). \end{aligned}$$

Therefore,

$$\lim_{n\to\infty} \frac{1}{n} I\left[\bigvee_{j=0}^{n-1} \mathbf{T}^j \xi\right](\omega) = \lim_{n\to\infty} \frac{1}{n} \sum_{j=0}^{n-1} (-\log f \circ z) \circ \mathbf{T}^j(\omega).$$

If we denote $-\log f \circ z$ by x, the limit on the right is exactly of the form to which the ergodic theorem applies.

Now $\mathbf{T}$ is ergodic, for suppose $C = \{\omega : \omega(j) = s_j,\ j \in G\}$ and $D = \{\omega : \omega(k) = t_k,\ k \in H\}$ are cylinder sets. Then if $i > \max H - \min G$,

$$\mathbf{T}^{-i} C \cap D = \{\omega : \omega(i+j) = s_j,\ j \in G\} \cap \{\omega : \omega(k) = t_k,\ k \in H\},$$

so that

$$\mu(\mathbf{T}^{-i} C \cap D) = \prod_{j \in G} f(s_j) \prod_{k \in H} f(t_k)$$
$$= \mu(C)\mu(D)$$

and

$$\lim_{i\to\infty} \mu(\mathbf{T}^{-i} C \cap D) = \mu(C)\mu(D).$$

Since the cylinder sets generate the σ-field one can show that this last equation implies that for all measurable sets A and B

$$\lim_{i\to\infty} \mu(\mathbf{T}^{-i} A \cap B) = \mu(A)\mu(B).$$

A transformation which satisfies this relation is said to be strongly mixing, and it is easy to see that strongly mixing transformations are ergodic, because if $\mathbf{T}^{-1}A = A$ and $\mathbf{T}$ is strongly mixing,

$$\mu(A)^2 = \lim_{i\to\infty} \mu(\mathbf{T}^{-i} A \cap A) = \mu(A)$$

and $\mu(A)$ is either zero or one.

Thus the system $(\Sigma(S), \mathfrak{F}, \mu, \mathbf{T})$ is strongly mixing and hence ergodic, and by the ergodic theorem

$$\lim_{n\to\infty} \frac{1}{n} \sum_{j=0}^{n-1} x \circ \mathbf{T}^{-j}(\omega) = E(x) \qquad \text{a.e. and } L_1.$$

However,

$$E(x) = \int_{\Sigma(S)} \mu(d\omega)(-\log f \circ z)(\omega)$$

$$= -\sum_{s \in S} f(s) \log f(s) = H(\xi).$$

Therefore we have that

$$\lim_{n\to\infty} \frac{1}{n} I\left[\bigvee_{j=0}^{n-1} \mathbf{T}^{j}\xi\right](\omega) = h(\mathbf{T}) \qquad \text{a.e. and } L_1,$$

and in this example $h(\mathbf{T}, \xi)$ [and, since ξ is a generating partition, $h(\mathbf{T})$] is actually a rate of information generation.

The Shannon–McMillan–Breiman theorem states that this is always the case.

THEOREM 2.53 (Shannon–McMillan–Breiman). *Let $(\Omega, \mathcal{F}, P, \mathbf{T})$ be a dynamical system with* **T** *ergodic. If ξ is a measurable partition such that $H(\xi) < \infty$ then*

$$\lim_{n\to\infty} \frac{1}{n} I\left[\bigvee_{j=0}^{n-1} \mathbf{T}^{-j}\xi\right] = h(\mathbf{T}, \xi) \qquad \text{a.e. and } L_1.$$

Proof. Since **T** is ergodic and $I(\xi/\bigvee_{j=1}^{\infty}\mathbf{T}^{-j}\xi)$ is a function in L_1 (by Theorem 2.18), the ergodic theorem implies that

$$\lim_{n\to\infty} \frac{1}{n+1} \sum_{k=0}^{n} I\left(\xi/\bigvee_{j=1}^{\infty} \mathbf{T}^{-j}\xi\right) \circ \mathbf{T}^{k}(\omega) = E\left\{ I\left(\xi/\bigvee_{j=1}^{\infty} \mathbf{T}^{-j}\xi\right)\right\}$$

both a.e. and L_1. Since $H(\xi) < \infty$, $E\{I(\xi/\bigvee_{j=1}^{\infty}\mathbf{T}^{-j}\xi)\}$, which is $H(\xi/\bigvee_{j=1}^{\infty}\mathbf{T}^{-j}\xi)$, is the rate of information generation $h(\mathbf{T}, \xi)$. Thus if we can show that

$$D(n) = \left| \frac{1}{n+1} I\left(\bigvee_{j=0}^{n} \mathbf{T}^{-j}\xi\right) - \frac{1}{n+1} \sum_{k=0}^{n} I\left(\xi \bigvee_{j=1}^{\infty} \mathbf{T}^{-j}\xi\right) \circ \mathbf{T}^{k} \right|$$

$$\to 0$$

a.e. and L_1, the theorem will be proven. By repeated application of (2.12) we get

$$I\left(\bigvee_{j=0}^{n} \mathbf{T}^{-j}\xi\right) = \sum_{k=0}^{n-1} I\left(\mathbf{T}^{-k}\xi/ \bigvee_{j=k+1}^{n} \mathbf{T}^{-j}\xi\right) + I(\mathbf{T}^{-n}\xi),$$

and applying (2.26) to each term on the right hand side gives

$$I\left(\bigvee_{j=0}^{n} \mathbf{T}^{-j}\xi\right) = \sum_{k=0}^{n} I\left[\xi/\bigvee_{j=1}^{n-k} \mathbf{T}^{-j}\xi\right] \circ \mathbf{T}^{k}$$

(where $I(\xi/\bigvee_{j=1}^{0}\mathbf{T}^{-j}\xi)\circ\mathbf{T}^n$ is to mean $I(\xi)\circ\mathbf{T}^n$ for this proof). Thus

$$D(n)\leqslant\frac{1}{n+1}\sum_{k=0}^{n}\left|I\left[\xi/\bigvee_{j=1}^{n-k}\mathbf{T}^{-j}\xi\right]-I\left(\xi/\bigvee_{j=1}^{\infty}\mathbf{T}^{-j}\xi\right)\right|\circ\mathbf{T}^k,$$

and the theorem will follow if we show the right hand side of this inequality converges to zero in L_1 and a.e.

The L_1 case is easy, since

$$\int_\Omega P(d\omega)\left|I\left[\xi/\bigvee_{j=1}^{n-k}\mathbf{T}^{-j}\xi\right]-I\left(\xi/\bigvee_{j=1}^{\infty}\mathbf{T}^{-j}\xi\right)\right|\circ\mathbf{T}^{-k}(\omega)$$
$$=\int_\Omega P(d\omega)\left|I\left[\xi/\bigvee_{j=1}^{n-k}\mathbf{T}^{-j}\xi\right]-I\left(\xi/\bigvee_{j=1}^{\infty}\mathbf{T}^{-j}\xi\right)\right|$$

by the change of variable formula and the fact that $\mathbf{T}$ is measure preserving. Theorem 2.18 now implies that this sequence of integrals converges to zero and hence $D(n)\to 0$ in L_1.

The a.e. case is slightly more difficult. To prove convergence in this case, let N be a fixed integer and define I_N by

$$I_N(\omega)=\sup_{m>N}\left|I\left(\xi/\bigvee_{j=1}^{m}\mathbf{T}^{-j}\xi\right)-I\left(\xi/\bigvee_{j=1}^{\infty}\mathbf{T}^{-j}\xi\right)\right|(\omega).$$

Then for $n>N$,

$$\frac{1}{n+1}\sum_{k=0}^{n}\left|I\left[\xi/\bigvee_{j=1}^{n-k}\mathbf{T}^{-j}\xi\right]-I\left(\xi/\bigvee_{j=1}^{\infty}\mathbf{T}^{-j}\xi\right)\right|(\omega)$$
$$\leqslant\frac{1}{n+1}\sum_{k=0}^{n-N-1}I_N\circ\mathbf{T}^k(\omega)+\frac{1}{n+1}\sum_{k=n-N}^{n}I_0\circ\mathbf{T}^k(\omega).\tag{2.56}$$

Since N is fixed and I_N is an L_1 function by Lemma 2.17, the ergodic theorem gives that

$$\lim_{n\to\infty}\frac{1}{n+1}\sum_{k=0}^{n-N-1}I_N\circ\mathbf{T}^k(\omega)=E(I_N)\qquad\text{a.e.}\tag{2.57}$$

Now,

$$\frac{1}{n+1}\sum_{k=n-N}^{n}I_0\circ\mathbf{T}^k(\omega)=\frac{1}{n+1}\left[I_0+I_0\circ\mathbf{T}+\cdots+I_0\circ\mathbf{T}^N\right]\circ\mathbf{T}^{n-N}(\omega),$$

so that if $J_N = I_0 + I_0 \circ \mathbf{T} + \cdots + I_0 \circ \mathbf{T}^N$,

$$\left| \frac{1}{n+1} \sum_{k=n-N}^{n} I_0 \circ \mathbf{T}^k \right| \leqslant \frac{1}{n+1} |J_N \circ \mathbf{T}^{n-N}(\omega)|.$$

Since

$$I_0 \leqslant \sup_n \left| I\left(\xi / \bigvee_{j=1}^{n} \mathbf{T}^{-j}\xi\right)\right| + I\left(\xi / \bigvee_{j=1}^{\infty} \mathbf{T}^{-j}\xi\right),$$

I_0 is an L_1 function and the ergodic theorem implies that

$$\frac{1}{k} J_k \to E(I_0) \qquad \text{a.e.},$$

and it follows that there exists M such that $|J_N| \leqslant N \cdot M$ a.e. Hence

$$\left| \frac{1}{n+1} \sum_{k=n-N}^{n} I_0 \circ \mathbf{T}^k \right| \leqslant \frac{N}{n+1} M \qquad \text{a.e.},$$

and it follows that

$$\lim_{n \to \infty} \frac{1}{n+1} \sum_{k=n-N}^{n} I_0 \circ \mathbf{T}^k = 0 \qquad \text{a.e.} \tag{2.58}$$

Using (2.57) and (2.58), if we take the limit in (2.56) as $n \to \infty$, we get

$$\lim_{n\to\infty} \frac{1}{n+1} \sum_{k=0}^{n} \left| I\left[\xi / \bigvee_{j=0}^{n-k} \mathbf{T}^{-j}\xi\right] - I\left(\xi / \bigvee_{j=0}^{\infty} \mathbf{T}^{-j}\xi\right) \circ \mathbf{T}^k(\omega) \right| \leqslant E(I_N)$$

for all N and almost all ω. The result now follows, since $I_N \downarrow 0$ a.e.

This theorem can be extended, with basically the same proof, to the case where $\mathbf{T}$ is not ergodic. However, in this extension $(1/n) I(\bigvee_{j=0}^{n-1} \mathbf{T}^{-j}\xi) \to f_\xi$ a.e. and L_1, where f_ξ is a function on Ω whose expected value is $h(\mathbf{T}, \xi)$. For a proof of this case see Parry [116].

The following corollary is usually called the equipartition property or equipartition theorem, because it loosely says that for ξ a measurable partition and all n sufficiently large, most of the atoms in $\xi^n = \bigvee_{j=0}^{n-1} \mathbf{T}^{-j}\xi$ have just about the same measure.

Suppose that ξ is a finite partition with K atoms. Then there are at most $K^n = e^{n \log K}$ atoms in the partition ξ^n. If each of these atoms is to have equal measure, then the measure of each must be $e^{-n\log K}$. The corollary will show that most of the space will be partitioned by sets each of whose measure is approximately $e^{-nh(\mathbf{T},\xi)}$.

COROLLARY 2.54. *If* ξ *is a measurable partition of the ergodic system* $(\Omega,\mathfrak{F},P,\mathbf{T})$ *and* $H(\xi)<\infty$, *then for every* $\delta>0$, *there exists an* N *such that for all* $n>N$ *there is a subset* $G(n)\subset\Omega_{\xi^n}$, *where* $\xi^n=\bigvee_{j=0}^{n-1}\mathbf{T}^{-j}\xi$, *such that*

$$P_{\xi^n}(G(n))>1-\delta$$

and for all $\bar{\omega}\in G(n)$

$$e^{-n[h(\mathbf{T},\xi)+\delta]}\leqslant P_{\xi^n}(\{\bar{\omega}\})\leqslant e^{-n[h(\mathbf{T},\xi)-\delta]}.$$

Proof. It follows from the theorem that

$$\lim_{m\to\infty}\frac{1}{m}I\left[\bigvee_{j=0}^{m-1}\mathbf{T}^{-j}\xi\right](\omega)=h(\mathbf{T},\xi)$$

both L_1 and a.e., so that the convergence is also in probability (i.e., in measure). Thus, there exists $N(\delta)$ such that if $n>N(\delta)$,

$$P\left\{\omega:\left|\frac{1}{n}I\left[\bigvee_{j=0}^{n-1}\mathbf{T}^{-j}\xi\right](\omega)-h(\mathbf{T},\xi)\right|>\delta\right\}<\delta,$$

or, replacing I by its definition,

$$P\left\{\omega:\sum_{A\in\xi^n}1_A(\omega)|-\log P(A)-nh(\mathbf{T},\xi)|>n\delta\right\}<\delta. \tag{2.59}$$

Take those atoms $A\in\xi^n$ such that

$$|-\log P(A)-nh(\mathbf{T},\xi)|>n\delta$$

to get the set $\Omega_{\xi^n}-G(n)$, i.e.,

$$G(n)=\{\mathbf{N}_{\xi^n}(A):|-\log P(A)-nh(\mathbf{T},\xi)|\leqslant n\delta\}.$$

Then $P_{\xi^n}\{\Omega_{\xi^n}-G(n)\}<\delta$ by the inequality (2.59). Also, if $\bar{\omega}\in G(n)$, then there is an atom $A\in\xi^n$ such that $P_{\xi^n}(\bar{\omega})=P(A)$ and

$$n[h(\mathbf{T},\xi)-\delta]\leqslant-\log P(A)\leqslant n[h(\mathbf{T},\xi)+\delta].$$

Therefore,

$$e^{-n[h(\mathbf{T},\xi)+\delta]} \leqslant P_{\xi^n}(\bar{\omega}) \leqslant e^{-n[h(\mathbf{T},\xi)-\delta]}.$$

Notice that this corollary implies that for each n sufficiently large the set $G(n)$ (called the set of good points) contains no more than $\exp\{n[h(\mathbf{T},\xi)+\delta]\}$ points, and no less than $(1-\delta)\exp\{n[h(\mathbf{T},\xi)-\delta]\}$ points. Therefore, if ξ is a partition with K atoms and $h(\mathbf{T},\xi)<\log K$ (which is the case unless ξ is independent for $\mathbf{T}$), the ratio of the number of points in $G(n)$ to the maximum number of points possible for Ω_{ξ^n} does not exceed

$$\frac{\exp[nh(\mathbf{T},\xi)+n\delta]}{\exp(n\log K)} = \exp\{n[h(\mathbf{T},\xi)+\delta-\log K]\},$$

and for δ sufficiently small this fraction approaches zero exponentially as $n\to\infty$.

Similarly, if $(\mathbf{T},\xi)$ and $(\bar{\mathbf{T}},\bar{\xi})$ are two processes with $h(\mathbf{T},\xi)<h(\bar{\mathbf{T}},\bar{\xi})$, and $G(n)$ and $\bar{G}(n)$ denote the sets of good points in the factor spaces associated with $\bigvee_{j=0}^{n-1}\mathbf{T}^{-j}\xi$ and $\bigvee_{j=0}^{n-1}\bar{\mathbf{T}}^{-j}\bar{\xi}$ respectively, then $|\bar{G}(n)|/|G(n)|$ increases exponentially as $n\to\infty$. (Here $|G(n)|$ denotes the cardinal number.) This observation underlies the proof of a number of theorems in information theory and ergodic theory.

2.11 Entropy as a Function of Distributions

In the preceding sections we have considered entropy as a function of random experiments modeled by either a probability space or a measurable partition of a Lebesgue space. In some applications, in particular to information theory (see McEliece [86]), entropy is treated as a function on the set of discrete probability distributions. From this point of view one can show (Theorem 2.57) that the negative of the entropy is a convex function, which is a property one expects entropy to have. In this section we indicate how the entropy we have discussed can be considered in this manner.

Recall that if S is a finite (or countably infinite) set, a nonnegative function f on S satisfying $\Sigma_{s\in S}f(s)=1$ was called a distribution function, or distribution, on S. Since any function on a finite set can be written as an n-tuple, we can consider all the possible distributions of a given finite set S as the collection of $|S|$-tuples of nonnegative real numbers whose sum is one. [From this point of view a distribution on S is a nonnegative vector in the space $R^{|S|}$ or $l_1(S)$.]

Definition 2.55. A *discrete probability distribution* is an N-tuple $(p_1,\ldots,p_N)$ of nonnegative real numbers such that $\Sigma_{i=1}^{N}p_i=1$.

If ξ is a finite measurable partition of a Lebesgue space, with N atoms, we can associate $N!$ discrete probability distributions with ξ, namely, the $N!$ orders which can be placed on the set $\{P(E): E \in \xi\}$. In case ξ is an ordered partition, then there is a unique discrete probability distribution associated with ξ.

Conversely, if $(p_1, p_2, \ldots, p_N)$ is a discrete probability distribution and $(\Omega, \mathfrak{F}, P)$ is a nonatomic Lebesgue space, there exists an ordered partition $\xi = \{A_1, A_2, \ldots, A_N\}$ of Ω whose associated distribution is $(p_1, p_2, \ldots, p_N)$. To obtain such a partition in Ω, define an ordered partition in the unit interval $(I, \mathfrak{L}, \lambda)$ by taking

$$E_k = \left(\sum_{i=0}^{k-1} p_i, \sum_{i=0}^{k} p_i \right), \qquad k = 1, 2, \ldots, N,$$

where p_0 is taken to be zero. Then since $(\Omega, \mathfrak{F}, P)$ is isomorphic to $(I, \mathfrak{L}, \lambda)$ we can define A_k to be the image of E_k under any connecting isomorphism.

Definition 2.56. Let $p = (p_1, \ldots, p_N)$ be a finite discrete probability distribution. The *entropy* of p, denoted by $H(p)$, is defined by

$$H(p) = -\sum_{i=1}^{N} p_i \log p_i.$$

Notice that if ξ is any partition and $(p_1, \ldots, p_N)$ is any one of the distributions associated with ξ, then $H(\xi) = H(p)$ and all of the results we have obtained for the entropy of finite measurable partitions can be translated into results for the entropy of discrete probability distributions.

The following result however is new, since the discrete probability distributions can be thought of as points in Euclidean space.

Recall that a subset K of a real linear space is convex if and only if for any two points $p_1, p_2 \in K$, the line joining p_1, p_2 (i.e., the set $\{ap_1 + (1-a)p_2 : a \in [0,1]\}$) is contained in K. A real valued function f on a convex subset K of a linear space is convex provided that for all p_1, p_2 in K and $a \in [0,1]$,

$$f(ap_1 + (1-a)p_2) \leqslant af(p_1) + (1-a)f(p_2).$$

In particular, a real valued function which is twice differentiable on an interval of the reals is convex provided its second derivative is nonnegative.

Let $\mathfrak{D}_N$ denote the set of all discrete probability distribution with N components. Then by an easy calculation it can be shown that $\mathfrak{D}_N$ is a convex subset of R^N. Since $\mathfrak{D}_N$ is also closed and bounded in R^N, it is compact.

THEOREM 2.57. *Entropy is a continuous function on the set $\mathfrak{D}_N$ of discrete probability distributions, thought of as a subset of R^N, and its negative is convex.*

Proof. Since $-x\log x$ is continuous on $[0,1]$, it is immediate that H is continuous on $\mathfrak{D}_N$. Since $x\log x$ is convex on $[0,1]$, if $a\in[0,1]$ and $p,q\in\mathfrak{D}_N$ then

$$\begin{aligned}-H(ap+(1-a)q)&=\sum_{i=1}^{N}\left[ap_i+(1-a)q_i\right]\log\left[ap_i+(1-a)q_i\right]\\&\leqslant\sum_{i=1}^{N}a\left[p_i\log p_i\right]+\sum_{i=1}^{N}(1-a)q_i\log q_i\\&=-aH(p)-(1-a)H(q),\end{aligned}$$

and we have that $-H$ is convex.

THEOREM 2.58. *For any $p\in\mathfrak{D}_N$,*

$$0\leqslant H(p)\leqslant\log N.$$

Moreover $H(p)=0$ if and only if one component of p is 1 (i.e., p is an extreme point of $\mathfrak{D}_N$), and $H(p)=\log N$ if and only if $p=(1/N,1/N,\ldots,1/N)$ (i.e., p is the centroid of $\mathfrak{D}_N$).

Proof. This is just a restatement of Theorem 2.3.

Now suppose that $S=\{1,2,\ldots,N\}$, and consider the sequence space $(\Sigma(S),\mathfrak{F})$. Let $\mathbf{T}$ be the shift on $\Sigma(S)$ and μ a $\mathbf{T}$-invariant probability measure on $(\Sigma(S),\mathfrak{F})$. The time zero partition ξ_0 of $\Sigma(S)$, whose atoms are the cylinder sets $\{\omega:\omega_0=i\}=C_i$, is an ordered partition, and the measure μ can be used to get a discrete distribution $p^0=(\mu(C_1),\mu(C_2),\ldots,\mu(C_N))$.

The partition $\xi_0\vee\mathbf{T}^{-1}\xi_0$ whose atoms are of the form $C_i\cap\mathbf{T}^{-1}C_j$ can be ordered by the lexicographic order so that it gives rise to a discrete distribution

$$p^{(2)}=\left(\mu\left(C_1\cap\mathbf{T}^{-1}C_1\right),\mu\left(C_1\cap\mathbf{T}^{-1}C_2\right),\ldots,\mu\left(C_N\cap\mathbf{T}^{-1}C_N\right)\right),$$

and in general we can obtain a discrete distribution $p^{(n)}$ from the partition $\bigvee_{j=0}^{n-1}\mathbf{T}^{-j}\xi_0$ by using lexicographic order.

It is clear from the definition that $H(p^{(n)})=H(\bigvee_{j=0}^{n-1}\mathbf{T}^{-j}\xi_0)$, so that we have

$$\lim_{n\to\infty}\frac{1}{n}H(p^{(n)})=h(\mathbf{T},\xi_0).$$

DEFINITION 2.59. If μ is a shift invariant measure on $(\Sigma(S), \mathfrak{F})$, where $S=\{1,2,\ldots, N\}$, the *entropy* of μ is defined by

$$h(\mu)= \lim_{n\to\infty} \frac{1}{n} H(p^{(n)}).$$

THEOREM 2.60. *If $S=\{1,2,\ldots, N\}$ and μ is any shift invariant probability on $(\Sigma(S), \mathfrak{F})$, then*

$$h(\mu) \leqslant - \sum_{i=1}^{N} p_i^{(0)} \log p_i^{(0)}$$

where $p_i^{(0)} = \mu\{\omega \in \Sigma(S): \omega_0 = i\}$. Moreover,

$$h(\mu) = - \sum_{i=1}^{N} p_i^{(0)} \log p_i^{(0)}$$

if and only if μ is a product measure obtained from the distribution $p^{(0)}$ on S.

Proof. This is a restatement of corollary 2.28, since $h(\mu)=h(\mathbf{T}, \xi_0)$.

COROLLARY 2.61. *If S and μ are as in the theorem, then*

$$h(\mu) \leqslant \log N,$$

with equality if and only if μ is a product measure obtained from an equidistribution on S.

Proof. Immediate, since $\Sigma_{i=1}^{N} p_i^{(0)} \log p_i^{(0)} \leqslant \log N$ with equality if and only if $p_i^{(0)} = 1/N$ for $i=1,2,\ldots, N$.

Notice that Theorem 2.60 (or Corollary 2.28) gives a characterization of independent stochastic sequences. Namely, $\{x_n\}$ is a independent sequence of identically distributed random variables in $(S, \mathbb{S})$ if and only if

$$\lim_{n\to\infty} \frac{1}{n} H(p^{(n)}) = H(p^{(0)}),$$

where $p^{(0)}$ is the distribution of x_0 [i.e., $p^{(0)}(i)=P(x_0^{-1}(i))$] and $p^{(n)}$ is the joint distribution of $\{x_0, x_1, \ldots, x_{n-1}\}$.

2.12 Examples

In this section we collect a number of examples of dynamical systems and specify the entropy of each. In cases where we have not already calculated the entropy, we either indicate the calculation or give a reference for it.

The first few examples show how the entropy of systems obtained in various ways from other systems can be obtained in terms of the entropy of these systems.

2.12.1 *Direct Products*

Let $\{(\Omega_i, \mathcal{F}_i, P_i, \mathbf{T}_i): i=1,2,\ldots,N\}$ be a finite collection of dynamical systems. They do not need to be invertible or ergodic. The direct product is the system $(\Omega, \mathcal{F}, P, \mathbf{T})$, where $(\Omega, \mathcal{F}, P)$ is the product measure space of the Ω_i, and $\mathbf{T}$ is defined on Ω by $\mathbf{T}(\omega_1, \omega_2, \ldots, \omega_N) = (\mathbf{T}_1(\omega_1), \ldots, \mathbf{T}_N(\omega_N))$.

The entropy of $\mathbf{T}$ is given by

$$h(\mathbf{T}) = \sum_{i=1}^{N} h(\mathbf{T}_i).$$

This is a consequence of Theorem 2.50.

2.12.2 *Skew Products*

Let $(\Omega, \mathcal{F}, P, \mathbf{T})$ be a dynamical system, and let f be a measurable function on Ω to the unit interval $(I, \mathcal{L}, \lambda)$. Define $\mathbf{T}_f$ on the product space $(\Omega \times I, \mathcal{F} \times \mathcal{L}, P \times \lambda)$ by

$$\mathbf{T}_f(\omega, y) = (\mathbf{T}\omega, (y + f(\omega))),$$

where $(y+f(\omega))$ denotes the fractional part of $y+f(\omega)$.

These transformations were first considered by Anzai [12], who showed that they were metric endomorphisms and gave conditions that would imply that they were ergodic and mixing. Their entropy was calculated by Abramov [2] and for any f is given by $h(\mathbf{T}_f) = h(\mathbf{T})$.

The transformation $\mathbf{T}_f$ is a special case of a more general transformation defined as follows. Let $(Y, \mathcal{Y}, \mu)$ be a probability space, and for each $\omega \in \Omega$ let $\mathbf{A}_\omega$ be a metric automorphism on $(Y, \mathcal{Y}, \mu)$ such that the map $(\omega, y) \to \mathbf{A}_\omega y$ of $(\Omega \times Y, \mathcal{F} \times \mathcal{Y})$ to $(Y, \mathcal{Y})$ is measurable. The skew product $\mathbf{P}$ on $(\Omega \times Y, \mathcal{F} \times \mathcal{Y}, P \times \mu)$ is defined by the equation $\mathbf{P}(\omega, y) = (\mathbf{T}\omega, \mathbf{A}_\omega y)$. If $\mathbf{A}_\omega y$ is taken to be $(y+f(\omega))$, we have the example just described. If $\mathbf{A}_\omega = \mathbf{A}$ for all ω, then the skew product $\mathbf{P}$ is just the direct product of $\mathbf{T}$ and $\mathbf{A}$. A formula relating $h(\mathbf{P})$, $h(\mathbf{T})$ and certain functions obtained from the entropy of partitions $\mathbf{A}_\omega^{-j}\xi$ of $(Y, \mathcal{Y}, \mu, \mathbf{A}_\omega)$ is given by Adler [5] and Abramov and Rohlin [3]. Also see Newton [88].

2.12.3 *Powers of Endomorphisms*

For any dynamical system $(\Omega, \mathcal{F}, P, \mathbf{T})$, if k is a positive integer and $\mathbf{T}^k$ denotes the composition of $\mathbf{T}$ with itself k times, then $(\Omega, \mathcal{F}, P, \mathbf{T}^k)$ is a dynamical system. We showed in Theorem 2.43 that $h(\mathbf{T}^k)=kh(\mathbf{T})$ for $k=0,1,2,\ldots,$ and if $\mathbf{T}$ is invertible that $h(\mathbf{T}^k)=|k|h(\mathbf{T})$ for $k=0,\pm 1,\pm 2,\ldots.$

2.12.4 *Flows*

A measurable flow is a collection $\{\mathbf{T}_t: t \text{ real}\}$ of metric automorphisms $\mathbf{T}_t$ on a Lebesgue space $(\Omega,\mathfrak{F},P)$ such that $\mathbf{T}_0$ is the identity, $\mathbf{T}_s\circ\mathbf{T}_t=\mathbf{T}_{s+t}$ for all real numbers s and t, and the map $(\omega,t)\rightarrow\mathbf{T}_t\omega$ of $(\Omega\times R,\mathfrak{F}\times\mathfrak{L})$ to $(\Omega,\mathfrak{F})$ is measurable. (R denotes the real numbers, and $\mathfrak{L}$ the Lebesgue sets in R.)

Using Theorem 2.43, it is easy to see that $h(\mathbf{T}_t)=|t|h(\mathbf{T}_1)$ for any rational t. Abramov [2] showed that this equality holds for all real t, and consequently the entropy of the flow $\{\mathbf{T}_t: t\in R\}$ is taken to be $h(\mathbf{T}_1)$. Kolomogoroff [69] had originally taken the entropy of a flow to be $\sup_{t>0}(1/t)h(\mathbf{T}_t)$.

Two flows $\{\mathbf{T}_t\}$ and $\{\mathbf{T}'_t\}$ on spaces $(\Omega,\mathfrak{F},P)$ and $(\Omega',\mathfrak{F}',P')$ respectively are isomorphic if there exists a metric isomorphism $\mathbf{S}:\Omega\rightarrow\Omega'$ such that $\mathbf{T}'_t\circ\mathbf{S}=\mathbf{S}\circ\mathbf{T}_t$ for all real t. It is clear that isomorphic flows must have the same entropy.

A Bernoulli flow is a flow in which $(\Omega,\mathfrak{F},P,\mathbf{T}_t)$ is a Bernoulli system for each t. (See Section 2.12.9, and Chapter 4.) The existence of Bernoulli flows is proven in [96], and Ornstein shows in [100] that all Bernoulli flows with finite entropy are isomorphic after a suitable time transformation. The results in this paper also imply that any flow $\{\mathbf{S}_t\}$ in which $\mathbf{S}_1$ is Bernoulli is a Bernoulli flow.

2.12.5 *Induced Automorphisms*

Let $(\Omega,\mathfrak{F},P,\mathbf{T})$ be a dynamical system, and let A be a set in $\mathfrak{F}$ with positive probability. For each $\omega\in A$ let $n_A(\omega)$ be the smallest positive integer k such that $\mathbf{T}^k(\omega)\in A$. Then

$$\{\omega\in A: n_A(\omega)=k\}=\{\omega\in A:\mathbf{T}\omega\notin A,\ldots,\mathbf{T}^{k-1}(\omega)\notin A,\mathbf{T}^k(\omega)\in A\}.$$

In case there is no such integer, define $n_A(\omega)=\infty$. The integer valued function n_A is called the first return time. Kac's recurrence theorem [59] states that if $\mathbf{T}$ is ergodic, then $\int_A P(d\omega)n_A(\omega)=1$.

The induced transformation, $\mathbf{T}_A$, is defined on the Lebesgue space $(A, A\cap\mathfrak{F}, P_A)$, where $P_A(E)=P(E)/P(A)$ for all $E\in A\cap\mathfrak{F}$, by

$$\mathbf{T}_A(\omega)=\mathbf{T}^{n_A(\omega)}(\omega).$$

These endomorphisms were defined by Kakutani [60] and are connected with the study of ergodic flows. We shall discuss this connection in Section

4.9. Their entropy was calculated for ergodic $\mathbf{T}$ by Abramov [1] and is given by

$$h(\mathbf{T}_A)=\frac{1}{P(A)}h(\mathbf{T}).$$

A proof of this formula can be found in Brown [27].

The following examples describe some specific dynamical systems.

2.12.6 *Periodic Automorphisms*

It is immediate from the definition of entropy that the identity $\mathbf{E}$ on any Lebesgue space has zero entropy. Suppose $(\Omega,\mathcal{F},P,\mathbf{T})$ is a dynamical system such that there exists an integer N with the property that $\mathbf{T}^N\omega=\omega$ for almost all $\omega\in\Omega$. Such a system is said to be periodic, and since $\mathbf{T}^N=\mathbf{E}$, it is immediate from Section 2.12.3 that periodic automorphisms have zero entropy.

2.12.7 *Rotations of the Circle*

Let T_1 denote the unit circle in Euclidean two-space, $\mathcal{H}_1$ the (completed) σ-field of subsets of T_1 generated by open arcs of T_1, and γ_1 the measure induced on $\mathcal{H}_1$ by the set function whose value on an open arc is the length of the arc divided by 2π. We may represent T_1 as the collection of complex numbers $\{e^{2\pi ix}:0\leqslant x<1\}$, and if f is defined on I by $f(x)=e^{2\pi ix}$, then f is a bijection of I onto T_1. It is easy to see that $f^{-1}(\mathcal{H}_1)=\mathcal{L}$ and $\gamma_1=\lambda\circ f^{-1}$, so that $(T_1,\mathcal{H}_1,\gamma_1)$ is isomorphic to $(I,\mathcal{L},\lambda)$.

For any angle a, consider the map of T_1 to itself which sends any point on the unit circle to the point obtained from the first by rotating the circle through the angle a. Specifically, for any real number a, let $\mathbf{R}_a$ be defined on T_1 by $\mathbf{R}_a(e^{2\pi ix})=e^{2\pi i(x+a)}$. It is clear that $\mathbf{R}_a$ is a metric automorphism of $(T_1,\mathcal{H}_1,\gamma_1)$ for each a.

In case a is a rational number, $\mathbf{R}_a$ is a periodic automorphism, and it follows that $h(\mathbf{R}_a)=0$. In case a is an irrational number, the partition ξ whose atoms are $\{e^{2\pi ix}:0\leqslant x<\frac{1}{2}\}$ and $\{e^{2\pi ix}:\frac{1}{2}\leqslant x<1\}$ has the property that $\bigvee_{j=0}^{\infty}\mathbf{R}_a^{-j}\xi=\varepsilon$. Since $\mathbf{R}_a$ is a metric automorphism, Corollary 2.41 tells us that $h(\mathbf{R}_a)=0$.

2.12.8 *Ergodic Automorphisms of Compact Abelian Groups*

Let G be a compact abelian group and m denote the Haar measure on the (completed) Borel subsets $\mathcal{B}$ of G. The Haar measure is a finite measure, since G is compact, and we may assume that it is a probability measure. If $\mathbf{A}$ is any (algebraic) automorphism of G, then $\mathbf{A}$ is a metric automorphism on $(G,\mathcal{B},m)$. To see this define the measure m' on $\mathcal{B}$ by

$m' = m \circ \mathbf{A}$. If $B \in \mathcal{B}$ and $g \in G$,

$$m'(B+g) = m(\mathbf{A}(B+g)) = m(\mathbf{A}(B) + \mathbf{A}(g)) = m(\mathbf{A}(B)),$$

since m is invariant under translation. Thus

$$m'(B+g) = m'(B),$$

and m' must be a constant multiple of m. Since both measures are probabilities, we must have $m = m' = m \circ \mathbf{A}$, and it follows that $\mathbf{A}$ is measure preserving.

A particular example of a compact abelian group with its Haar measure is $(T_1, \mathcal{H}_1, \gamma_1)$ of Section 2.12.7. There are only two measurable group automorphisms of T_1, namely the identity and complex conjugation, both of which have zero entropy. Neither of these automorphisms is ergodic.

Other examples are given by the toral groups with their Haar measure. Specifically, let $(T_n, \mathcal{H}_n, \gamma_n)$ be the direct product of n copies of $(T_1, \mathcal{H}_1, \gamma_1)$. The group automorphisms of T_n can be represented by $n \times n$ matrices M with integer entries. In case the determinate of M is ± 1, then the group automorphism $\mathbf{A}(M)$ defined by

$$\mathbf{A}(M)(e^{2\pi i x_1}, \ldots, e^{2\pi i x_n}) = (e^{2\pi i y_1}, \ldots, e^{2\pi i y_n}),$$

where $y_j = \sum_{k=1}^{n} M_{jk} x_k$ for $j = 1, 2, \ldots, n$, is a metric automorphism of $(T_n, \mathcal{H}_n, \gamma_n)$.

The automorphisms associated with matrices none of whose eigenvalues are roots of unity are ergodic. The entropy of such automorphisms is given by

$$h(\mathbf{A}(M)) = \sum_{i=1}^{k} \log |a_i|,$$

where $\{a_i : i = 1, 2, \ldots, k\}$ are those eigenvalues of M with absolute value greater than one.

This result is proven by Sinai for $n = 2$ in [142], and the proof for the general case is given by Berg in [17].

Katznelson [63] showed that these finite toral automorphisms are Bernoulli systems (see Section 2.12.9 and Definition 4.9), and shortly thereafter Aoki and Totoki [13], Chu [30], and Lind [78] independently extended this result to infinite toral automorphisms. In 1977, Lind [80] proved that ergodic (algebraic) automorphisms of compact abelian groups are Bernoulli and indicated that his methods could be extended to the nonabelian case. This same result has been obtained independently using a different method by Miles and Thomas [83–85]. In [80] Lind shows that the set of values for the entropy of group automorphisms is either the set of nonnegative reals or is countable, depending upon the answer to a 40 year old unsolved problem of Lehmer in algebraic number theory. Namely, if $p(x)=\Pi_i(x-\lambda_i)$ is a monic polynomial with integer coefficients and constant term ± 1, can $\Sigma_{|\lambda_i|>1}\log|\lambda_i|$ be arbitrarily small?

2.12.9 *Bernoulli Shifts*

Let $S=\{1,2,\dots,k\}$, and $\{f(i): i\in S\}$ be a discrete probability distribution on S. The system $(\Sigma(S),\mathcal{F},\mu,\mathbf{B})$, where $(\Sigma(S),\mathcal{F},\mu)$ is the Lebesgue space of doubly infinite sequences of elements from S with the product measure defined in Example 1.3 and where $\mathbf{B}$ is the shift [i.e., $(\mathbf{B}(\omega))_j=\omega_{j+1}$], is called a Bernoulli shift. We showed in Example 2.40 that the entropy of a Bernoulli shift is given by $h(\mathbf{B})=-\Sigma_{i=1}^k f(i)\log f(i)$. The major portion of Chapter 4 is devoted to a study of these systems.

2.12.10 *Markov Shifts*

These dynamical systems are constructed in the same way as Bernoulli shifts except that a Markov measure is used in place of the product measure. This measure is obtained from an initial probability distribution f and a matrix A of transition probabilities by the construction outlined in Example 1.5. Specifically, let $S=\{1,2,\dots,k\}$ and A be a $k\times k$ matrix with nonnegative entries a_{ij} such that $\Sigma_{i=1}^k a_{ij}=1$ for $j=1,2,\dots,k$, and let $\{f(i): i\in S\}$ be a discrete probability distribution on S such that $\Sigma_{i=1}^k f(i)a_{ij}=f(j)$ for $j=1,2,\dots,k$.

Let $G=\{g_0<g_1<\cdots<g_N\}$ be a finite set of integers. Define a function P_G on cylinder sets of the form

$$C_G(i_0,i_1,\dots,i_N)=\{\omega\in\Sigma(S):\omega_{g_0}=i_0,\dots,\omega_{g_N}=i_N\}$$

where $i_0,i_1,\dots,i_N$ are selected from S, by

$$P_G(C_G(i_0,i_1,\dots,i_N))=f(i_0)a_{i_0i_1}^{(g_1-g_0)}a_{i_1i_2}^{(g_2-g_1)}\cdots a_{i_{N-1}i_N}^{(g_N-g_{N-1})},$$

where $a_{ij}^{(l)}$ denotes the i,jth entry of A^l, the lth power of the matrix A. P_G can be extended by usual extension techniques to the σ-field generated by the cylinder sets based on G, so that P_G is a probability measure on this σ-field. The family of measures $\{P_G: G \text{ a finite subset of } Z\}$ satisfies the Kolmogoroff consistency conditions. By the Kolmogoroff extension there is a unique probability measure μ defined on the σ-field generated by the collection of cylinder sets with finite base which coincides with P_G on any cylinder set based on G. This measure μ is the Markov measure associated with the initial distribution f and transition matrix A.

Let $\mathbf{M}$ denote the shift on $\Sigma(S)$, i.e., $(\mathbf{M}(\omega))(j)=\omega(j+1)$. Since $\Sigma_{i=1}^k f(i)a_{ij}=f(j)$, it is easy to show that $\mu(\mathbf{M}^{-1}C_G)=\mu(C_G)$ for any cylinder set, and it follows that **M** is measure preserving. The system $(\Sigma(S), \mathfrak{F}, \mu, \mathbf{M})$ is a Markov shift.

One can see easily that $\xi_0 = (\{\omega: \omega(0)=i\}: i=1,2,\ldots,k)$ is a generating partition for the system, and it is also easy to show that $\mu(\{\omega(0)=j\}|\{\omega(-1)=i, \omega(-2)=i_{-2},\ldots,\omega(-N)=i_{-N}\} = a_{ij} = \mu\ (\{\omega(0)=j\}\,|\,\{\omega(-1)=i\})$ for any $N>1$. Thus

$$H\left[\xi_0 | \bigvee_{j=1}^{N} \mathbf{M}^j \xi_0\right] = H(\xi_0 | \mathbf{M}\xi_0) \text{ for all } N=1,2,\ldots$$

and

$$\begin{aligned} h(\mathbf{M}) = h(\mathbf{M}^{-1}, \xi_0) &= \lim_{N\to\infty} H\left[\xi_0 | \bigvee_{j=1}^{N} \mathbf{M}^j \xi_0\right] \\ &= H(\xi_0 / \mathbf{M}\xi_0) \\ &= -\sum_{i=1}^{k}\sum_{j=1}^{k} f(i) a_{ij} \log a_{ij}. \end{aligned}$$

2.12.11 *S-Automorphisms*

Let S be a finite set and $\{p_i : i\in S\}$ a probability distribution on S. For any permutation σ of the integers, define a metric automorphism $\mathbf{T}_\sigma$ on $(\Sigma(S), \mathfrak{F}, \mu)$, the space of doubly infinite sequences of elements from S with product measure, by the equations

$$(\mathbf{T}_\sigma \omega)_j = \omega_{\sigma(j)}, \qquad j \in Z.$$

The dynamical system $(\Sigma(S), \mathfrak{F}, \mu, \mathbf{T}_\sigma)$ is ergodic if and only if σ contains only infinite cycles in its disjoint cycle decomposition (see Standish [149]). The entropy of this transformation is given by

$$h(\mathbf{T}_\sigma) = -k(\sigma) \sum_{i\in S} p_i \log p_i,$$

where $k(\sigma)$ denotes the number (possibly infinite) of infinite disjoint cycles in σ. Moreover, the systems are ergodic if and only if they are Bernoulli (Martin [82]).

The following examples describe systems which are not invertible.

2.12.12 *Unilateral Shifts*

For each positive integer r define the function $\mathbf{T}_r$ on $(I, \mathfrak{L}, \lambda)$, the unit interval with Lebesgue measure, by

$$\mathbf{T}_r x = (rx)$$

where (y) denotes the fractional part of y.

By considering intervals it is not too hard to show that $\mathbf{T}_r$ is a metric endomorphism. The partition ξ whose atoms are the intervals $(j/r, j+1/r)$ for $j=0,1,\ldots,r-1$ is such that $\bigvee_{j=0}^{\infty}\mathbf{T}_r^{-j}\xi = \varepsilon\,(\text{mod } 0)$, and the Kolmogoroff–Sinai theorem gives that $h(\mathbf{T}_r)=h(\mathbf{T}_r,\xi)$. By calculation one can show that ξ is an independent partition, i.e., $\mathbf{T}_r^{-j}\xi$ is independent of $\bigvee_{l=0}^{j-1}\mathbf{T}_r^{-l}\xi$ for all l, and consequently that $h(\mathbf{T}_r,\xi)=H(\xi)$. Thus

$$\begin{aligned} h(\mathbf{T}_r) &= -\sum_{i=0}^{n-1}\frac{1}{r}\log\frac{1}{r} \\ &= \log r. \end{aligned}$$

Another way of calculating $h(\mathbf{T}_r)$ is to notice that $(I, \mathfrak{L}, \lambda, \mathbf{T}_r)$ is isomorphic to $(\Sigma'(0,\ldots,r-1), \mathfrak{F}, \mu_f, \mathbf{S})$ where Σ' denotes the collection of one sided sequences $\omega'=(a_0,a_1,a_2,\ldots)$, $0\leqslant a_j\leqslant r-1$; μ_f is product measure obtained from the distribution $f(i)=1/r$ for $0\leqslant i\leqslant r-1$; and $(\mathbf{S}\omega')_i=\omega'_{i+1}$ is a shift. The isomorphism is given by assigning x to $(a_0,a_1,\ldots)$ if and only if $x=\sum_{j=0}^{\infty}a_j/r^j$. That is, $.a_0a_1a_2\cdots$ is the expansion of x in the base r.

2.12.13 *Continued Fraction Transformations*

Define $\mathbf{G}$ on I by $\mathbf{G}(x)=(1/x)$. It is clear that $\mathbf{G}$ is a measurable transformation on $(I,\mathfrak{L})$ to itself, but $\mathbf{G}$ does not preserve Lebesgue measure. There is, however, a probability measure μ defined on $\mathfrak{L}$ which is absolutely continuous with respect to λ and which is preserved by $\mathbf{G}$ (see [20]). This measure is given by $\mu(E)=\int_E(1+x)^{-1}(\log 2)^{-1}dx$ for any $E\in\mathfrak{L}$. The dynamical system $(I,\mathfrak{L},\mu,\mathbf{G})$ has an entropy calculated by Rohlin [125] to be

$$h(\mathbf{G})=\frac{\pi^2}{6\log 2}.$$

Just as the systems $(I,\mathfrak{L},\lambda,\mathbf{T}_r)$ are isomorphic to one sided shifts, so is the system $(I,\mathfrak{L},\mu,\mathbf{G})$ isomorphic to a one sided shift of sequences of integers. The connection between a point x in I and a sequence $(a_0,a_1,a_2,\ldots)$ of integers is given by the continued fraction representation of x, i.e., $x \to (a_0, a_1, \ldots)$ if and only if $x = \lim_{n\to\infty} x_n$, where $x_n = (1 + (1 + \cdots + (1 + a_n^{-1})^{-1} \cdots)^{-1})^{-1}$, and there are $n+1$ parentheses in this expression. The map **G** was first studied by Gauss. See also Hartman [58] and Parry [110].

2.12.14 *f-Transformations*

The examples to be described are generalizations of Sections 2.12.12 and 2.12.13. Their ergodic properties were studied by Renyi [120] and Hartman [58]; their entropy has been calculated by Rohlin [125] and Parry [111].

Let f be a positive monotone real valued function. For each positive real number x let $\{a_n(x)\}$ and $\{r_n(x)\}$ be defined inductively by

$$a_0(x) = [x], \qquad r_0(x) = (x),$$

$$a_{n+1}(x) = [f^{-1}(r_n(x))], \qquad r_{n+1}(x) = (f^{-1}(r_n(x))),$$

where $[x]$ is the integral part of x, and (x) is the fractional part.

Renyi shows in [120] that under certain conditions on f every real number in I has an extension of the form

$$x = \lim_{n\to\infty} \big(a_0(x) + f\big(a_1(x) + f\big(a_2(x) + \cdots\big)\big)\big) \tag{2.60}$$

where there are $n+1$ parentheses. Notice that if $f(x) = 1/x$, (2.60) gives the continued fraction representation of x, and if $f(x) = xr^{-1}$ for r an integer, (2.60) gives the r-adic expansion of x.

Renyi further shows that under his stated conditions on f there exists a measure μ on $(I, \mathfrak{L})$ which is absolutely continuous with respect to Lebesgue measure and which is invariant with respect to the transformation $\mathbf{T}_f$ defined on I by $\mathbf{T}_f x = (f^{-1}(x))$. He shows that $(I, \mathfrak{L}, \mu, \mathbf{T}_f)$ is an ergodic dynamical system.

This dynamical system is isomorphic to a one sided shift on sequences of integers where the connecting isomorphism is obtained by assigning x to the sequence $(a_0(x), \ldots, a_n(x), \cdots)$.

The entropy of the dynamical systems $(I, \mathfrak{L}, \mu, \mathbf{T}_f)$ is calculated by Rohlin in [125]. Parry developed a formula for calculating the entropy of certain stochastic processes which can be applied to these dynamical systems. This formula gives

$$h(\mathbf{T}_f) = \int_0^1 \log\left|\frac{df^{-1}}{dx}\right| g(x)\,dx,$$

where the invariant measure μ for $\mathbf{T}_f$ is given by

$$\mu(E)=\int_E g(x)\,dx,$$

provided that the partition $\xi=(\{x\in I: a_0(x)=n\}, n\in Z^+)$ is a generating partition for $\mathbf{T}_f$ and $\mathbf{T}_f$ is a strongly ergodic endomorphism, i.e., $\mathbf{T}_f^{-1}E\subset E$ implies that $\mu(E)=0$ or $\mu(E)=1$.

Applying this formula to $f(x)=1/x$ and $f(x)=x/r$, for r an integer, gives respectively the entropy of the continued fraction transformation and the unilateral shift of Sections 2.12.12 and 2.12.13. Other special cases of f-transformations, called β-transformations, are given by the functions $f_1(x)=x/\beta$ for $\beta>1$; $f_2(x)=x-\alpha$ for α irrational; and $f_3(x)=x/\beta-\alpha/\beta$ for $\beta>1$, $0<\alpha<1$. For these functions we get

$$\mathbf{T}_{f_1}(x)=(\beta x), \qquad h(\mathbf{T}_{f_1})=\log\beta,$$
$$\mathbf{T}_{f_2}(x)=(x+\alpha), \qquad h(\mathbf{T}_{f_2})=0,$$
$$\mathbf{T}_{f_3}(x)=(\beta x+\alpha), \qquad h(\mathbf{T}_{f_3})=\log\beta.$$

The value for the entropy is obtained from Parry's formula by noting that the invariant measure for each of these endomorphisms is Lebesgue measure. [The formula for $h(\mathbf{T}_{f_2})$ is only valid for α and β which make $\mathbf{T}_{f_2}$ strongly ergodic.] See [110], [111] for details.

2.13 Sequence Entropy and r-Entropy.

In this section we shall give a generalization of the Kolmogoroff–Sinai invariant and a generalization of the rate of information generation which have some usefulness. We shall not study them in any detail, being content to give the definitions and indicate their uses.

The first generalization was given by Kushnirenko's [73] modification of a definition due to Kirilov [67]. It consists of calculating the rate of information generation along a subsequence of times.

DEFINITION 2.62. Let $(\Omega, \mathscr{F}, P, \mathbf{T})$ be a dynamical system and $A=\{n_j\}$ a sequence of positive integers. The *A-entropy* of $\mathbf{T}$, or *sequence entropy* of $\mathbf{T}$ along A, denoted by $h_A(\mathbf{T})$, is defined by

$$h_A(\mathbf{T})=\sup\{h_A(\mathbf{T},\xi):\xi \text{ a finite partition}\},$$

where

$$h_A(\mathbf{T},\xi)=\lim_{l\to\infty}\frac{1}{l}H\left(\bigvee_{j=1}^{l}\mathbf{T}^{n_j}\xi\right).$$

It is easy to see that $h_A(\mathbf{T})$ is an isomorphism invariant of the dynamical system and that $h_A(\mathbf{T}) \geqslant h(\mathbf{T})$ for any sequence A. It is this property which makes the sequence entropy useful, since it can be used to distinguish nonisomorphic dynamical systems with zero entropy. Kushnirenko [73] used sequence entropy along the sequence $\{2^j\}$ to show that a horocycle flow on a compact two dimensional orientable manifold of constant negative curvature is not isomorphic to its Cartesian square. Both the flow (i.e., the automorphism obtained from the flow at $t=1$) and its square have zero entropy and continuous spectra. In the same paper it was shown that a system has discrete spectrum (see Chapter 4) if and only if its sequence entropy along every sequence is zero. Saleski [135, 136] has used sequence entropy to study various types of mixing, and Walters [161] has used it to obtain invariant sub-σ-algebras of the system. See also Newton [89, 90].

The second generalization comes from coding with a fidelity criterion. Suppose that the outcomes of a probability space Ω_N are sequences of length N whose components are from a finite set $\{a_1, a_2, \ldots, a_k\}$. Each point $\omega = (a_{i_1}, \ldots, a_{i_N})$ can be thought of as a message. Let d be defined by $d(x, y) = 1$ if $x \neq y$ and 0 otherwise. Now define d on $\Omega_N \times \Omega_N$ by $d(\omega, \bar{\omega}) = \sum_{i=1}^N d(\omega_i, \bar{\omega}_i)$, where ω_i denotes the ith coordinate of ω. One sees immediately that d indicates in how many places the two messages ω and $\bar{\omega}$ have different letters, i.e., how many mistakes are made if the message $\bar{\omega}$ is used in place of ω. A fidelity criterion would require that no more than a certain fraction of mistakes be allowed. (See Section 3.6.)

This concept was used by Posner, Rodemich, and Rumsey [119], who defined the ε, r entropy of a probability space which is also a metric space by using partitions of $1-\varepsilon$ of the space (i.e., disjoint subsets of the space whose union has measure no less than $1-\varepsilon$), whose atoms have diameter no more than r. Feldman [39] has expanded on this to obtain an entropy of automorphisms which has applications to measure preserving actions of continuous groups. Basically what he does is to use ε, r entropy on the factor spaces obtained from the partitions $\bigvee_{j=0}^N \mathbf{T}^{-j}\xi$ and allow N to approach infinity.

Definition 2.63. Let $(\Omega, \mathfrak{F}, P, \mathbf{T})$ be a dynamical system and $\xi = \{\xi(1), \xi(2), \ldots, \xi(k)\}$ be a finite measurable partition. Denote the partition $\bigvee_{j=0}^N \mathbf{T}^{-j}\xi$ by ξ^N, and consider the factor space $(\Omega_{\xi^N}, \mathfrak{F}_{\xi^N}, P_{\xi^N})$. For each $\omega \in \Omega_{\xi^N}$ there is a unique sequence $(i_0, i_1, \ldots, i_N)$ such that $\mathbf{N}_{\xi^N}^{-1}(\omega) = \xi(i_0) \cap \mathbf{T}^{-1}\xi(i_1) \cap \cdots \cap \mathbf{T}^{-N}\xi(i_N)$. Denote this sequence by $\mathbf{M}_N(\omega)$.

Let $\varepsilon > 0$ and $r > 0$ be given. For each N, a (ξ, N, r) *partition* is a finite collection $\eta = \{\eta(1), \eta(2), \ldots, \eta(l)\}$ of disjoint subsets of Ω_{ξ^N} such that

$$\sup\left\{ \frac{1}{N} d(\mathbf{M}_N(\omega), \mathbf{M}_N(\bar{\omega})) : \omega, \bar{\omega} \in \eta(i) \right\} \leqslant r$$

for each $i=1,2,\ldots,l$. The ε, r *entropy* of $(\Omega_{\xi^N}, \mathcal{F}_{\xi^N}, P_{\xi^N})$, denoted by $H_{\varepsilon,r}(\xi^N)$, is defined by

$$H_{\varepsilon,r}(\xi^N)=\inf\left\{-\sum_{i=1}^{l} P_{\xi^N}(\eta(i))\log P_{\xi^N}(\eta(i))\right\},$$

where the infimum is taken over all (ξ, N, r) partitions η of Ω_{ξ^N} such that $P_{\xi^N}(\bigcup_i \eta(i)) \geqslant 1-\varepsilon$. Posner et al. [119] have shown this infimum is assumed.

The r-entropy of $\mathbf{T}$ with respect to ξ is given by

$$h_r(\mathbf{T},\xi)=\sup_{\varepsilon>0}\limsup_{N\to\infty}\frac{1}{N}H_{\varepsilon,r}(\xi^N).$$

The r-entropy has the following properties:

R1. $h_r(\mathbf{T},\xi)\leqslant h(\mathbf{T},\xi)$,
R2. $h_r(\mathbf{T},\xi)=0$ if $r\geqslant 1$,
R3. $h_r(\mathbf{T},\xi)$ is a monotone increasing function of r,
R4. if $\xi_1 \leqslant \xi_2$, then $h_r(\mathbf{T},\xi_1)\leqslant h_r(\mathbf{T},\xi_2)$,
R5. $h(\mathbf{T})=\sup\{h_r(\mathbf{T},\xi): \xi \text{ a finite partition}\}$.

These properties are proven in [39], where a Shannon–McMillan theorem for r-entropy, which is a type of second order theorem, is also proven. By modifying the definition of the metric d used in defining (ξ, N, r) partitions, an r-entropy is obtained which can be used to get the same type of Shannon–McMillan theorem for ergodic aperiodic actions of finite products of the reals. This same r-entropy is also used to obtain the isomorphism theorem (Theorem 4.39) with Bernoulli replaced by finitely determined for these actions by methods similar to those used in Chapter 4 for metric automorphisms.

CHAPTER 3

Information Theory

3.1 A Model of an Information System

Information theory is concerned with constructing a mathematical model for systems which transmit information and then analyzing this model. The object of this analysis is to develop techniques to reproduce at one point (the destination) a message, or an adequate approximation to a message, which has been chosen at another point (the source) and transmitted over a channel.

Fundamental to this problem is a measure of the information transmitted by such a system. It is only in terms of quantity or rate of information processed by a system that one can judge the effectiveness of the system. Central to the notion of quantity of information is an interpretation of the idea of entropy. This interpretation equates the removal of uncertainty with the gain in information. Since entropy is a numerical measure of uncertainty, this interpretation of information gives entropy its central position. The interpretation and the resulting theories were initiated by C. E. Shannon [138] in his fundamental paper "A Mathematical Theory of Communication" published in 1948.

In this chapter we shall describe a standard model of an information system and show how the notion of entropy provides a quantitative basis for measuring the information processed by a system. We shall focus on the construction of the various models, and the definitions and theorems necessary to understand these models.

A standard representation of an information system is given in Figure 3.1. This model of an information or communication system is sufficiently general to include most systems encountered while remaining simple enough for analysis. The encoder and decoder are frequently further

ENCYCLOPEDIA OF MATHEMATICS and Its Applications, Gian-Carlo Rota (ed.).
Vol. 12: Nathaniel F. Martin and James W. England, Mathematical Theory of Entropy.
ISBN 0-201-13511-6

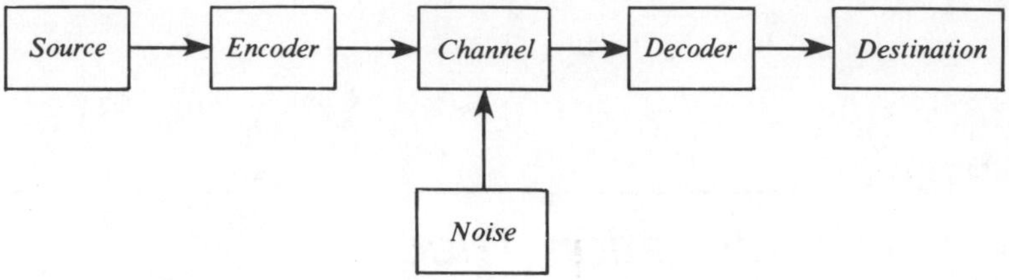

Figure 3.1.

divided into source encoder and channel encoder and into channel decoder and source decoder, respectively. This has the effect of making the design of the channel encoder and decoder almost independent of the source encoder and decoder.

The source is a person or machine that produces the information to be transmitted. The encoder is a device that changes the form of the output of the source to a form that can be transmitted over the channel. If the encoder is divided into a source and channel encoder, the source encoder changes the output of the source over some time interval into a finite set of messages, usually binary data, which is then encoded by the channel encoder (usually in a one to one manner) for transmission over the channel. The channel is a medium that connects the source to the destination. The decoder converts the output of the channel into a form that can be used at the destination.

There are two types of difficulties that can arise in this scheme. One is that *noise* can occur in the channel as it transmits the message, so that errors in transmission are produced. The channel decoder must decide, by examining the received message over some period of time, what message was sent. The source decoder then changes the form of the message it is given by the channel decoder into a form suitable at the destination. Another problem frequently encountered is that the source may produce information at a rate that exceeds the capacity of the channel. The source encoder must select or classify messages to be sent over the channel, using a fidelity criterion which measures the relative seriousness of the possible errors. Thus the source encoder and channel decoder are complex, having to make decisions in order to implement many to one functions, whereas the source decoder and channel encoder are usually relatively simple, having to implement one to one functions.

It is not clear that separating the various components of a communication system, as we have done, does not impose limitations on the system. It is a result of the theory that under general conditions the limitations are few (Blasburg and Van Blerkom [21]).

The problem of transmitting information over a noisy channel is dealt with in a fundamental theorem of information theory, which states that it is possible to transmit information through a noisy channel at any rate less than the capacity of the channel with an arbitrarily small probability of error. The notion of entropy is used to define the rate at which information is processed and hence the capacity of a channel. The proof of this theorem is nonconstructive (it does not provide a specific procedure for coding), but much work has been done in recent years in constructing effective codes to implement the results of this theorem.

A converse to the noisy channel coding theorem gives a minimum distortion that must take place when transmitting information through a channel at a rate that exceeds its capacity. In order to minimize the effect of this distortion it is necessary to develop a scheme to select the messages to be transmitted according to their importance at the destination. This is done by associating with a source-destination pair a function, called the rate-distortion function, which has the following interpretation. It is possible to design a communication system that reproduces the output of a source at the destination with an average distortion less than or equal to d if and only if the capacity of the channel joining the source to the destination exceeds the value of the rate-distortion function at d. After discussing the noisy channel coding theorem, we shall give a brief discussion of a type of source coding which has arisen from the work of D. S. Ornstein on the isomorphism problem (see Chapter 4). Since a detailed discussion of the rate-distortion function, including Shannon's source coding theorem, is given by McEliece [86] and involves no new interpretation of entropy, we shall not discuss it here. The only discussion of source coding we give will be a treatment of sliding-block codes in Section 3.6.

3.2 The Source

A *discrete source* is a stochastic sequence in a finite set S, called the source alphabet, with parameter set Z, the integers. The adjective discrete refers to the fact that the source alphabet is finite. In Section 1.7 we saw that a stochastic sequence in a set S can be described in terms of the quadruple $(\Sigma(S), \mathfrak{F}_S, \mu, \mathbf{T}_S)$, where $\Sigma(S)$ is the set of all doubly infinite sequences of elements of S, $\mathfrak{F}_S$ is the product σ-field, and μ is the probability obtained from the joint distributions of the process [i.e., $(\Sigma(S), \mathfrak{F}_S, \mu)$ is the realization or path space of the sequence]. The map $\mathbf{T}_S$ is the shift transformation, and in general μ may not be $\mathbf{T}_S$-invariant. (We shall not use the subscript S except when more than one system is involved.) For $\omega \in \Sigma(S)$ we shall think of ω_n, the nth coordinate of ω, as the letter produced by the source at time n, $(\omega_k, \omega_{k+1}, \ldots, \omega_{k+l})$ as a source "word" of length l, and $\omega = (\ldots, \omega_{-1}, \omega_0, \omega_1, \ldots)$ as a source message. Given an alphabet S, $\Sigma(S)$ and $\mathbf{T}$ will remain fixed, while the probability measure μ will change in order to represent different sources with the same alphabet. Therefore, we adopt the usual custom and denote a source by

$[\Sigma(S), \mu]$. Of course, this model is only for the output of the source; we are uninterested in the mechanism that *produces* this output. With this model of a source we can view Examples 1.3 and 1.5 and the examples in Section 1.7 as discrete sources. Discrete sources are classified in terms of their associated shift transformations. The source $[\Sigma(S), \mu]$ is said to be *stationary* provided $(\Sigma(S), \mathcal{F}_S, \mu, \mathbf{T}_S)$ is a dynamical system, i.e., $\mathbf{T}_S$ is a metric automorphism, so that $\mu\mathbf{T}_S^{-1} = \mu$. (This condition implies that the stochastic sequence is stationary.) In our terminology, a stationary source is one that has the same probability of producing a particular source word of length l in the time interval from 0 to l as it has of producing this same word in the time interval from time k to time $k+l$, for all $k \in Z$ (see Section 1.7). In this chapter we consider only stationary sources. Therefore, this condition becomes part of the definition of a source.

In order to conveniently apply the definitions and theorems of the previous chapters, we let ξ_S denote the time-zero partition of $\Sigma(S)$. The atoms of this partition are sets of the form $\{\omega \in \Sigma(S) | \omega_0 = s\} = (\omega_0 = s)$ for $s \in S$. Thus a source word $(\omega_k, \omega_{k+1}, \ldots, \omega_{k+n})$ is simply an atom of the partition $\bigvee_{j=k}^{k+n} \mathbf{T}^{-j}\xi_S$. (Recall that the factor space associated with ξ_S is isomorphic to the source alphabet S with its distribution.) We use the partition ξ_S to define the entropy of the source as the average rate at which the source produces information. In Chapter 2 we noted that $H(\xi_S)$ is the average amount of information in the experiment ξ_S, which in our setting is the average amount of information produced by the source at time zero. Continuing with this interpretation, $H(\bigvee_{j=0}^{n-1} \mathbf{T}^{-j}\xi_S)$ is the average amount of information produced by the source during the time interval from 0 to $n-1$. Thus if we insist that the source produce one letter per time interval, $(1/n)H(\bigvee_{j=0}^{n-1} \mathbf{T}^{-j}\xi_S)$ is the average rate of information produced per unit time during this time interval. Thus the natural definition of the entropy of the source $[\Sigma(S), \mu]$, as the average rate of information produced per unit time, is $\lim_{n\to\infty}(1/n)H(\bigvee_{j=0}^{n-1} \mathbf{T}^{-j}\xi_S)$. In Chapter 2 we saw that this limit always exists, and we denoted it by $h(\mathbf{T}, \xi_S)$. Since the partition ξ_S generates $\mathcal{F}_S$ under the shift $\mathbf{T}$, Theorem 2.39 implies that $h(\mathbf{T}, \xi_S) = h(\mathbf{T})$. Thus, we define the *entropy of the source* $[\Sigma(S), \mu]$ to be the entropy of its shift transformation $h(\mathbf{T})$.

The source $[\Sigma(S), \mu]$ is called *memoryless* provided the collection of partitions $\{\mathbf{T}^i\xi_S | i \in Z\}$ of $\Sigma(S)$ is an independent sequence of partitions, or the process $(\mathbf{T}, \xi_S)$ is an independent process. The entropy of a memoryless source is simply $H(\xi_S)$ (see Example 2.40). The source is a *Markov source* provided the process $(\mathbf{T}, \xi_S)$ is a Markov process (see Section 2.12.10).

The source $[\Sigma(S), \mu]$ is an *ergodic source* provided the transformation $\mathbf{T}_S$ is ergodic. Recall that an automorphism $\mathbf{T}$ is ergodic provided it has only trivial invariant sets. Notice that this is a property which is invariant under isomorphisms, so that if $[\Sigma(S), \mu]$ is an ergodic source, any other source $[\Sigma(F), \mu']$ isomorphic to it is also ergodic.

Another property similar to ergodicity is the *Bernoulli* property. A dynamical system $(\Omega, \mathfrak{F}, P, \mathbf{T})$ or the automorphism $\mathbf{T}$ is said to be Bernoulli provided the system is isomorphic to a Bernoulli shift (see Section 2.12.9). A source $[\Sigma(S), \mu]$ is Bernoulli provided $\mathbf{T}_S$ is Bernoulli. Thus a Bernoulli system is any dynamical system which is isomorphic to the shift on the path space of some doubly infinite sequence of independent identically distributed random variables. It is important to note the difference between a memoryless or Markov source on the one hand and a Bernoulli or ergodic source on the other. The former are properties of both the transformation and the partition, i.e. of the process $(\mathbf{T}, \xi_S)$, while the latter are properties of the transformation alone. For example, every memoryless (or mixing Markov) source is Bernoulli, while it is possible for the source to be Bernoulli and yet for the process $(\mathbf{T}, \xi_S)$ not to be an independent process. (See Chapter 4 for a discussion of this point.)

3.3 Coding

The output of a discrete source is a sequence of letters from a finite alphabet chosen according to the probability measure that determines the source. In order to transmit this output over some channel, we need to encode these messages into a usually different alphabet. We wish to do this in such a way that the message after transmission can be recovered, at least with a high probability of success. If A is the alphabet we use to encode the source $[\Sigma(S), \mu]$, then $(\Sigma(S), \mathfrak{F}_A)$ will serve as a reproducing space, where $\mathfrak{F}_A$ is the product σ-field on $\Sigma(S)$. A code is to be a rule which associates messages from $\Sigma(S)$ with messages from $\Sigma(A)$. Precisely, a *code* is a measurable function from $\Sigma(S)$ to $\Sigma(A)$. We specialize codes by placing conditions on the functions which represent them. We shall usually insist that codes be independent of time, that is, stationary. This means if ϕ is a code from $\Sigma(S)$ to $\Sigma(A)$, then $\phi \circ \mathbf{T}_S = \mathbf{T}_A \circ \phi$. We say that a code $\phi : \Sigma(S) \to \Sigma(A)$ is *invertible with respect to* μ provided there exists a subset Σ' of $\Sigma(S)$ with $\Sigma' \in \mathfrak{F}_S$, $\mu(\Sigma') = 1$, $\phi(\Sigma') \in \mathfrak{F}_A$ and such that ϕ is one to one on Σ'. This means that we can uniquely recover any message from Σ' that is emitted by the source. In terms of Definition 2.35, the existence of a code ϕ which is invertible with respect to μ is equivalent to an isomorphism of the dynamic systems $(\Sigma(S), \mathfrak{F}_S, \mathbf{T}_S, \mu)$ and $(\Sigma(A), \mathfrak{F}_A, \mathbf{T}_A, \mu\phi^{-1})$. Therefore, we can restate isomorphism theorems of dynamical systems in terms of the existence of codes. In particular (Corollary 2.38), the entropy is an isomorphism invariant for dynamical systems. Thus, if $[\Sigma(S), \mu]$ is a source with entropy h, if $\Sigma(A)$ is a reproducing space with an alphabet A containing n elements, and if ϕ is an invertible (with respect to μ) code from $\Sigma(S)$ to $\Sigma(A)$, it follows that the entropy $h_{\mu\phi^{-1}}$ of the dynamical system $(\Sigma(A), \mathfrak{F}_A, \mathbf{T}_A, \mu\phi^{-1})$ must equal h. However, Theorem 2.51 tells us that $h(\mathbf{T}_A) \leqslant \log n$ for any stationary measure in $\mathfrak{F}_A$. Hence a necessary condition for there to exist an invertible code from $[\Sigma(S), \mu]$ to $\Sigma(A)$ is that

$h(\mathbf{T}_S) \leqslant \log n$. In Chapter 4 we show that entropy is a complete invariant for Bernoulli shifts. Thus if $[\Sigma(S), \mu]$ is a Bernoulli source with entropy $h \leqslant \log n$, then we can find a measure ν on $\mathcal{F}_A$ which is stationary with respect to $\mathbf{T}_A$ such that $(\Sigma(A), \mathcal{F}_A, \mathbf{T}_A, \nu)$ is Bernoulli and $h(\mathbf{T}_A) = h$. Thus the shifts $\mathbf{T}_S$ and $\mathbf{T}_A$ with measures μ and ν, respectively are isomorphic. Hence if $[\Sigma(S), \mu]$ is a Bernoulli source, then there exists an invertible code from $\Sigma(S)$ to $\Sigma(A)$ if and only if the entropy of $[\Sigma(S), \mu]$ is less than or equal to $\log n$. Billingsley [20] was one of the first to indicate the connection between the isomorphism problem for Bernoulli shifts and (noiseless source) coding.

The type of code we have discussed to this point (i.e., an isomorphism) is not meaningful in a practical or engineering sense. The problem is that before we can determine anything about $\phi(\omega)$ we must have complete knowledge of $\omega \in \Sigma(S)$—complete future knowledge as well as past. Hence in proving the various coding theorems it is important to restrict the class of codes we consider. We will return to this topic in the context of these theorems.

3.4 The Channel

A channel is a device that operates on inputs from a source of a particular type and produces an output of another type for the destination. A channel is determined by the set of possible inputs and outputs together with a conditional probability distribution on the set of outputs. The channel is *discrete* if the input and output alphabets are finite. Let A and B denote the input and output alphabets, respectively. For each input message $\omega \in \Sigma(A)$ we are given a probability measure $P(\omega,\ )$ on the outputs $\Sigma(B)$. For $\omega \in \Sigma(A)$ and $C \in \mathcal{F}_B$ we interpret $P(\omega, C)$ as the probability that the output message belongs to C given that the input messages was ω. We also assume that for each $C \in \mathcal{F}_B$ the function $P(\ , C): \Sigma(A) \to \mathbf{R}$ is $\mathcal{F}_A$-measurable. We denote a channel by $[\Sigma(A), P(\omega,\ ), \Sigma(B)]$. Notice that if for each $\omega \in \Sigma(A)$ there is an $\eta \in \Sigma(B)$ such that $P(\omega, \{\eta\}) = 1$, then the resulting channel is simply an invertible code from $\Sigma(A)$ to $\Sigma(B)$. We shall always insist that the channel $[\Sigma(A), P(\omega,\ ), \Sigma(B)]$ be *stationary*, i.e., $P(\mathbf{T}_A\omega, \mathbf{T}_B C) = P(\omega, C)$ for all $\omega \in \Sigma(A)$ and $C \in \mathcal{F}_B$.

In order to simplify our discussion, we shall further restrict our discussion to a class of channels called memoryless. A discrete channel is *memoryless* provided the output letter at a given time depends only upon the corresponding input letter. If we let ξ_A and ξ_B be the time zero partitions of $\Sigma(A)$ and $\Sigma(B)$, respectively, then the condition for a channel to be memoryless is that for all $n \in Z$ and for all sets $C \in \mathbf{T}_B^n \xi_B$ the function $P(\ , C)$ is $\mathbf{T}_A^n \xi_A\hat{}$-measurable. Thus the conditional probabilities $P(\omega,\ )$ for a memoryless channel with $A = \{1, 2, \ldots, n\}$ and $B = \{1, 2, \ldots, m\}$ are determined by an m by n matrix C, where C_{ij} is the conditional probability of receiving i as output, given that the input to the channel was j. For each $\omega=(\ldots,j_{-1},j_0,j_1,\ldots)\in\Sigma(A)$ the measure $P(\omega,\ )$ is determined by

$$P(\omega,\{\bar{\omega}\in\Sigma(B):\bar{\omega}_k=i_k,p\leqslant k\leqslant q\})=\prod_{k=p}^{q}C_{i_kj_k}.$$

We now put a probability measure μ on the input space $\mathcal{F}_A$ of the channel, so that $[\Sigma(A),\mu]$ is a source. Using the measure space $(\Sigma(A),\mathcal{F}_A,\mu)$ and the measurable space $(\Sigma(B),\mathcal{F}_B)$ together with the channel measures $\{P(\omega,\ ):\omega\in\Sigma(A)\}$, we can apply Theorem 1.15 to obtain a measure p on $(\Sigma(A)\times\Sigma(B),\mathcal{F}_A\times\mathcal{F}_B)$. The measure p then induces a measure q on $(\Sigma(B),\mathcal{F}_B)$ if we define q to be the p-measure of sets of the form $\Sigma(A)\times C$ for $C\in\mathcal{F}_B$. Thus

$$q(C)=p(\Sigma(A)\times C)\qquad\text{for}\quad C\in\mathcal{F}_B.$$

This measure is called a marginal density. In case the channel is memoryless we have

$$\begin{aligned}
&p(\{\omega:\omega_k=j_k,p\leqslant k\leqslant q\}\times\{\eta:\eta_k=i_k,p\leqslant k\leqslant q\})\\
&\qquad=\prod_{k=p}^{q}C_{i_kj_k}\mu(\{\omega:\omega_k=j_k,p\leqslant k\leqslant q\}),\\
&q(\{\eta:\eta_k=i_k,p\leqslant k\leqslant q\})\\
&\qquad=\sum_{(j_p,\ldots,j_q)}\prod_{k=p}^{q}C_{i_kj_k}\mu(\{\omega:\omega_k=j_k,p\leqslant k\leqslant q\}).
\end{aligned}$$

If the source $[\Sigma(A),\mu]$ and the channel $[\Sigma(A),P(\omega,\ ),\Sigma(B)]$ are both stationary, then a straightforward calculation shows that the measures p and q are preserved by the shifts $\mathbf{T}_{A\times B}$ and $\mathbf{T}_B$, respectively. Thus we can apply the results concerning entropy to all three shifts: $\mathbf{T}_A$, $\mathbf{T}_{A\times B}$, and $\mathbf{T}_B$. In Section 3.2 we defined the entropy rate of the source $[\Sigma(A),\mu]$ to be $h(\mathbf{T}_A)$ because, since ξ_A is a generating partition, $h(\mathbf{T}_A)$ is equal to the "intuitively correct" definition $\lim_{n\to\infty}(1/n)H(\bigvee_{j=0}^{n-1}\mathbf{T}_A^{-j}\xi_A)$. We proceed as we did in Section 3.2 to define the rate at which the memoryless channel $[\Sigma(A),P(\omega,\ ),\Sigma(B)]$ processes information about the source $[\Sigma(A),\mu]$.

Given the time zero partition ξ_A of $\Sigma(A)$, the partition $\xi_A\times\Sigma(B)$ is a partition of $\Sigma(A)\times\Sigma(B)$ with the property that the processes $(\mathbf{T}_A,\xi_A)$ and $(\mathbf{T}_{A\times B},\xi_A\times\Sigma(B))$ are equivalent. Thus we shall use the less cumbersome notation $(\mathbf{T}_A,\xi_A)$ for the process $(\mathbf{T}_{A\times B},\xi_A\times\Sigma(B))$, and similarly $(\mathbf{T}_B,\xi_B)$ for $(\mathbf{T}_{A\times B},\Sigma(A)\times\xi_B)$.

In Section 2.5 we defined the mutual information between two partitions, ξ and η, to be $I(\xi;\eta)=H(\xi)-H(\xi/\eta)$, and we noted that this is a numerical measure of the average gain in information about ξ if we know the result of η. It is this idea we wish to use in measuring the rate of information processed by the channel. As before, we let $\xi_A^{(n)} = \bigvee_{j=0}^{n-1}\mathbf{T}_A^{-j}\xi_A$, and $\xi_B^{(n)} = \bigvee_{j=0}^{n-1}\mathbf{T}_B^{-j}\xi_B$ for each positive integer n. Thus $I(\xi_A^{(n)}, \xi_B^{(n)})$ is the average gain in information about the source by knowing the output over the time interval from 0 to $n-1$. Since $I(\xi_A^{(n)}; \xi_B^{(n)}) = H(\xi_A^{(n)}) - H(\xi_A^{(n)}/\xi_B^{(n)})$, this is the average amount of information produced by the source over the time interval from 0 to $n-1$ minus the average remaining uncertainty about the source after receiving the output in this time interval. Thus dividing this number by n results in the rate at which information about the source is processed by the channel over the appropriate time interval. Hence we define the *rate of information about the source* $[\Sigma(A), \mu]$ *processed by the channel* $[\Sigma(A), P(\omega, \ ), \Sigma(B)]$, also called rate of transmission of the channel, to be

$$R(\mu, P) = \lim_{n\to\infty} \frac{1}{n} I(\xi_A^{(n)}; \xi_B^{(n)}).$$

Since $I(\xi_A^{(n)}; \xi_B^{(n)}) = H(\xi_A^{(n)}) + H(\xi_B^{(n)}) - H(\xi_A^{(n)} \vee \xi_B^{(n)})$ by Equation (2.25), we can apply Equation (2.45) to get that $R(\mu, P)$ exists and that

$$R(\mu, P) = h(\mathbf{T}_A, \xi_A) + h(\mathbf{T}_B, \xi_B) - h(\mathbf{T}_{A\times B}, \xi_A \times \xi_B).$$

Since ξ_A, ξ_B and $\xi_A \times \xi_B$ are generating partitions, we have

$$R(\mu, P) = h(\mathbf{T}_A) + h(\mathbf{T}_B) - h(\mathbf{T}_{A\times B}).$$

The *rate of equivocation* or *equivocation* of the channel is defined to be the number

$$\lim_{n\to\infty} \frac{1}{n} H(\xi_A^{(n)}/\xi_B^{(n)}) = \lim_{n\to\infty} \frac{1}{n}\left[H(\xi_A^{(n)} \times \xi_B^{(n)}) - H(\xi_B^{n})\right]$$

$$= h(\mathbf{T}_{A\times B}) - h(\mathbf{T}_B).$$

Notice that the sum of the rate of transmission of a channel and its rate of equivocation is the entropy of the source. Thus the rate of transmission of a channel increases as its equivocation decreases. The equivocation is also closely related to the probability that the channel makes an error in transmission (Fano's inequality; see Ash [14]).

The usual situation is that the source alphabet is not the same as the input alphabet for the channel, and therefore it must be coded into the channel. There is a straightforward way to deal with this situation in the context of our previous discussion. Let $[\Sigma(S), \mu]$ be a source and

$[\Sigma(A), P(\omega, \ ), \Sigma(B)]$ be a channel. If $\phi: \Sigma(S) \to \Sigma(A)$ is a code, then we can construct a (compound) channel $[\Sigma(S), P(\phi(\omega), \ ), \Sigma(B)]$. We use the measures μ and $P(\phi(\omega), \ )$ and Theorem 1.15 to obtain a measure p on $\mathfrak{F}_S \times \mathfrak{F}_B$. The rate of transmission of the channel for the source $[\Sigma(S), \mu]$ is $R(\mu, P(\phi(\omega), \ ))$. Thus there is no loss in generality in assuming that the space of the source is the same as the input space of the channel.

The calculation of the rate of transmission of a channel and source is in general quite difficult. However, in case both the source and the channel are memoryless it is easy to calculate the transmission rate. Assume that $A = \{1,2,\dots,n\}$, $B = \{1,2,\dots,m\}$, and $C = (C_{ij})$ is the m by n channel matrix for the channel $[\Sigma(A), P(\omega, \ ), \Sigma(B)]$, and let $\mu = (\mu_1, \dots, \mu_n)$ be a probability distribution on A. In this case we have

$$p(i_0, i_1, \dots, i_k; j_0, j_1, \dots, j_k) = \prod_{l=0}^{k} C_{j_l i_l} \mu_{i_l} = \prod_{l=0}^{k} p(i_l, j_l),$$

so that $(\mathbf{T}_{A\times B}, \xi_A \times \xi_B)$ is an independent process. The definition of the marginal density q on $\mathfrak{F}_B$ implies that $(\mathbf{T}_B, \xi_B)$ is also an independent process. [The process $(\mathbf{T}_A, \xi_A)$ was assumed independent.] In addition, all three partitions ξ_A, ξ_B, and $\xi_A \times \xi_B$ generate their respective spaces. Thus, by Theorem 2.39 and Corollary 2.28 $h(\mathbf{T}_A) = H(\xi_A)$, $h(\mathbf{T}_B) = H(\xi_B)$, and $h(\mathbf{T}_{A\times B}) = H(\xi_A \vee \xi_B)$, so that in this case

$$R(\mu, P) = H(\xi_A) + H(\xi_B) - H(\xi_A \vee \xi_B).$$

If we keep the channel $[\Sigma(A), P(\omega, \ ), \Sigma(B)]$ fixed and allow the measure μ to vary over the set of stationary measures on $\mathfrak{F}_A$, then the rate of transmission $R(\mu, P)$ is simply a real valued function of μ. The *capacity of the channel*, $[\Sigma(A), P(\omega, \ ), \Sigma(B)]$, denoted by $C(P)$, is the supremum of all such rates, so

$$C(P) = \sup_{\mu} R(\mu, P).$$

For a general channel it is not known if there exists a measure μ on $\Sigma(A)$ such that $C(P) = R(\mu, P)$. In case the channel is memoryless there is a measure $\mu \in \mathfrak{F}_A$ so that $C(P) = R(\mu, P)$. To see this let $[\Sigma(A), \mu]$ be a source, and let $\mu_i = \mu(\{\omega \in \Sigma(A) : \omega_0 = i\})$ (i.e., μ_i is a distribution on the alphabet A). We define the function $\phi(\mu_1, \dots, \mu_n) = H(\xi_A) + H(\xi_B) - H(\xi_A \vee \xi_B)$. (Note that this is not equal to $R(\mu, P)$ unless the source $[\Sigma(A), \mu]$ is memoryless.) The function ϕ is a continuous function on a compact subset of $\mathbf{R}^n$ (see Section 2.11), and as such attains its maximum on this set. Let $(\bar{\mu}_1,\ldots,\bar{\mu}_n)$ be a point of this set at which ϕ attains its maximum. Use the distribution $\{\bar{\mu}_i\}$ on A to define the product measure $\bar{\mu}$ on $(\Sigma(A),\mathfrak{F}_A)$ as in Example 1.3. Then $[\Sigma(A),\bar{\mu}]$ is a memoryless source. Memoryless sources are clearly stationary, so $C(P)\geqslant\phi(\bar{\mu}_1,\bar{\mu}_2,\ldots,\bar{\mu}_n)$. Let μ be any stationary probability measure on $\Sigma(A)$. Since $I(\xi;\eta)$ is symmetric,

$$R(\mu,P)=\lim_{n\to\infty}\frac{1}{n}I(\xi_B^{(n)};\xi_A^{(n)})$$

$$=\lim_{n\to\infty}\frac{1}{n}\left[H(\xi_B^{(n)})-H(\xi_B^{(n)}/\xi_A^{(n)})\right].$$

Now note that in the case under consideration

$$H(\xi_B^{(n)}/\xi_A^{(n)})=-\sum_{i_0\ldots i_{n-1}}\sum_{j_0\ldots j_{k-1}}\left(\prod_{k=0}^{n-1}C_{j_ki_k}\mu_{i_k}\right)\log\prod_{k=0}^{n-1}C_{j_ki_k}$$

$$=-\sum_{i_0\ldots i_{n-1}}\sum_{j_0\ldots j_{k-1}}\left(\prod_{k=0}^{n-1}C_{j_ki_k}\mu_{i_k}\right)\left(\sum_{k=0}^{n-1}\log C_{j_ki_k}\right)$$

$$=\sum_{k=0}^{n-1}\left(C_{j_ki_k}\mu_{i_k}\log C_{j_ki_k}\right)\left(\sum_i\sum_j\prod_{l\neq k}C_{j_li_l}\mu_{i_l}\right)$$

$$=nH(\xi_B/\xi_A).$$

By repeated use of Corollary 2.12, we have

$$H(\xi_B^{(n)})=H\left[\bigvee_{j=0}^{n-1}\mathbf{T}^{-j}\xi_B\right]$$

$$\leqslant H(\xi_B)+H(\mathbf{T}^{-1}\xi_B)+\cdots+H(\mathbf{T}^{-(n-1)}\xi_B)$$

$$=nH(\xi_B).$$

Hence $(1/n)[H(\xi_B^{(n)})-H(\xi_B^{(n)}/\xi_A^{(n)})]\leqslant\phi(\mu_1,\ldots,\mu_n)$. This implies $R(\mu,P)\leqslant\phi(\bar{\mu}_1,\ldots,\bar{\mu}_n)$. Thus $C(P)\leqslant\phi(\bar{\mu}_1,\ldots,\bar{\mu}_n)$, and this together with our first observation proves $C(P)=\phi(\bar{\mu}_1,\ldots,\bar{\mu}_n)$. Therefore in case the channel is memoryless, its capacity is achieved by a memoryless source.

Channels are classified in terms of the rate at which they transmit information about the source. For example, if the equivocation is zero for all input distributions (which happens if and only if $C(P)=\log n$, where A

contains n elements) the channel is said to be *lossless*. The following is an example of a lossless channel. Take $A=\{1,2,3,4\}$, $B=\{1,2\}$, and let

$$C=\begin{bmatrix} 0 & \frac{1}{2} \\ \frac{1}{3} & 0 \\ \frac{1}{3} & 0 \\ \frac{1}{3} & 0 \\ 0 & \frac{1}{2} \end{bmatrix}$$

be the channel matrix of a memoryless channel. Let μ be any stationary probability measure on $(\Sigma(A), \mathcal{F}_A)$. Let $\mu_i=\mu\{\omega\in\Sigma(A): \omega_0=i\}$ for all $i=1,2$.

Using the channel matrix C and the source measure μ, we define the measures p and q on the channel and output as before. Then

$$H(\xi_A/\xi_B)=\sum_{j=1}^{2} q(j)\sum_{i=1}^{4}\frac{p(\{i,j\})}{p(\Sigma(A)\times\{j\})}\log\frac{p(\{i,j\})}{p(\Sigma(A)\times\{j\})}$$

Notice that for all $j\in B$ and $i\in A$ we have

$$\frac{p(\{i,j\})}{p(\Sigma(A)\times\{j\})}=\frac{\mu_i C_{ji}}{\sum_i \mu_i C_{ji}}=0 \text{ or } 1,$$

so $H(\xi_A/\xi_B)=0$. If we apply Corollary 2.12, we have

$$\begin{aligned} H(\xi_A^{(n)}/\xi_B^{(n)}) &\leq \sum_{j=0}^{n-1} H\left[\mathbf{T}^{-j}\xi_A \Big/ \bigvee_{j=0}^{n-1}\mathbf{T}^{-j}\xi_B\right] \\ &\leq \sum_{i=0}^{n-1} H(\mathbf{T}^{-j}\xi_A/\mathbf{T}^{-j}\xi_B) \\ &= \sum_{i=0}^{n-1} H(\xi_A/\xi_B)=0. \end{aligned}$$

Thus $R(\mu, P)=H(\xi_A)$ for any stationary input measure and the channel is lossless. If $\xi_A^{(\infty)}=\bigvee_{j=0}^{\infty}\mathbf{T}^{-j}\xi_A$ and $\xi_B^{(\infty)}=\bigvee_{j=0}^{\infty}\mathbf{T}^{-j}\xi_B$, then $H(\xi_A^{(\infty)}/\xi_B^{(\infty)})$ is the equivocation, which in this case is zero. Theorem 2.7 gives in this case that $\xi_A^{\infty}\leq\xi_B^{\infty}$. In other words, for a lossless channel, the output determines the input. If $C_{ji}=0$ or 1 for all $i\in A$ and $j\in B$, then the memoryless channel is said to be *deterministic*. For example, if $A=\{1,2\}$, $B=\{1,2,3,4\}$ and if

$$C=\begin{pmatrix} 0 & 0 & 1 & 1 \\ 1 & 1 & 0 & 0 \end{pmatrix},$$

then a 1 always goes to either a 3 or a 4, while a 2 always goes to a 1 or a 2. A channel that is both deterministic and lossless is called *noiseless*. Examples of other types of channels, including nonmemoryless, can be found in Ash [14], Gallager [43], and McEliece [86].

For a more general class of channels it is possible to have different types of capacity depending upon how the type of source is restricted. That is, we could have one number if we restricted ourselves to stationary sources, and another (of necessity not exceeding the first) if we restricted ourselves to ergodic sources. However, in the case of memoryless channels these numbers are equal, since we showed that the stationary capacity is attained by a memoryless (and hence ergodic) source.

3.5 The Noisy Channel Coding Theorem

We have now considered all the concepts needed to state the noisy channel coding theorem and understand its proof. This theorem gives operational significance to the notion of the capacity of a channel.

THEOREM 3.1. *Let* $[\Sigma(A), P(\omega,\ ), \Sigma(B)]$ *be a discrete memoryless channel with capacity* C *and let* $[\Sigma(S), \mu]$ *be an ergodic source with entropy* h. *If* $h<C$, *then for* $\varepsilon>0$ *there exists a code* $\phi: \Sigma(S)\to\Sigma(A)$ *such that the rate of transmission of the source over the channel,* $R(\mu\phi^{-1}, P)$, *is greater than* $h-\varepsilon$. *If* $h>C$, *then there exists no code* ϕ *for which* $R(\mu\phi^{-1}, P)=h$.

There are a number of different statements of this theorem, the form of which usually depends upon whether one wishes to measure the effectiveness of a channel in terms of its equivocation or probability of error. The particular form of the statement will frequently involve the type of code used in its proof. Proofs of this theorem for a class of codes called block codes can be found in Shannon [138], Gallager [43], or Billingsley [20]. A proof using sliding block codes can be found in Gray and Ornstein [53].

We complete this section with a short discussion of the proof of the fundamental theorem. The first task in the proof is to construct a decision scheme from which the code can be defined. This is done by examining the channel without reference to a particular source. That is, given the memoryless channel $[\Sigma(A), P(\omega,\ ), \Sigma(B)]$ with channel matrix C, then the conditional probabilities of output words given a particular input word depend only on C. This observation gives us the following scheme for transmitting a message through the channel. For a large integer k, if we transmit the code word having k ones followed by k twos (assuming $A=\{1,2,\dots,n\}$), then the frequency distribution within the first k elements of the received message should be very close to the first column of C, while the frequency distribution of the last k elements of the received message should be very close to the second column of C. Now, if we send the code word obtained by first sending k twos and then k ones, then the frequency distributions should first look like the second column of C and then the first column of C. Therefore, if these columns of C are different, then if we choose k large enough we should be able to distinguish between these two input messages by examining the outputs. The capacity of the channel is determined by the differences between the columns of C. That is, the columns of C are identical if and only if the capacity of the channel is zero. Thus, we simply have to see how the lengths of the code words are related to the capacity of the channel. Feinstein [37] formalized this procedure in the following theorem.

THEOREM 3.2. *Let* $[\Sigma(A), P(\omega,\ ), \Sigma(B)]$ *be a discrete memoryless channel with capacity* C. *For* $0<\varepsilon<C$ *there exists a positive integer* K *such that if* $k>K$, *then* A^k *(the product of* k *copies of* A*) contains* N *words* $\omega_1, \omega_2, \dots, \omega_N$, *and* B^k *(the product of* k *copies of* B*) can be partitioned into* N *corresponding sets* $U_1, U_2, \dots, U_N$ *such that*

$$p\{u\in U_i : \omega=\omega_i\}>1-\varepsilon, \qquad i=1,2,\dots,N,$$

and $N>e^{k(C-\varepsilon)}$.

This theorem gives us the following decision scheme. If we receive the word u (of length k), we determine which of the sets U_i contains u. Having done this, we should guess that the code word ω_i was transmitted. This scheme will have probability of error less then ε for a given source, provided we can code the source into $\Sigma(A)$ in such a way that we only send code words from our list $\omega_1, \dots, \omega_n$. Thus, we would like to show that for a given source with entropy less than C we can code it into $\Sigma(A)$ so that the resulting measure on A^k, for properly chosen k, has the measure of the set $\{y\in A^k : y\in\{\omega_1,\dots,\omega_N\}\}$ equal to 1. This structure gives rise to a type of code called a k-block code. A *k-block code* ϕ from $\Sigma(S)$ to $\Sigma(A)$ is a code that is determined by a (super) code $\phi' : \Sigma(S^k)\to\Sigma(A^k)$. There is a natural correspondence between messages in $\Sigma(S)$ and in $\Sigma(S^k)$, given as follows: $(\dots,\omega_{-1},\omega_0,\omega_1,\dots)\in\Sigma(S)$ corresponds to

$$\omega'=(\dots,\omega'_{-1},\omega'_0,\omega'_1,\dots), \text{where } \omega'_n=(\omega_{kn},\omega_{kn+1},\dots,\omega_{kn+k-1}).$$

With these ideas the proof is finished in the following manner. We choose k large enough so that we can apply Feinstein's theorem and so that the equipartition theorem (Corollary 2.54) holds. In this case we have by the equipartition theorem that there exists a set $E_k \subset S^k$ such that $\mu\{S^k - E_k\} < \varepsilon$ and if $x \in E_k$ then $\mu(\{x\}) > e^{-k(h+\varepsilon)}$, where h denotes the entropy of the ergodic source $[\Sigma(S), \mu]$. Now, A^k contains N code words, where $N > e^{k(C-\varepsilon)}$. Because $\mu(E_k) < 1$, E_k contains at most $e^{k(h+\varepsilon)}$ words. If we have chosen ε small enough $[\varepsilon < (C-h)/2]$, then there are more code words in A^k than source words in E_k. Thus there exists a function $\phi' : S^k \to \{\omega_1, \ldots, \omega_n\} \in A^k$ that is one to one on E_k and sends all words in $S^k - E_k$ to one word. This function gives rise to a k-block code from $\Sigma(S)$ to $\Sigma(A)$. By a careful analysis of the equivocation, primarily using Fano's theorem [14], we can show that the equivocation is small.

The argument given for the noisy channel coding theorem is not satisfactory from a practical, or constructive, point of view. Block codes, such as those used above, are hard to construct and usually hard to analyze. The noisy channel coding theorem should therefore be viewed as an existence theorem with a nonconstructive proof. The problem of constructing codes which can actually be implemented and whose effectiveness can be analyzed is formidable. McEliece [86] devotes the second half of his volume in this series to coding theory, and the reader interested in these problems should consult that work.

3.6 Source Coding

In Section 3.1 we noted that if the source produces information at a rate which exceeds the capacity of the channel, then the overall operation of coding the source into the channel can be factored into source coding and channel coding. The object of source coding is to map the source into an approximation of itself which has an entropy rate that does not exceed the capacity of the channel.

Most of the theory of source coding [86] has used block codes. In this section we discuss a type of code, called a sliding block code, which comes from an adaptation of a technique used by Ornstein in proving the isomorphism theorem (Theorem 4.38). We shall give a noiseless source coding theorem to describe this class of codes, and then a theorem about source coding with a fidelity criterion. The proof of this latter theorem involves a construction similar to that used in the proof of Theorem 4.38, but the proof is easier and can serve as motivation for the necessity portion of the isomorphism theorem. We end the section with a particularly simple example of a sliding block code. This example is also a type of code which is often used in modern ergodic theory. The ideas involved in sliding block codes, arising as they do from work on the isomorphism problem, have demonstrated a deep connection between coding theory and the theory of approximation of stochastic processes.

At the end of Section 3.3 we noted that codes of the type that arise from isomorphisms between dynamical systems are usually not practical because they involve knowing the entire message before we can know any part of its coded form. In proving the noisy channel coding theorem we attempted to overcome this difficulty by using block codes. However, besides the problems mentioned in the last paragraph of Section 3.5, these codes are not stationary and are usually sensitive to errors made by the channel. In addition a number of the techniques used in practice are not covered by the theory of block codes. The notion of sliding block codes and its extension to finitary codes seem to be of some value for practical application.

Most of the notations and results from measure theory needed to understand this section have been developed. The one notion which has not been introduced and will be needed is a distance function, $\bar{d}$, between sources. This function measures how well two stochastic processes can be matched up at a single time if they are connected by a stationary channel. Specifically, assume we are given two sources (i.e. stationary processes), $[\Sigma(S), \mu]$ and $[\Sigma(S), \nu]$ with the same alphabet S. As we have indicated above, a stationary channel joining these sources can be viewed as a shift invariant measure p on $\mathcal{F}_S \times \mathcal{F}_S$ such that for each $A \in \mathcal{F}_S$ we have $p(\Sigma(S) \times A) = \nu(A)$ and $p(A \times \Sigma(S)) = \mu(A)$. Measures with this property are said to have the "right marginals". Let $\mathcal{C}$ denote the class of all such measures. The $\bar{d}$-distance between the sources $[\Sigma(S), \mu]$ and $[\Sigma(S), \nu]$ is defined by the equation

$$\bar{d}([\Sigma(S), \mu], [\Sigma(S), \nu]) = \inf\{p\{(\omega, \bar{\omega}) : \omega_0 \neq \bar{\omega}_0\} : p \in \mathcal{C}\}.$$

Suppose $S = \{s_1, s_2, \ldots, s_n\}$ is a finite alphabet; and let ξ_0 denote the time zero partition of $\Sigma(S)$, and $d_\mu(\xi_0)$ and $d_\nu(\xi_0)$ the discrete probability distributions associated with the (ordered) partition ξ_0 and measures μ and ν respectively. That is,

$$d_\mu(\xi_0) = (\mu\{\omega : \omega_0 = s_1\}, \ldots, \mu\{\omega : \omega_0 = s_n\})$$

and

$$d_\nu(\xi_0) = (\nu\{\omega : \omega_0 = s_1\}, \ldots, \nu\{\omega : \omega_0 = s_n\}).$$

It is easy to show that

$$\bar{d}([\Sigma(S), \mu], [\Sigma(S), \nu]) \leq |d_\mu(\xi_0) - d_\nu(\xi_0)|,$$

where $|d_\mu(\xi_0) - d_\nu(\xi_0)| = \sum_{k=1}^{n} |\mu\{\omega : \omega_0 = s_k\} - \nu\{\omega : \omega_0 = s_k\}|$ is just the l^1 norm in R^n.

Actually, if the sources are Bernoulli, or independent sources, and ξ_0 is the independent generator, then

$$\bar{d}([\Sigma(S),\mu],[\Sigma(S),\nu])=|d_\mu(\xi_0)-d_\nu(\xi_0)|,$$

which we now show.

Define a distribution vector $p=(p_{ij}:1\leqslant i\leqslant n,\ 1\leqslant j\leqslant n)$ as follows. Assume that $\xi_0=(\{\omega:\omega_0=s_k\}:1\leqslant k\leqslant n)$ has been ordered so that

$$\mu(\{\omega:\omega_0=s_k\})\leqslant\nu(\{\omega:\omega_0=s_K\})\quad\text{if}\quad 1\leqslant k\leqslant l,$$

$$\mu(\{\omega:\omega_0=s_k\})>\nu(\{\omega:\omega_0=s_k\})\quad\text{if}\quad l+1\leqslant k\leqslant n.$$

Let μ_i and ν_i denote respectively the μ- and ν-measures of the ith atom of the partition ξ_0. Define

$$p_{ii}=\begin{cases}\mu_i & \text{if} \quad i\leqslant l,\\ \nu_i & \text{if} \quad i>l,\end{cases}$$

and for $i\neq j$,

$$p_{ij}=\begin{cases}0 & \text{if} \quad 1\leqslant i\leqslant l, 1\leqslant j\leqslant n,\\ 0 & \text{if} \quad l+1\leqslant i\leqslant n, l+1\leqslant j\leqslant n,\\ a_{ij} & \text{if} \quad l+1\leqslant i\leqslant n, 1\leqslant j\leqslant l,\end{cases}$$

where $\{a_{ij}:l+1\leqslant i\leqslant n, 1\leqslant j\leqslant l, i\neq j\}$ is any set of nonnegative numbers such that $\sum_{i=l+1}^{n}a_{ij}=\nu_j-\mu_j$ for $j=1,2,\ldots,l$ and $\sum_{j=1}^{l}a_{ij}=\mu_i-\nu_i$ for $i=l+1,\ldots,n$. [Notice there is considerable choice left in the selection of the $l(n-l)$ numbers a_{ij}.] If we form the independent process $(\mathbf{T}_s\times\mathbf{T}_s,\xi_0\times\xi_0)$ by using the distribution on $S\times S$ given by $p(s_i,s_j)=p_{ij}$, it is easily seen that $p\in\mathcal{C}$ and

$$p(\{(\omega,\bar{\omega}):\omega_0\neq\bar{\omega}_0\})=\sum_{i\neq j}p_{ij}=|d_{\xi_0}(\mu)-d_{\xi_0}(\nu)|.$$

This shows that at least for independent processes the $\bar{d}$-distance between sources is a measure of how well two sources can be matched up by a stationary channel.

In general, computing the $\bar{d}$-distance between two stationary processes is not easy [74]. We shall return to a discussion of the $\bar{d}$-metric and a natural generalization of it in the context of our discussion of source coding with a fidelity criterion. In the next chapter, we shall use the $\bar{d}$-metric in a somewhat different form. It is not immediate that these various forms are equivalent. A proof of their equivalence is given in [52].

Let a source $[\Sigma(S),\mu]$ be given, and let $(\Sigma(A),\mathfrak{F}_A)$ be a reproducing space. That is, A is the reproducing alphabet and $\mathfrak{F}_A$ denotes the product σ-field in $\Sigma(A)$. We denote the Cartesian product of k copies of S by S^k. For each positive integer N, a *sliding block encoder* of block length N is a function $f^{(N)}$ on S^{2N+1} to A. We can use the function $f^{(N)}$ to define a function ψ from $\Sigma(S)$ to $\Sigma(A)$ by taking

$$(\psi(\omega))_n=f^{(N)}(\omega_{n-N},\dots,\omega_n,\dots,\omega_{n+N})$$

for $n=0,\pm 1,\pm 2,\dots$. The term sliding block is used because one can visualize the encoding process (via $f^{(N)}$) by way of the diagram in Figure 3.2. The source message ω is moved each time unit by one letter through a shift register, and at each time the encoded letter $[\psi(\omega)]_n$ represents a reproduction of the source letter at the center of the register.

This definition also works as well for $N=\infty$. In this case $f^{(\infty)}$ is a map on $\Sigma(S)$ to A and is called an infinite length sliding block encoder. The encoded sequence $\psi(\omega)$ corresponding to a source message ω is given by $[\psi(\omega)]_n=f^{(\infty)}(\mathbf{T}_S^n\omega)$, where $\mathbf{T}_S$ is the shift on $\Sigma(S)$. Of course the function ψ is a code in the sense of Section 3.3. Conversely, any code (i.e., metric isomorphism) ψ from $\Sigma(S)$ to $\Sigma(A)$ defines a unique infinite length sliding block encoder $f^{(\infty)}$ by $f^{(\infty)}(\omega)=[\psi(\omega)]_0$. In addition every infinite length sliding block encoder $f^{(\infty)}$ defines a partition of $\Sigma(S)$ containing as many atoms as there are elements in the alphabet A if one takes the ith atom of

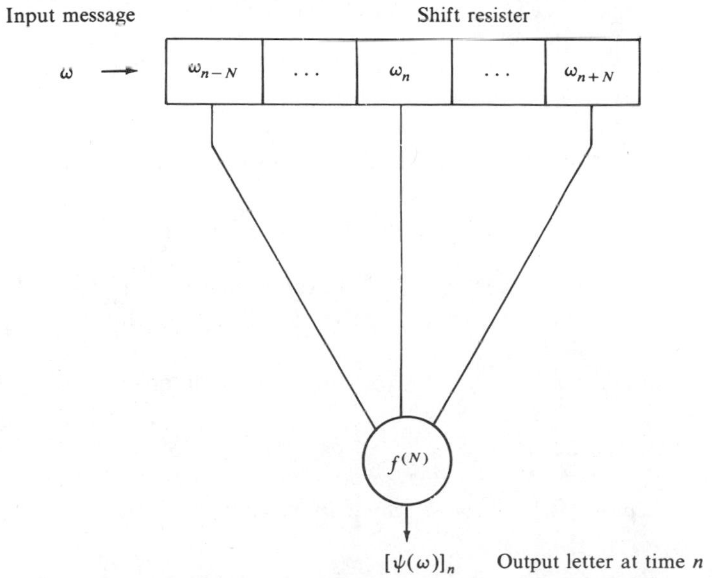

Figure 3.2

the partition to be the inverse image under $f^{(\infty)}$ of the ith letter in the alphabet A. Conversely, an ordered partition ξ of $\Sigma(S)$ containing as many atoms as there are elements in the alphabet A defines an infinite sliding block encoder $f^{(\infty)}$ if one takes $f^{(\infty)}(\omega)$ to be a_i if and only if $\omega \in \xi(i)$, the ith atom of the partition ξ. (Note that we are implicitly assuming the alphabet A is also ordered so that a_i is the ith letter of the alphabet.)

In the same way a sliding block encoder of length N is uniquely associated with a partition of S^{2N+1} which contains as many atoms as there are elements of the alphabet A. Furthermore, there is a one to one correspondence between elements of S^{2N+1} and atoms of $\bigvee_{j=-N}^{N} \mathbf{T}_S^j \xi_S$. It follows from Lemma 1.10 that any measurable partition of $\Sigma(S)$ may be approximated as well as we wish by a partition whose atoms are sets in $(\bigvee_{j=-N}^{N} \mathbf{T}^j \xi_S)^{\wedge}$, provided N is sufficiently large. This observation stated in terms of encoders becomes

LEMMA 3.3 [49]. *Given a source* $[\Sigma(S), \mu]$, *an infinite sliding block encoder* $f^{(\infty)}: \Sigma(S) \to A$, *and* $\varepsilon > 0$, *there exists a positive integer* $N = N(\varepsilon, f^{(\infty)})$ *and a sliding block encoder of length* N, $f^{(N)}: S^{2N+1} \to A$, *such that*

$$\mu\left(\left\{\omega \in \Sigma(S) : f^{(\infty)}(\omega) \neq f^{(N)}(\omega_{-N}, \ldots, \omega_0, \ldots, \omega_N)\right\}\right) \leqslant \varepsilon.$$

Proof. Let η denote the partition of $\Sigma(S)$ associated with $f^{(\infty)}$. By Lemma 1.10 there exists an N and a partition $\bar{\eta}$ with as many atoms as η such that $\bar{\eta} \leqslant \bigvee_{j=-N}^{N} \mathbf{T}_S^j \xi_S$, and $\Sigma_i \mu(\eta(i) \triangle \bar{\eta}(i)) \leqslant \varepsilon$. Define $f^{(N)}$ on S^{2N+1} to $A = \{a_1, a_2, \ldots, a_n\}$ by

$$f^{(N)}(s_0, s_1, \ldots, s_{2N+1}) = a_i \text{ iff } \quad \{\omega : \omega_{-N} = s_0, \ldots, \omega_N = s_{2N+1}\} \subset \bar{\eta}(i).$$

It is clear that this is a sliding block encoder of length N and

$$\mu\left(\left\{\omega : f^{(\infty)}(\omega) \neq f^{(N)}(\omega_{-N}, \ldots, \omega_N)\right\}\right) \leqslant \varepsilon.$$

This lemma says that $f^{(\infty)}$ and $f^{(N)}$ each applied to the source $[\Sigma(S), \mu]$ produce the same letter at any given time with probability at least $1 - \varepsilon$.

The second observation we make gives a bound on the number of output symbols that can be in error due to a single error.

THEOREM 3.4. *Let* $f^{(N)}: S^{2N+1} \to A$ *be a sliding block encoder of length* N, *and let* $\{W_n\}$ *and* $\{V_n\}$ *be two stationary sequences defined on the same probability space* $(\Omega, \mathfrak{F}, P)$ *with values in* S. *Then*

$$\mathrm{P}\left\{f^{(N)}(W_{-N}, \ldots, W_0, \ldots, W_N) \neq f^{(N)}(V_{-N}, \ldots, V_0, \ldots, V_N)\right\} \leqslant (2N+1)\mathrm{P}\{W_0 \neq V_0\}.$$

Proof. The proof is obtained by the following calculation.

$$\begin{aligned}
\mathrm{P}\{f^{(N)}(W_{-N},\dots,W_N)\neq f^{(N)}(V_{-N},\dots,V_N)\}
&= P\{\omega:(W_{-N}(\omega),\dots,W_N(\omega))\neq(V_{-N}(\omega),\dots,V_N(\omega))\}\\
&\leqslant P\left(\bigcup_{i=-N}^{N}\{\omega: W_i(\omega)\neq V_i(\omega)\}\right)\\
&\leqslant (2N+1)P\{\omega: W_0(\omega)\neq V_0(\omega)\}\\
&= (2N+1)\mathrm{P}\{W_0\neq V_0\}.
\end{aligned}$$

In order to state and prove a theorem for noiseless sliding block source coding we need to introduce the notion of a source encoder-decoder pair $(f_E^{(N)}, f_D^{(M)})$. As might be expected, this is just a pair of sliding block encoders with $f_E^{(N)}: S^{2N+1}\to A$ and $f_D^{(M)}: A^{2M+1}\to S$. The errors made in using a encoder-decoder pair can be thought of as noise. Let $\mathfrak{S}$ denote the set of all points $\omega\in\Sigma(S)$ for which an error is made in using the encoder-decoder pair—i.e.,

$$\mathfrak{S}=\{\omega\in\Sigma(S): \omega_0\neq f_D^{(M)}(f_E^{(N)}\circ \mathbf{N}^N\circ \mathbf{T}_S^{-M}(\omega),\dots, f_E^{(N)}\circ \mathbf{N}^N\circ \mathbf{T}_S^{-M}(\omega))\},$$

where $\mathbf{N}^N:\Sigma(S)\to S^{2N+1}$ is defined by projection, i.e., $\mathbf{N}^N(\omega)=(\omega_{-N},\dots,\omega_N)$. Then the pair is said to be ε-noiseless provided $\mu(\mathfrak{S})\leqslant\varepsilon$. A noiseless pair is one for which $\mu(\mathfrak{S})=0$, i.e., the probability of making an error in decoding is zero.

THEOREM 3.5 [49]. *If two sources $[\Sigma(S),\mu]$ and $[\Sigma(A),\nu]$ are isomorphic, then there exists an infinite length noiseless encoder-decoder pair $(f_E^{(\infty)}, f_D^{(\infty)})$ such that the encoded process is $[\Sigma(A),\nu]$. Furthermore, given $\varepsilon>0$ there exists a finite length ε-noiseless encoder-decoder pair $(f_E^{(N)}, f_D^{(M)})$ such that the encoded process is within ε of $[\Sigma(A),\nu]$ in the $\bar{d}$-distance.*

Proof. Since $[\Sigma(S),\mu]$ and $[\Sigma(A),\nu]$ are isomorphic, there exists a code $\phi:\Sigma(S)\to\Sigma(A)$ (see Section 3.3). Let $f_E^{(\infty)}$ and $f_D^{(\infty)}$ denote the infinite length sliding block encoders corresponding to ϕ and ϕ^{-1} respectively. We apply Lemma 3.3 to $f_D^{(\infty)}$ to obtain a finite length sliding block encoder $f_D^{(M)}: A^{2M+1}\to S$ such that

$$\nu(\{y\in\Sigma(A): f_D^{(\infty)}(y)\neq f_D^{(M)}(y_{-M},\dots,y_M)\})\leqslant\varepsilon/2.$$

Since ϕ is an isomorphism,

$$\begin{aligned}
&\mu(\{x\in\Sigma(S): f_D^{(\infty)}(\phi(x))\neq f_D^{(M)}((\phi(x))_{-M},\dots,(\phi(x))_M)\})\\
&\qquad=\nu(\{y\in\Sigma(A): f_D^{(\infty)}(y)\neq f_D^{(M)}(y_{-M},\dots,y_M)\})\\
&\qquad\leqslant\varepsilon/2. \qquad (3.1)
\end{aligned}$$

Now use Lemma 3.3 again applied to $f_E^{(\infty)}$ to choose a finite length encoder $f_E^{(N)}$ such that

$$\mu\big(\{x\in\Sigma(S): f_E^{(\infty)}(x)\neq f_E^{(N)}(x_{-N},\dots,x_N)\}\big)\leq\frac{\varepsilon}{4M+2}. \tag{3.2}$$

Define the map $z:\Sigma(S)\to S$ by $z(x)=f_D^{(M)}((\phi(x))_{-M},\dots,(\phi(x))_M)$, so that $z(x)$ is the decoded letter using the finite decoder and the infinite encoder. Likewise let $\hat{x}:\Sigma(S)\to S$ be defined by

$$\hat{x}(x)=f_D^{(M)}\big(f_E^{(N)}\circ\mathbf{N}^N\circ\mathbf{T}_S^{-M}(x),\dots,f_E^{(N)}\circ\mathbf{N}^N\circ\mathbf{T}_S^{M}(x)\big),$$

so that $\hat{x}(x)$ is the decoded letter using the finite encoder-decoder pair.

Let $d: S\times S\to\{0,1\}$ be defined by $d(x,y)=0$ if $x=y$ and $d(x,y)=1$ if $x\neq y$. Then

$$\mu(\mathcal{E})=\int_{\Sigma(S)}\mu(dx)\,d(x_0,\hat{x}(x))$$

$$\leq\int_{\Sigma(S)}\mu(dx)\,d(x_0,z(x))+\int_{\Sigma(S)}\mu(dx)\,d(z(x),\hat{x}(x)). \tag{3.3}$$

If we define the stationary processes $\{W_n\}$ and $\{V_n\}$ by $W_n(x)=f_E^{(\infty)}\circ\mathbf{T}_S^n(x)$ and $V_n(x)=f_E^{(N)}\circ\mathbf{N}^N\circ\mathbf{T}_S^n(x)$, we can apply Theorem 3.4 to $\{W_n\}$, $\{V_n\}$, and $f_D^{(M)}$ to obtain

$$\int_{\Sigma(S)}\mu(dx)\,d(z(x),\hat{x}(x))=\mu(\{x: z(x)\neq\hat{x}(x)\})$$

$$\leq(2M+1)\mu\{x: W_0(x)\neq V_0(x)\}$$

$$=(2M+1)\mu\big(\{x: f_E^{(\infty)}(x)\neq f_E^{(N)}(x_{-N},\dots,x_N)\}\big).$$

The inequality (3.2) then gives that

$$\int_{\Sigma(S)}\mu(dx)\,d(z(x),\hat{x}(x))\leq\varepsilon/2. \tag{3.4}$$

Since ϕ is an isomorphism and $f_E^{(\infty)}$ is its associated infinite length sliding block encoder, we have that

$$\mu\{x\in\Sigma(S): x_0\neq z(x)\}$$

$$=\mu\{x: f_D^{(\infty)}(\phi(x))\neq f_D^{(M)}((\phi(x))_{-M},\dots,(\phi(x))_M)\}$$

and the inequality (3.1) gives

$$\int_{\Sigma(S)}\mu(dx)\,d(x,z(x))\leq\varepsilon/2. \tag{3.5}$$

Combining the inequalities (3.4) and (3.5) with (3.3) gives $\mu(\mathcal{E}) \leqslant \varepsilon$.

Furthermore, by noting that the stationary process defined by $f_E^{(\infty)}$ (i.e., $\{W_n\}$ above) is the process defined by the source $[\Sigma(A), \nu]$, the inequality (3.2) implies that the encoded process defined by $f_E^{(N)}$ is within $\varepsilon/(4M+2)$ of that defined by $[\Sigma(A), \nu]$ in the $\bar{d}$-distance, and the theorem is proven.

By combining this theorem with the Ornstein isomorphism theorem (sufficiency of entropy for isomorphism of Bernoulli systems; see Theorem 4.38) we obtain the following corollary.

COROLLARY 3.6. *If* $[\Sigma(S), \mu]$ *and* $[\Sigma(A), \nu]$ *are Bernoulli sources with the same entropy, then there exists an infinite length noiseless encoder-decoder pair such that the encoded process is* $[\Sigma(A), \nu]$. *Furthermore for every* $\varepsilon > 0$ *there is a finite length* ε*-noiseless encoder-decoder pair such that the encoded process is within* ε *of* $[\Sigma(A), \nu]$ *in the* $\bar{d}$*-distance.*

In order to interpret Theorem 3.5 in the setting of source coding, that is, coding a source into a channel in such a way that entropy is reduced, we take the second source of Theorem 3.5, $[\Sigma(A), \nu]$, to be an independent, identically distributed sequence of equally likely letters, i.e., a Bernoulli shift with uniform distribution, so that $h(\mathrm{T}_A) = \log k$ if A has k letters. Such a choice for $[\Sigma(A), \nu]$ is the most efficient because it has the least possible redundancy (i.e. maximal entropy). With this choice of $[\Sigma(A), \nu]$, Theorem 3.5 states that the source $[\Sigma(S), \nu]$ can be encoded in an ε-noiseless way into a process arbitrarily close to $[\Sigma(A), \nu]$ in the $\bar{d}$-distance. For example any source with entropy equal to one bit per symbol can be encoded into a process which is arbitrarily close in the $\bar{d}$-distance to an independent coin toss with a fair coin. Furthermore this coding can be done in such a way that it may be decoded with arbitrarily small probability of making an error.

We now turn our attention to source coding with a fidelity condition. As indicated in Section 3.1, we shall not discuss the usual distortion rate function. Instead we discuss the concept of a fidelity criterion with the notion of a $\bar{\rho}$-distance between stationary processes [50]. This is a natural generalization of the $\bar{d}$-distance we discussed above. The connection between the $\bar{\rho}$-distance and the distortion rate function is considered in detail in [51].

Assume we are given an ergodic source $[\Sigma(S), \mu]$ on a finite alphabet S. Let A be a reproducing alphabet with reproducing space $(\Sigma(A), \mathcal{F}_A)$. A single letter nonnegative distortion measure is a nonnegative function ρ defined on $S \times A$. For (s, a) given, $\rho(s, a)$ is thought of as the penality or distortion made by reproducing the source symbol s as a.

Let $f^{(N)}: S^{2N+1} \to A$ be a given sliding block encoder, and $\{\tilde{X}_n\}$ the stationary stochastic process defined on $[\Sigma(S), \mu]$ by

$$\tilde{X}_n(\omega) = f^{(N)}(\omega_{-N}, \ldots, \omega_N).$$

If ρ is a single letter nonnegative distortion measure, the average distortion of the sliding block code $f^{(N)}$ is given by

$$\rho(f^{(N)}) = E(\rho(\omega_0, \tilde{X}_0))$$
$$= \int_{\Sigma(S)} \mu(d\omega)\rho(\omega_0, \tilde{X}_0(\omega)).$$

Notice that the realization space of the process $\tilde{X}_n$[i.e., the space of sequences $\{\tilde{X}_n(\omega)\}_{n=-\infty}^{+\infty}$] is $\Sigma(A)$ and hence induces a measure ν on $(\Sigma(A), \mathfrak{F}_A)$. The space $(\Sigma(A), \mathfrak{F}_A, \nu, \mathbf{T}_A)$, where $\mathbf{T}_A$ is the shift, is the reproducing process, and we shall call the entropy of this process the entropy of the sliding block encoder. That is, the entropy of $f^{(N)}$, denoted by $h(f^{(N)})$, is given by $h(f^{(N)}) = h(\mathbf{T}_A)$.

Since the object of source coding is to map the source into an approximation of itself which has entropy less than that of the source, we need a measure of how good an approximation we have in terms of ρ. This is done by using a quantity known as the optimal performance theoretically attainable (OPTA), which is defined as follows.

Given a positive number R (the maximum rate allowed) and a block length $2N+1$, define $\delta(R, N)$ by

$$\delta(R, N) = \inf\{\rho(f^{(N)})\},$$

where the infimum is over all encoders $f^{(N)}$ such that $h(f^{(N)}) \leqslant R$. Then the OPTA, $\delta(R)$, is defined by

$$\delta(R) = \inf\{\delta(R, N) : N \geqslant 0\}.$$

One sees from the definition that $\delta(R)$ is the smallest average distortion per time unit attainable by using a finite length sliding block encoder over a channel with transmission rate R.

Note that $\delta(R) = \lim_{N\to\infty} \delta(R, N)$ and δ is a continuous function of R.

If $[\Sigma(S), \mu]$ and $[\Sigma(A), \nu]$ are two sources, and ρ a given single letter nonnegative distortion measure on $S \times A$, the $\bar{\rho}$-distance between these sources is defined by

$$\bar{\rho}([\Sigma(S), \mu], [\Sigma(A), \nu]) = \inf \int_{\Sigma(S)\times\Sigma(A)} p[d(x, y)]\rho(x_0, y_0),$$

where the infimum is taken over all stationary measures p on $\mathfrak{F}_A \times \mathfrak{F}_A$ such that $p(\Sigma(S) \times E) = \nu(E)$ and $p(E \times \Sigma(A)) = \mu(E)$. The $\bar{d}$-metric considered earlier in this section is a special case of this metric with $\rho(x, y) = 0$ if $x = y$ and 1 otherwise.

We are now ready to consider the source coding subject to a fidelity criterion theorem.

THEOREM 3.7 [50]. *If $[\Sigma(S), \mu]$ is an ergodic process, S finite, and ρ is a single letter nonnegative distortion measure, then*

$$\delta(R) = \inf\{\bar{\rho}([\Sigma(S), \mu], [\Sigma(A), \nu])\},$$

where the infimum is taken over all process $[\Sigma(A),\nu]$ *with* A *finite and* $h(\mathbf{T}_A)\leqslant R$.

This theorem states that the optimal attainable distortion using a sliding block source encoder is given by the $\bar{\rho}$-distance between the source process and any process with entropy no more than the given rate.

It is immediate from the definition of $\delta(R)$ that

$$\delta(R)\geqslant \inf\{\bar{\rho}([\Sigma(A),\mu],[\Sigma(A),\nu])\},$$

since if $f^{(N)}$ is a finite length encoder such that $\rho(f^{(N)})$ is within ε of $\delta(R)$, then it induces a measure $\hat{\mu}$ on $\Sigma(A)$ such that the entropy of $[\Sigma(A),\hat{\mu}]$ does not exceed R and $\bar{\rho}([\Sigma(S),\mu],[\Sigma(A),\hat{\mu}])\leqslant\delta(R)+\varepsilon$.

The reverse inequality follows from the following lemma.

LEMMA 3.8. *If* $[\Sigma(S),\mu]$ *and* $[\Sigma(A),\nu]$ *are ergodic sources with finite alphabets,* ρ *is a single letter nonnegative distortion measure, and* $\delta>0$, *there exists an integer* N_0 *such that for all* $N\geqslant N_0$ *there is a sliding block encoder* $f^{(N)}$ *for* $[\Sigma(S),\mu]$ *such that*

$$\rho(f^{(N)})\leqslant\bar{\rho}([\Sigma(S),\mu],[\Sigma(A),\nu])+\delta$$

and

$$h(f^{(N)})\leqslant h(\mathbf{T}_A)+\delta.$$

The proof of this lemma involves an argument which is quite a bit different from that used in the usual block source coding theorem. Those proofs are obtained by randomly generating a set of codebooks and then proving that there exists at least one codebook in the set that works nearly optimally. The proof for sliding block encoders involves constructing a good picture of a joint process "inside" a process representing the source. This picture, called a stack, in turn gives rise to a sliding block encoder. This technique resembles the one used in proving the isomorphism theorem (see Section 4.5). While this construction again has limited practical appeal, it has led recently to a class of codes which have the possibility of being implementable.

The object we wish to use in the proof of Lemma 3.8 is called an (ε,n)-stack. Its existence is discussed in detail in Section 4.5 of the next chapter, and so we simply fix the notation at this point.

Let $(\Omega,\mathcal{F},P,\mathbf{T})$ be an invertible dynamical system, and ξ a finite ordered partition of Ω with atoms denoted by $\xi(i)$ for $i=1,2,\ldots,k$. The discrete probability distribution $(P(\xi(1)),\ldots,P(\xi(k)))$ is called the distribution of the partition and is denoted by $d(\xi)$. Given any set $E\in\mathcal{F}$, $E\cap(\bigvee_{j=0}^{n-1}\mathbf{T}^{-j}\xi)$ is an ordered partition of E, induced by the partition $\bigvee_{j=0}^{n-1}\mathbf{T}^{-j}\xi$ given the lexicographic order. If $P(E)>0$, then $d(E\cap(\bigvee_{j=0}^{n-1}\mathbf{T}^{-j}\xi))$ is the distribution of this partition in the space $(E,\mathcal{F}_E,P_E)$. The strong form of the

Kakutani-Rohlin theorem (Theorem 4.31) states that if $(\Omega, \mathcal{F}, P, T)$ is an ergodic system and ξ is a finite partition of Ω, then for every positive number c and every positive integer n, there exists a set $E \in \mathcal{F}$ such that $E, \mathbf{T}E, \ldots, \mathbf{T}^{n-1}E$ are disjoint, $P(\bigcup_{j=0}^{n-1}\mathbf{T}^j E) \geqslant 1-c$, and $d(\bigvee_{j=0}^{n-1}\mathbf{T}^{-j}\xi) = d(E \cap \bigvee_{j=0}^{n-1}\mathbf{T}^{-j}\xi)$. Intuitively this says that $1-c$ of the space Ω can be partitioned into n disjoint sets that are shifts of a base set that is independent of the partition $\bigvee_{j=0}^{n-1}\mathbf{T}^{-j}\xi$.

A (c, n)-*stack* is a partition σ of Ω into $n+1$ sets, $\sigma(0), \sigma(1), \ldots, \sigma(n)$, such that $\mathbf{T}^j\sigma(0) = \sigma(j)$ for $j = 0, \ldots, n-1$ and $P(\sigma(n)) < c$. A *strong* (c, n)-*stack* is a (c, n)-stack σ together with a partition ξ such that $d(\bigvee_{j=0}^{n-1}\mathbf{T}^j\xi) = d(\sigma(0) \cap \bigvee_{j=0}^{n-1}\mathbf{T}^j\xi)$.

The hypothesis of ergodicity in the Kakutani-Rohlin theorem is not necessary. Halmos [56] gives a proof which only requires that the metric automorphism be aperiodic, i.e., the set of periodic points has measure zero. The strong form of the Kakutani-Rohlin theorem is obtained from the Kakutani-Rohlin theorem and it is also valid for aperiodic automorphisms. The reason we interject these comments is that in the proof of Lemma 3.8 we need the strong form of the Kakutani-Rohlin theorem for an automorphism $\mathbf{T}$ which is not necessarily ergodic but is aperiodic. In particular, even if $\mathbf{T}_A$ and $\mathbf{T}_S$ are ergodic, the product $\mathbf{T}_S \times \mathbf{T}_A$ does not have to be ergodic, but it is aperiodic.

Proof of Lemma 3.8. Let $[\Sigma(S), \mu]$ and $[\Sigma(A), \nu]$ be ergodic, $\delta > 0$, and p a stationary measure on $\mathcal{F}_S \times \mathcal{F}_A$ with the right marginals such that

$$\int_{\Sigma(S)\times\Sigma(A)} p[d(x,y)]\rho(X_0(x), Y_0(y)) \leqslant \bar{\rho}([\Sigma(S), \mu], [\Sigma(A), \nu]) + \delta/3.$$

[Here X_0 and Y_0 denote projection onto the zeroth coordinate in $\Sigma(S)$ and $\Sigma(A)$ respectively.]

Let $\mathbf{T}$ denote the metric automorphism on $(\Sigma(S)\times\Sigma(A), \mathcal{F}_S \times \mathcal{F}_A, p)$ defined by $\mathbf{T}(x,y) = (\mathbf{T}_S(x), \mathbf{T}_A(y)) = \mathbf{T}_S \times \mathbf{T}_A(x,y)$. Let ξ and η be the partitions of $\Sigma(S)\times\Sigma(A)$ such that $\xi \cap \Sigma(S)$ is the time zero partition in $\Sigma(S)$ and $\eta \cap \Sigma(A)$ is the time zero partition in $\Sigma(A)$. That is, $\xi(i) = \{(x,y) : X_0(x) = s_i\}$ for $i = 1, 2, \ldots, l$ and $\eta(j) = \{(x,y) : Y_0(y) = a_j\}$ for $j = 1, 2, \ldots, k$.

Now $\xi \vee \eta$ is a generating partition for $\mathbf{T}$, $\mathbf{T}_S$ is isomorphic to the factor isomorphism $\mathbf{T}_{\xi^\infty}$, where $\xi^\infty = \bigvee_{i=-\infty}^{+\infty}\mathbf{T}^i\xi$ and $\mathbf{T}_A$ is isomorphic to the factor isomorphism $\mathbf{T}_{\eta^\infty}$. Moreover, $\mathbf{T}$ is aperiodic (since $\mathbf{T}_S$ and $\mathbf{T}_A$ are ergodic) and

$$\int_{\Sigma(S)\times\Sigma(A)} p[d(x,y)]\rho(X_0(x), Y_0(y)) = \sum_{j=1}^{k}\sum_{i=1}^{l} \rho(s_i, a_j)p(\xi(i) \cap \eta(j)).$$

Because $\mathbf{T}_A$ is isomorphic to $\mathbf{T}_{\eta^\infty}$ and η is a finite partition,

$$h(\mathbf{T}_A)=h(\mathbf{T},\eta)=\lim_{n\to\infty}\frac{1}{n}H\left(\bigvee_{i=0}^{n-1}\mathbf{T}^{-i}\eta\right).$$

Let $0<\delta<e^{-1}$ be given, and choose m so large that

$$\left|\frac{1}{m}H\left(\bigvee_{i=0}^{m-1}\mathbf{T}^{-i}\eta\right)-h(\mathbf{T}_A)\right|\leqslant\frac{\delta}{3}.$$

Choose $\varepsilon>0$ so small and n so large that

$$kl\rho_{\max}\varepsilon\leqslant\frac{\delta}{3}$$

and

$$l^m\left(\varepsilon+\frac{m-1}{n}\right)\leqslant\frac{\delta}{3},$$

where $\rho_{\max}=\max\{\rho(s_i,a_j):1\leqslant i\leqslant l,\ 1\leqslant j\leqslant k\}$.

Let σ be a strong (ε,n)-stack on $(\Sigma(S)\times\Sigma(A),\mathfrak{F}_S\times\mathfrak{F}_A,p,\mathbf{T})$ associated with the partition $\xi\vee\eta$. Thus $p(\bigcup_{i=0}^{n-1}\mathbf{T}^i\sigma(0))\geqslant1-\varepsilon$, and using the measure p to obtain distributions,

$$d\left(\sigma(0)\cap\bigvee_{i=0}^{n-1}\mathbf{T}^i(\xi\vee\eta)\right)=d\left(\bigvee_{i=0}^{n-1}\mathbf{T}^i(\xi\vee\eta)\right).\tag{3.6}$$

Since $\mathbf{T}_{\xi^\infty}$ is isomorphic to $\mathbf{T}_S$,

$$\begin{aligned}d\left(\sigma(0)\cap\bigvee_{i=0}^{n-1}\mathbf{T}^i\xi\right)&=d\left(\bigvee_{i=0}^{n-1}\mathbf{T}^i\xi\right)\\&=d\left(\bigvee_{i=0}^{n-1}\mathbf{T}_S^i\xi_0\right),\end{aligned}\tag{3.7}$$

where ξ_0 denotes the time zero partition in $\Sigma(S)$.

Because of (3.7) the strong (ε,n)-stack σ defined using the partition $\xi\vee\eta$ may be viewed as a strong (ε,n)-stack for the partition ξ. Denote this stack by σ_ξ. Now construct a strong Rohlin (ε,n)-stack σ' on $(\Sigma(S),\mathfrak{F}_S,\mu,\mathbf{T}_S)$ with the partition ξ_0 so that

$$d\left(\sigma'(0)\cap\bigvee_{i=0}^{n-1}\mathbf{T}_S^{-i}\xi_0\right)=d\left(\bigvee_{i=0}^{n-1}\mathbf{T}_S^i\xi_0\right).\tag{3.8}$$

Combining (3.7) and (3.8) gives

$$d\left(\sigma(0)\cap\bigvee_{i=0}^{n-1}\mathbf{T}^{i}\xi\right)=d\left(\sigma'(0)\cap\bigvee_{i=0}^{n-1}\mathbf{T}_S^{i}\xi_0\right). \tag{3.9}$$

When two stacks σ_ξ and σ' satisfy a relationship such as (3.9) they are said to be isomorphic, and we write $\sigma_\xi\sim\sigma'$. Because of Equation (3.9), corresponding atoms of the two partitions have that same measure. Since any nonatomic space can be partitioned so that the distribution of the partition is any preassigned discrete probability distribution it follows that there exists a partition $\eta_0=(\eta_0(1),\ldots,\eta_0(k))$ of $\bigcup_{i=0}^{n-1}\mathbf{T}_S^i\sigma'(0)$ with the property that

$$d\left(\sigma(0)\cap\bigvee_{i=0}^{n-1}\mathbf{T}^{-i}(\xi\vee\eta)\right)=d\left(\sigma'(0)\cap\bigvee_{i=0}^{n-1}\mathbf{T}_S^{i}(\xi_0\vee\eta_0)\right), \tag{3.10}$$

which implies that

$$d\left(\sigma(0)\cap\bigvee_{i=0}^{n-1}\mathbf{T}^{-i}\eta\right)=d\left(\sigma'(0)\cap\bigvee_{i=0}^{n-1}\mathbf{T}_S^{i}\eta_0\right), \tag{3.11}$$

and in terms of the notation given above, σ_ξ is isomorphic to σ'_{η_0}.

Extend η_0 in any manner so that it is a partition of $\Sigma(S)$ rather than just $\bigcup_{i=0}^{n-1}\sigma'(i)$. Notice that by combining (3.10) and (3.6) we have

$$p\left(\xi(i)\cap\eta(j)\cap\bigcup_{i=0}^{n-1}\mathbf{T}^{-i}\sigma(0)\right)=p(\xi(i)\cap\eta(j))$$

and

$$\mu\left(\xi_0(i)\cap\eta_0(j)\cap\bigcup_{i=0}^{n-1}\mathbf{T}_S^{i}\sigma'(0)\right)=p\left(\xi(i)\cap\eta(j)\cap\bigcup_{i=0}^{n-1}\mathbf{T}^{-i}\sigma(0)\right)$$

for all i and j. Furthermore $\mu(\bigcup_{i=0}^{n-1}\mathbf{T}_S^i\sigma'(0))\geqslant 1-\varepsilon$. Thus $|\mu(\xi_0(i)\cap\eta_0(j))-p(\xi(i)\cap\eta(j))|\leqslant\varepsilon$ for all i and j, and we have

$$\begin{aligned}\rho(\xi_0,\eta_0)&=\sum_{i,j}\rho(s_i,a_j)\mu(\xi_0(i)\cap\eta_0(j))\\&\leqslant\sum_{i,j}\rho(s_i,a_j)p(\xi(i)\cap\eta(j))+\varepsilon\sum_{i,j}\rho(s_i,a_j)\\&\leqslant\bar{\rho}([\Sigma(S),\mu],[\Sigma(A),\nu])+\tfrac{2}{3}\delta.\end{aligned} \tag{3.12}$$

We now apply Lemma A of the appendix of [49] to obtain

$$\frac{1}{m}H\left(\bigvee_{i=0}^{m-1}\mathbf{T}_S^i\eta_0\right)\leqslant\frac{1}{m}H\left(\bigvee_{i=0}^{m-1}\mathbf{T}^{-i}\eta\right)+l^m\left(\varepsilon+\frac{m-1}{n}\right)$$

$$\leqslant h(\mathbf{T}_A)+\tfrac{2}{3}\delta. \tag{3.13}$$

We note that this proves the lemma for an infinite length sliding block encoder defined by the partition η_0, i.e., $f^{(\infty)}(x)=a_i$ if and only if $x\in\eta_0(i)$. We restate (3.12) and (3.13) in terms of $f^{(\infty)}$ to obtain the conclusions of the lemma for $f^{(\infty)}$:

$$\rho(f^{(\infty)})=\sum_{i,j}\rho(s_i,a_j)\mu(\xi_0(i)\cap\eta_0(j))$$

$$\leqslant\bar{\rho}([\Sigma(S),\mu],[\Sigma(A),\nu])+\tfrac{2}{3}\delta, \tag{3.12'}$$

$$h(f^{(\infty)})\leqslant\lim\frac{1}{m}H\left(\bigvee_{i=0}^{m-1}\mathbf{T}_S^{-i}\eta_0\right)$$

$$\leqslant h(\mathbf{T}_A)+\tfrac{2}{3}\delta. \tag{3.13'}$$

Since ξ_0 is a generating partition for $(\Sigma(S),\mathfrak{F}_S,\mu,\mathbf{T}_S)$ and η_0 is an $\mathfrak{F}_S$ measurable partition, given $\delta'>0$, there exists $N>0$ and a partition $\bar{\eta}_0=(\bar{\eta}_0(1),\ldots,\bar{\eta}_0(k))$ with $\bar{\eta}_0\leqslant\bigvee_{-N}^{N}\mathbf{T}_S^i\xi_0$ and

$$|\bar{\eta}_0-\eta_0|=\sum_{i=1}^{k}\mu(\bar{\eta}_0(i)\,\triangle\,\eta_0(i))\leqslant\delta'.$$

It follows from Theorem 4.23 that δ' may be chosen small enough and N large enough so thatq

$$|h(\mathbf{T}_S,\eta_0)-h(\mathbf{T}_S,\bar{\eta}_0)|\leqslant\delta/3.$$

For each i and j,

$$\xi_0(i)\cap\bar{\eta}_0(j)\subset(\xi_0(i)\cap\eta_0(j))\cup(\eta_0(j)\,\triangle\,\bar{\eta}_0(j))$$

and

$$\mu(\xi_0(i)\cap\bar{\eta}_0(j))\leqslant\mu(\xi_0(i)\cap\eta_0(j))+\mu(\eta_0(j)\,\triangle\,\bar{\eta}_0(j)).$$

Thus

$$\begin{aligned}\rho(\xi_0,\bar{\eta}_0)&=\sum_{i,j}\rho(s_i,a_j)\mu(\xi_0(i)\cap\bar{\eta}_0(j))\\&\leqslant\sum_{i,j}\rho(s_i,a_j)\mu(\xi_0(i)\cap\eta_0(j))+|\eta_0-\bar{\eta}_0|\rho_{\max}\\&\leqslant\bar{\rho}([\Sigma(S),\mu],[\Sigma(A),\nu])+\tfrac{2}{3}\delta+\delta'\rho_{\max}.\end{aligned}$$

Hence, if in addition to the above choice of δ' we require that $\delta'\rho_{\max}\leqslant\delta/3$, we have

$$\begin{aligned}h(\mathbf{T}_S,\bar{\eta}_0)&\leqslant h(\mathbf{T}_S,\eta_0)+\delta/3\\&\leqslant h(\mathbf{T}_A)+\delta\end{aligned}\tag{3.14}$$

and

$$\rho(\xi_0,\bar{\eta}_0)\leqslant\bar{\rho}([\Sigma(S),\mu],[\Sigma(A),\nu])+\delta.\tag{3.15}$$

Since $\bar{\eta}_0\leqslant\bigvee_{i=-N}^{N}\mathbf{T}_S^i\xi_0$, we can define $f^{(N)}: S^{2N+1}\to A$ by

$$f^{(N)}(s_{j_{-N}},\ldots,s_{j_N})=a_n\quad\text{iff}\quad\bigcap_{i=-N}^{N}\mathbf{T}_S^{i+N+1}\xi_0(j_i)\subset\bar{\eta}_0(n).$$

As we did for $f^{(\infty)}$ defined above, we restate (3.14) and (3.15) in terms of $f^{(N)}$:

$$\begin{aligned}h(f^{(N)})&\leqslant h(\mathbf{T}_A)+\delta,\\\rho(f^{(N)})&\leqslant\bar{\rho}([\Sigma(S),\mu],[\Sigma(A),\nu])+\delta,\end{aligned}$$

and the lemma is proven.

Proof of Theorem 3.7. We have already observed that the only thing we need to prove is $\delta(R)\leqslant\inf\{\bar{\rho}([\Sigma(S),\mu],[\Sigma(A),\nu])\}=r$. Let $\varepsilon>0$ be given, and choose a stationary measure $\bar{\nu}$ on $\Sigma(A)$ such that $h_{\bar{\nu}}(\mathbf{T}_A)\leqslant R$ and

$$\bar{\rho}([\Sigma(S),\mu],[\Sigma(A),\bar{\nu}])\leqslant r+\varepsilon.$$

Apply Lemma 3.8 to the pair $[\Sigma(S),\mu],[\Sigma(A),\bar{\nu}]$ to obtain a function $f^{(N)}$ with N sufficiently large so that

$$\begin{aligned}\rho(f^{(N)})&\leqslant r+\tfrac{3}{2}\varepsilon,\\h(f^{(N)})&\leqslant R+\varepsilon,\end{aligned}$$

so that $\delta(R)+\varepsilon\leqslant r\leqslant\delta(R)$ for all $\varepsilon>0$. Since $\delta(R)$ is continuous, the theorem follows.

We end this section with an example of a sliding block encoder. The example we give is a simple adaptation of an isomorphism described in [6]. Other examples of sliding-block encoders may be found in [49], [6], and [65]. In fact, in [140] Shields and Neuhoff give a discussion of how block codes and sliding block encoders are connected and how one may convert from one to the other. The reason we chose the particular example given below is that in addition to being an example of sliding block encoder, it is an example of what is called a finitary isomorphism (see [65]).

Example 3.9. Let $S=\{1,2,3,4,5,6\}$. We define a measure on $(\Sigma(S),\mathcal{F}_S)$ so that $(\mathbf{T}_S, \xi_S)$ is a Markov process (see Section 2.12.10). Let $p=(\frac{1}{6},\frac{1}{6},\frac{1}{6},\frac{1}{6},\frac{1}{6},\frac{1}{6})$, and M be the transition matrix

$$M=\begin{bmatrix} 0 & .5 & 0 & .5 & 0 & 0 \\ .5 & 0 & 0 & 0 & 0 & .5 \\ 0 & .5 & 0 & .5 & 0 & 0 \\ 0 & 0 & .5 & 0 & .5 & 0 \\ .5 & 0 & 0 & 0 & 0 & .5 \\ 0 & 0 & .5 & 0 & .5 & 0 \end{bmatrix}.$$

As usual, M_{ij} is the probability of a transition from i to j. The measure μ induced on $\Sigma(S)$ by p and M is defined on cylinder sets by

$$\mu(\xi_S(i_0)\cap\mathbf{T}_S^{-1}\xi_S(i_1)\cap\cdots\cap\mathbf{T}_S^{-k}\xi_S(i_k))=p_{i_0}M_{i_0i_1}\cdots M_{i_{k-1}i_k}.$$

and extended to $\mathcal{F}_S$ in the usual manner. The entropy of $\mathbf{T}_S$ with respect to μ is $1=\log_2 2$ in bits (see Section 2.12.10). Let $A=\{a,b\}$, and define ν on $(\Sigma(A),\mathcal{F}_A)$ so that $(\mathbf{T}_A,\xi_A)$ is an independent identically distributed process, with $\nu(\{y: y_0=a\})=\nu(\{y: y_0=b\})=\frac{1}{2}$.

We define an infinite length sliding block encoder-decoder pair and then restrict to a finite length pair as in the proof of the theorem. Define $h: S\times S\to A$ by

$$h(1,2)=h(2,1)=h(4,3)=h(3,2)=h(5,1)=h(6,3)=a,$$
$$h(1,4)=h(2,6)=h(4,5)=h(3,4)=h(5,6)=h(6,5)=b.$$

Thus there are two types of transitions, "a" and "b" transitions. In fact, the mapping h defines a length 2 sliding block encoder and induces an isomorphism $\phi_h: \Sigma(S)\to\Sigma(A)$ on a subset of $\Sigma(S)$ of measure 1 by $(\phi_h(x))_i=h(x_{i-1},x_i)$. It is in the decoder that we see the distinction between the finite length and the infinite length.

The idea of the decoder is quite simple. For $y\in\Sigma(A)$, if $y_0=a$, then we know an "a" transition took place and we have limited our choices for the corresponding $x_{-1}x_0$ to one of the pairs $\{(1,2(2,1),(4,3),(3,2),(5,1),$

(6,3)}. Furthermore, notice that as soon as we know which "a" transition took place, then (with probability 1) we can calculate the rest of the coordinates of the source message. Finally we notice that if we see the string *aaba*, then we know the last source symbol was 3, and from now on we can calculate the message, because we know which "a" or "b" transition took place. The last statements are easy to verify, so we leave them to the reader. Using this scheme, the decoder is defined as follows:

Given the element $y \in \Sigma(A)$, we look through its past $\ldots, y_{-3}, y_{-2}, y_{-1}$ until we find the first occurrence of the key, *aaba*. Knowing that the corresponding source letter was 3, we can work our way back to y_0 and determine which source letter was sent to x_0. Formally,

$$f_D^{(\infty)}(y) = x_0,$$

where

1. $x_0 = 3$ if $y_{-4}y_{-3}y_{-2}y_{-1} = aaba$;
2. if k is the smallest positive integer such that $y_{-k-3}y_{-k-2}y_{-k-1}y_{-k} = aaba$, then x_0 is the right hand letter of the unique source word $(3, x_{-k+1}, \ldots, x_0)$ corresponding to $(y_{-k}, y_{-k+1}, \ldots, y_0)$;
3. if there is no such k, then x_0 is equally likely to be any one of the six possible y_0-transitions.

This infinite length decoder is made to have length N by restricting k to lie in the set $\{1,2,\ldots, N\}$. The ergodic theorem assures us that for $N = \infty$, the probability of occurrence of event 3 is zero. That is, the probability of the set of all points in $\Sigma(S)$ for which the key *aaba* occurs infinitely often in their past is 1. The probability that a word of length N does not contain *aaba* is asymptotic to a positive function f such that for sufficiently large N, $f(N) \leqslant (0.97)^N$. Thus while the probability converges to zero, it does so rather slowly.

CHAPTER 4

Ergodic Theory

4.1 Introduction

Ergodic theory has its origins in the attempt to explain the macroscopic characteristics of physical systems, in particular thermodynamical systems of gases, in terms of the behavior of the microscopic structure of the system. This problem, along with other physical problems, led to what has been known as the "many body problem" in mathematics, and mathematical research on this problem led to what is now known as ergodic theory.

For example, if a gas is considered to be a large collection of molecules (thought of as point masses) which are in motion, such characteristics of the gas as its pressure, temperature, and volume should be determined by the dynamic behavior of these molecules, i.e., their positions and momenta as functions of time.

If such a system is conservative, i.e., its total energy does not change with time, then the Hamiltonian theory of dynamical systems can be used to obtain transformations on manifolds in a high dimensional Euclidean space called phase space. These manifolds in phase space consist of those states of the gas (generalized coordinates of position and momentum of each molecule) with the same total energy. The transformations preserve the measure induced by Lebesgue measure on the manifold; their construction was sketched in Section 2.8.

It is impossible to determine the microscopic state of a gas at an instant of time, so that even if the Hamilton equations of motion could be solved to find the transformation explicitly, it would not be possible to predict exactly the future states of the gas. However, it is possible to select a probability distribution on the states which depends on such measurable quantities as energy and temperature and gives the probability that the gas is in a certain collection of states.

ENCYCLOPEDIA OF MATHEMATICS and Its Applications, Gian-Carlo Rota (ed.).
Vol. 12: Nathaniel F. Martin and James W. England, Mathematical Theory of Entropy.
ISBN 0-201-13511-6

This probability distribution determines a measure on the manifolds of constant energy and is invariant under the transformations determined by the Hamilton system of equations. In this way a measure preserving transformation **T** on a probability space $(\Omega, \mathfrak{F}, P)$ is obtained. This dynamical system $(\Omega, \mathfrak{F}, P, \mathbf{T})$ can be used as a model for studying the dynamic behavior of the gases.

Ergodic theory in its most abstract form consists of the study of measure preserving transformations. In this chapter we discuss the problems in ergodic theory which led to the development of the entropy of dynamical systems. We also discuss certain classes of dynamical systems which can be characterized by entropy considerations. In particular we discuss K-systems and Bernoulli systems, and we shall prove that entropy is a complete isomorphism invariant for Bernoulli systems.

Throughout this chapter we assume that all dynamical systems are invertible and the underlying Lebesgue space is nonatomic.

4.2 Unitary Operator of a System and Bernoulli Shifts

In [70] Koopman developed a technique for associating a unitary operator on a Hilbert space with each metric automorphism of a measure space. This technique in effect, replaces a nonlinear system with a linear system. It was used very effectively by Halmos and von Neumann [57] in studying dynamical systems. In this section we shall discuss some of this work and indicate how it led indirectly to the notion of the entropy of systems.

Suppose $(\Omega, \mathfrak{F}, P, \mathbf{T})$ is a dynamical system. If we define $^*\mathbf{T}$ on the collection of $\mathfrak{F}$-measurable functions by $(^*\mathbf{T}f)(\omega) = (f \circ \mathbf{T})(\omega)$, then $^*\mathbf{T}$ is a linear transformation. In particular, if $^*\mathbf{T}$ is restricted to $L^2(\Omega, \mathfrak{F}, P)$, the Hilbert space of square-summable functions with norm $\|f\|_2^2 = \int P(d\omega)|f(\omega)|^2$, then since $P(\mathbf{T}^{-1}E) = P(E)$ for all $E \in \mathfrak{F}$, the change of variables formula shows that $\|^*\mathbf{T}f\|_2 = \|f\|_2$ for all $f \in L^2$, and it follows that $^*\mathbf{T}$ is a linear isometry on L^2. Since **T** is invertible, $^*\mathbf{T}$ has an inverse and $^*\mathbf{T}$ is a unitary operator.

Recall that linear operators $\mathbf{B}_1$ and $\mathbf{B}_2$ on a Hilbert space are said to be unitarily equivalent if there exists a unitary operator **H** such that $\mathbf{H} \circ \mathbf{B}_1 = \mathbf{B}_2 \circ \mathbf{H}$. The equivalence classes of unitarily equivalent operators within the collection of unitary operators can be completely determined by the spectral theory of operators.

Now suppose $(\Omega, \mathfrak{F}, P, \mathbf{T})$ and $(\Omega', \mathfrak{F}', P', \mathbf{T}')$ are two isomorphic dynamical systems and **S** denotes a metric automorphism such that $\mathbf{S} \circ \mathbf{T} = \mathbf{T}' \circ \mathbf{S}$. Then $^*\mathbf{S}$ is a unitary operator and $^*\mathbf{S} \circ {}^*\mathbf{T}' = {}^*\mathbf{T} \circ {}^*\mathbf{S}$, so that $^*\mathbf{T}$ and $^*\mathbf{T}'$ are unitarily equivalent. If it were also the case that the unitary equivalence of $^*\mathbf{T}$ and $^*\mathbf{T}'$ implied that $\mathbf{T}$ and $\mathbf{T}'$ were isomorphic, then isomorphism problems in ergodic theory could be handled completely by using spectral theory.

If $\mathbf{H}$ is a linear operator on a Hilbert space, the set of complex numbers λ such that $\mathbf{H}-\lambda\mathbf{I}$ ($\mathbf{I}$ is the identity operator) does not have a bounded inverse is called the *spectrum* of the operator $\mathbf{H}$. In case $\mathbf{H}$ is unitary, the spectrum is a subset of the unit circle, i.e., $|\lambda|=1$ for all λ in the spectrum. A complex number λ is called an *eigenvalue* of $\mathbf{H}$ if there exists a nonzero element f, called an *eigenfunction*, such that $(\mathbf{H}-\lambda\mathbf{I})f=0$. Clearly eigenvalues, if they exist, are points in the spectrum of $\mathbf{H}$, but there can be other elements in the spectrum besides eigenvalues.

A system $(\Omega, \mathfrak{F}, P, \mathbf{T})$ or the automorphism $\mathbf{T}$ is said to have *discrete* spectrum if $L^2(\Omega, \mathfrak{F}, P)$ is spanned by eigenfunctions of $^*\mathbf{T}$, and is said to have *continuous* spectrum if 1 is the only eigenvalue of $^*\mathbf{T}$. (Notice that if f is a constant, then $^*\mathbf{T}f=f$, so that 1 is always an eigenvalue.)

Halmos and von Neumann [57] showed that if $\mathbf{T}$ and $\mathbf{T}'$ have discrete spectrum and they are unitarily equivalent, then they are isomorphic. Thus within the class of systems with discrete spectrum, unitary equivalence is enough to determine isomorphism. Halmos [56] shows that this is not true in general by constructing two transformations without discrete spectrum which are unitarily equivalent but are not isomorphic.

There is an interesting class of ergodic dynamical systems which for a time were all known to be unitarily equivalent but resisted every effort to determine whether they were also isomorphic. This is the class of *Bernoulli shifts*. These systems are defined in Section 2.12.9, and one will notice that the distinguishing feature of systems in the class is the distribution function f. These dynamical systems are called Bernoulli shifts because they are models of sequences of identically distributed independent random variables with distribution f. All of these systems have continuous spectrum, and they are all unitarily equivalent.

In 1948 Kakutani considered using the entropy to solve this problem but was unable to find an effective way of calculating it, and the problem remain unsolved until 1958. In that year Kolmogoroff [69] defined the entropy function we have been discussing and gave a formula for the entropy of Bernoulli shifts in terms of the distribution function which showed that all Bernoulli shifts are not isomorphic. (The reader may recall that in Example 2.40 we used the entropy to show that Bernoulli shifts with uniform distributions on two and three points are not isomorphic.) Sinai [142] made a slight, but very significant, modification in Kolmogoroff's definition, and a revival of research in ergodic theory occurred which has produced some extremely deep and fundamental results. In particular, the work of Ornstein in showing that the isomorphism classes of Bernoulli shifts are determined by entropy has given new insights into old problems in ergodic theory.

Before discussing the isomorphism theorem we shall analyze a class of systems defined by Kolmogoroff which includes the Bernoulli shifts and whose members are characterized by the entropy. These systems are models of stochastic processes which satisfy the zero-one law, and there used to be some reason to believe that they were isomorphic to Bernoulli shifts. The construction of such systems which were not isomorphic to Bernoulli shifts was not accomplished until 1973, when Ornstein used techniques in the construction that he had developed to prove the isomorphism theorem.

4.3 *K*-Systems and *K*-Automorphisms

We begin by giving some notation which will be useful in the development of the rest of the chapter:

$$\xi^n = \bigvee_{j=0}^{n-1} \mathbf{T}^j\xi \qquad \text{for all} \quad n \geqslant 0,$$

$$\xi^+ = \bigvee_{j=0}^{\infty} \mathbf{T}^j\xi,$$

$$\xi^{-n} = \bigvee_{j=1}^{n} \mathbf{T}^{-j}\xi \qquad \text{for all} \quad n>0,$$

$$\xi^- = \bigvee_{j=1}^{\infty} \mathbf{T}^{-j}\xi,$$

$$\xi^\infty = \xi^+ \vee \xi^- = \bigvee_{j=-\infty}^{+\infty} \mathbf{T}^{-j}.$$

Bernoulli shifts will be denoted by **B** together with a given probability vector $p=(p_1, p_2, \ldots, p_k)$. Thus the symbol $(\mathbf{B}; p_1, \ldots, p_k)$ denotes the dynamical system $(\Sigma(S), \mathfrak{F}, \mu, \mathbf{B})$, where $S=\{1, \ldots, k\}$, μ is the product measure determined by the distribution function $f(i)=p_i$, and **B** is defined by $(\mathbf{B}\omega)(j)=\omega(j+1)$. $(\mathbf{B}; p_1, \ldots, p_k)$ will be called a Bernoulli k-shift with distribution $p=(p_1, \ldots, p_k)$.

Suppose ξ_0 is the "time zero" partition of a Bernoulli k-shift $(\mathbf{B}, p)$, i.e., the atoms of ξ_0 consists of sets of the form $\{\omega: \omega(0)=i\}$ for $i=1,2,\ldots,k$. Then ξ_0 is an ordered partition with discrete probability distribution p (see Section 2.11). Moreover, the collection $\{\mathbf{B}^j\xi_0: j\in Z\}$ of measurable partitions is independent, and ξ_0 is a generating partition, i.e., $\xi_0^\infty = \varepsilon$. (As we shall see in Section 4.5, the existence of a partition ξ of a dynamical system

$(\Omega, \mathfrak{F}, P, \mathbf{T})$ which is independent and generating is necessary and sufficient for the dynamical system to be isomorphic to a Bernoulli shift.)

Consider the partition $\bigwedge_{n=0}^{\infty}\bigvee_{j=n}^{\infty}\mathbf{B}^{-j}\xi_0$. This partition was discussed in Section 1.8, where it was considered as the collection of outcomes in the infinitely distant future, i.e., outcomes which are not determined by any finite number of the random variables in the process $(\mathbf{B}, \xi_0)$. It is called the tail of the process and will be denoted by $\text{Tail}(\mathbf{B}, \xi_0)$. Notice that if $\{\eta_k\}$ is an independent collection of partitions, then $\bigvee_{k\in S}\eta_k$ and $\bigvee_{k\in T}\eta_k$ are independent and so are $\bigwedge_{k\in S}\eta_k$ and $\bigwedge_{k\in T}\eta_k$, provided the index sets S and T have no points in common. Since $\{\mathbf{B}^j\xi_0\}$ is an independent sequence, if $k \leqslant N$, then $\xi_0^{-n}\vee\xi_0^n$ is independent of $\bigvee_{j=k}^{N}\mathbf{B}^{-j}\xi_0$ for all $n<k$. Thus $\xi_0^{-n}\vee\xi_0^n$ is independent of $\bigvee_{j=k}^{\infty}\mathbf{B}^{-j}\xi_0$ for all $n<k$, and $\xi_0^{-n}\vee\xi_0^n$ is independent of $\bigwedge_{r=k}^{\infty}\bigvee_{j=r}^{\infty}\mathbf{B}^{-j}\xi_0$ for all $n<k$. Since $\text{Tail}(\mathbf{B}, \xi_0) = \bigwedge_{r=k}^{\infty}\bigvee_{j=r}^{\infty}\mathbf{B}^{-j}\xi_0$ for any k, we have that $\xi_0^{-n}\vee\xi_0^n$ is independent of $\text{Tail}(\mathbf{B}, \xi_0)$ for all n and hence ξ_0^{∞} and $\text{Tail}(\mathbf{B}, \xi_0)$ are independent. Since ξ_0^{∞} is the point partition, any event A in $[\text{Tail}(\mathbf{B}, \xi_0)]^{\wedge}$ is also in $(\xi_0^{\infty})^{\wedge}$, and A is independent of itself. Therefore, $P(A\cap A) = P(A)P(A)$, and $P(A)$ is either zero or one. It follows that $\text{Tail}(\mathbf{B}, \xi_0)$ is the trivial partition. (This result is known in probability theory as the zero-one law.)

Recall that each measurable partition ξ of a dynamical system $(\Omega, \mathfrak{F}, P, \mathbf{T})$ gives rise to a stochastic process $(\mathbf{T}, \xi)$. We have just seen that for a Bernoulli shift $\mathbf{B}$, there is a partition ξ_0 such that events in the far distant future of $(\mathbf{B}, \xi_0)$ are deterministic. Suppose that the tail of a process $(\mathbf{T}, \xi)$ is trivial. It would seem plausible that if we consider a finite measurable partition η of the factor spaces $(\Omega_{\xi^\infty}, \mathfrak{F}_{\xi^\infty}, P_{\xi^\infty}, \mathbf{T}_{\xi^\infty})$, then the events in the tail of $(\mathbf{T}_{\xi^\infty}, \eta)$ should also be trivial. If this were the case, then every partition η of a Bernoulli shift $\mathbf{B}$ would have a trivial tail even though the sequence of partitions $\{\mathbf{B}^j\eta\}$ is not an independent sequence. This statement is indeed true and follows from a deep result of Sinai and Rohlin concerning the connection between tails of processes and the Pinsker partition π (cf. Theorem 2.52). Systems with the property that every process in the system has a trivial tail are called K-systems and Bernoulli shifts are examples of K-systems. Before developing these ideas we prove two lemmas which will be needed in the development.

Lemma 4.1. *Let $(\Omega, \mathfrak{F}, P, \mathbf{T})$ be an invertible dynamical system, and ξ, η, and γ be measurable partitions such that $\xi \leqslant \eta$ and $H(\eta\vee\gamma/\eta^-) < \infty$. Then*

$$\lim_{k\to\infty} H(\xi/\eta^-\vee\mathbf{T}^{-k}\gamma^-) = H(\xi/\eta^-).$$

Proof. By Theorems 2.21 and 2.24 we have that

$$\frac{1}{n}H(\eta^n/\eta^-\vee\gamma^-) = \frac{1}{n}\sum_{k=0}^{n-1} H(\eta/\eta^-\vee\mathbf{T}^{-k}\gamma^-).$$

Since $H(\eta/\eta^-)\leqslant H(\eta\vee\gamma/\eta^-)<\infty$, Lemma 2.25 implies that

$$\lim_{n\to\infty}\frac{1}{n}\sum_{k=0}^{n-1}H(\eta/\eta^-\vee\mathbf{T}^{-k}\gamma^-)=H(\eta/\eta^-). \tag{4.1}$$

Since $\mathbf{T}^{-k}\gamma^-$ is decreasing, $H(\eta/\eta^-\vee\mathbf{T}^{-k}\gamma^-)$ is an increasing sequence and hence has a limit, which from (4.1) must be $H(\eta/\eta^-)$. Thus the lemma is proven if $\xi=\eta$.

By Theorem 2.21, for $\xi\leqslant\eta$,

$$\begin{aligned}H(\xi/\eta^-\vee\mathbf{T}^{-k}\gamma^-)&=H(\eta/\eta^-\vee\mathbf{T}^{-k}\gamma^-)-H(\eta/\xi\vee\eta^-\vee\mathbf{T}^{-k}\gamma^-)\\&\geqslant H(\eta/\eta^-\vee\mathbf{T}^{-k}\gamma^-)-H(\eta/\xi\vee\eta^-).\end{aligned}$$

Thus

$$\begin{aligned}\lim_{k\to\infty}H(\xi/\eta^-\vee\mathbf{T}^{-k}\gamma^-)&\geqslant H(\eta/\eta^-)-H(\eta/\xi\vee\eta^-)\\&=H(\xi/\eta^-).\end{aligned}$$

Since $H(\xi/\eta^-)\geqslant H(\xi/\eta^-\vee\mathbf{T}^{-k}\gamma^-)$ for all k, the reverse inequality is satisfied and the lemma is proven.

LEMMA 4.2. *The Pinsker partition π is refined by the tail of any generating partition.*

Proof. Suppose ξ is a partition such that $H(\xi/\xi^-)<\infty$. Let $\{\eta_k\}$ be a sequence of finite partitions such that $\eta_k\uparrow\pi$. Then $H(\xi\vee\eta_k/\xi^-)<\infty$ and by Theorem 2.33, $H(\xi\vee\eta_k/\xi^-\vee\eta_k^-)=H(\eta_k/\eta_k^-\vee\xi^\infty)+H(\xi/\xi^-)$, and we have

$$H(\xi/\xi^-\vee\eta_k^-)+H(\eta_k/\xi\vee\xi^-\vee\eta_k^-)=H(\eta_k/\eta_k^-\vee\xi^\infty)+H(\xi/\xi^-).$$

Since $\eta_k\leqslant\pi$, $H(\eta_k/\eta_k^-)=0$ and we have

$$H(\xi/\xi^-\vee\eta_k^-)=H(\xi/\xi^-),$$

for all k. Taking the limit as $k\to\infty$ gives

$$H(\xi/\xi^-\vee\pi)=H(\xi/\xi^-). \tag{4.2}$$

Now let ζ be a partition such that $\zeta^\infty = \bigvee_{j=-\infty}^{+\infty} \mathbf{T}^{-j}\zeta = \varepsilon$, and let $\zeta_0 = \lim_{k\to\infty} \mathbf{T}^{-k}\zeta^- = \mathrm{Tail}(\mathbf{T}, \xi)$. Since $\zeta_0^- = \zeta_0$, if ξ is any partition with finite entropy, $H(\xi \vee \zeta_0 / \xi^- \vee \zeta_0^-) = H(\xi/\xi^- \vee \zeta_0^-) \leqslant H(\xi) < \infty$. Therefore

$$\begin{aligned} H(\xi/\xi^- \vee \zeta_0) &= H(\xi/\xi^- \vee \zeta_0^-) \\ &= H(\xi \vee \zeta_0 / \xi^- \vee \zeta_0^-) \\ &= H(\xi \vee \zeta_0 / \xi^- \vee \zeta_0^- \vee \pi) \\ &= H(\xi/\xi^- \vee \zeta_0 \vee \pi). \end{aligned}$$

Since the Pinsker partitions for all powers of $\mathbf{T}$ are the same this last equation gives

$$H\left(\xi/\left(\bigvee_{j=1}^{\infty} T^{-jp}\xi\right) \vee \zeta_0\right) = H\left(\xi/\left(\bigvee_{j=1}^{\infty} T^{-jp}\xi\right) \vee \zeta_0 \vee \pi\right)$$

for all $p = 0, \pm 1, \pm 2, \ldots$. If $\xi \leqslant \mathbf{T}^p\zeta^-$ for some p, then $\mathbf{T}^{-jp}\xi \leqslant \mathbf{T}^{-j}\zeta^-$ and we have $\bigwedge_p \bigvee_{j=1}^{\infty} T^{-jp}\xi \vee \zeta_0 = \zeta_0$. Thus if $\xi_n \leqslant \mathbf{T}^n\zeta^-$,

$$H(\xi_n/\zeta_0) = H(\xi_n/\zeta_0 \vee \pi) \tag{4.3}$$

by Theorem 2.20. If ξ is any measurable partition with finite entropy there exist finite partitions $\xi_n \uparrow \xi$ such that $\xi_n \leqslant \mathbf{T}^{-n}\zeta^-$ and taking the limit on n in the last equation gives $H(\xi/\zeta_0) = H(\xi/\zeta_0 \vee \pi)$ for any measurable partition ξ with finite entropy. Then if ξ is a partition with finite entropy such that $\xi \leqslant \pi$, we have $H(\xi/\zeta_0) = 0$ and $\xi \leqslant \zeta_0$. Consequently $\pi \leqslant \zeta_0$ and the lemma is proven.

Definition 4.3. An invertible dynamical system $(\Omega, \mathfrak{F}, P, \mathbf{T})$ is a *K*-system if every finite measurable partition has a trivial tail. An automorphism is a *K-automorphism* if it is the automorphism of a *K*-system.

This is not the usual definition given for a *K*-system (see [123], [124], [125]) although it is equivalent to the usual definition, as we shall show in a moment. First we derive the result due to Rohlin and Sinai [128] mentioned above which associates the Pinsker partition (cf. Theorem 2.52) with *K*-automorphisms. Recall that the Pinsker partition is the maximal invariant partition whose factor system has zero entropy. It follows from the properties of the Pinsker partition π associated with a given system that every nontrivial factor of the system has positive entropy if and only if $\pi = \nu$. Such systems are said to have completely positive entropy. What Rohlin and Sinai showed was that a system is a *K*-system if and only if it has completely positive entropy. We now prove a result which connects the

Pinsker partition and tails of processes. The result on completely positive entropy follows immediately from this.

LEMMA 4.4. *If* $(\Omega, \mathcal{F}, P, \mathbf{T})$ *is an invertible dynamical system, then*

$$\pi = \bigvee \{\mathrm{Tail}(\mathbf{T}, \xi) : \xi \text{ finite}\}.$$

Proof. Choose $\{\xi_k\}$ such that ξ_k are finite and $\xi \uparrow \pi$. Then since $\xi_k \leqslant \pi$, we have $H(\xi_k / \xi_k^-) = 0$. This implies that $\xi_k \leqslant \xi_k^-$ and consequently $\mathbf{T}^{-n}\xi_k \leqslant \mathbf{T}^{-n}\xi_k^-$ for all $n \geqslant 0$. Thus $\xi_k^- \leqslant \mathrm{Tail}(\mathbf{T}, \xi_k)$ for all k. Since $\xi_k^- \uparrow \pi$, we have

$$\pi \leqslant \bigvee_{k=1}^{\infty} \mathrm{Tail}(\mathbf{T}, \xi_k) \leqslant \bigvee \{\mathrm{Tail}(\mathbf{T}, \xi) : \xi \text{ finite}\}.$$

Next suppose α, ξ are finite and $\alpha \leqslant \mathrm{Tail}(\mathbf{T}, \xi)$. Since $\mathrm{Tail}(\mathbf{T}, \xi)$ is invariant, we have $\alpha^{\infty} \leqslant \mathrm{Tail}(\mathbf{T}, \xi) \leqslant \xi^-$. By Theorem 2.33

$$H(\alpha \vee \xi / \alpha^- \vee \xi^-) = H(\alpha / \alpha^-) + H(\xi / \alpha^{\infty} \vee \xi^-),$$

and since $\alpha \leqslant \xi^-$ and $\alpha^- \leqslant \xi^-$,

$$H(\xi / \xi^-) = H(\alpha / \alpha^-) + H(\xi / \xi^-).$$

Thus, since $H(\xi / \xi^-) < \infty$, we have $H(\alpha / \alpha^-) = 0$, and by the definition of π, $\alpha \leqslant \pi$. Therefore $\mathrm{Tail}(\mathbf{T}, \xi) \leqslant \pi$ for each finite ξ, and we have that

$$\pi \geqslant \bigvee \{\mathrm{Tail}(\mathbf{T}, \xi) : \xi \text{ finite}\}.$$

THEOREM 4.5. *An invertible dynamical system is a K-system if and only if its Pinsker partition is the trivial partition, or equivalently, if and only if it has completely positive entropy.*

COROLLARY 4.6. *If* $\mathbf{T}$ *is a K-automorphism, then for every integer* k, $\mathbf{T}^k$ *is a K-automorphism and every factor of* $\mathbf{T}$ *is a K-automorphism.*

Proof. If $\mathbf{T}^{-1}\zeta \leqslant \zeta$ and $\xi \leqslant \zeta$ is such that $\mathbf{T}^{-1}\xi \leqslant \xi$, then $(\mathbf{T}_\zeta)_\xi$ is isomorphic to $\mathbf{T}_\xi$. Thus if $\mathbf{T}$ is a K-automorphism,

$$h\left[(\mathbf{T}_\zeta)_\xi \right] = h(\mathbf{T}_\xi) > 0$$

and $\mathbf{T}_\zeta$ has completely positive entropy.

Also, since $(\mathbf{T}^k)_\xi = (\mathbf{T}_\xi)^k$, Theorem 2.43 gives

$$h(\mathbf{T}_\xi^k) = |k|\,h(\mathbf{T}_\xi) > 0,$$

and $\mathbf{T}^k$ has completely positive entropy.

As a consequence of the corollary we have that not only is the tail of every finite process $(\mathbf{T}, \xi)$ in a K-system trivial, but the "backward" tail of the process, i.e. $\bigwedge_{n=0}^{\infty} \bigvee_{j=n}^{\infty} \mathbf{T}^j \xi$, is also trivial. This is because $\mathbf{T}^{-1}$ is a K-automorphism and hence $\mathrm{Tail}(\mathbf{T}^{-1}, \xi)$ is trivial. This partition represents outcomes in the far distant past of the process.

In a different direction notice that, since $\mathrm{Tail}(\mathbf{T}, \xi)$ is refined by π for any finite partition and automorphism $\mathbf{T}$, Lemma 4.4 tells us that the factor automorphism associated with the tail of any process $(\mathbf{T}, \xi)$ is deterministic, provided of course ξ is finite.

The next result is the key to proving that Definition 4.3 is equivalent to Kolmogoroff's original definition. Notice that this lemma also produces a measurable generating partition. However, the difficulty with this generating partition is that it may easily be nondenumerable.

Lemma 4.7. *If $(\Omega, \mathcal{F}, P, \mathbf{T})$ is an invertible dynamical system, there exists a measurable partition α such that $\alpha^\infty = \varepsilon$, $\mathrm{Tail}(\mathbf{T}, \alpha) = \pi(\mathbf{T})$, and $h(\mathbf{T}) = H(\alpha/\alpha^-)$.*

Proof. Let $\{\xi_k\}$ be a sequence of partitions with finite entropy such that $\xi_k \uparrow \varepsilon$. We define inductively a sequence $\{n_k\}$ of positive integers such that for any positive integer m

$$H\left[\bigvee_{k=1}^{l} \mathbf{T}^{-n_k}\xi_k \Big/ \left(\bigvee_{k=1}^{m-1} \mathbf{T}^{-n_k}\xi_k\right)^{-}\right] - H\left(\bigvee_{k=1}^{l} \mathbf{T}^{-n_k}\xi_k \Big/ \left(\bigvee_{k=1}^{m} \mathbf{T}^{-n_k}\xi_k\right)^{-}\right)$$
$$\leqslant \frac{1}{l}\cdot\frac{1}{2^{m-l}} \qquad (4.4)$$

for $l = 1, 2, \ldots, m-1$. The induction depends on Lemma 4.1 and goes as follows.

Assume we have integers $n_1, n_2, \ldots, n_{q-1}$ such that the inequalities (4.4) are satisfied for any positive integer $m \leqslant q-1$. Let α_l denote $\bigvee_{k=1}^{l} \mathbf{T}^{-n_k}\xi_k$ for $l = 1, 2, \ldots, q-1$. Since $\alpha_l \leqslant \alpha_{q-1}$ and $H(\alpha_l) < \infty$, Lemma 4.1 implies that for each l

$$H(\alpha_l/\alpha_{q-1}^-) - H(\alpha_l/\alpha_{q-1}^- \vee \mathbf{T}^{-n}\xi_q^-) \to 0$$

as $n \to \infty$. Thus there exist integers $n_{l,q}$, $l=1,2,\ldots,q-1$, such that

$$H(\alpha_l/\alpha_{q-1}^-) - H(\alpha_l/\alpha_{q-1}^- \vee \mathbf{T}^{-n}\xi_q^-) < \frac{1}{l}\cdot\frac{1}{2^{q-l}}$$

for all $n \geq n_{l,q}$. Let $n_q = \max\{n_{l,q} : l=1,2,\ldots,q-1\}$. Then

$$H(\alpha_l/\alpha_{q-1}^-) - H(\alpha_l/\alpha_{q-1}^- \vee \mathbf{T}^{-n_q}\xi_q^-) \leq \frac{1}{l}\cdot\frac{1}{2^{q-l}}$$

for $n \geq n_q$ and $l=1,2,\ldots,q-1$. Since

$$\begin{aligned}
\alpha_{q-1}^- \vee \mathbf{T}^{-n_q}\xi_k^- &= \bigvee_{j=1}^{\infty}\bigvee_{k=1}^{q-1} \mathbf{T}^{-n_k-j}\xi_k \vee \bigvee_{j=n_q+1}^{\infty} \mathbf{T}^{-j}\xi_q \\
&= \bigvee_{k=1}^{q-1} \mathbf{T}^{-n_k}\left(\bigvee_{j=1}^{\infty}\mathbf{T}^{-j}\xi_k\right) \vee T^{-n_q}\left(\bigvee_{j=1}^{\infty}\mathbf{T}^{-j}\xi_q\right) \\
&= \bigvee_{k=1}^{q} \mathbf{T}^{-n_k}\left(\bigvee_{j=1}^{\infty}\mathbf{T}^{-j}\xi_k\right) \\
&= \left(\bigvee_{k=1}^{q}\mathbf{T}^{-n_k}\xi_k\right)^- = \alpha_q^-,
\end{aligned}$$

we have

$$H(\alpha_l/\alpha_{q-1}^-) - H(\alpha_l/\alpha_q^-) < \frac{1}{l}\cdot\frac{1}{2^{q-l}} \qquad \text{for} \quad l=1,2,\ldots,q-1,$$

and the induction is complete.

Now if $l<q$ are fixed positive integers, summing the equations (4.4) gives

$$\begin{aligned}
H(\alpha_l/\alpha_l^-) - H(\alpha_l/\alpha_q^-) &< \sum_{m=l+1}^{q}\left[H(\alpha_l/\alpha_{m-1}^-) - H(\alpha_l/\alpha_m^-)\right] \\
&< \frac{1}{l}.
\end{aligned}$$

Let $\alpha = \bigvee_{l=1}^{\infty}\alpha_l = \bigvee_{l=1}^{\infty} = \bigvee_{k=1}^{l}\mathbf{T}^{-n_k}\xi_k$. Then $\alpha_q^- \uparrow \alpha^-$, and since $H(\alpha_l/\alpha_q^-) \leq H(\alpha_l) \leq \sum_{k=1}^{l} H(\xi_k) < \infty$ for any $l<q$, we have that $H(\alpha_l/\alpha_q^-) \downarrow H(\alpha_l/\alpha^-)$ as $q \to \infty$. Therefore

$$H(\alpha_l/\alpha_l^-) - H(\alpha_l/\alpha^-) \leq \frac{1}{l} \qquad \text{for} \quad l=1,2,\ldots.$$

Thus

$$\lim_{l\to\infty}\left[H(\alpha_l/\alpha_l^-)-H(\alpha_l/\alpha^-)\right]=0. \tag{4.5}$$

Given $l>0$,

$$\alpha_l^\infty=\bigvee_{j=-\infty}^{+\infty}\mathbf{T}^{-j}\bigvee_{k=1}^{l}\mathbf{T}^{-n_k}\xi_l$$

$$=\bigvee_{k=1}^{l}\bigvee_{j=-\infty}^{+\infty}\mathbf{T}^{-n_k-j}\xi_k\geqslant\xi_l,$$

and since $\xi_l\uparrow\varepsilon$, it follows that $\alpha_l^\infty\uparrow\varepsilon$ as $l\to\infty$. Thus

$$\varepsilon=\bigvee_{l=1}^{\infty}\bigvee_{j=-\infty}^{+\infty}\mathbf{T}^{-n_k}\xi_k=\bigvee_{j=-\infty}^{\infty}\bigvee_{l=1}^{\infty}\mathbf{T}^{-n_k}\xi_k=\alpha^\infty,$$

and Corollary 2.48 gives that

$$\lim_{l\to\infty}H(\alpha_l/\alpha_l^-)=\lim_{l\to\infty}h(\mathbf{T},\alpha_l)=h(\mathbf{T}).$$

Also since $\alpha_l\uparrow\alpha$,

$$\lim_{l\to\infty}H(\alpha_l/\alpha^-)=H(\alpha/\alpha^-).$$

Equation (4.5) now gives us that $H(\alpha/\alpha^-)=h(\mathbf{T})$.

All that remains to be proven is that Tail$(\mathbf{T},\alpha)$ is the Pinsker partition π. It follows from Lemma 4.2 that $\pi\leqslant$ Tail$(\mathbf{T},\alpha)$.

To obtain the reverse inequality let $\xi\leqslant$ Tail$(\mathbf{T},\alpha)$ with $H(\xi)<\infty$. Then for any k, $\mathbf{T}^k\xi\leqslant$ Tail$(\mathbf{T},\alpha)$, so that $\xi^\infty\leqslant$ Tail$(\mathbf{T},\alpha)$. But

$$\alpha^-=\bigvee_{j=1}^{\infty}\mathbf{T}^{-j}\alpha\geqslant\bigvee_{j=k}^{\infty}\mathbf{T}^{-j}\alpha\geqslant\operatorname{Tail}(\mathbf{T},\alpha),$$

so $\xi^\infty\leqslant\alpha^-$. Since $H(\xi\vee\alpha_p/\alpha_p^-)<\infty$ for all p, Theorem 2.33 gives

$$\begin{aligned}H(\xi/\xi^-)&=H(\xi\vee\alpha_p/\xi^-\vee\alpha_p^-)-H(\alpha_p/\alpha_p^-\vee\xi^\infty)\\&\leqslant H(\alpha_p/\alpha_p^-\vee\xi)+H(\xi/\alpha_p^-\vee\xi^-)-H(\alpha_p/\alpha_p^-\vee\xi^\infty)\\&\leqslant H(\alpha_p/\alpha_p^-)+H(\xi/\alpha_p^-)-H(\alpha_p/\alpha^-)\\&\leqslant\frac{1}{p}+H(\xi/\alpha_p^-).\end{aligned}$$

Taking the limit as $p \to \infty$ gives

$$H(\xi/\xi^-) \leqslant H(\xi/\alpha^-) = 0.$$

Thus $\xi \leqslant \pi$. Take a sequence $\{\xi_k\}$ of partitions with finite entropy such that $\xi_k \uparrow \mathrm{Tail}(\mathbf{T}, \eta)$. Then

$$\mathrm{Tail}(\mathbf{T}, \eta) = \bigvee_{k=1}^{\infty} \xi_k \leqslant \pi$$

and the lemma is proven.

THEOREM 4.8. *An invertible dynamical system* $(\Omega, \mathfrak{F}, P, \mathbf{T})$ *is a K-system if and only if there exists a measurable partition* η *such that*

$$\bigvee_{j=-\infty}^{+\infty} \mathbf{T}^{-j}\eta = \varepsilon, \qquad \text{i.e.} \quad \eta^{\infty} = \varepsilon, \tag{4.6}$$

and

$$\bigwedge_{n=1}^{\infty} \bigvee_{j=n}^{\infty} \mathbf{T}^{-j}\eta = \nu, \qquad \text{i.e.} \quad \mathrm{Tail}(\mathbf{T}, \eta) = \nu. \tag{4.7}$$

Proof. Suppose there exists a partition η satisfying the conditions. By Lemma 4.2, $\pi \leqslant \mathrm{Tail}(\mathbf{T}, \eta) = \nu$ and $\mathbf{T}$ is a K-automorphism.

Next suppose $\mathbf{T}$ is a K-automorphism. By Lemma 4.7 there exists η such that $\eta^{\infty} = \varepsilon$ and $\mathrm{Tail}(\mathbf{T}, \eta) = \pi$. Since $\pi = \nu$ by Theorem 4.5, the result is proven.

The usual definition of a K-automorphism is an automorphism which satisfies (4.6) and (4.7). It is easy to see from the theorem that Bernoulli shifts are K-automorphisms. Just take the time zero partition ξ_0 to be the generating partition with trivial tail. It is also immediate that any dynamical system which is isomorphic to a K-system is also a K-system, and hence any system which is isomorphic to a Bernoulli shift is a K-system. As we mentioned in the last section, it was thought for some time that every K-system was the isomorph of a Bernoulli shift, but this was proven to be false by Ornstein [97]. It has subsequently been shown [103] that there exist a nondenumerable number of nonisomorphic K-automorphisms with equal finite entropy no one of which is isomorphic to a Bernoulli shift.

To make a clear distinction between Bernoulli shifts and a dynamical system which is isomorphic to a Bernoulli shift, we introduced the term Bernoulli system in Chapter 3. For emphasis we repeat the definition here.

DEFINITION 4.9. A dynamical system $(\Omega, \mathcal{F}, P, \mathbf{T})$ is a *Bernoulli system* if it is isomorphic to a Bernoulli shift.

To illustrate the difference between a Bernoulli system and a Bernoulli shift, consider the following example.

Example 4.10 (*The baker's transformation*). Let $(I^2, \mathfrak{L}^2, \lambda^2)$ denote the unit square with Lebesgue measure. This is a Lebesgue space, and we shall define a transformation $\mathbf{T}$ of I^2 to itself in a geometric fashion. This transformation is called the baker's transformation because it is said to be similar to the process used by a baker when he is kneading dough.

Transform the unit square by a linear transformation which sends I^2 to the rectangle $[0,\frac{1}{2}]\times[0,2]$. Then cut this rectangle along the line $x=1$ and translate the right half of the rectangle to the top of the left half. The baker's transformation $\mathbf{T}$ is the composition of these two transformations, as shown in Figure 4.1.

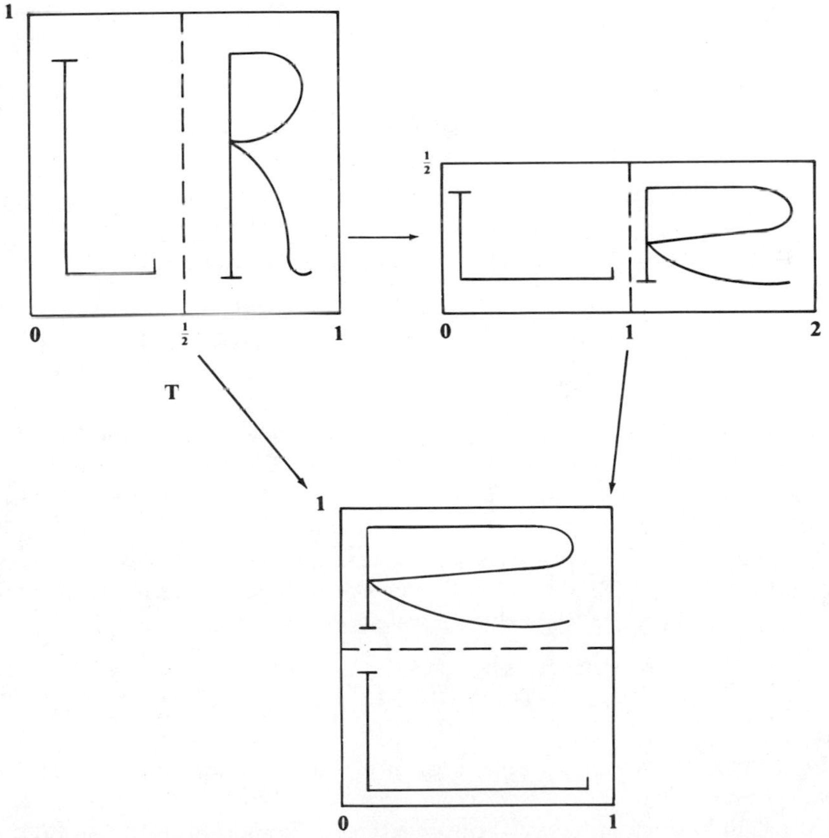

Figure 4.1

The analytic definition is given by

$$\mathbf{T}(x,y)=\begin{cases}\left(2x,\tfrac{1}{2}y\right), & 0\leqslant x\leqslant\tfrac{1}{2},\\ \left((2x),\left(\tfrac{1}{2}(y+1)\right)\right), & \tfrac{1}{2}<x<1,\end{cases}$$

where (x) denotes the fractional part of x.

To see that the system $(I^2,\mathcal{L}^2,\lambda^2,\mathbf{T})$ is a Bernoulli system, we shall indicate how it is isomorphic to $(\mathbf{B};\frac{1}{2},\frac{1}{2})$, a Bernoulli 2-shift with distribution $(\frac{1}{2},\frac{1}{2})$. Consider the partition $\xi=\{C_0,C_1\}$, where $C_0=[0,\frac{1}{2})\times[0,1)$ and $C_1=[\frac{1}{2},1)\times[0,1)$. These are marked in Figure 4.1 by L and R respectively. By consideration of the action of $\mathbf{T}$ one can see that

$$\begin{aligned}
\mathbf{T}^{-1}C_0&=\left\{\left[0,\tfrac{1}{4}\right)\times[0,1)\right\}\cup\left\{\left[\tfrac{1}{2},\tfrac{3}{4}\right)\times[0,1)\right\},\\
\mathbf{T}^{-1}C_1&=\left\{\left[\tfrac{1}{4},\tfrac{1}{2}\right)\times[0,1)\right\}\cup\left\{\left[\tfrac{3}{4},1\right)\times[0,1)\right\},\\
\mathbf{T}C_0&=[0,1)\times\left[0,\tfrac{1}{2}\right),\\
\mathbf{T}C_1&=[0,1)\times\left[\tfrac{1}{2},1\right),\\
\mathbf{T}^2C_0&=\left\{[0,1)\times\left[0,\tfrac{1}{4}\right)\right\}\cup\left\{[0,1)\times\left[\tfrac{1}{2},\tfrac{3}{4}\right)\right\},\\
\mathbf{T}^2C_1&=\left\{[0,1)\times\left[\tfrac{1}{4},\tfrac{1}{2}\right)\right\}\cup\left\{[0,1)\times\left[\tfrac{3}{4},1\right)\right\}.
\end{aligned}$$

Thus the atoms of $\mathbf{T}^{-1}\xi\vee\xi\vee\mathbf{T}\xi\vee\mathbf{T}^2\xi$ consist of the rectangles

$$\left[\frac{j}{4},\frac{j+1}{4}\right)\times\left[\frac{k}{4},\frac{k+1}{4}\right)\qquad\text{with } j,k=0,1,2,3.$$

In general the atoms of $\bigvee_{l=-K}^{K}\mathbf{T}^{-l}\xi$ will consist of rectangles with vertices at dyadic rationals and hence $\xi^\infty=\varepsilon$ (mod 0), where ε is the point partition in I^2.

It is also easy to convince oneself that the partition $\{\mathbf{T}^l\xi_0: l=0,\pm1,\pm2,\dots\}$ are independent, so we can get an isomorphism between $(I^2,\mathcal{L}^2,\lambda^2,\mathbf{T})$ and $(\mathbf{B};\frac{1}{2},\frac{1}{2})$ as follows: For almost all $z\in I^2$, there is a unique sequence $\{\omega_l\}_{l=-\infty}^{+\infty}$, where ω_l is either zero or one, such that

$$\{z\}=\bigcap_{l=-\infty}^{+\infty}\mathbf{T}^{-l}C_{\omega_l}.$$

The map which assigns z to this sequence is an isomorphism between the two systems.

We shall have more to say about this type of isomorphism in Section 4.5 when we discuss Ornstein's fundamental lemma. Before doing this, however, we give another characterization of K-automorphisms, in terms of a probabilistic relationship between partitions which may be thought of as a type of approximate independence between experiments.

The proof we gave that the tail of the time zero partition ξ_0 of a Bernoulli shift was trivial depended upon the independence of the sequence $\{\mathbf{T}^j\xi_0\}_{j=-\infty}^{+\infty}$, but we have subsequently seen that every finite partition η in a Bernoulli shift has a trivial tail even though the sequence $\{\mathbf{T}^j\eta\}$ may not be independent. This suggests that the dependence between these experiments tends to disappear as time passes. That is actually the case, not only for Bernoulli shifts but for K-automorphisms in general, and hence for Bernoulli systems as well as shifts. The condition is defined in terms of the following concept, which is due to Ornstein [93].

DEFINITION 4.11. Let ξ and η be measurable partitions of a Lebesgue space $(\Omega,\mathcal{F},P)$ with ξ countable. For c a positive real number, ξ is *c-independent* of η, denoted by $\xi \overset{c}{\perp} \eta$, if there exists a set $Q\in\eta^\wedge$ such that $P(Q)\geqslant 1-c$ and

$$\sum_{A\in\xi} |P^\eta(\omega,A)-P(A)|<c \qquad \text{a.e. on } Q. \tag{4.8}$$

In case η is also countable (4.8) can be written as

$$\sum_{A\in\xi}\left|\frac{P(A\cap B)}{P(B)}-P(A)\right|<c$$

for all $B\in\eta$ except for a collection of atoms whose total measure is less than c. A sequence $\{\xi^i\}$ is c-independent if $\xi^n \overset{c}{\perp} \bigvee_{i=1}^{n-1}\xi^i$ for all n.

LEMMA 4.12. *If ξ is a finite measurable partition of an invertible dynamical system $(\Omega,\mathcal{F},P,\mathbf{T})$, then* Tail$(\mathbf{T},\xi)$ *is trivial if and only if for every positive integer M and positive number c there exists an integer $N=N(M,c)$ such that*

$$\bigvee_{i=-M}^{M}\mathbf{T}^{-i}\xi \overset{c}{\perp} \bigvee_{j=M+n}^{\infty}\mathbf{T}^{-j}\xi$$

for all $n\geqslant N$.

Proof. Suppose first that ξ satisfies the condition. Let A be any event in Tail$(\mathbf{T},\xi)^\wedge$ with positive measure. We shall show that $P(A)=1$.

Let c be a given positive number. Since Tail$(\mathbf{T},\xi)$ is refined by $\xi^\infty=\bigvee_{j=-\infty}^{+\infty}\mathbf{T}^{-j}\xi$, we have $A\in(\xi^\infty)^\wedge$, and by Lemma 1.10 there exists an integer M and a set B_M with $B_M\in(\bigvee_{j=-M}^{M}\mathbf{T}^{-j}\xi)^\wedge$ such that $P(A\,\triangle B_M)<c$.

Since ξ is finite, $\bigvee_{j=-M}^{M}\mathbf{T}^{-j}\xi$ is a finite partition and $B_M=\bigcup_{j=1}^{K}B_j$, where B_j are atoms of this partition. Thus

$$c>P(A\,\triangle B_M)=\sum_{j=1}^{K}P(A\cup B_j)-\sum_{j=1}^{K}P(A\cap B_j),$$

so that

$$-\sum_{j=1}^{K}P(A\cap B_j)<-\sum_{j=1}^{K}P(B_j)+c. \tag{4.9}$$

Also, if B is any atom of $\bigvee_{j=-M}^{M}\mathbf{T}^{-j}\xi$ with $B\cap B_M=\varnothing$, then $A\cap B\subset\Omega-B_M$, so that

$$\sum_{B\cap B_M=\varnothing}P(A\cap B)=P\Big(A\cap\bigcup B\Big)\leqslant P(A-B_M)<c. \tag{4.10}$$

Now there exists an integer $N=N(M,c)$ such that for all $n\geqslant N$

$$\bigvee_{j=-M}^{M}\mathbf{T}^{-j}\xi\overset{c}{\perp}\bigvee_{j=M+n}^{\infty}\mathbf{T}^{-j}\xi.$$

Let $\zeta(n)=\bigvee_{j=M+n}^{\infty}\mathbf{T}^{-j}\xi$ and $\eta=\bigvee_{j=-M}^{M}\mathbf{T}^{-j}\xi$. Then for each $n\geqslant N$, there exists a set $Q_n\in\zeta(n)^{\wedge}$ such that $P(Q_n)\geqslant 1-c$ and

$$\sum_{B\in\eta}|P^{\zeta(n)}(\omega,B)-P(B)|<c$$

for almost all $\omega\in Q_n$.

Since $A\in\zeta(n)^{\wedge}$ for all n, Equation (1.5) gives

$$\sum_{B\in\eta}|P(A\cap B)-P(A)P(B)|=\sum_{B}\left|\int_A P(d\omega)\{P^{\zeta(n)}(\omega,B)-P(B)\}\right|$$

$$\leqslant\int_A P(d\omega)\sum_{B\in\eta}|P^{\zeta(n)}(\omega,B)-P(B)|$$

$$<\int_{Q_n}P(d\omega)\sum_{B\in\eta}|P^{\zeta(n)}(\omega,B)-P(B)|+P(\Omega-Q_n).$$

Since for all $n\geqslant N$ the right hand side of this inequality is less than $2c$, we have

$$\sum_{B\in\eta}|P(A\cap B)-P(A)P(B)|<2c. \tag{4.11}$$

Now

$$0 \leqslant P(A) - P(A)^2 = \sum_{B \in \eta} [P(A \cap B) - P(A)P(A \cap B)]$$

$$= \sum_{j=1}^{K} \{P(A \cap B_j) - P(A)P(A \cap B_j)\}$$

$$+ \sum_{B \cap B_M = \varnothing} P(A \cap B).$$

Applying the inequalities (4.9) and (4.10), we get

$$P(A) - P(A)^2 \leqslant \sum_{j=1}^{K} [P(A \cap B_j) - P(A)P(B_j)] + 2c.$$

Since c was arbitrary, $P(A) = P(A)^2$ and $P(A) = 1$.

Conversely suppose $\mathrm{Tail}(\mathbf{T}, \xi)$ is trivial. Let $\zeta(n) = \bigvee_{j=n}^{\infty} \mathbf{T}^{-j}\xi^{-}$. Since $\zeta(n) \downarrow \mathrm{Tail}(\mathbf{T}, \xi)$, the martingale theorem (cf. Section 1.8) implies that

$$\lim_{n \to \infty} P^{\zeta(n)}(\omega, B) = P(B) \qquad \text{a.e.}$$

for every set $B \in \mathfrak{F}$. Let M and $c > 0$ be given. Since ξ is finite, $\bigvee_{j=-M}^{M} \mathbf{T}^{-j}\xi$ is finite. Suppose this partition contains L atoms. For each $B \in \bigvee_{j=-M}^{M} \mathbf{T}^{-j}\xi$ there exists an integer $N(M, c, B)$ such that

$$|P^{\zeta(M+n)}(\omega, B) - P(B)| < c/L$$

for all $n \geqslant N(M, c, B)$ and almost all ω in Ω. If $N = \max\{N(M, c, B) : B \in \bigvee_{j=-M}^{M} \mathbf{T}^{-j}\xi\}$, we have that

$$\bigvee_{j=-M}^{M} \mathbf{T}^{-j}\xi \overset{c}{\perp} \bigvee_{j=M+n}^{\infty} \mathbf{T}^{-j}\xi$$

for all $n \geqslant N$.

THEOREM 4.13. *An invertible dynamical system $(\Omega, \mathfrak{F}, P, \mathbf{T})$ is a K-system if and only if for each finite partition ξ, positive integer M, and real number $c > 0$, there exists an integer N such that*

$$\bigvee_{j=-M}^{M} \mathbf{T}^{-j}\xi \overset{c}{\perp} \bigvee_{j=M+n}^{\infty} \mathbf{T}^{-j}\xi$$

for all $n \geqslant N$.

COROLLARY 4.14. *An invertible dynamical system $(\Omega, \mathfrak{F}, P, \mathbf{T})$ with finite entropy is a K-system if and only if there exists a finite generating partition ξ such that for every positive integer M and real number $c>0$, there exists an integer N such that*

$$\bigvee_{j=-M}^{M} \mathbf{T}^{-j}\xi \overset{c}{\perp} \bigvee_{j=M+n}^{\infty} \mathbf{T}^{-j}\xi$$

for all $n \geqslant N$.

Proof. The only thing which is not clear in the proof of this result is how one can obtain a finite generating partition. This can be done for any ergodic dynamical system with finite entropy. For a proof see Krieger [71], Smorodinsky [148], or Denker [33].

The reader will also notice that the condition in Theorem 4.13 is a type of asymptotic independence condition. Various types of asymptotic independence for dynamical systems have been defined in ergodic theory under the name of mixing. For a classical treatment of mixing in ergodic theory see Halmos [56], and for the relationship between *K*-automorphisms and mixing see Smorodinsky [148] or Sucheston [150, 151].

Pinsker had conjectured that any ergodic metric automorphism with positive entropy was isomorphic to a product of a *K*-automorphism and an automorphism with zero entropy. This was shown to be false by Ornstein [98] when he used his example of a *K*-automorphism without a square root to obtain a counterexample. The argument is simple and goes as follows:

Let $\mathbf{T}$ be a *K*-automorphism without a square root acting on the unit interval $(I, \mathfrak{L}, \lambda)$ with Lebesgue measure. Define the automorphism $\hat{\mathbf{T}}$ on $\{a, b\} \times I$ by

$$\hat{\mathbf{T}}(x,y) = \begin{cases} (b,y) & \text{if } x=a, \\ (a,\mathbf{T}y) & \text{if } x=b, \end{cases}$$

where a uniform distribution is assumed on $\{a, b\}$. It is easy to see that $\hat{\mathbf{T}}^2(x,y)=(x,\mathbf{T}y)$. Thus if $\hat{\mathbf{T}}=\mathbf{H}\times\mathbf{K}$, where $\mathbf{H}$ has zero entropy, and $\mathbf{K}$ is a *K*-automorphism, then $\hat{\mathbf{T}}^2 \cong \mathbf{H}^2 \times \mathbf{K}^2 \cong \mathbf{I}\times\mathbf{T}$, so that $\mathbf{K}^2=\mathbf{T}$, contrary to the assumption that $\mathbf{T}$ did not have a square root.

It was subsequently shown by Ornstein [99] that there is a mixing automorphism which does not satisfy Pinsker's conjecture.

A modification of the Pinsker property has been given by Thouvenot [158]. A system $(\Omega, \mathfrak{F}, P, \mathbf{T})$ has the *weak Pinsker property* if there exists a sequence $\{\xi_n\}$ of invariant measurable partitions such that $\xi_n \geqslant \xi_{n+1}$, $\lim_{n\to\infty} h(\mathbf{T}_{\xi_n})=0$, and for each n there exists an independent partition β_n

such that β_n^∞ and ξ_n are independent and $\beta_n^\infty \vee \xi_n = \varepsilon$. (Notice that this says that for each n, $\mathbf{T}$ is isomorphic to the product $\mathbf{T}_{\beta_n^\infty} \times \mathbf{T}_{\xi_n}$, and the partitions ξ_n are complemented in the terminology of Section 4.8.) Thouvenot has shown that if a system has the weak Pinsker property, then so has every factor, and the class of automorphisms which are products of a Bernoulli system and some other system have the weak Pinsker property. (See Section 4.8 for more information on such systems.)

4.4 Spaces of Ordered Partitions, Weak Independence, and Weak Dependence

In this section we shall introduce some metrics on the set of all finite ordered partitions of a Lebesgue space which will allow us to make approximation arguments. We shall also introduce refinements of the ideas developed in Section 1.3 and in Chapter 2 concerning the relationship between the partial order in this set and independence or dependence of experiments. These refinements are fundamental to the development of the Ornstein theory.

Throughout the remainder of this chapter all partitions of Lebesgue spaces Ω will be finite ordered partitions (except in certain limiting cases). If ξ is such a partition which has k atoms, we shall always consider the factor space Ω_ξ to be the set $\{0,1,2,\ldots,k-1\}$ by identifying the ith atom C_i with the integer i. With this convention the canonical projection map $\mathbf{N}_\xi$ will always take its values in an initial segment of the nonnegative integers, and the ith atom of ξ can be represented by $\mathbf{N}_\xi^{-1}(i)$.

The factor probability P_ξ on the space $\Omega_\xi = \{0,1,\ldots,k-1\}$ will then be determined by the discrete probability vector

$$d(\xi) = \big(P(\mathbf{N}_\xi^{-1}(0)),\ldots, P(\mathbf{N}_\xi^{-1}(k-1))\big).$$

Notice that if ξ is a finite ordered partition of a Lebesgue space, then $(\Omega_\xi, P_\xi) = (\{0,1,\ldots,k-1\}, d(\xi))$ is a source alphabet as discussed in Chapter 3.

For the Lebesgue space $(\Omega, \mathfrak{F}, P)$ let $\mathfrak{Z}_k(\Omega)$ denote the set of all (mod 0) equivalence classes of finite ordered partitions with no more than k atoms, and denote by $\mathfrak{Z}(\Omega)$ the union over all k of $\mathfrak{Z}_k(\Omega)$. We now give three ways of measuring distance between points in $\mathfrak{Z}(\Omega)$.

Definition 4.15. The *distribution distance* between ξ and η in $\mathfrak{Z}(\Omega)$ is the l_1-distance between $d(\xi)$ and $d(\eta)$ and is denoted by $|d(\xi) - d(\eta)|$, i.e.,

$$|d(\xi) - d(\eta)| = \sum_{j=0}^{k-1} |P(\mathbf{N}_\xi^{-1}(j)) - P(\mathbf{N}_\eta^{-1}(j))|. \tag{4.12}$$

The *partition distance*, or partition metric between ξ and η, denoted by $|\xi-\eta|$, is given by

$$|\xi-\eta| = \sum_{j=0}^{k-1} P\left[\mathbf{N}_\xi^{-1}(j) \triangle \mathbf{N}_\eta^{-1}(j)\right]. \tag{4.13}$$

In Equations (4.12) and (4.13), $k=\max\{|\xi|,|\eta|\}$, and if one partition has fewer atoms than the other, we adjoin empty sets to the smaller partition.

The *Rohlin distance* on $\mathfrak{Z}(\Omega)$ is defined by

$$R(\xi,\eta)=H(\xi/\eta)+H(\eta/\xi). \tag{4.14}$$

LEMMA 4.16. *The distribution and Rohlin distances are pseudometrics, and the partition distance is a metric.*

If $(\Omega, \mathfrak{F}, P)$ *is a Lebesgue space, then* $\mathfrak{Z}_k(\Omega)$ *is a complete metric space with respect to both the distribution and partition distances.*

Finally, for all $\xi, \eta \in \mathfrak{Z}(\Omega)$,

$$|d(\xi)-d(\eta)| \leqslant |\xi-\eta|.$$

Proof. It is a well-known fact (Halmos [55]) that the measure algebra of a measure μ is a complete metric space with respect to the metric $\rho(C,D)=\mu(C \triangle D)$. Since $|\xi-\eta|=\sum_{i=0}^{k-1}\rho(\mathbf{N}_\xi^{-1}(i) \triangle \mathbf{N}_\eta^{-1}(i))$, it follows that $\mathfrak{Z}_k(\Omega)$ is a complete metric space with respect to the partition metric.

The other statements are immediate from the definitions.

Recall that in Section 1.3 we indicated how one can think of partitions as experiments whose outcomes were the atoms of the partition. From this point of view $\xi \leqslant \eta$ indicated that the experiment ξ was completely determined by η or, stated another way, ξ was totally dependent on η. We further showed that ξ is refined by η if and only if the average uncertainty about ξ given the experiment η is zero, i.e., $\xi \leqslant \eta$ iff $H(\xi/\eta)=0$.

An approximate form of dependence of this type can be defined using the metrics just introduced. This quantitative form of dependence is obtained by requiring the partition ξ to be close in the partition metric to a partition which is refined by η. The definition is given below, after which we show that this type of dependence is characterized by requiring $H(\xi/\eta)$ to be small.

DEFINITION 4.17. Let ξ and η be partitions in $\mathfrak{Z}(\Omega)$, and c be a positive real number. We say that ξ is *c-refined* by η, denoted by $\xi \overset{c}{\leqslant} \eta$, if there exists a partition ξ' such that $\xi' \leqslant \eta$ and $|\xi-\xi'|<c$.

THEOREM 4.18. *For every $c>0$ and positive integer $k>1$, there exist $d>0$ such that if $\xi\in\mathfrak{Z}_k(\Omega)$ and $H(\xi/\eta)<d$, then $\xi \overset{c}{\leqslant} \eta$.*

Proof. Let $c>0$ and k be given. Let d_1 be less than $c/2k$ and so small that $t\in[0,e^{-1})$ with $|t\log t|<d_1$ implies $t<c/2k$, and that $t\in(e^{-1},1]$ with $|t\log t|<d_1$ implies $1-t<c/2k$.

Take $d=d_1^2$. Let $\xi=\{A_1, A_2,\dots, A_k\}$ be in $\mathfrak{Z}_k(\Omega)$, and η be any partition such that $H(\xi/\eta)<d$. Then

$$d_1^2>\int_\Omega P(d\omega)\left\{-\sum_{i=1}^k P^\eta(\omega, A_i)\log P^\eta(\omega, A_i)\right\}$$

$$\geqslant\int_{E(d_1)} P(d\omega)\left\{-\sum_{i=1}^k P^\eta(\omega, A_i)\log P^\eta(\omega, A_i)\right\},$$

where $E(d_1)=\{\omega: -\sum_{i=1}^k P^\eta(\omega, A_i)\log P^\eta(\omega, A_i)\geqslant d_1\}$. Thus $P(E(d_1))\leqslant d_1$, and for all $\omega\notin E(d_1)$

$$-\sum_{i=1}^k P^\eta(\omega, A_i)\log P^\eta(\omega, A_i)<d_1.$$

By the choice of d_1,

$$\left\{\omega: P^\eta(\omega, A_i)<\frac{c}{2k}\right\}\cup\left\{\omega: P^\eta(\omega,\Omega-A_i)<\frac{c}{2k}\right\}$$

contains $\Omega-E(d_1)$ and hence has measure greater than $1-d_1$. Thus

$$P\left(\left\{\omega: \frac{c}{2k}\leqslant P^\eta(\omega, A_i)\leqslant 1-\frac{c}{2k}\right\}\right)<d_1.$$

For each $i=1,2,\dots, k$ let

$$B_i=\left\{\omega: P^\eta(\omega, A_i)<\frac{c}{2k}\right\}\cup\left\{\omega: P^\eta(\omega,\Omega-A_i)<\frac{c}{2k}\right\}.$$

Then B_i is $\hat{\eta}$-measurable and

$$P(A_i\triangle B_i)=\int_{\Omega-B_i} P(d\omega)P^\eta(\omega, A_i)+\int_{B_i} P(d\omega)P^\eta(\omega,\Omega-A_i)$$

$$<d_1+\frac{c}{2k}<\frac{c}{k}.$$

Thus

$$\sum_{i=1}^{k} P(A_i \triangle B_i) < c.$$

Define the partition $\xi_i' = \{B_i'\}$ where $B_i' = B_i - \bigcup_{j<i} B_j$. Since the B_i are $\eta^{\wedge}$-sets, so are the B_i' and hence $\xi' \leqslant \eta$. Moreover

$$|\xi' - \xi| \leqslant \sum_{i=1}^{k} P(A_i \triangle B_i) < c,$$

and the theorem is proven.

COROLLARY 4.19. *For every $c > 0$ and partitions $\xi, \eta \in \mathfrak{Z}_k(\Omega)$ there exists $d > 0$ such that if* $\max\{H(\xi/\eta), H(\eta/\xi)\} < d$, *then* $|\xi - \eta| < c$.

Proof. Let c' be selected less than c and smaller than the measure of any atom in ξ or η with positive measure. Select d small enough so that $H(\xi/\eta) < d$ implies $\xi \overset{c'}{\leqslant} \eta$ and $H(\eta/\xi) < d$ implies $\eta \overset{c'}{\leqslant} \xi$. Thus if $\max\{H(\xi/\eta), H(\eta/\xi)\} < d$, there exist $\xi' \leqslant \eta$ with $|\xi' - \xi| < c'$. Since c' is less than the measure of any atom of ξ with positive measure, ξ' contains at least as many atoms of positive measure as ξ. Since $\xi' \leqslant \eta$, we have that ξ contains no more atoms of positive measure than η. Using the same argument, since $\eta \overset{c'}{\leqslant} \xi$, we have that η contains no more atoms than ξ and hence ξ and η have the same number of nonzero atoms. But ξ' is refined by η and has at least as many atoms as ξ. Thus $\xi' = \eta$ (mod 0) and $|\xi - \eta| = |\xi' - \xi| < c' < c$.

LEMMA 4.20. *For every $c > 0$ and positive integer $k > 1$ there exists a $d > 0$ such that if $\xi, \eta \in \mathfrak{Z}_k(\Omega)$ with $|\xi - \eta| < d$, then* $\max\{H(\xi/\eta), H(\eta/\xi)\} < c$.

Proof. Let c and k be given. Since $-t\log t$ is uniformly continuous on $[0,1]$, there exists $d_1 > 0$ such that $|t_1 - t_2| < d_1$ implies that $|t_1 \log t_1 - t_2 \log t_2| < c(k+1)^{-1}$. Let d_2 be smaller than d_1 and $c(k+1)^{-1}$, and take d to be d_2^2.

Let ξ and η be partitions in $\mathfrak{Z}_k(\Omega)$ such that $|\xi - \eta| < d$. If $\xi = \{A_1, \dots, A_k\}$ and $\eta = \{B_1, \dots, B_k\}$, we have

$$\begin{aligned}
\sum_{i=1}^{k} \int_\Omega P(d\omega) |P^\eta(\omega, A_i) - 1_{B_i}(\omega)| &\leqslant \sum_{i=1}^{k} \int_\Omega P(d\omega) |P^\eta(\omega, A_i) - P^\eta(\omega, B_i)| \\
&\leqslant \sum_{i=1}^{k} \int_\Omega P(d\omega) E^\eta(|1_{A_i} - 1_{B_i}|) \\
&= |\xi - \eta| < d_2^2.
\end{aligned}$$

If $E=\{\omega:\Sigma_{i=1}^{k}|P^{\eta}(\omega, A_i)-1_{B_i}(\omega)|\geqslant d_2\}$, then $P(E)\leqslant d_2$ by the previous inequality, and we have that

$$\sum_{i=1}^{k}|P^{\eta}(\omega, A_i)-1_{B_i}(\omega)|<d_2 \tag{4.15}$$

except on an η-set of measure less than d_2. Since $d_2<d_1$, by (4.15) and the choice of d_1

$$\sum_{i=1}^{k}|P^{\eta}(\omega, A_i)\log P^{\eta}(\omega, A_i)-1_{B_i}(\omega)\log 1_{B_i}(\omega)|<\frac{kc}{k+1}$$

except on a η-set of measure less than d_2. Thus

$$\begin{aligned} H(\xi/\eta)&=\int_{\Omega}P(d\omega)\left\{-\sum_{i=1}^{k}P^{\eta}(\omega, A_i)\log P^{\eta}(\omega, A_i)\right\}\\ &=\int_{\Omega-E}P(d\omega)\left\{\sum_{i=1}^{k}|P^{\eta}(\omega, A_i)\log p^{\eta}(\omega, A_i)\right.\\ &\quad\left.-1_{B_i}(\omega)\log 1_{B_i}(\omega)|\right\}\\ &\quad+\int_{E}P(d\omega)\left\{\sum_{i=1}^{k}|P^{\eta}(\omega, A_i)\log P^{\eta}(\omega, A_i)\right.\\ &\quad\left.-1_{B_i}(\omega)\log 1_{B_i}(\omega)|\right\}\\ &\leqslant\frac{kc}{k+1}+d_2<c. \end{aligned}$$

The same reasoning shows that $H(\eta/\xi)<c$.

COROLLARY 4.21. *The topological space determined by the Rohlin pseudometric on $\mathfrak{Z}_k(\Omega)$ is homeomorphic to the space determined by the partition metric on $\mathfrak{Z}_k(\Omega)$.*

LEMMA 4.22. *For every $c>0$ and positive integer k there exists $d>0$ such that if ξ and η are partitions in $\mathfrak{Z}_k(\Omega)$ with $\xi \overset{d}{\leqslant} \eta$, then $H(\xi/\eta)<c$.*

Proof. Let d be the number in Lemma 4.20 associated with c, and suppose $\xi \overset{d}{\leqslant} \eta$. Then there exist $\xi'\leqslant\eta$ with $|\xi'-\xi|<d$ and hence $H(\xi/\xi')<c$. However,

$$H(\xi/\eta)\leqslant H(\xi/\xi')<c.$$

Theorem 4.23. *Let* $(\Omega, \mathfrak{F}, P, \mathbf{T})$ *be a dynamical system. The rate of information generation by* $\mathbf{T}$ *is uniformly continuous on* $\mathfrak{Z}_k(\Omega)$ *and continuous on* $\mathfrak{Z}(\Omega)$ *with respect to the partition metric (and consequently with respect to the distribution and Rohlin pseudometrics).*

Proof. This follows immediately from Corollary 4.21 and the inequality

$$|h(\mathbf{T},\xi)-h(\mathbf{T},\eta)| \leqslant H(\xi/\eta)+H(\eta/\xi),$$

which is obtained from Lemma 2.29.

Corollary 4.24. *If* $(\Omega, \mathfrak{F}, P, \mathbf{T})$ *is a dynamical system on a nonatomic Lebesgue space and* ξ *is any partition in* $\mathfrak{Z}_k(\Omega)$, *then* $h(\mathbf{T},\ )$ *takes on every value between* 0 *and* $h(\mathbf{T},\xi)$.

Proof (Brown [27]). Suppose $\xi=\{A_1, A_2,\dots, A_k\}$ and $P(A_1)<1$. For each $t\in[0,1)$ let ξ_t be that partition $\{A_{t1}, A_{t2},\dots, A_{tk}\}$ where

$$P(A_{t1})=1-t[1-P(A_1)],$$

$$P(A_{tj})=\frac{1-P(A_{t1})}{1-P(A_1)}P(A_j), \qquad j=2,3,\dots,k.$$

Since $h(\mathbf{T},\ )$ is continuous in distribution, $h(\mathbf{T},\xi_t)$ is a continuous map of $[0,1]$ onto $[0, h(\mathbf{T},\xi)]$. The intermediate value property of continuous functions completes the proof.

The reader will notice that Theorem 4.18 and Lemma 4.22 give a result analogous to Theorem 2.23. These two theorems can be interpreted as saying that approximate dependence of experiments can be characterized by conditional entropy.

In the last section we introduced a notion of approximate independence, which we now show can also be characterized by conditional entropy. Recall that Theorem 2.9 states that ξ and η are independent if and only if $H(\xi)=H(\xi/\eta)$. The notion of approximate independence will be characterized by requiring $H(\xi)$ to be close to $H(\xi/\eta)$. The proof we give is due to Smorodinsky [148].

Lemma 4.25. *For every* $c>0$ *there exists* $d>0$ *such that if* $\{x_i\}$ *and* $\{y_i\}$ *are nonnegative real numbers with* $1\geqslant \Sigma x_i \geqslant \Sigma y_i$ *and* $\Sigma x_i \log x_i y_i^{-1}<d$, *then* $\Sigma|x_i-y_i|<c$.

Proof. Let $\rho(t)=t-1-\log t$ for $t\in(0,\infty)$. Let $c>0$ be given. Since ρ decreases on $(0,1]$ and increases on $(1,\infty)$, one can use the continuous inverses of ρ over these intervals to find d_1 such that if $\rho(t)<d_1$ then $|t-1|<c/4$. Notice that $\rho(t)\geqslant 0$ for all t.

Take $d=\min\{c/4, d_1^2\}$. Suppose $\{x_i\}$ and $\{y_i\}$ are sequences of nonnegative real numbers satisfying the hypotheses of the lemma. We may also assume without loss of generality that all x_i and y_i are nonzero.

For each i, set $t_i=y_i/x_i$ and $\rho_i=\rho(t_i)$. Then

$$d_1^2>\sum x_i \log x_i y_i^{-1}=\sum x_i-\sum y_i+\sum x_i\rho_i,$$

and we have that $\Sigma x_i\rho_i \leqslant d_1^2$. Let E denote those indices i such that $\rho_i \geqslant d_1$, and E' the remaining indices. Thus

$$d_1^2>\sum_E x_i\rho_i \geqslant d_1 \sum_E x_i$$

and

$$\sum_E x_i \leqslant d_1.$$

Also if $i\in E'$, then $\rho(t_i)<d_1$ implies by the choice of d_1 that $|y_i/x_i-1|<c/4$, and it follows that $\Sigma_{E'}|x_i-y_i|<c/4$. Therefore,

$$\begin{aligned}\sum |x_i-y_i| &= \sum_E |x_i-y_i|+\sum_{E'}|x_i-y_i| \\ &< \sum_E x_i+\sum_E y_i+\frac{c}{4}.\end{aligned}$$

However,

$$\begin{aligned}\sum_E y_i &= \sum y_i-\sum_{E'} y_i \leqslant \sum x_i-\sum_{E'} y_i \\ &= \sum_{E'}(x_i-y_i)+\sum_E x_i \\ &< \frac{c}{4}+d_1,\end{aligned}$$

and hence

$$\sum |x_i-y_i|<2d_1+\frac{c}{2}<c.$$

THEOREM 4.26. *For every $c>0$ there exists $d>0$ such that if ξ is a countable partition and ζ any measurable partition with $H(\xi)-H(\xi/\zeta)<d$, then ξ is c-independent of ζ.*

Proof. Let $c>0$ be given. Let d_1 be less than the d of Lemma 4.25 and c. Take $d=d_1^2$. Let ξ be a countable partition, and ζ any partition such that $H(\xi)-H(\xi/\zeta)<d$.

Then, using Lemma 2.8,

$$d_1^2>H(\xi)-H(\xi/\zeta)$$

$$=\int_{\Omega_\zeta} P(d\bar{\omega})\left\{\sum_{A\in\xi} P^\zeta(A|\bar{\omega})\log P^\zeta(A|\bar{\omega})P(A)^{-1}\right\}.$$

$$\geqslant\int_E P(d\bar{\omega})\left\{\sum_{A\in\xi} P^\zeta(A|\bar{\omega})\log P^\zeta(A|\bar{\omega})P(A)^{-1}\right\}\geqslant d_1 P_\zeta(E),$$

where $E=\{\bar{\omega}\in\Omega_\zeta : \Sigma_A P^\zeta(A|\bar{\omega})\log P^\zeta(A|\bar{\omega})P(A)^{-1}\geqslant d_1\}$. Thus $P_\zeta(E)<d_1<c$, and for almost all $\bar{\omega}\notin E$

$$\sum_A P^\zeta(A|\bar{\omega})\log P^\zeta(A|\bar{\omega})P(A)^{-1}<d_1.$$

It now follows from Lemma 4.25 that for almost all $\bar{\omega}\notin E$

$$\sum_{A\in\xi}|P^\zeta(A|\bar{\omega})-P(A)|<c$$

and ξ is c-independent of ζ.

THEOREM 4.27. *For every $c>0$ and integer $k>1$ there exists $d>0$ such that if $\xi\in\mathfrak{Z}_k(\Omega)$ and ξ is d-independent of ζ, then $H(\xi)-H(\xi/\zeta)<c$.*

Proof. Let $c>0$ and k be given. Select d_1 so small that $|t_1-t_2|<d_1$ implies that $|t_1\log t_1-t_2\log t_2|<c(k+1)^{-1}$. Let $\xi\in\mathfrak{Z}_k(\Omega)$ be given, and take any ζ such that ξ is d-independent of ζ, where $d=\min\{d_1, ec/2(k+1)\}$.

Let B be a ζ-set with measure less than d such that

$$\sum_{A\in\xi}|P^\zeta(\omega,A)-P(A)|<d\leqslant d_1 \qquad \text{a.e. on } \Omega-B,$$

and by choice of d_1

$$\sum_{A\in\xi}|P(A)\log P(A)-P^\zeta(\omega,A)\log P^\zeta(\omega,A)|<\frac{kc}{k+1}$$

a.e. on $\Omega - B$. Consequently,

$$H(\xi) - H(\xi/\zeta) \leqslant \int_{\Omega - B} + \int_B P(d\omega)\left\{ \sum_{A \in \xi} |P(A)\log P(A) - P^{\zeta}(\omega, A)\log P^{\zeta}(\omega, A)| \right\}$$

$$< \frac{2}{e}\mu(B) + \frac{kc}{k+1}$$

$$< c.$$

4.5 Coding and Ornstein's Fundamental Lemma

In Section 1.7 we indicated how a measurable partition ξ of a dynamical system induces a stochastic process. Recall that the path space of this process is isomorphic to the factor system obtained from $\bigvee_{j=-\infty}^{+\infty} \mathbf{T}^{-j}\xi$, and consequently if ξ is a generating partition, the path space of the process $(\mathbf{T}, \xi)$ is isomorphic to the original system.

The path space consists of sequences of elements from Ω_ξ, so if ξ is a finite ordered partition, the points in the path space are sequences $(\ldots, i_{-2}, i_{-1}, i_0, i_1, \ldots)$ of integers $i_j \in \Omega_\xi$. The map which sends $\omega \in \Omega$ to $(i_n)_{-\infty}^{+\infty}$ if and only if $\mathbf{T}^{-n}\mathbf{N}_\xi(\omega) = i_n$ is an isomorphism between the factor space associated with $\bigvee_{j=-\infty}^{+\infty} \mathbf{T}^{-j}\xi$ and the sequence space $\Sigma(\Omega_\xi)$. If the reader will refer back to Example 4.10 he will see a specific example of such an isomorphism.

Now suppose that $(\Omega, \mathfrak{F}, P, \mathbf{T})$ is an invertible ergodic dynamical system and ξ is an independent generating partition. It is clear that the induced system $(\Sigma(\Omega_\xi), \mathbf{B})$ is a Bernoulli shift, and conversely if $(\Omega, \mathfrak{F}, P, \mathbf{T})$ is a Bernoulli system, there exists an independent generating partition. (Just use the image under the isomorphism of the time zero partition in the isomorphic shift.)

Therefore, if we are looking for isomorphisms between Bernoulli shifts, we may try to build them up from the independent generating partitions. This can be accomplished if and only if the joint distributions are the same. In order to say what the same joint distributions mean, we need to put an order on the common refinement of several partitions. This is accomplished by using the lexicographic order on the set of n-tuples of integers.

For example, if $\xi = \{A_0, A_1, A_2\}$ and $\eta = \{B_0, B_1\}$, then $\xi \vee \eta = \{C_0, C_1, C_2, C_3, C_4, C_5\}$, where

$$C_i = \begin{cases} A_0 \cap B_i & \text{for } i = 0, 1, \\ A_1 \cap B_{i-2} & \text{for } i = 2, 3, \\ A_2 \cap B_{i-4} & \text{for } i = 4, 5, \end{cases}$$

whereas $\eta\vee\xi=\{D_j: j=0,1,\ldots,5\}$, where

$$D_j=\begin{cases} B_0\cap A_j & \text{for } j=0,1,2,\\ B_1\cap A_{j-3} & \text{for } j=3,4,5.\end{cases}$$

With this convention $\Omega_{\xi\vee\eta}=\{0,1,2,3,4,5\}$, and we may define the distribution of $\xi\vee\eta$ to be

$$d(\xi\vee\eta)=(P(C_0),P(C_1),\ldots,P(C_5)).$$

Notice that $d(\xi\vee\eta)$ does not necessarily equal $d(\eta\vee\xi)$.

To obtain a method for going back and forth between the factor spaces Ω_{ξ^i} for ordered partitions ξ^i, $i=0,1,\ldots,n$, and the factor space associated with the ordered partition $\bigvee_{i=0}^n\xi^i$, we introduce the following map.

Definition 4.28. Let $\xi^i=(A_0^i,A_1^i,\ldots,A_{k_i}^i)$ for $i=1,2,\ldots,n$ be finite ordered partitions. For $(l_0,l_1,\ldots,l_n)\in\Omega_{\xi^1}\times\Omega_{\xi^2}\times\cdots\times\Omega_{\xi^n}$ let $\lambda(l_1,l_2,\ldots,l_n)=l$ if and only if $(l_1,l_2,\ldots,l_n)$ is the lth n-tuple in the lexicographic order. It is easy to see that λ is a bijection to $\Omega_{\bigvee_1^n\xi^i}=\{0,1,2,\ldots,k^1k^2\ldots k^n-1\}$. The inverse of this map will be denoted by $\mathbf{M}_{\bigvee_1^n\xi^i}$.

Notice that $\bigvee_{i=1}^n\xi^i$ is an ordered partition so that $\mathbf{N}_{\bigvee_1^n\xi^i}$ takes its values in $\Omega_{\bigvee_1^n\xi^i}$ and for any $\omega\in\Omega$

$$[\mathbf{M}_{\bigvee\xi^i}(\mathbf{N}_{\bigvee\xi^i}(\omega))]_j=\mathbf{N}_{\xi^j}(\omega).$$

Thus

$$\mathbf{N}_{\bigvee\xi^i}^{-1}(l)=\mathbf{N}_{\xi^1}^{-1}(l_0)\cap\mathbf{N}_{\xi^2}^{-1}(l_1)\cap\cdots\cap\mathbf{N}_{\xi^n}^{-1}(l_{n-1})$$

if and only if $\mathbf{M}_{\bigvee\xi^i}(l)=(l_0,l_1,\ldots,l_{n-1})$. In particular, if ξ is a partition of $(\Omega,\mathfrak{F},P,\mathbf{T})$ and $\zeta=\bigvee_{j=0}^{n-1}\mathbf{T}^{-j}\xi$, then $\mathbf{M}_\zeta(l)$ is known as the ξ n-name of l in $\Omega_{\xi^{-n}}$, or of any ω in $\mathbf{N}_\zeta^{-1}(l)$.

Now let $(\Omega,\mathfrak{F},P,\mathbf{T})$ and $(\overline{\Omega},\overline{\mathfrak{F}},\overline{P},\overline{\mathbf{T}})$ be invertible dynamical systems and let $\bar{\xi}$ be a generating partition for the $\overline{\mathbf{T}}$-system. Suppose we can find a partition ξ of the $\overline{\mathbf{T}}$-system such that for every $n=0,1,2,\ldots$

$$d\left(\bigvee_{j=-n}^{n}\mathbf{T}^j\xi\right)=d\left(\bigvee_{j=-n}^{n}\overline{\mathbf{T}}^j\bar{\xi}\right).\tag{4.16}$$

This equation states that the identity map between the discrete probability spaces (Ω_n,P_n) and $(\overline{\Omega}_n,\overline{P}_n)$, where Ω_n is the factor space associated with

$\bigvee_{j=-n}^{+n}\mathbf{T}^j\xi$ and similarly for $\bar{\Omega}_n$, is measure preserving. Notice that Ω_n and $\bar{\Omega}_n$ are always the same set of integers but the discrete distributions could be different. If $n>m$, then $\Omega_m \supset \Omega_n$ and $\bar{\Omega}_m \supset \bar{\Omega}_n$, so that the maps between Ω_n and $\bar{\Omega}_n$ extend to a measure preserving map between the factor spaces associated with $\bigvee_{j=-\infty}^{+\infty}\mathbf{T}^j\xi$ and $\bigvee_{j=-\infty}^{+\infty}\bar{\mathbf{T}}^j\bar{\xi}$, the maps on these spaces obtained from $\mathbf{T}$ and $\bar{\mathbf{T}}$ respectively commute with this measure preserving map, and hence it is an isomorphism between the two factor systems. However, the factor system associated with $\bigvee_{j=-\infty}^{+\infty}\bar{\mathbf{T}}^j\bar{\xi}$ is isomorphic to $(\bar{\Omega}, \bar{\mathfrak{F}}, \bar{P}, \bar{\mathbf{T}})$, since $\bar{\xi}$ is a generating partition.

What we have then is that the existence of a partition ξ satisfying (4.16) implies that $(\bar{\Omega}, \bar{\mathfrak{F}}, \bar{P}, \bar{\mathbf{T}})$ is (isomorphic to) a factor of $(\Omega, \mathfrak{F}, P, \mathbf{T})$. In case ξ is a generating partition, then the two systems are isomorphic.

Now suppose the $\bar{\mathbf{T}}$-system is a Bernoulli system and $\bar{\xi}$ is an independent generator. If we can find a partition ξ of the $\mathbf{T}$-system which satisfies (4.16), then since $\{\bar{\mathbf{T}}^j\bar{\xi}\}$ is an independent sequence, Equation (4.16) will imply that ξ is an independent partition. In case ξ is a generating partition, then $(\Omega, \mathfrak{F}, P, \mathbf{T})$ is isomorphic to the Bernoulli system $(\bar{\Omega}, \bar{\mathfrak{F}}, \bar{P}, \bar{\mathbf{T}})$.

In particular, if $p=(p_1, p_2, \dots, p_k)$ is a finite discrete probability distribution, we may consider the Bernoulli shift $(\mathbf{B}, p)$ as the $\bar{\mathbf{T}}$-system above, and try to find a partition ξ of a given system $(\Omega, \mathfrak{F}, P, \mathbf{T})$ which is independent and such that $d(\xi)=p$. Since ξ is independent, (4.16) will be satisfied, where $\bar{\xi}$ is the time zero partition in the shift $(\mathbf{B}, p)$.

In 1962 Sinai [143, 144] proved that if $p=(p_1, \dots, p_k)$ is any finite probability distribution and $(\Omega, \mathfrak{F}, P, \mathbf{T})$ is an ergodic invertible dynamical system whose entropy is not exceeded by $H(p)$, then there exists an independent partition ξ for the $\mathbf{T}$-system such that $d(\xi)=p$. If one has two Bernoulli systems with the same entropy, then by considering the distribution of the independent generator of one of the systems as the finite probability distribution in Sinai's result, there exists an independent partition of the other system with this distribution and the factor system induced by this partition is isomorphic to the first system.

If one could modify the independent partition in such a way that the new partition was still independent and had the same distribution, but was now a generator, then the two Bernoulli systems would be isomorphic. In 1969 Ornstein [93] developed a technique of constructing partitions from other partitions by a coding process which allowed him to do exactly this.

We now describe this method and then give a proof of Ornstein's fundamental lemma. To simplify the notation, we use $\xi(i)$ rather than $\mathbf{N}_\xi^{-1}(i)$ to denote the ith atom of a finite ordered partition ξ. The following concept was introduced earlier. (cf. Section 3.6.)

Definition 4.29. Let $(\Omega, \mathfrak{F}, P, \mathbf{T})$ be an invertible dynamical system. For any positive real number c and positive integer n, a partition σ is called a (c, n)-stack if σ contains $n+1$ atoms such that

$$\mathbf{T}^j\sigma(0)=\sigma(j), \qquad 0\leqslant j\leqslant n-1,$$

and

$$P\sigma(n)<c.$$

If σ is a (c, n)-stack the space Ω can be visualized as a set $\sigma(n)$ together with a stack of n intervals of the same measure one above the other. The map $\mathbf{T}$ sends each level of this stack onto the level above it, as shown in Figure 4.2. Each level in the stack is indexed by a point in Ω_σ, and the P_σ-measures of the points $0, 1, 2, \ldots, n-1$ are equal.

The following lemma is fundamental to the further development. Its proof is based on an ingenious geometric representation of an ergodic dynamical system due to Kakutani, called a skyscraper. We will describe this representation before stating and proving the lemma.

Let $(\Omega, \mathfrak{F}, P, \mathbf{T})$ be an ergodic, invertible dynamical system. Let A_0 be a measurable set with positive measure. For each $k>0$ define

$$A_0^k=\left\{\omega\in A_0 : \mathbf{T}^k\omega\in A_0,\ \mathbf{T}^j\omega\notin A_0,\ 0<j<k\right\}.$$

If we consider $\mathbf{T}^k\omega$ to be the position at time k of a particle which was at ω at time zero, then $\bigcup_{k=1}^{\infty}A_0^k=(\bigcup_{k=1}^{\infty}\mathbf{T}^{-k}A_0)\cap A_0$ can be thought of as the set of positions in A_0 with the property that a particle placed at one of them will eventually return to A_0. We call this set the set of points of A_0 which *return* to A_0. The set A_0^k consists of those points which return for the first time at time k.

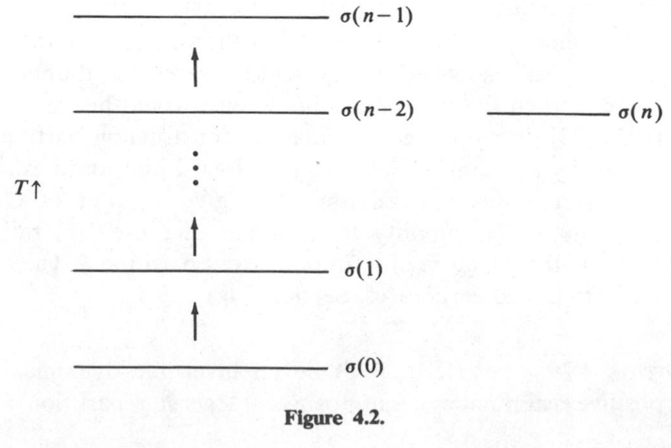

Figure 4.2.

Suppose $P(A_0 - \bigcup_{k=1}^{\infty} A_0^k) = P(A_0 \cap \bigcap_{k=1}^{\infty} \mathbf{T}^{-k}(\Omega - A_0)) > 0$. The sets $\mathbf{T}^{-j}(A_0 \cap \bigcap_{k=1}^{\infty} \mathbf{T}^{-k}(\Omega - A_0))$ are all disjoint and have the same measure. But this implies that $P(\Omega) = \infty$. Hence $P(A_0 - \bigcup_{k=1}^{\infty} A_0^k) = 0$, so that $\bigcup_{k=1}^{\infty} A_0^k = A_0$ a.e. and almost all points of A_0 return to A_0. (This is the Poincaré recurrence theorem.)

If k is any positive integer, the sets $\{\mathbf{T}^j A_0^k\}_{j=0}^{k-1}$ are disjoint, and since A_0^k for $k = 1, 2, \ldots$ are disjoint, we have that $\{\mathbf{T}^j A_0^k : k = 1, 2, \ldots, \ 0 \leqslant j \leqslant k-1\}$ is a pairwise disjoint collection of sets.

Let $\Omega' = \bigcup_{k=1}^{\infty} \bigcup_{j=0}^{k-1} \mathbf{T}^j A_0^k = \bigcup_{j=1}^{\infty} \mathbf{T}^j A_0$. Then $\mathbf{T}^{-1}\Omega' \subset \Omega'$. However, $\Omega' - \mathbf{T}^{-1}\Omega'$ has measure zero, because otherwise $\mathbf{T}^{-k}(\Omega' - \mathbf{T}^{-1}\Omega')$ would form a countable infinite collection of pairwise disjoint sets each with the same positive measure, which is impossible, since $P(\Omega') \leqslant P(\Omega) = 1$. Thus $\mathbf{T}^{-1}\Omega' = \Omega'$ (mod 0), and since $\mathbf{T}$ is ergodic, $P(\Omega') = 1$. Thus $\Omega' = \Omega$ (mod 0).

What we have proved in the last paragraph is that the collection $\{\mathbf{T}^j A_0^k : k = 0, 1, 2, \ldots, \ 0 \leqslant j \leqslant k-1\}$ is a (mod 0) partition of Ω'. Moreover this partition has the property that certain atoms are carried onto others by $\mathbf{T}$. If we represent each atom by an interval with the atoms $\{\mathbf{T}^j A_0^k\}_{j=0}^{k-1}$ stacked above each other as in Figure 4.3, we have what is known as a Kakutani skyscraper. In this diagram one can think of $\mathbf{T}$ sending a point in any interval directly upward to the interval above it, and somewhere into A_0 if there is no interval above it.

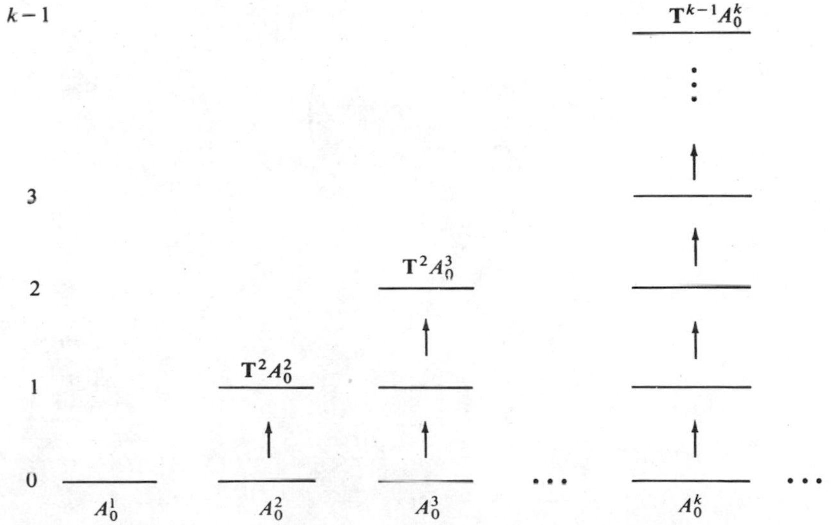

Figure 4.3.

THEOREM 4.30 (Kakutani-Rohlin). *If $(\Omega, \mathfrak{F}, P, \mathbf{T})$ is an ergodic, invertible, dynamical system on a nonatomic space, then for every $c > 0$ and positive integer n there exists a (c, n)-stack in Ω.*

Proof. Let A_0 be a measurable set in Ω such that $0<P(A_0)<cn^{-1}$, and consider the Kakutani skyscraper based on A_0. Define

$$F=\bigcup_{j=n}^{2n-1} A_0^j \cup \bigcup_{j=2n}^{3n-1} \left(A_0^j \cup \mathbf{T}^n A_0^j\right) \cup \cdots$$

$$\cup \bigcup_{j=kn}^{kn-1} \left(A_0^j \cup \cdots \cup \mathbf{T}^{(k-1)n} A_0^j\right)$$

$$=\bigcup_{k=1}^{\infty} \bigcup_{j=kn}^{(k+1)n-1} \bigcup_{l=0}^{(k-1)n} \mathbf{T}^l A_0^j.$$

The set F is indicated on the Kakutani skyscraper in Figure 4.4. One can see using the skyscraper that $F, TF, \ldots, \mathbf{T}^{n-1}F$ are disjoint and

$$\Omega-\bigcup_{j=0}^{n-1} \mathbf{T}^j F=\left[A_0^1 \cup \left(A_0^2 \cup \mathbf{T} A_0^2\right) \cup \cdots \cup \left(A_0^{n-1} \cup \cdots \cup \mathbf{T}^{n-2} A_0^{n-1}\right)\right]$$

$$\cup \mathbf{T}^n\left[A_0^{n+1} \cup \left(A_0^{n+2} \cup \mathbf{T} A_0^{n+2}\right) \cup \cdots\right.$$

$$\left.\cup \left(A_0^{2n-1} \cup \cdots \cup \mathbf{T}_0^{n-2} A_0^{2n-1}\right)\right] \cdots$$

$$=\bigcup_{k=0}^{\infty} \mathbf{T}^{kn}\left(\bigcup_{j=1}^{n-1} \bigcup_{l=0}^{j-1} \mathbf{T}^l A_0^{kn+j}\right).$$

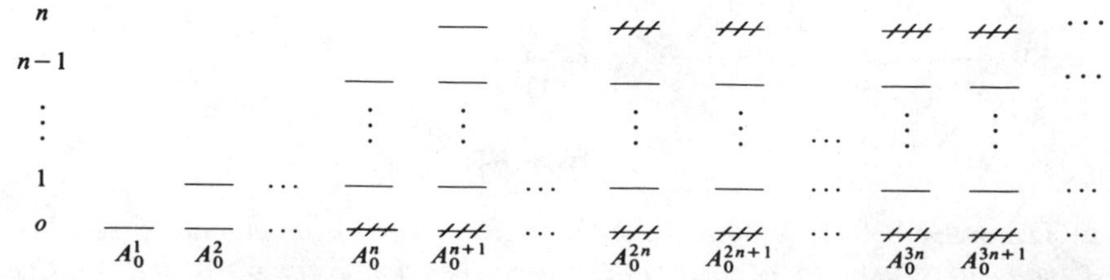

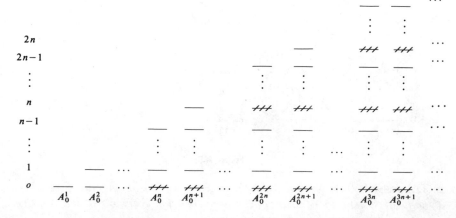

Figure 4.4.

Since $\mathbf{T}$ is a metric automorphism,

$$P\left(\Omega-\bigcup_{j=0}^{n-1}\mathbf{T}^jF\right)=\sum_{k=0}^{\infty}\sum_{j=1}^{n-1}jP\left(A_0^{kn+j}\right)\leqslant nP(A_0)<c.$$

So if we take $\sigma(0)=F$, $\sigma(j)=\mathbf{T}^jF$, and $\sigma(n)=\Omega-\cup_{j=0}^{n-1}\mathbf{T}^jF$, then σ is a (c,n)-stack.

Suppose that ξ is a partition in $(\Omega,\mathfrak{F},P,\mathbf{T})$ and σ is a (c,n)-stack in the system. Each of the levels in σ is a Lebesgue space $(\sigma(j),\sigma(j)\cap\mathfrak{F}, P^{\sigma}(\ |j))$ where $P^{\sigma}(\ |j)$ denotes the member $P^{\sigma}(\ \ |\sigma(j))$ of the canonical family of measures associated with $\sigma(j)$. If we let $\mathbf{T}P^{\sigma}(\ |j)$ denote the measure $P^{\sigma}(\ |j)\circ\mathbf{T}^{-1}$ then the jth level space can be written as $(\mathbf{T}^j\sigma(0),\mathbf{T}^jP^{\sigma}(\ |0))$. The partition ξ induces an ordered partition ξ_j in each Lebesgue space $(\mathbf{T}^j\sigma(0),\mathbf{T}^jP^{\sigma}(\ |0))$ which is given by $\xi_j=\{\xi(i)\cap\mathbf{T}^j\sigma(0):i\in\Omega_\xi\}$ and $d(\xi_j)=(\mathbf{T}^jP^{\sigma}(\xi(i)|0):i\in\Omega_\xi)=(P^{\sigma}(\mathbf{T}^{-j}\xi(i)|0):i\in\Omega_\xi)$.

For each $j=0,1,\ldots,n-1$, $\mathbf{T}^{-j}\xi_j$ is a partition of $(\sigma(0),P^{\sigma}(\ |0))$ and so is $\bigvee_{j=0}^{n-1}\mathbf{T}^{-j}\xi_j$. However, notice that $\bigvee_{j=0}^{n-1}\mathbf{T}^{-j}\xi_j=(\bigvee_{j=0}^{n-1}\mathbf{T}^{-j}\xi)\cap\sigma(0)$. By a strengthening of the Kakutani-Rohlin theorem one can obtain the following.

THEOREM 4.31. *If $(\Omega,\mathfrak{F},P,\mathbf{T})$ is an invertible ergodic system and ξ is a finite partition of Ω, then for any real number $c>0$ and positive integer n there exists a (c,n)-stack σ such that if $\zeta=\bigvee_{j=0}^{n-1}\mathbf{T}^{-j}\xi$, then for each $l\in\Omega_\zeta$*

$$P^{\sigma}(\zeta(l)|0)=P(\zeta(l)).$$

That is, $d(\bigvee_{j=0}^{n-1}\mathbf{T}^{-j}\xi\cap\sigma(0))=d(\bigvee_{j=0}^{n-1}\mathbf{T}^{-j}\xi)$.

A proof is indicated in Shields [139, p. 22].

Suppose we have a stack σ and partition ξ in Ω which satisfy the conclusion of Theorem 4.31. For each $l\in\Omega_\zeta$ the atoms

$$\left\{\mathbf{T}^i\left[\left[\bigvee_{j=0}^{n-1}\mathbf{T}^{-j}\xi\right](l)\cap\sigma(0)\right]:i=0,1,\ldots,n-1\right\}$$

are pairwise disjoint sets in distinct levels of the stack σ all with the same measure. This collection is called the lth column of the stack. Notice that there are n atoms in a column.

The map $\mathbf{M}_\zeta$ which sends points in Ω_ζ to n-tuples of elements from Ω_ξ (recall that $\zeta=\bigvee_{j=0}^{n-1}\mathbf{T}^{-j}\xi$) may be used to assign a label selected from Ω_ξ to each atom in the lth column as follows: Assign l_i to

$\mathbf{T}^i[(\bigvee_{j=0}^{n-1}\mathbf{T}^{-j}\xi)(l)\cap\sigma(0)]$ if and only if l_i is the ith component of $\mathbf{M}_\zeta(l)$ (see Figure 4.5). The first column in this stack is associated with the second atom of $\bigvee_{j=0}^{3}\mathbf{T}^{-j}\xi\cap\sigma(0)$, and $\mathbf{M}_\zeta(2)=0010$. (We start counting with zero.)

By assigning the n-tuple of integers $\mathbf{M}_\zeta(l)=(l_0,\dots,l_{n-1})$ to the set $\bigcup_{i=0}^{n-1}\mathbf{T}^i(\zeta(l)\cap\sigma(0))$ in Ω, we have coded points in a portion of the space, namely $\Omega_1=\bigcup_{i=0}^{n-1}\sigma(i)$, to sequences of elements from Ω_ξ. If $(\Omega_\xi, d(\xi))$ is thought of as an alphabet with distribution $d(\xi)$ on the letters, we have assigned words of length n from this alphabet to most of the space Ω (provided c is small).

The map $\mathbf{M}_\zeta$ is a way of assigning words of length n from the alphabet $(\Omega_\xi, d(\xi))$ to points in (Ω_ζ, P_ζ). It is exactly this map which gives us the assignment of points in Ω to such words. Suppose that Φ is any one to one map from Ω_ζ to words of length n from some alphabet (S,p) where $S=\{0,1,\dots,\bar{k}-1\}$ and p is a discrete probability distribution on S. Using Φ in the same way that we used $\mathbf{M}_\zeta$, we can label the atoms in each level of the lth column with an element from the alphabet (S,p) and thereby assign to each point of the set $\bigcup_{i=0}^{n-1}\mathbf{T}^i(\zeta(l)\cap\sigma(0))$ a word $(s_0,s_1,\dots,s_{n-1})$ from the alphabet S. Now using this labeling from S, we can construct another partition η of Ω_1 such that $\Omega_\eta=S$. Just take the rth atom of η to be the union of all column levels whose Φ-index is r, i.e.,

$$\eta(r)=\bigcup_{i,l}\mathbf{T}^i(\zeta(l)\cap\sigma(0))$$

where the union is over all i,l such that $(\Phi(l))_i=r$.

This construction gives a partition whose factor sample space Ω_η coincides with S, but there is no reason to expect the distribution $d(\eta)$ to be related in any way to p. This is because the maps Φ and $\mathbf{M}_\zeta$ are not exactly the same kind of map in the sense that $\mathbf{M}_\zeta$ maps the probability space $(\Omega_\zeta, d(\zeta))$ to the probability space $(\times_{i=0}^{n-1}\Omega_\xi, P_\zeta)$ in a measure preserving

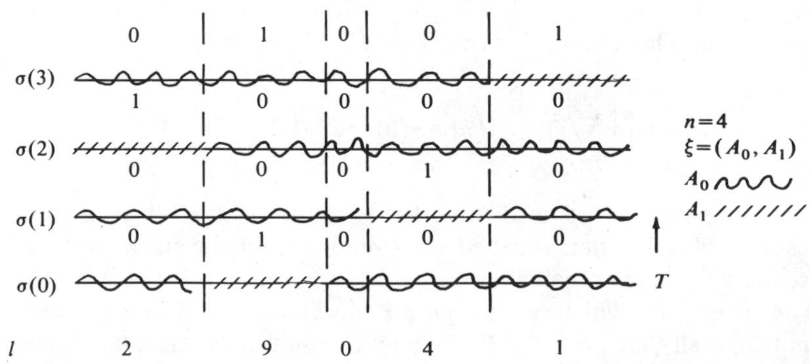

Figure 4.5

way and thus reconstructing ξ from $\mathbf{M}_\xi$ gives exactly $(\Omega_\xi, d(\xi))$. However, we know nothing concerning the relationship between Φ and the measure P. If we use Φ as a map from (Ω_ξ, μ) to $(\times S, p^n)$, where p^n denotes the product measure obtained from p and μ is the measure on Ω_ξ induced by Φ, then we obtain a factor space (Ω_η, p) isomorphic to (S, p). By using the law of large numbers, the Shannon-McMillan-Breiman theorem, and the Kakutani-Rohlin theorem, Ornstein was able to define a map Φ so that not only was p close to $d(\eta)$ (as distributions) but also the partition η was close to ξ in partition distance. This allowed a series of modifications which led to an independent partition with given distribution which was also a generator.

We shall now give a proof of Ornstein's fundamental lemma. This proof is based on Shields's treatment in [139] and depends on the following lemmas.

In the last section we used $\bigvee_{j=1}^{n}\mathbf{T}^{-j}\xi$ quite often and denoted this common refinement by ξ^{-n}. For the rest of this chapter, we shall need $\mathbf{T}\xi^{-n}=\bigvee_{j=0}^{n-1}\mathbf{T}^{-j}\xi$ rather than ξ^{-n} and shall use the symbol ${}^{1}\xi^{-n}$ for $\mathbf{T}\xi^{-n}$.

LEMMA 4.32. *Let $S=\{0,1,\ldots,k-1\}$ and p be a discrete probability distribution on S. For every $d>0$ and invertible ergodic system $(\Omega, \mathfrak{F}, P, \mathbf{T})$ with $h(\mathbf{T}) \geqslant H(p)$ there exists a partition $\eta \in \mathfrak{Z}_k(\Omega)$ such that*

$$|d(\eta)-p|<d \tag{4.17}$$

and

$$0<H(p)-h(\mathbf{T},\eta)<d. \tag{4.18}$$

Proof. Let $d>0$ be given and select $d_1<d/6$. By Corollary 4.24 there exists a partition $\xi_1 \in \mathfrak{Z}(\Omega)$ such that

$$2d_1<H(p)-h(\mathbf{T},\xi_1)<4d_1. \tag{4.19}$$

Select $\bar{d}$ so small that $|\zeta-\zeta'|<\bar{d}$ implies that $|h(\mathbf{T},\zeta)-h(\mathbf{T},\zeta')|<d_1$, and $\tilde{d}$ so small that $|d(\zeta)-d(\nu)|<\tilde{d}$ implies that $H(\zeta)<d_1$. Take $d_2=\min\{[H(p)-h(\mathbf{T},\xi_1)]/2, \bar{d}/4, \tilde{d}/4, d/(4k+1)\}$. Let ξ_0 denote the time zero partition in the Bernoulli shift $(\Sigma(S), \mu_p, \mathbf{B})$, and remember that $(\Sigma(S)_{\xi_0}, d(\xi_0))=(S,p)$.

By the equipartition property (Corollary 2.54) there exists N_1 such that for all $n \geqslant N_1$

$$\exp\{-n[H(p)+d_2]\}<\mu_p\{{}^{1}\xi_0^{-n}(\mathbf{N}_{{}^{1}\xi_0^{-n}}(s))\}<\exp\{-n[H(p)-d_2]\} \tag{4.20}$$

for all $s \in \Sigma(S)-\tilde{B}_0(n)$ where $\tilde{B}_0(n)$ is a ${}^{1}\xi_0^{-n}$-set with $\mu_p(\tilde{B}_0(n))<d_2$.

By the ergodic theorem (Theorem 1.24) and the fact that a.e. convergence implies almost uniform convergence, there exists an integer N_2 such that for $n \geqslant N_2$,

$$\sum_{i \in S} \left| \frac{1}{n} \sum_{j=0}^{n-1} 1_{\xi_0(i)}(\mathbf{B}^j s) - p_i \right| < d_2 \tag{4.21}$$

for all $s \in \Sigma(S) - E_0(n)$, where $E_0(n)$ is a ${}^1\xi_0^{-n}$-set such that $\mu_p(E_0(n)) < d_2$. Take $B_0(n) = \tilde{B}_0(n) \cup E_0(n)$.

Use the equipartition property again but this time apply it to the system $(\Omega, \mathfrak{F}, P, \mathbf{T})$ to obtain an integer N_3 such that for all $n > N_3$

$$\exp\{-n[h(\mathbf{T}, \xi_1) + d_2]\} < P({}^1\xi_1^{-n}(\mathbf{N}_{{}^1\xi_1^{-n}}(\omega)))$$

$$< \exp\{-n[h(\mathbf{T}, \xi_1) - d_2]\} \tag{4.22}$$

for all $\omega \in \Omega - B(n)$, where $B(n)$ is a ${}^1\xi_1^{-n}$-set with $P(B(n)) < d_2$.

Since $d_2 < \frac{1}{2}[H(p) - h(\mathbf{T}, \xi_1)]$, there exists an integer N_4 such that for all $n \geqslant N_4$

$$4 \exp\{-n[H(p) - h(\mathbf{T}, \xi_1) - 2d_2]\} < 1 - 2d_2.$$

Now select $n > \max\{N_1, N_2, N_3, N_4, 2\tilde{d}^{-1}\}$ and define the sets $G_0(n)$ and $G_1(n)$ in $\Sigma(S)_{{}^1\xi_0^{-n}}$ and $\Omega_{{}^1\xi_1^{-n}}$ respectively by

$$G_0(n) = \{r : {}^1\xi_0^{-n}(r) \subset \Sigma(S) - B_0(n)\},$$

$$G_1(n) = \{l : {}^1\xi_1^{-n}(l) \subset \Omega - B(n)\}.$$

By the definition of $B_0(n)$ and $B(n)$ we have that $\mu_{{}^1\xi_0^{-n}}(G_0(n)) > 1 - 2d_2$ and $P_{{}^1\xi_1^{-n}}(G_1(n)) > 1 - d_2$. Moreover

$$\frac{|G_0(n)|}{|G_1(n)|} > (1 - 2d_2) \exp\{n[H(p) - h(\mathbf{T}, \xi_1) - 2d_2]\},$$

where $|\ |$ denotes the number of points. Since $n \geqslant N_4$, we have that

$$|G_0(n)| > 4|G_1(n)| \tag{4.23}$$

and there are at least four times as many points in $G_0(n)$ as in $G_1(n)$.

Now suppose s_1 and s_2 are points in ${}^1\xi_0^{-n}(r)$ for some $r \in \Sigma(S)_{{}^1\xi_0^{-n}}$. Then for $j = 0, 1, \ldots, n-1$, $\mathbf{N}_{\xi_0} \circ \mathbf{B}^j(s_1) = \mathbf{N}_{\xi_0} \circ \mathbf{B}^j(s_2)$ and this common value is the jth letter from S of the word $\mathbf{M}_{{}^1\xi_0^{-n}}(r)$. Thus $\Sigma_{j=0}^{n-1} 1_{\xi_0(i)}(\mathbf{B}^j s)$ is constant on each atom ${}^1\xi_0^{-n}(r)$ of ${}^1\xi_0^{-n}$ and is equal to the frequency of occurrence of the letter $i \in S$ in the word $\mathbf{M}_{^1\xi_0^{-n}}(r)$. Thus if $f_i(n,r)$ denotes the number of i's in the word $\mathbf{M}_{^1\xi_0^{-n}}(r)$, Equation (4.21) becomes

$$\sum_{i \in S} \left| \frac{1}{n} f_i(n,r) - p_i \right| < d_2. \tag{4.24}$$

We are now ready to construct a stack which we shall use for coding as was described earlier. By the strong form of Rohlin's theorem (Theorem 4.31) there exists a (d_2, n)-stack σ' in $(\Omega, \mathfrak{F}, P, \mathbf{T})$ such that

$$d(^1\xi_1^{-n} \cap \sigma'(0)) = d(^1\xi_1^{-n}).$$

Replace the stack σ' by the stack σ whose levels consist of atoms $\mathbf{T}^j[^1\xi_1^{-n}(l) \cap \sigma'(0)]$ for $l \in G_1(n)$ and $j = 0, 1, \ldots, n-1$. This is done by taking

$$\sigma(0) = \sigma'(0) \cap \bigcup_{l \in G_1(n)} {^1\xi_1^{-n}(l)},$$

$$\sigma(j) = \mathbf{T}^j\sigma(0), \qquad j = 1, 2, \ldots, n-1,$$

$$\sigma(n) = \Omega - \bigcup_{j=0}^{n-1} \sigma(j).$$

Since $P_{^1\xi^{-n}}(G_1(n)) > 1 - d_2$ and $P(\bigcup_{j=0}^{n-1} \mathbf{T}^j\sigma'(0)) > 1 - d_2$ we have that $P(\sigma(n)) < 2d_2$. Thus σ is a $(2d_2, n)$-stack, and using the partition ξ_1 we obtain columns in this stack which are indexed by $G_1(n)$.

Since there are more points in $G_0(n)$ than in $G_1(n)$, there exists a one to one map ϕ on $G_1(n)$ into $G_0(n)$ which induces a map Φ on the collection of words $\mathbf{M}_{^1\xi_1^{-n}}(l)$ into the collection of words $\mathbf{M}_{^1\xi_0^{-n}}(r)$, where $l \in G_1(n)$, $r \in G_0(n)$, defined by

$$\Phi \mathbf{M}_{^1\xi_1^{-n}}(l) = \mathbf{M}_{^1\xi_0^{-n}}(\phi l), \qquad l \in G_1(n).$$

Define the partition η by the coding process outlined above using Φ. Specifically, for any $i \in S$, take

$$A_i = \bigcup \mathbf{T}^j(\sigma(0) \cap {^1\xi_1^{-n}(l)}),$$

where the union is extended over all $j \in \{0, 1, 2, \ldots, n-1\}$ and $l \in G_1(n)$ such that the jth letter in $\Phi \mathbf{M}_{^1\xi_1^{-n}}(l)$ is i. Enlarge each set A_i to a set, which we still call A_i, by a subset of $\sigma(n)$ so that $\{A_1, \ldots, A_k\}$ is a partition of Ω. This is the required partition η.

We now show that η satisfies the conditions (4.17) and (4.18).

First (4.17). For each $l\in G_1(n)$, let $C(l)$ denote the column over $\sigma(0)\cap {}^1\xi_1^{-n}(l)$, i.e.

$$C(l)=\bigcup_{j=0}^{n-1} \mathbf{T}^j\left[{}^1\xi_1^{-n}(l)\cap\sigma(0)\right],$$

and let $\Omega_1=\cup_{l\in G_1(n)}C(l)$. Recall that $\Omega-\Omega_1=\sigma(n)$ and hence $P(\Omega-\Omega_1)<2d_2$.

Since

$$\begin{aligned}P(A_i\cap C(l))&=f_i(n,\phi l)P({}^1\xi_1^{-n}(l)\cap\sigma(0))\\&=\frac{1}{n}f_i(n,\phi l)P(C(l)),\end{aligned}$$

Equation (4.24) gives that for each $l\in G_1(n)$

$$\sum_{i\in S}|P(A_i\cap C(l))-p_iP(C(l))|<d_2P(C(l)).$$

Therefore

$$\begin{aligned}|d(\eta)-p|&=\sum_i|P(A_i)-p_i|\\&\leqslant\sum_{i\in S}\quad\sum_{l\in G_1(n)}|P(A_i\cap C(l))-p_iP(C(l))|\\&\quad+\sum_{i\in S}|P(A_i\cap\sigma(n))-p_iP(\sigma(n))|\\&<\sum_{l\in G_1(n)}d_2P(C(l))+\sum_{i\in S}4d_2\\&<(1+4k)d_2\leqslant d.\end{aligned}$$

To see that (4.18) is satisfied, notice that the column levels $\mathbf{T}^j({}^1\xi_1^{-n}(l(\cap\sigma(0))$ associated with ξ_1 and the column levels $\mathbf{T}^j({}^1\eta^{-n}(l)\cap(\sigma(0))$ associated with η for $l\in G_1(n)$ and $j=0,1,\ldots,n-1$ are the same sets. Thus $\xi_1\cap\Omega_1$ consists of unions of sets of the form

$$\mathbf{T}^j\left[{}^1\eta^{-n}(l)\cap\sigma(0)\right]\qquad\text{for }\ j=0,1,2,\ldots,n-1,\quad l\in G_1(n)$$

which are atoms of the partition

$$\left\{{}^1\eta^{-n}\cap\sigma(0);\left[\mathbf{T}\,{}^1\eta^{-n}\right]\cap\sigma(1);\ldots;\left[\mathbf{T}^{n-1}\,{}^1\eta^{-n}\right]\cap\sigma(n-1)\right\}$$

of the space $(\Omega_1, \Omega_1 \cap \mathfrak{F})$. Since

$$\mathbf{T}^j({}^1\eta^{-n}) \cap \sigma(j) = \bigvee_{k=j}^{j-n+1} \mathbf{T}^k \eta \cap \sigma(j) \leqslant \bigvee_{k=-n+1}^{n-1} \mathbf{T}^k \eta \cap \sigma(j)$$

for $j = 0, 1, 2, \ldots, n-1$, we have that

$$\xi_1 \cap \Omega_1 \leqslant \left\{ \bigvee_{k=-n+1}^{n-1} \mathbf{T}^k \eta \cap \sigma(0); \ldots; \bigvee_{k=-n+1}^{n-1} \mathbf{T}^k \eta \cap \sigma(n-1) \right\}.$$

Define

$$\xi_1' = \{\xi_1(i) \cap \Omega_1 : i \in \Omega_{\xi_1}\} \cup \{\sigma(n)\},$$

$$\eta' = \{\eta(i) \cap \Omega_1 : i \in S\} \cap \{\sigma(n)\}.$$

Then

$$\xi_1' \leqslant \left\{ \bigvee_{k=-n+1}^{n-1} \mathbf{T}^k \eta \cap \sigma(0); \ldots; \bigvee_{k=-n+1}^{n-1} \mathbf{T}^k \eta \cap \sigma(n-1); \bigvee_{k=-n+1}^{n-1} \mathbf{T}^k \eta \cap \sigma(n) \right\},$$

or

$$\xi_1' \leqslant \bigvee_{k=-n+1}^{n-1} \mathbf{T}^k \eta \vee \sigma.$$

If σ_0 is taken to be the partition $\{\sigma(0), \Omega - \sigma(0)\}$, then

$$\sigma = \bigvee_{k=0}^{n-1} \mathbf{T}^k \sigma_0 \leqslant \bigvee_{k=-n+1}^{n-1} \mathbf{T}^k \sigma_0.$$

Thus,

$$\xi_1' \leqslant \bigvee_{j=-n+1}^{n-1} \mathbf{T}^j(\eta \vee \sigma_0), \tag{4.25a}$$

and similarly

$$\eta' \leqslant \bigvee_{j=n+1}^{n-1} \mathbf{T}^j(\xi_1 \vee \sigma_0). \tag{4.25b}$$

Also,

$$|\xi_1 - \xi_1'| < \sum_{A \in \xi_1} P(A - A \cap \Omega_1) + P(\sigma(n)) \leqslant 4d_2 < \bar{d}$$

and $|\eta - \eta'| < \bar{d}$.

By choice of $\bar{d}$ we have that

$$\begin{aligned} |h(\mathbf{T}, \xi_1) - h(\mathbf{T}, \xi_1')| &< d_1, \\ |h(\mathbf{T}, \eta) - h(\mathbf{T}, \eta')| &< d_1. \end{aligned} \tag{4.26}$$

Moreover, by (4.25),

$$\begin{aligned} h(\mathbf{T}, \xi_1') &\leqslant h(\mathbf{T}, \eta \vee \sigma_0) < h(\mathbf{T}, \eta) + H(\sigma_0) < h(\mathbf{T}, \eta) + d_1, \\ h(\mathbf{T}, \eta') &\leqslant h(\mathbf{T}, \xi_1 \vee \sigma_0) < h(\mathbf{T}, \xi) + H(\sigma_0) < h(\mathbf{T}, \xi_1) + d_1. \end{aligned} \tag{4.27}$$

Here we have used the fact that $H(\sigma_0) < d_1$, since $P(\sigma(0)) < \frac{1}{n} \leqslant \frac{\tilde{\delta}}{2}$ so that $|d(\sigma_0) - d(\nu)| < 2n^{-1} < \tilde{d}$. We get from (4.26) and (4.27) that

$$\begin{aligned} h(\mathbf{T}, \xi_1') - d_1 < h(\mathbf{T}, \xi_1) < h(\mathbf{T}, \xi_1') + d_1 < h(\mathbf{T}, \eta) + 2d_1, \\ h(\mathbf{T}, \eta') - d_1 < h(\mathbf{T}, \eta) < h(\mathbf{T}, \eta') + d_1 < h(\mathbf{T}, \xi_1) + 2d_1, \end{aligned}$$

so that

$$\begin{aligned} H(p) - h(\mathbf{T}, \xi_1) - 2d_1 &< H(p) - h(\mathbf{T}, \eta) \\ &< H(p) - h(\mathbf{T}, \xi_1) + 2d_1, \end{aligned}$$

and the inequality (4.19) gives

$$0 < H(p) - h(\mathbf{T}, \eta) < 6d_1 < d.$$

The next step in the proof of Ornstein's fundamental lemma is to show how one can modify partitions which have distributions close to a given distribution in such a way that the resulting partition is close in the partition distance to the given partition. This is done by selecting a map ϕ used in the previous lemma in a very particular way. In order to pick the map correctly we use a way of measuring distance between two sequences of partitions that is given by what is known as the $\bar{d}$-metric. We shall not say much about this metric, being content to define it and use it in the proof of the next lemma. For a careful and readable discussion of the $\bar{d}$ metric see Shields [139]. For applications of the $\bar{d}$-metric to stochastic sequences and probability theory see Ornstein [101].

DEFINITION 4.33. Let $(\Omega_1, \mathfrak{F}_1, P_1)$, $(\Omega_2, \mathfrak{F}_2, P_2)$, and $(\bar{\Omega}, \bar{\mathfrak{F}}, \bar{P})$ be Lebesgue spaces, and $\{\xi_1^i\}_{i=1}^n$ and $\{\xi_2^i\}_{i=1}^n$ be sequences of partitions in $\mathfrak{Z}_k(\Omega_1)$ and $\mathfrak{Z}_k(\Omega_2)$ respectively. Then $\bar{d}_n(\{\xi_1^i\}, \{\xi_2^i\})$ is defined to be

$$\inf\left\{\frac{1}{n}\sum_{i=1}^{n}|\eta_1^i-\eta_2^i|\right\},$$

where the infimum is taken over all sequences of partitions $\{\eta_1^i\}_1^n$ and $\{\eta_2^i\}_1^n$ in $\mathfrak{Z}_k(\bar{\Omega})$ such that $d(\bigvee_{i=1}^n \eta_1^i)=d(\bigvee_{i=1}^n \xi_1^i)$ and $d(\bigvee_{i=1}^n \eta_2^i)=d(\bigvee_{i=1}^n \xi_2^i)$.

The next lemma gives a condition on two sequences of partitions which are uniformly close in distribution to insure that they are close in the $\bar{d}$-metric.

LEMMA 4.34. *Let $(\Omega_j, \mathfrak{F}_j, P_j)$ for $j=1,2$ be nonatomic Lebesgue spaces, and $\{\xi_j^i\}_{i=1}^n$ be sequences of partitions from $\mathfrak{Z}_k(\Omega_j)$, $j=1,2$. If*

$$\{\xi_1^i\}_{i=1}^n \quad \textit{is independent},$$

$$\{\xi_2^i\}_{i=1}^n \quad \textit{is c-independent},$$

and

$$|d(\xi_1^i)-d(\xi_2^i)|<c \qquad \textit{for} \quad i=1,2,\ldots,n,$$

then

$$\bar{d}_n(\{\xi_1^i\}_1^n, \{\xi_2^i\}_1^n)<4c.$$

Proof. The proof is obtained by induction and depends on the well-known fact that if Ω is a nonatomic probability space and $(p_1,\ldots,p_k)=p$ is a given probability distribution, then there exists a partition $\xi\in\mathfrak{Z}_k(\Omega)$ such that $d(\xi)=p$. A minor extension of this result will produce the following:

1.A If ξ_1 and ξ_2 are partitions in $\mathfrak{Z}_k(\Omega_1)$ and $\mathfrak{Z}_k(\Omega_2)$ respectively then there exist partitions η_1 and η_2 in $\mathfrak{Z}_k(\bar{\Omega})$ such that $d(\eta_j)=d(\xi_j)$, $j=1,2$ and $|\eta_1-\eta_2|=|d(\xi_1)-d(\xi_2)|$.

This statement implies that the lemma is true for $n=1$. Now assume the lemma is true for $n=m$, and let $(\xi_j^i\}_1^{m+1}$ be partitions from $\mathfrak{Z}_k(\Omega_j)$, $j=1,2$, which satisfy the hypothesis of the lemma. Let $\{\eta_j^i\}_1^m$, $j=1,2$, be partitions from $\mathfrak{Z}_k(\bar{\Omega})$ such that

$$d\left(\bigvee_{i=1}^{m}\eta_j^i\right)=d\left(\bigvee_{i=1}^{m}\xi_j^i\right), \qquad j=1,2,$$

and

$$\frac{1}{m}\sum_{i=1}^{m}|\eta_1^i-\eta_2^i|<4c.$$

Since $\{\xi_2^i\}_{i=1}^{m+1}$ are c-independent, ξ_2^{m+1} is c-independent of $\bigvee_{i=1}^m\xi_2^i$, and hence there exists a $\bigvee_{i=1}^m\xi_2^i$-set E_m such that $P_2(E_m)>1-c$ and

$$\sum_{l=p}^{k-1}|P^{\bigvee_1^m\xi_2^i}(\omega,\xi_2^{m+1}(l))-P(\xi_2^{m+1}(l))|<c, \tag{4.28}$$

a.e. on E_m. This inequality implies that for each atom B_2 of $\bigvee_{i=1}^m\xi_2^i$ which is contained in E_m we have

$$|d(\xi_2^{m+1}\cap B_2)-d(\xi_2^{m+1})|<c.$$

Since $\{\xi_1^i\}_{i=1}^{m+1}$ is independent,

$$|d(\xi_1^{m+1}\cap B_1)-d(\xi_1^{m+1})|=0$$

for any atom B_1 in $\bigvee_{i=1}^m\xi_1^i$. It now follows from the third hypothesis that

$$|d(\xi_2^{m+1}\cap B_2)-d(\xi_1^{m+1}\cap B_1)|<2c$$

for any $\bigvee_{i=1}^m\xi_2^i$-atom $B_2\subset E_m$ and any $\bigvee_{i=1}^m\xi_1^i$-atom B_1.

Let $E_m'=\mathbf{N}_{\bigvee_{i=1}^m\xi_2^i}(E_m)$. For $r\in E_m'\subset\Omega_{\bigvee_{i=1}^m\xi_2^i}$ and $s\in\Omega_{\bigvee_{i=1}^m\xi_1^i}$ consider the subsets $F(r)=(\bigvee_{i=1}^m\eta_2^i)(r)$ and $F(s)=(\bigvee_{i=1}^m\eta_1^i(s)$ contained in $(\overline{\Omega},\overline{\mathfrak{F}},\overline{P})$. With the relativized measure in this space, $F(r)\cap F(s)$ is a nonatomic Lebesgue space.

Consider the partitions $\xi_2^{m+1}\cap B_2(r)$ and $\xi_1^{m+1}\cap B_1(s)$ of the spaces obtained from the atoms $B_2(r)=(\bigvee_{i=1}^m\xi_2^i)(r)$ and $B_1(s)=(\bigvee_{i=1}^m\xi_1^i)(s)$ in Ω_1 and Ω_2 respectively.

Now apply statement A1 to the spaces $B_1(s)$, $B_2(r)$, $F(r)\cap F(s)$ with appropriate partitions to obtain partitions $\eta_1^{m+1}\cap F(r)\cap F(s)$ and $\eta_2^{m+1}\cap F(r)\cap F(s)$ such that

$$\begin{aligned}d(\eta_1^{m+1}\cap F(r)\cap F(s))&=d(\xi_1^{m+1}\cap B_1(s)),\\ d(\eta_2^{m+1}\cap F(r)\cap F(s))&=d(\xi_2^{m+1}\cap B_2(r))\end{aligned} \tag{4.29}$$

and

$$|\eta_2^{m+1}\cap F(r)\cap F(s)-\eta_1^{m+1}\cap F(r)\cap F(s)|<2c. \tag{4.30}$$

For $r \in \Omega_{\bigvee_{i=1}^{m} \xi_2^i} - E_m'$, take $\eta_1^{m+1} \cap F(r) \cap F(s)$ and $\eta_2^{m+1} \cap F(r) \cap F(s)$ to be any partition such that (4.29) holds. Since $P(E_m) \geqslant 1-c$, (4.30) implies that

$$|\eta_2^{m+1} - \eta_1^{m+1}| < 4c,$$

and the lemma is proven.

We are now ready to proceed with the lemma which allows one to select a partition close in both distribution and partition metrics to a given partition.

LEMMA 4.35. *Let $S = \{0, 1, \ldots, k-1\}$ and p be a discrete probability distribution on S. For every $c > 0$ there exists $d' > 0$ such that if $(\Omega, \mathfrak{F}, P, \mathbf{T})$ is any invertible ergodic dynamical system with entropy no smaller than $H(p)$, then for every $\xi \in \mathfrak{Z}_k(\Omega)$ satisfying*

$$|d(\xi) - p| \leqslant d' \quad \textit{and} \quad 0 \leqslant H(p) - h(\mathbf{T}, \xi) \leqslant d',$$

it is true that for every $d > 0$ there exists a partition $\eta \in \mathfrak{Z}_k(\Omega)$ such that

$$|d(\eta) - p| \leqslant d, \qquad 0 \leqslant H(p) \quad h(\mathbf{T}, \eta) \leqslant d,$$

and

$$|\xi - \eta| \leqslant c.$$

Proof. We may replace the hypothesis $H(p) - h(\mathbf{T}, \xi) \geqslant 0$ by the condition $H(p) - h(\mathbf{T}, \xi) > 0$ without loss of generality. For, if ξ is any partition in $\mathfrak{Z}_k(\Omega)$ and $H(p) = h(\mathbf{T}, \xi)$, then replace ξ by another partition ξ' such that $h(\mathbf{T}, \xi') > h(\mathbf{T}, \xi)$ whose atoms are obtained by modifying atoms of ξ with sets from $(\bigvee_{j=-\infty}^{+\infty} \mathbf{T}^j \xi)^\wedge$, and proceed with the construction using ξ'. If no such modification exists, the required partition η can be any partition in $\mathfrak{Z}_k(\Omega)$ such that $d(\eta) = p$ and $|\eta - \xi| < c$.

Let $c > 0$ be given and take $c' < c^2/64$. Select d_1' so small that $H(\zeta) - H(\zeta/\zeta') < d_1'$ implies that ζ is c'-independent of ζ' (Theorem 4.26). Let d_2' be so small that $|d(\zeta) - p| < d_2'$ implies that $|H(\zeta) - H(p)| < d_1'/2$ (Theorem 2.57). Take $d' = \min\{d_1'/2, d_2', c'\}$.

Now let $(\Omega, \mathfrak{F}, P, \mathbf{T})$ be a given ergodic invertible system $d > 0$ be a given real number which we assume to be less than c', and $\xi \in \mathfrak{Z}_k(\Omega)$ be such that $|d(\xi) - p| \leqslant d'$ and $0 < H(p) - h(\mathbf{T}, \xi) \leqslant d'$.

Take $d_1 < d/6$, and select $\tilde{d} > 0$ so small that $|\xi - \zeta| < \tilde{d}$ implies that $H(\xi/\zeta) < d_1$ (Lemma 4.20). As in Lemma 4.32, select $\xi' \in \mathfrak{Z}(\Omega)$ such that

$$3d_1 < H(p) - h(\mathbf{T}, \xi') < 4d_1$$

and $|\xi - \xi'| < \tilde{d}$. Then if $\xi_1 = \xi \vee \xi'$, Lemma 2.29 implies that

$$2d_1 < H(p) - h(\mathbf{T}, \xi_1) < 4d_1.$$

Now proceed as in Lemma 4.23, using the partition ξ_1 to obtain the integers N_1, N_2, N_3, N_4, the real number d_2 (selected as in Lemma 4.32 with the additional requirement that it be smaller than $\sqrt{c'}$), and the integer $n > \max\{N_1, N_2, N_3, N_4, 2\tilde{d}^{-1}\}$, to obtain the sets $G_0(n) \subset \Sigma(S)_{{}^1\xi_0^{-n}}$ and $G_1(n) \subset \Omega_{{}^1\xi_1^{-n}}$ with

$$P_{{}^1\xi_1^{-n}}(G_1(n)) > 1 - d_2, \qquad \mu_{{}^1\xi_0^{-n}}(G_0(n)) > 1 - 2d_2,$$

and for points in these sets (4.20), (4.21), (4.22), (4.23), and (4.24) all hold.

We are going to replace ξ_1 by ξ and proceed with the coding using ξ. Thus we need to replace $G_1(n)$ by a set of good points $G(n)$ from $\Omega_{{}^1\xi^{-n}}$. This is easily accomplished, since $\xi \leqslant \xi_1$ and hence the map $\mathbf{N}_{{}^1\xi_1^{-n}, {}^1\xi^{-n}}$ from $\Omega_{{}^1\xi_1^{-n}}$ to $\Omega_{{}^1\xi^{-n}}$ (defined in Section 1.3) can be used to obtain $G(n)$; just take $G(n) = \mathbf{N}_{{}^1\xi_1^{-n}, {}^1\xi^{-n}}(G_1(n))$. We then have that

$$P_{{}^1\xi^{-n}}(G(n)) > 1 - d_2 \quad \text{and} \quad |G_0(n)| \geqslant 4|G(n)|.$$

Now using the strong form of Kakutani-Rohlin's theorem (Theorem 4.31), there exists a (d_2, n)-stack $\bar{\sigma}$ in $(\Sigma(S), \mathfrak{F}_S, \mu, \mathbf{B})$ such that

$$d({}^1\xi_0^{-n} \cap \bar{\sigma}(0)) = d({}^1\xi_0^{-n}) \tag{4.31}$$

and, as in Lemma 4.32, a $(2d_2, n)$-stack in $(\Omega, \mathfrak{F}, P, \mathbf{T})$ such that

$$d({}^1\xi^{-n} \cap \sigma(0)) = d({}^1\xi^{-n}), \tag{4.32}$$

and the columns obtained in the stack σ from the partition ξ are indexed by points in $G(n)$.

Since ξ satisfies the hypotheses, we have

$$H(\xi) - h(\mathbf{T}, \xi) < d_1'.$$

Thus for any $m > 0$

$$H(\mathbf{T}^{-m}\xi) - H\left[\mathbf{T}^{-m}\xi / \bigvee_{j=0}^{m-1} \mathbf{T}^{-j}\xi\right] < d_1',$$

and by choice of d_1', $\{\mathbf{T}^{-j}\xi\}$ is a c'-independent sequence. Moreover, $\{\mathbf{B}^{-j}\xi_0\}$ is an independent sequence, and one can easily show that these two facts together with (4.31) and (4.32) imply that

$$\{\mathbf{T}^{-i}\xi\cap\sigma(0)\} \quad \text{is } c'\text{-independent in}\,(\sigma(0), P^{\sigma}(\ |0)),$$
$$\{\mathbf{B}^{-i}\xi_0\cap\bar{\sigma}(0)\} \quad \text{is independent in}\,(\bar{\sigma}(0), P^{\bar{\sigma}}(\ |0)),$$

and for any $i=0,1,2,\dots,n-1$

$$|d(\mathbf{T}^{-i}\xi\cap\sigma(0))-d(\mathbf{B}^{-i}\xi_0\cap\bar{\sigma}(0))|=|d(\xi)-p|<c'.$$

Thus applying Lemma 4.34 we have that

$$\bar{d}_n(\{\mathbf{T}^{-i}\xi\cap\sigma(0)\}_{i=0}^{n-1},\{\mathbf{B}^{-i}\xi_0\cap\bar{\sigma}(0)\}_{i=0}^{n-1})<4c', \tag{4.33}$$

so that there are partitions $\zeta^i\in\mathfrak{Z}_k(\sigma(0))$ for $i=0,1,\dots,n-1$ such that

$$d\left(\bigvee_{i=0}^{n-1}\zeta^i\right)=d({}^1\xi_0^{-n}\cap\bar{\sigma}(0)) \tag{4.34}$$

and

$$\frac{1}{n}\sum_{i=0}^{n-1}|\mathbf{T}^{-i}\xi\cap\sigma(0)-\zeta^i|\leqslant 4c'. \tag{4.35}$$

For each $i=0,1,\dots,n-1$, $\mathbf{T}^i\zeta^i$ is a partition of the ith level of the stack σ, and if ξ_* is the partition whose jth atom is the set $\bigcup_{i=0}^{n-1}\mathbf{T}^i\zeta^i(j)$ for $j=0,1,\dots,k-1$, then ξ_* is a partition of $\bigcup_{i=0}^{n-1}\mathbf{T}^i\sigma(0)-\Omega-\sigma(n)$ such that

$$\xi_*\cap\mathbf{T}^i\sigma(0)=\mathbf{T}^i\zeta^i.$$

It follows from (4.34) and (4.35) that

$$d({}^1\xi_*^{-n}\cap\sigma(0))=d({}^1\xi_0^{-n}\cap\bar{\sigma}(0)) \tag{4.36}$$

and

$$\frac{1}{n}\sum_{i=0}^{n-1}|\xi\cap\mathbf{T}^i\sigma(0)-\xi_*\cap\mathbf{T}^i\sigma(0)|\leqslant 4c'. \tag{4.37}$$

Because of (4.36), the spaces $([\sigma(0)]_{{}^1\xi_*^{-n}}, P^{\sigma}_{{}^1\xi_*^{-n}}(\ |0))$ and $([\bar{\sigma}(0)]_{{}^1\xi_0^{-n}}, P^{\bar{\sigma}}_{{}^1\xi_0^{-n}}(\ |0))$ are the same space, so we may consider $G_0(n)$ as a subset of $\Omega_{{}^1\xi_*^{-n}}$, and the ξ_* n-name, $\mathbf{M}_{\xi_*^{-n}}(l')$, for $l'\in G_0(n)$ is meaningful.

We shall now define a subset A of $G(n)$ and a one to one map ϕ from $G(n)$ to $G_0(n)$ such that

$$P\Big(\bigcup_{l\in A} {}^1\xi^{-n}(l)\cap\sigma(0)\Big)\geqslant\big[1-6\sqrt{c'}\,\big]P(\sigma(0)) \tag{4.38}$$

and for each $l\in A$

$$\operatorname{Ham}\{\mathbf{M}_{{}^1\xi^{-n}}(l),\mathbf{M}_{{}^1\xi_0^{-n}}(\phi l)\}<nc', \tag{4.39}$$

where Ham denotes the Hamming metric. [If $a=(a_1,\dots,a_n)$ and $b=(b_1,\dots,b_n)$, then Ham $\{a,b\}$ is the number of places where the n-tuples disagree.] To this end, for each $l\in G(n)$ take

$$A'(l)=\Big\{l'\in G_0(n):\operatorname{Ham}\big\{\mathbf{M}_{{}^1\xi_*^{-n}}(l'),\mathbf{M}_{{}^1\xi^{-n}}(l)\big\}\leqslant 2n\sqrt{c'}\,\Big\},$$

and define A to be the set of all $l\in G(n)$ such that

$$P\Big(\bigcup_{l'\in A'(l)} {}^1\xi_*^{-n}(l')\cap{}^1\xi^{-n}(l)\cap\sigma(0)\Big)>\tfrac{1}{2}P({}^1\xi^{-n}(l)\cap\sigma(0)),$$

i.e., l is in A if and only if its associated atom in ${}^1\xi_*^{-n}\cap\sigma(0)$ is more than half covered by atoms from ${}^1\xi_*^{-n}\cap\sigma(0)$.

Before defining ϕ, we show that (4.38) is satisfied. Let E be the set of points in $\sigma(0)$ such that

$$\operatorname{Ham}\Big\{\mathbf{M}_{{}^1\xi_*^{-n}}\big(\mathbf{N}_{{}^1\xi_*^{-n}}(\omega)\big),\mathbf{M}_{{}^1\xi^{-n}}\big(\mathbf{N}_{{}^1\xi^{-n}}(\omega)\big)\Big\}>2n\sqrt{c'}\,.$$

For $i=0,1,2,\dots,n-1$ let E_i denote the set of ω in $\sigma(0)$ such that the ith coordinate of $\mathbf{M}_{{}^1\xi_*^{-n}}(\mathbf{N}_{{}^1\xi_*^{-n}}(\omega))$ is different from the ith coordinate of $\mathbf{M}_{{}^1\xi^{-n}}(\mathbf{N}_{{}^1\xi^{-n}}(\omega))$. Thus

$$E_i=\mathbf{T}^{-i}\bigcup_{j=0}^{k-1}\big(\{\xi_*(j)\cap\mathbf{T}^i\sigma(0)\}\triangle\{\xi(j)\cap\mathbf{T}^i\sigma(0)\}\big),$$

and applying (4.37), we get

$$\sum_{i=0}^{n-1}P(E_i)\leqslant 4nc'P(\sigma(0)). \tag{4.40}$$

However, $2n\sqrt{c'}\,1_E \leqslant \Sigma_{i=0}^{n-1} 1_{E_i}$, so that integrating this inequality and applying (4.40) gives

$$P(E)\leqslant 2\sqrt{c'}\,P(\sigma(0)).$$

Now let $B_*(l)$ denote the union over all l' in $A'(l)$ of the atoms $1_{\xi_*^{-n}(l')\cap\sigma(0)}$, and let $\overline{B}_*(l)$ denote the union of the remaining atoms $1_{\xi_*^{-n}(l')\cap\sigma(0)}$. Then

$$\begin{aligned}\sum_{l\notin A} P({}^1\xi^{-n}(l)\cap\sigma(0)) &= \sum_{l\notin A} P\big({}^1\xi^{-n}(l)\cap B_*(l)\cap\sigma(0)\big)\\ &\quad+\sum_{l\notin A} P\big({}^1\xi^{-n}(l)\cap \overline{B}_*(l)\cap\sigma(0)\big)\\ &\leqslant \sum_{l\notin A} \tfrac{1}{2}P({}^1\xi^{-n}(l)\cap\sigma(0))+P(E).\end{aligned}$$

Thus

$$\sum_{l\notin A} P({}^1\xi^{-n}(l)\cap\sigma(0))\leqslant 2P(E)\leqslant 2\sqrt{c'}\,P(\sigma(0)),$$

and we have that

$$\begin{aligned}\sum_{l\in A} P({}^1\xi^{-n}(l)\cap\sigma(0)) &\geqslant P\Big(\bigcup_{l\in G(n)} {}^1\xi^{-n}(l)\cap\sigma(0)\Big)-4\sqrt{c'}\,P(\sigma(0))\\ &>(1-2d_2-4\sqrt{c'}\,)P(\sigma(0))\\ &>(1-6\sqrt{c'}\,)P(\sigma(0)).\end{aligned}$$

By the choice of n we have that $\exp n[H(p)-h(\mathbf{T},\xi)-2d_2]$ is greater than 4, and it follows from (4.20) and (4.22) that

$$P({}^1\xi^{-n}(l)\cap\sigma(0))>4P\big({}^1\xi_*^{-n}(l')\cap\sigma(0)\big)$$

for each $l\in G(n)$ and $l'\in G_0(n)$, so at least four atoms associated with points in $G_0(n)$ are needed to cover an atom associated with a point in $G(n)$.

Therefore, given any t elements $l_1, l_2,\dots, l_t$ in A, there are at least t elements $l_1',\dots, l_t'$ in $G_0(n)$ such that

$${}^1\xi_*^{-n}(l_i)\cap {}^1\xi^{-n}(l_i')\cap\sigma(0)\neq\varnothing, \tag{4.41}$$

and by the definition of A,

$$\text{Ham}\left\{\mathbf{M}_{{}^1\xi^{-n}}(l_i), \mathbf{M}_{{}^1\xi_*^{-n}}(l_i')\right\} \leqslant 2n\sqrt{c'}\ . \tag{4.42}$$

Now for any $l \in A$ and $l' \in G_0(n)$ we say that l "knows" l' if and only if ${}^1\xi_*^{-n}(l) \cap {}^1\xi^{-n}(l') \cap \sigma(0)$ is not empty and the Hamming distance between the ξ n-name and the ξ_* n-name is less than $2n\sqrt{c'}$. The previous paragraph shows that this relationship satisfies the hypothesis of Hall's matching lemma [37] and consequently there exists a one to one function ϕ on A to $G_0(n)$ such that l "knows" ϕl. Define ϕ on $G(n)-A$ to $G_0(n)-\phi(A)$ in any fashion.

The partition η is now defined in the same way as was done in Lemma 4.32 using the map ϕ. The conditions $|d(\eta)-p| \leqslant d$ and $0 \leqslant H(p)-h(\mathbf{T},\eta) \leqslant d$ follow as in that lemma.

To see that $|\eta-\xi|<c$, which will complete the proof, note that for each $l \in A$, if $C(l)=\bigcup_{j=0}^{n-1}({}^1\xi^{-n}(l)\cap \mathbf{T}^j\sigma(0))$, there can be no more than $2n\sqrt{c'}$ indices i such that $\xi(i)\cap C(l) \neq \eta(i) \cap C(l)$. Thus

$$\begin{aligned}\sum_{i=0}^{k-1} P([\xi(i)\cap C(l)] \triangle [\eta(i)\cap C(l)]) &\leqslant 2n\sqrt{c'}\, P({}^1\xi^{-n}(l)\cap\sigma(0)) \\ &< 2\sqrt{c'}\, P(C(l)).\end{aligned} \tag{4.43}$$

Let $\Omega_1 = \bigcup_{l\in G(n)} C(l)$. Then using (4.43) and (4.38),

$$\begin{aligned}|\xi\cap\Omega_1 - \eta\cap\Omega_1| &= \sum_{i=0}^{k-1} \frac{P([\xi(i)\triangle\eta(i)]\cap\Omega_1)}{P(\Omega_1)} \\ &= \sum_{i=0}^{k-1}\sum_{l\in A} \frac{P([\xi(i)\triangle\eta(i)]\cap C(l))}{P(\Omega_1)} \\ &\quad + \sum_{i=0}^{k-1}\sum_{l\notin A} \frac{P([\xi(i)\triangle\eta(i)]\cap C(l))}{P(\Omega_1)} \\ &< 2\sqrt{c'} \sum_{l\in A} \frac{P(C(l))}{P(\Omega_1)} + 6\sqrt{c'} \sum_{l\notin A} \frac{P(C(l))}{P(\Omega_1)} \\ &< 6\sqrt{c'}\ .\end{aligned}$$

Since $P(\Omega-\Omega_1)<2d_2$, we have

$$|\xi-\eta| < 6\sqrt{c'} + 2d_2 < 8\sqrt{c'} < c.$$

We are now ready to prove the fundamental lemma. Its proof is obtained by the use of Lemma 4.35 to obtain a Cauchy sequence of partitions in $\mathfrak{Z}_k(\Omega)$ with the partition metric.

LEMMA 4.36 (Ornstein's fundamental lemma). *Let* $S=\{0,1,\dots,k-1\}$, *and p be a discrete probability distribution on S. For every* $c>0$ *there exist* $d>0$ *such that for any invertible ergodic system* $(\Omega,\mathfrak{F},P,\mathbf{T})$ *whose entropy is not exceeded by* $H(p)$ *and any* $\xi\in\mathfrak{Z}_k(\Omega)$ *satisfying*

$$|d(\xi)-p|\leqslant d \quad \textit{and} \quad 0\leqslant H(p)-h(\mathbf{T},\xi)\leqslant d,$$

there exists an independent partition η *in* $\mathfrak{Z}_k(\Omega)$ *with distribution p whose partition distance from* ξ *does not exceed c.*

Proof. Let $c>0$ be given, and for each $n=1,2,\dots$, let d'_n be the d' associated with $c/2^n$ by Lemma 4.35. By induction, using Lemma 4.35, obtain partitions $\eta_n\in\mathfrak{Z}_k(\Omega)$ such that

$$|d(\eta_n)-p|\leqslant d'_{n+1} \tag{4.44}$$

$$0\leqslant H(p)-h(\mathbf{T},\eta_n)\leqslant d'_{n+1} \tag{4.45}$$

$$|\eta_n-\eta_{n+1}|<c/2^n. \tag{4.46}$$

Since $\mathfrak{Z}_k(\Omega)$ is a complete metric space in the partition metric, (4.46) implies that $\eta=\lim_{n\to\infty}\eta_n$ exists. Since $d'_n<c/2^n$, the continuity of $h(\mathbf{T},\ )$ and the expression (4.45) imply that $h(\mathbf{T},\eta)=H(p)$. The continuity of $H(\ )$ in the distribution metric with (4.46) implies that $H(p)=H(\eta)$, so that $h(\mathbf{T},\eta)=H(\eta)$, and it follows from Corollary 2.28 that η is an independent partition.

4.6 The Isomorphism Theorem for Bernoulli Systems

In this section we shall give a proof of the isomorphism theorem for Bernoulli systems which is based on Ornstein's fundamental lemma and the following lemma, due essentially to Ornstein.

LEMMA 4.37. *Let* $(\Omega_1,\mathfrak{F}_1,P_1,\mathbf{T}_1)$ *and* $(\Omega_2,\mathfrak{F}_2,P_2,\mathbf{T}_2)$ *be Bernoulli systems with independent generators* ξ_1 *and* ξ_2 *respectively. If* $\eta_1\in\mathfrak{Z}_k(\Omega_1)$ *is such that*

$$d\left(\bigvee_{i=0}^{n}\mathbf{T}_1^{-i}\eta_1\right)=d\left(\bigvee_{i=0}^{n}\mathbf{T}_2^{-i}\xi_2\right),\qquad n=0,1,\dots,$$

then for every $c>0$ there exists a partition $\eta_1' \in \mathfrak{Z}_k(\Omega_1)$ and an integer K such that

$$d\left(\bigvee_{i=0}^{n} \mathbf{T}_1^{-i}\eta_1'\right) = d\left(\bigvee_{i=0}^{n} \mathbf{T}_2^{-i}\xi_2\right), \tag{4.47}$$

$$\xi_1 \overset{c}{\leqslant} \bigvee_{-K}^{K} \mathbf{T}_1^i \eta_1', \tag{4.48}$$

$$|\eta_1' - \eta_1| \leqslant c. \tag{4.49}$$

The idea of the proof is to select a partition η which is refined by $\bigvee_{i=-\infty}^{+\infty}\mathbf{T}_1^i\eta_1$ such that $d(\bigvee_{i=0}^{n}\mathbf{T}_1^{-i}\eta) = d(\bigvee_{i=0}^{n}\mathbf{T}_1^{-i}\eta_1)$ and η_1 is c-refined by $\bigvee_{-N}^{N}\mathbf{T}_1^i\eta$ for some integer N and small c. Then for sufficiently large K and some small c', η will be c'-refined by $\bigvee_{i=-K}^{K}\mathbf{T}_1^i\eta_1$.

Next, for sufficiently large n take an n-stack σ_1 in $(\Omega_1, \mathfrak{F}_1, P_1, \mathbf{T}_1)$ and an n-stack $\bar{\sigma}_1$ in the factor space associated with $\bigvee_{i=-\infty}^{+\infty}\mathbf{T}_1^i\eta_1$ such that

$$d\left(\bigvee_{i=0}^{n-1} \mathbf{T}_1^{-i}\xi_1 \cap \sigma_1(0)\right) = d\left(\bigvee_{i=0}^{n-1} \mathbf{T}_1^{-i}\eta_1 \cap \bar{\sigma}_1(0)\right).$$

Using these stacks together with the partitions ξ_1 and η_1, obtain atoms, as was done in the coding technique, which are reassembled to obtain a partition η_1^* such that

$$d\left(\bigvee_{i=0}^{n-1} \mathbf{T}_1^{-i}(\xi_1 \vee \eta_1^*) \cap \sigma_1(0)\right) = d\left(\bigvee_{i=0}^{n-1} \mathbf{T}_1^{-i}(\eta \vee \eta_1) \cap \bar{\sigma}_1(0)\right).$$

This can be done in such a way that η_1^* will be close enough to η_1 to apply the fundamental lemma to modify η_1^* and obtain by this modification the required partition. The details of this process are worked out by Shields [139].

THEOREM 4.38 (Kolmogoroff-Ornstein). *Bernoulli systems with finite generators are isomorphic if and only if they have the same entropy.*

Proof. As we pointed out in Section 4.2, the necessity of the condition was proven by Kolmogoroff [69] and it follows from Corollary 2.38. Thus we shall only give here a proof of the sufficiency (which, as we have said, was proven by Ornstein [93]). For this purpose let $(\Omega_1, \mathfrak{F}_1, P_1, \mathbf{T}_1)$ and $(\Omega_2, \mathfrak{F}_2, P_2, \mathbf{T}_2)$ be two Bernoulli systems with independent generators ξ_1 and ξ_2 respectively, and suppose $h(\mathbf{T}_1) = h(\mathbf{T}_2)$.

Apply Lemma 4.32, using $S=(\Omega_2)_{\xi_2}$ with the discrete distribution $p=d(\xi_2)$ to obtain a partition $\eta^{(0)}$ of $(\Omega_1, \mathcal{F}_1, P_1, \mathbf{T}_1)$ such that

$$|d(\eta^{(0)})-d(\xi_2)|\leqslant d$$

and

$$0\leqslant H(\xi_2)-h(\mathbf{T}_1,\eta^{(0)})\leqslant d,$$

where d is the number in the fundamental lemma associated with 1. Applying the fundamental lemma, there exists a partition $\eta^{(1)}$ such that

$$\{\mathbf{T}_1^i\eta^{(1)}\} \text{ is independent,} \tag{4.50}$$

$$d(\eta^{(1)})=d(\xi_2), \tag{4.51}$$

$$|\eta^{(0)}-\eta^{(1)}|\leqslant 1. \tag{4.52}$$

The statements (4.50) and (4.51) imply that $d(\bigvee_{i=0}^{n}\mathbf{T}_1^{-i}\eta^{(1)})=d(\bigvee_{i=0}^{n}\mathbf{T}_2^{-i}\xi_2)$ for every n. By Lemma 4.37, there exists $\eta^{(2)}$ and K_2 such that

$$d\left(\bigvee_{j=0}^{n}\mathbf{T}_1^{-j}\eta^{(2)}\right)=d\left(\bigvee_{j=0}^{n}\mathbf{T}_2^{-j}\xi_2\right), \tag{4.53}$$

$$\xi_1 \text{ is } \tfrac{1}{2} \text{ refined by } \bigvee_{-K_2}^{K_2}\mathbf{T}_1^{j}\eta^{(2)}, \tag{4.54}$$

$$|\eta^{(2)}-\eta^{(1)}|\leqslant \tfrac{1}{2}. \tag{4.55}$$

Proceeding in this fashion, we obtain by induction a sequence $\{\eta^{(l)}\}$ of partitions and an increasing sequence of integers $\{K_l\}$ such that

$$d\left(\bigvee_{j=0}^{n}\mathbf{T}_1^{-j}\eta^{(l)}\right)=d\left(\bigvee_{j=0}^{n}\mathbf{T}_2^{-j}\xi_2\right), \qquad n,l=0,1,2,\ldots, \tag{4.56}$$

$$\xi_1 \text{ is } 1/2^{l-1} \text{ refined by } \bigvee_{j=-K_{l-1}}^{K_{l-1}}\mathbf{T}_1^{-j}\eta^{(l)}, \tag{4.57}$$

$$|\eta^{(l)}-\eta^{(l-1)}|\leqslant\frac{1}{2^{l-1}(2K_{l-1}+1)}. \tag{4.58}$$

Since $\Sigma_{l=1}^{\infty}1/2^{l-1}(2K_{l-1}+1)$ converges, (4.58) implies that $\{\eta^{(l)}\}$ is a Cauchy sequence in the partition metric space and hence $\eta=\lim_{l\to\infty}\eta^{(l)}$ exists.

By (4.56) we have for each n that

$$\left|d\left(\bigvee_{j=0}^{n}\mathbf{T}_1^{-j}\eta\right)-d\left(\bigvee_{j=0}^{n}\mathbf{T}_2^{-j}\xi_2\right)\right|=\left|d\left(\bigvee_{j=0}^{n}\mathbf{T}_1^{-j}\eta\right)-d\left(\bigvee_{j=0}^{n}\mathbf{T}_1^{-j}\eta^{(l)}\right)\right|$$

$$\leqslant\left|\bigvee_{j=0}^{n}\mathbf{T}_1^{-j}\eta-\bigvee_{j=0}^{n}\mathbf{T}_1^{-j}\eta^{(l)}\right|$$

$$\leqslant(n+1)|\eta-\eta^{(l)}|.$$

Since $|\eta-\eta^{(l)}|\to 0$ as $l\to\infty$, we have that $d(\bigvee_{j=0}^{n}\mathbf{T}_1^{-j}\eta)=d(\bigvee_{j=0}^{n}\mathbf{T}_2^{-j}\xi_2)$ for all n. It follows from this that $\{\mathbf{T}_1^{j}\eta\}$ is independent and $d(\eta)=d(\xi_2)$.

All that remains is to prove that η is a generating partition for $\mathbf{T}_1$. To do this notice that if $i<n$, (4.58) implies that

$$\left|\bigvee_{j=-K_i}^{K_i}\mathbf{T}_1^{j}\eta^{(n)}-\bigvee_{j=-K_i}^{K_i}\mathbf{T}_1^{j}\eta^{(i)}\right|\leqslant\sum_{l=i-1}^{n-1}\left|\bigvee_{-K_i}^{K_i}\mathbf{T}_1^{j}\eta^{(l+1)}-\bigvee_{-K_i}^{K_i}\mathbf{T}_1^{j}\eta^{(l)}\right|$$

$$\leqslant\sum_{l=i-1}^{n-1}(2K_i+1)\frac{c}{2^l(2K_l+1)}$$

$$<\sum_{l=i}^{\infty}\frac{c}{2^{l-1}}=r_i.$$

Also (4.57) implies that there exists a partition ζ_i which is refined by $\bigvee_{j=-K_i}^{K_i}\mathbf{T}_1^{j}\eta^{(i)}$ such that $|\xi_1-\zeta_i|\leqslant 1/2^{i-1}$. Thus if ζ_n is any partition which is refined by $\bigvee_{j=-K_i}^{K_i}\mathbf{T}_1^{j}\eta^{(n)}$, then

$$|\xi_1-\zeta_n|\leqslant|\xi_1-\zeta_i|+\left|\bigvee_{j=-K_i}^{K_i}\mathbf{T}_1^{j}\eta^{(n)}-\bigvee_{j=-K_i}^{K_i}\mathbf{T}_1^{j}\eta^{(i)}\right|$$

$$<r_i,$$

and it follows that ξ_1 is r_i refined by $\bigvee_{j=-K_i}^{K_i}\mathbf{T}_1^{j}\eta^{(n)}$ for $i<n$. Taking n to ∞ gives that ξ_1 is r_i refined by $\bigvee_{j=-K_i}^{K_i}\mathbf{T}_1^{j}\eta$ for all i, and since $r_i\to 0$ as $i\to\infty$, it follows that ξ_1 is refined by $\bigvee_{j=-\infty}^{\infty}\mathbf{T}_1^{j}\eta$. But ξ_1 is a generator, so that

$$\varepsilon=\bigvee_{j=-\infty}^{+\infty}\mathbf{T}^{j}\xi_1\leqslant\bigvee_{j=-\infty}^{+\infty}\mathbf{T}^{j}\eta\leqslant\varepsilon$$

and η is a generator.

We have only proven that equal entropy implies isomorphism in the class of Bernoulli shifts with finite generators. This was Ornstein's original result [93], but he soon extended the theorem to Bernoulli systems with infinite entropy [94]. Since Krieger's theorem [71] on generators always insures that a Bernoulli system with finite entropy has a finite generator, it is true that entropy is a complete isomorphism invariant for Bernoulli systems.

THEOREM 4.39 (Kolmogoroff-Ornstein). *A necessary and sufficient condition for two Bernoulli systems to be isomorphic is that they have the same entropy.*

COROLLARY 4.40. *The largest class of ergodic invertible dynamical systems for which the entropy is a complete isomorphism invariant is the class of Bernoulli systems.*

Proof. Let $\mathfrak{E}$ denote the class of all ergodic invertible dynamical systems for which the entropy is a complete isomorphism invariant. The Kolmogoroff-Ornstein theorem implies that $\mathfrak{E}$ contains all Bernoulli systems. In case $(\Omega, \mathfrak{F}, P, \mathbf{T})$ is a system in $\mathfrak{E}$, Ornstein's fundamental lemma implies that there exists a Bernoulli shift whose entropy is $h(\mathbf{T})$. Since both $(\Omega, \mathfrak{F}, P, \mathbf{T})$ and the Bernoulli shift are in $\mathfrak{E}$, we have that the system is isomorphic to a Bernoulli shift and consequently is a Bernoulli system.

4.7 Characterization of Bernoulli Systems

Now that we have shown that the entropy is a complete isomorphism invariant for Bernoulli systems, and this is the largest class for which the entropy is complete, it is important to obtain a technique for determining whether a given system or class of systems is Bernoulli. As one can see from Example 4.10, there are systems with no immediate connection with stationary processes which are Bernoulli.

We have already used one internal criterion (i.e. involving the system only) for determining that a system is Bernoulli, namely that there exists an independent generating partition. There are many partitions associated with a dynamical system, and it is a formidable problem to decide whether there is one that not only is independent but also generates.

Soon after Ornstein proved his first isomorphism theorem, he and Friedman [41] showed that mixing Markov chains were Bernoulli systems and consequently that the entropy is a complete isomorphism invariant for these systems. The result was obtained by showing that if a system has a generating partition for which stretches of iterates of the partitions are almost independent, then it has an independent generating partition. This type of almost independence is called the weak Bernoulli property.

DEFINITION 4.41. A finite partition ξ of an ergodic dynamical system $(\Omega, \mathfrak{F}, P, \mathbf{T})$ is *weak Bernoulli* if for every $c>0$ there exists $N>0$ such that $\bigvee_{i=-m}^{0}\mathbf{T}^i\xi$ is c-independent of $\bigvee_{i=N}^{N+m}\mathbf{T}^i\xi$ for $m=0,1,2,\ldots$.

Example 4.42 (*Mixing Markov shift*). If the transition matrix A of a Markov shift $(\Sigma(S), \mathfrak{F}, \mu, \mathbf{M})$ (see Section 2.12.10) has all of its entries positive and if $\lim_{n\to\infty} a_{ij}^{(n)}$ exists for all i, j, then the system is a mixing Markov chain and the time zero partition $\xi_0 = (\{\omega : \omega(0) = i\} : i \in S)$ is a weak Bernoulli partition.

The fact that mixing Markov chains are Bernoulli systems again illustrates the distinction between a Bernoulli shift and a Bernoulli system. There is *some* generating partition of the space $\Sigma(S)$ which is independent, but clearly the time zero partition is not independent. It need not even be the case that the independent generating partition is obtained from a finite set of coordinate functions of the process $(\mathbf{M}, \xi_0)$.

Subsequent to the Friedman-Ornstein result a modification of weak Bernoulli was developed in connection with the study of Bernoulli flows [96] (also see Section 2.12.4) and was shown to imply the existence of an independent partition.

DEFINITION 4.43. A finite partition ξ of a dynamical system $(\Omega, \mathfrak{F}, P, \mathbf{T})$ is a *very weak Bernoulli partition* if for every $c>0$, there exist $N>0$ such that for every $m \geqslant 1$ there is a collection $\mathcal{Q}_m$ of atoms of $\bigvee_{j=-m}^{-1}\mathbf{T}^j\xi$ such that $P(\bigcup_{A\in\mathcal{Q}_m} A) > 1-c$ and $\bar{d}_N(\{\mathbf{T}^i\xi \cap A\}_{i=0}^{N-1}, \{\mathbf{T}^i\xi\}_{i=0}^{N-1}) < c$ for all $A \in \mathcal{Q}_m$.

THEOREM 4.44. *The following statements are equivalent*:

4.44.1. *The ergodic dynamical system* $(\Omega, \mathfrak{F}, P, \mathbf{T})$ *is a Bernoulli system.*
4.44.2. *There exists a weak Bernoulli generator* ξ *in* $(\Omega, \mathfrak{F}, P, \mathbf{T})$.
4.44.3. *There exists a very weak Bernoulli generator in* $(\Omega, \mathfrak{F}, P, \mathbf{T})$.

The proof of the equivalence of statements 4.44.1 and 4.44.2 is in Friedman and Ornstein [41], and that of statements 4.44.1 and 4.44.3 is in Ornstein [96].

The weak Bernoulli and very weak Bernoulli concepts have proved very effective is showing that specific dynamical systems are Bernoulli. In particular Katznelson [63] used very weak Bernoulli partitions to show that ergodic automorphisms of the n-torus (see Section 2.12.8) are Bernoulli systems. They can also be used to show that geodesic flows of constant negative curvature are Bernoulli flows.

An external criterion (i.e. one involving collections of dynamical systems) for a system to be Bernoulli was developed from a result that Shields [139] calls the Ornstein copying theorem. This result is important in the proof of Lemma 4.35, and basically says the following: Suppose ξ is a partition in a system $(\Omega, \mathfrak{F}, P, \mathbf{T})$ whose joint distributions, i.e. $d(\bigvee_{j=0}^{n}\mathbf{T}^{-j}\xi)$, are close enough to the joint distributions of an independent partition ξ' in a system $(\Omega', \mathfrak{F}', P', \mathbf{T}')$, and the entropy of the process $(\mathbf{T}, \xi)$ is close enough to the entropy of $(\mathbf{T}', \xi')$. Then the processes are close in the $\bar{d}$-metric. The condition derived from this result is called finitely determined and was introduced by Ornstein in [95] and [96].

DEFINITION 4.45. Let $(\Omega, \mathfrak{F}, P, \mathbf{T})$ be an invertible dynamical system. A partition $\xi \in \mathfrak{Z}_k(\Omega)$ is *finitely determined* if for every $c > 0$ there exists an integer $N > 0$ and a real number $d > 0$ such that for every ergodic system $(\Omega', \mathfrak{F}', P', \mathbf{T}')$ whose entropy is not exceeded by $h(\mathbf{T}, \xi)$ and every partition $\xi' \in \mathfrak{Z}_k(\Omega')$ such that

$$\left| d\left(\bigvee_{i=0}^{N-1} \mathbf{T}^{i}\xi \right) - d\left(\bigvee_{i=0}^{N-1} \mathbf{T}'^{i}\xi' \right) \right| < d$$

and

$$0 \leqslant h(\mathbf{T}, \xi) - h(\mathbf{T}', \xi') \leqslant d,$$

we have

$$\sup_n \bar{d}_n\left(\{\mathbf{T}^{i}\xi\}_{i=0}^{n-1}, \{\mathbf{T}'^{i}\xi'\}_{i=0}^{n-1} \right) < c.$$

By a technique similar to the proof of the isomorphism theorem, Ornstein proved that entropy is a complete isomorphism invariant for systems with finitely determined generating partitions, and hence they are Bernoulli systems. (Brown [27] uses finitely determined partitions throughout his proof of the isomorphism theorem.)

The Ornstein copying theorem (Shields [139, p. 54]) implies that independent partitions are finitely determined, and thus we have the following theorem.

THEOREM 4.46. *An invertible ergodic dynamical system is Bernoulli if and only if it has a finitely determined generating partition.*

A real advantage of finitely determined partitions is that not only are the independent generating partitions of Bernoulli systems finitely determined, but every finite partition of a Bernoulli system is finitely determined. Compare this with the fact that Bernoulli systems have partitions which are neither independent nor weak Bernoulli (Smorodinsky [147]).

Notice that every partition in a Bernoulli system being finitely determined implies that every factor of a Bernoulli system is Bernoulli, since every factor of a Bernoulli system is a factor space associated with $\bigvee_{j=-\infty}^{+\infty}\mathbf{T}^j\xi$ for some partition ξ. However, it is not in general the case that every factor space of an arbitrary invertible ergodic system is obtained from $\bigvee_{j=-\infty}^{+\infty}\mathbf{T}^j\xi$ for some finite ξ.

The ultimate connection between internal criteria (independent, weak Bernoulli, very weak Bernoulli) and the external criterion (finitely determined) was obtained by Ornstein and Weiss [105] when they proved that a finitely determined partition is also very weak Bernoulli, and consequently every partition of a Bernoulli system is very weak Bernoulli. Thus the problem of deciding whether a system is Bernoulli is reduced to determining for a particular system whether any conveniently selected generating partition, for example, the time zero partition in a stochastic process, is very weak Bernoulli.

4.8 Relative Isomorphism

In this section we shall consider isomorphisms between Bernoulli systems which induce isomorphisms between given factors of the systems. Such isomorphisms will be called relative isomorphisms.

Throughout the section all systems will be invertible, be ergodic, and have finite entropy. A measurable partition ζ of a system $(\Omega, \mathfrak{F}, P, \mathbf{T})$ is invariant provided $\mathbf{T}\zeta=\zeta$ (mod 0), so that the factor $\mathbf{T}_\zeta$ is an automorphism of the factor space. Because of this property invariant partitions are sometimes called factors. It is not required that an invariant partition be finite or countable, and in most cases the invariant partitions are of the form $\beta^\infty=\bigvee_{i=-\infty}^{\infty}\mathbf{T}^i\beta$, where β is a finite partition. In particular, if ζ is an invariant partition of a Bernoulli system, then $\mathbf{T}_\zeta$ is Bernoulli and there exists an independent partition β such that $\zeta=\beta^\infty$.

An invariant partition ζ is said to be *complemented* if there exists an invariant partition γ, called the complement of ζ, such that ζ and γ are independent and $\zeta\vee\gamma$ is the point partition ε. Notice that if a system has a complemented invariant partition, then it is isomorphic to the product of the factors associated with the partition and its complement. In particular if a Bernoulli system has a complemented invariant partition, then it splits into the product of two Bernoulli systems, and conversely the product of two Bernoulli systems is a Bernoulli system with a complemented invariant partition.

Suppose $(\Omega, \mathfrak{F}, P, \mathbf{T})$ and $(\bar{\Omega}, \bar{\mathfrak{F}}, \bar{P}, \bar{\mathbf{T}})$ are two systems with invariant partitions ζ and $\bar{\zeta}$ respectively. A *relative isomorphism* (with respect to ζ and $\bar{\zeta}$) is a metric isomorphism $\mathbf{R}$ of Ω to $\bar{\Omega}$ such that $\mathbf{R}\circ\mathbf{T}=\bar{\mathbf{T}}\circ\mathbf{R}$ and $\mathbf{R}(\zeta)=\bar{\zeta}$. (Compare this with Definition 2.35.) Two systems with invariant partitions are said to be *relatively isomorphic* if they are connected by a relative isomorphism. The following theorem gives a connection between complemented partitions and relative isomorphisms.

THEOREM 4.47. *Let* $(\Omega, \mathcal{F}, P, \mathbf{T})$ *and* $(\bar{\Omega}, \bar{\mathcal{F}}, \bar{P}, \bar{\mathbf{T}})$ *be Bernoulli systems with invariant partitions* ζ *and* $\bar{\zeta}$. *If* ζ *and* $\bar{\zeta}$ *are complemented, then they are relatively isomorphic if and only if* $h(\mathbf{T})=h(\bar{\mathbf{T}})$ *and* $h(\mathbf{T}_\zeta)=h(\bar{\mathbf{T}}_{\bar{\zeta}})$. *If the systems are relatively isomorphic and one partition is complemented, so is the other.*

Proof. Suppose ζ and $\bar{\zeta}$ are complemented with complements γ and $\bar{\gamma}$, $h(\mathbf{T})=h(\bar{\mathbf{T}})$, and $h(\mathbf{T}_\zeta)=h(\bar{\mathbf{T}}_{\bar{\zeta}})$. Then

$$h(\mathbf{T}_\zeta)+h(\mathbf{T}_\gamma)=h(\mathbf{T})=h(\bar{\mathbf{T}})=h(\mathbf{T}_{\bar{\zeta}})+h(\bar{\mathbf{T}}_{\bar{\gamma}})$$

so $h(\mathbf{T}_\gamma)=h(\bar{\mathbf{T}}_{\bar{\gamma}})$, and since these are factors of a Bernoulli system, they are Bernoulli, and it follows from Ornstein's theorem that $\mathbf{T}_\gamma$ and $\bar{\mathbf{T}}_{\bar{\gamma}}$ are isomorphic. Denote this isomorphism by $\mathbf{R}_2$. Also, $\mathbf{T}_\zeta$ and $\bar{\mathbf{T}}_{\bar{\zeta}}$ are isomorphic, and if $\mathbf{R}_1$ denotes the isomorphism connecting them, the isomorphism $\mathbf{R}_1 \times \mathbf{R}_2$ induces a relative isomorphism between the original systems.

In case there is a relative isomorphism $\mathbf{R}$ between the systems and ζ is complemented with complement γ, then $\mathbf{R}(\gamma)$ is a complement for $\bar{\zeta}$.

Notice this theorem says that entropy is a complete relative isomorphism invariant within the class of Bernoulli systems with complemented invariant partitions. One can view this as a relative version of the Kolmogoroff-Ornstein isomorphism theorem, so that for relative isomorphisms, Bernoulli systems with complemented invariant partitions are analogous to Bernoulli systems for isomorphisms. This analogy was exposed by the deep results of Thouvenot [156] where he defined relative versions of "finitely determined" and proved relative versions of many of Ornstein's lemmas. In particular he proved the following version of Ornstein's fundamental lemma (Lemma 4.36).

THEOREM 4.48. *Let* $S=\{0,1,2,\ldots,k-1\}$, *and* p *be a discrete probability distribution on* S. *Let* $(\Omega, \mathcal{F}, P, \mathbf{T})$ *be an ergodic system whose entropy is not exceeded by* $H(p)+h(\mathbf{T},\eta)$ *where* η *is some finite partition of* Ω. *For every* $c>0$ *there exists* $d>0$ *such that if* ξ *is a measurable partition of* Ω *with* k *atoms such that*

$$|d(\xi)-p|\leqslant d$$

and

$$|h(\mathbf{T},\eta)+H(p)-h(\mathbf{T},\xi)|\leqslant d,$$

then there exists an independent partition β with k atoms and distribution p such that β^∞ and η^∞ are independent and the partition distance between β and ξ does not exceed c.

This result is proven in [156], where one also finds the following definition of relatively finite determined.

DEFINITION 4.49. Let $(\Omega, \mathfrak{F}, P, \mathbf{T})$ be an ergodic system with finite partitions ξ and η. The partition ξ is said to be *finitely determined relative to* η or η-*conditionally finitely determined* if for every $c>0$ there is a $d>0$ and positive integer N such that for any ergodic system $(\overline{\Omega}, \overline{\mathfrak{F}}, \overline{P}, \overline{\mathbf{T}})$ and partitions $\bar{\xi}$ and $\bar{\eta}$ of $\overline{\Omega}$ with

$$d\left(\bigvee_{i=0}^{m} \overline{\mathbf{T}}^i \bar{\eta}\right) = d\left(\bigvee_{i=0}^{m} \mathbf{T}^i \eta\right), \qquad m=0,1,2,\ldots,$$

$$\left| d\left(\bigvee_{i=0}^{N} \overline{\mathbf{T}}^i (\bar{\xi} \vee \bar{\eta})\right) - d\left(\bigvee_{i=0}^{N} \mathbf{T}^i (\xi \vee \eta)\right)\right| \leqslant d,$$

$$\left| h(\mathbf{T}, \xi\vee\eta) - h(\overline{\mathbf{T}}, \bar{\xi}\vee\bar{\eta})\right| \leqslant d,$$

we have for any n

$$\frac{1}{n+1} \sum_{i=0}^{n} |\alpha^i - \bar{\alpha}^i| < c,$$

where $\alpha^i, \bar{\alpha}^i, \beta^i$ for $i=0,1,\ldots,n$ are finite partitions of a Lebesgue space (X, B, μ) such that

$$d\left(\bigvee_{i=0}^{n} \overline{\mathbf{T}}^i (\bar{\xi} \vee \bar{\eta})\right) = d\left(\bigvee_{i=0}^{n} (\alpha^{-i} \vee \beta^i)\right)$$

and

$$d\left(\bigvee_{i=0}^{n} \mathbf{T}^i (\xi \vee \eta)\right) = d\left(\bigvee_{i=0}^{n} (\alpha^i \vee \beta^i)\right).$$

Thouvenot shows that this condition characterizes complemented invariant partitions of Bernoulli systems. Specifically, he proves the following two theorems.

THEOREM 4.50. *Let $(\Omega, \mathfrak{F}, P, \mathbf{T})$ be an ergodic system and β be a finite independent partition of Ω. Suppose γ is a finite partition such that β^∞ and γ^∞*

are independent and $(\beta\vee\gamma)^\infty=\varepsilon$. *If* ξ *is any finite partition of* Ω, *then* ξ *is finitely determined relative to* γ.

THEOREM 4.51. *Let* $(\Omega,\mathfrak{F},P,\mathbf{T})$ *be an ergodic system with* β *a finite independent partition of* Ω. *Suppose* γ *is a finite partition such that* β^∞ *and* γ^∞ *are independent and* $(\beta\vee\gamma)^\infty=\varepsilon$. *If* ξ *is any finite partition of* Ω, *there exists an independent partition* $\bar\beta$ *such that* $(\bar\beta\vee\gamma)^\infty=(\xi\vee\gamma)^\infty$ *and* $\bar\beta^\infty$ *is independent of* γ^∞.

The last theorem implies that if a Bernoulli system has a complemented invariant partition, then every factor system has a complemented invariant partition.

Thouvenot [157] also gave a relative version of very weak Bernoulli partitions and showed that a partition that is relatively very weak Bernoulli is relatively finitely determined.

These results of Thouvenot led Ornstein to the analogy between Bernoulli systems and Bernoulli systems with a complemented factor and resulted in an analog for K-systems, which we now explain. (See the introduction to [102].)

Ornstein and Weiss [105] had shown that if $(\Omega,\mathfrak{F},P,\mathbf{T})$ is a K-system and ζ_0, ζ_1, and ζ_2 are invariant partitions of Ω such that ζ_0 is strictly refined by ζ_1, ζ_0 is independent of ζ_2, and $h(\mathbf{T}_{\zeta_0})=h(\mathbf{T}_{\zeta_1})$, then ζ_1 is also independent of ζ_2. Now if the system is Bernoulli and ζ_0 is complemented, then there exists ζ_2 which is independent of ζ_0 and $\zeta_0\vee\zeta_2=\varepsilon$. If ζ_1 is any partition strictly finer than ζ_0, then $h(\mathbf{T}_{\zeta_1})>h(\mathbf{T}_{\zeta_0})$, for otherwise $\zeta_1\vee\zeta_2$ is a partition strictly finer than the point partition. Call an invariant partition *maximal for its entropy* if the entropy of any factor automorphisms whose associated invariant partition is strictly finer than the given partition is greater than the entropy of the factor automorphism determined by this invariant partition, i.e., ζ is maximal for its entropy if $\bar\zeta>\zeta$ implies that $h(\mathbf{T}_{\bar\zeta})>h(\mathbf{T}_\zeta)$. We thus have the following.

THEOREM 4.52. *If* ζ_0 *is a complemented invariant partition of a Bernoulli system, then* ζ_0 *is maximal for its entropy.*

A Bernoulli system with an invariant partition maximal for its entropy is analogous to a K-automorphism. One can see the analogy by recalling that K-automorphisms are characterized by having no nontrivial factors with zero entropy (Theorem 4.5). If one thinks of an invariant partition ζ as corresponding to a zero entropy system if $h(\mathbf{T}_\zeta)=h(\mathbf{T})$, the analogy becomes clear. Theorem 4.52 is then an analog of the fact that Bernoulli systems are K-systems.

The analogy is strengthened by an example of Ornsteins' [102] of a noncomplemented invariant partition which is maximal for its entropy, an analog of the example of a K-system which is not Bernoulli. This example is produced by taking the skew product of a Bernoulli automorphism with a two member family one of which is a non-Bernoulli K-automorphism. Swanson [153] has shown that Ornstein's example gives rise to an uncountable family $\{(\Omega_i, \mathfrak{F}_i, P_i, \mathbf{T}_i) : i \in I\}$ of Bernoulli shifts with invariant partitions ξ_i such that ξ_i^∞ is maximal for its entropy and $(\mathbf{T}_i)_{\xi_i^\infty}$ is isomorphic to $(\mathbf{T}_j)_{\xi_j^\infty}$ for all $i, j \in I$, but there is no relative isomorphism (with respect to ξ_i^∞ and ξ_j^∞) between $(\Omega_i, \mathfrak{F}_i, P_i, \mathbf{T}_i)$ and $(\Omega_j, \mathfrak{F}_j, P_j, \mathbf{T}_j)$ unless $i = j$.

That Bernoulli systems with complemented invariant partitions do behave differently from Bernoulli systems is shown by a result of Thouvenot [157] which, loosely speaking, says that there exists a Bernoulli system with complemented invariant partition with the property that any factor of the system with complemented invariant partition and full entropy is relatively isomorphic to the system.

The results concerning relative properties have been extended to countable partitions by Lind [80].

4.9 Special Flows and Equivalence Theory

Isomorphism of systems is an equivalence relation on the collection of all invertible ergodic dynamical systems, and the theorem of Ornstein tells us that if we only consider the subcollection of Bernoulli systems (or equivalently, finitely determined systems), then the entropy of the system is a complete isomorphism invariant and each equivalence class can be represented by a Bernoulli shift $(\Sigma(S), \mathfrak{F}, \mu, \mathbf{B})$ with the correct entropy.

There is another equivalence relation on the collection of all systems which is associated with flows (see Section 2.12.4) and has been studied recently with great success using modifications of the methods discussed in Section 4.7. In the present section we shall give a brief discussion of this relation and indicate some recent results.

If $\{\mathbf{T}_t : -\infty < t < \infty\}$ is a flow with the property that $\mathbf{T}_t E = E$ for all t implies E has measure zero or one, then $\{\mathbf{T}_t\}$ is said to be *ergodic*. There is a method of representing ergodic flows in terms of single ergodic metric automorphisms and a real valued integrable function on the measure space of the automorphism. This representation, called a special flow, was discovered by Ambrose [10] and is defined as follows.

Definition 4.53. Let $(X, \mathfrak{B}, \mu)$ be a measure space and $\mathbf{T}$ an ergodic metric automorphism on X. Let h be a positive integrable function on X, and let Ω denote the subset $\{(x, s) : x \in X,\ 0 \leq s < h(x)\}$ of $\Omega \times R$. If λ denotes Lebesgue measure on R, then $(\mu \times \lambda)(\Omega) = \int_X \mu(dx) h(x)$, and the restriction of $\mu \times \lambda$ to Ω is a probability if we normalize by the integral of h. Let $(\Omega, \mathfrak{F}, P)$ denote the probability space obtained by this normalized restriction. The *special flow* on $\mathbf{T}$ under h, denoted by $\{\mathbf{T}_t^h\}$, is defined on $(\Omega, \mathcal{F}, P)$ by

$$\mathbf{T}_t^h(x,s) = \left(\mathbf{T}^n x, s+t-\sum_{k=0}^{n-1} h(\mathbf{T}^j x)\right)$$

$$\text{if} \quad \sum_{k=0}^{n-1} h(\mathbf{T}^k x) - s \leqslant t < \sum_{k=0}^{n} h(\mathbf{T}^k x) - s,$$

$$\mathbf{T}_t^h(x,s) = (x, s+t)$$

$$\text{if} \quad -s \leqslant t < h(x) - s,$$

$$\mathbf{T}_t^h(x,s) = \left(\mathbf{T}^{-n} x, s+t+\sum_{k=1}^{n} h(\mathbf{T}^{-k} x)\right)$$

$$\text{if} \quad -\sum_{k=0}^{n} h(\mathbf{T}^{-k} x) - s \leqslant t < -\sum_{k=0}^{n-1} h(\mathbf{T}^{-k} x) - s$$

for $n = 1, 2, 3, \ldots$.

For intuitive purposes one can visualize a special flow as moving each point in the area under the graph of the function h directly upward with unit speed until it reaches the graph of h, at which time it is reflected instantaneously to a position on the floor determined by $\mathbf{T}$. (See Figure 4.6.)

Ambrose [10] showed that any measurable ergodic flow is isomorphic to a special flow. In 1943 Kakutani [60] defined an equivalence relation for

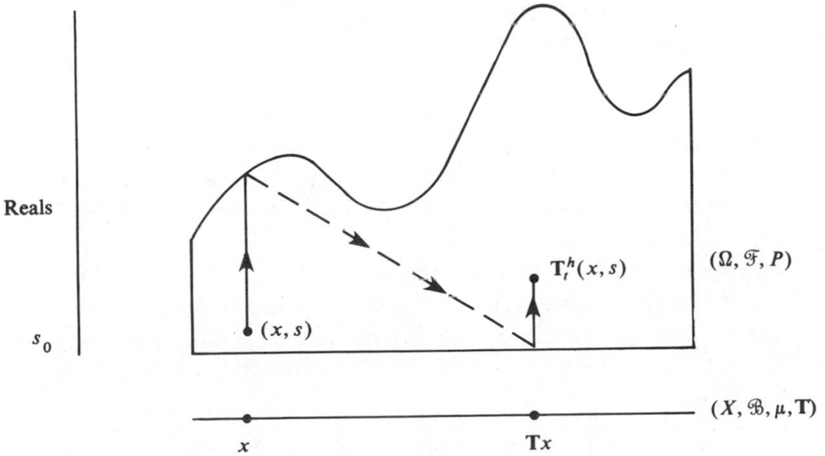

Figure 4.6

metric automorphism which has the property that special flows are isomorphic if and only if the metric automorphisms in their bases are equivalent. This relation is now known as Kakutani equivalence or monotone equivalence.

Recall the Kakutani skyscraper construction described in Section 4.5. Suppose $\mathbf{T}$ is an ergodic automorphism on $(X, \mathfrak{B}, \mu)$, and A is a subset of X with positive measure. For each integer k let

$$A^k = \{x \in A : \mathbf{T}^k x \in A, \mathbf{T}^j x \notin A, 0 < j < k\}.$$

The Kakutani skyscraper is constructed on A, and we showed in Section 4.5 that A is the union of the disjoint sets A^k. Define the function r_A by

$$r_A(x) = k \qquad \text{if} \quad x \in A^k.$$

This function is defined almost everywhere on A and is called the first return time. In the Kakutani skyscraper built on A, $r_A(x)$ represents the number of levels in the stack which contains x in its base, so that

$$\begin{aligned}\int_A r_A \, d\mu &= \sum_{k=1}^{\infty} k\mu(A^k) \\ &= \sum_{k=1}^{\infty} \sum_{j=0}^{k-1} \mu(\mathbf{T}^j A^k) = \mu(X).\end{aligned}$$

The transformation induced by $\mathbf{T}$ on A, denoted by $\mathbf{T}_A$, is defined by

$$\mathbf{T}_A(x) = \mathbf{T}^{r_A(x)}(x).$$

Notice that the induced transformation tells one where a point on the roof of a Kakutani skyscraper goes under the action of $\mathbf{T}$, and the Kakutani skyscraper is analogous to a special flow built on $\mathbf{T}_A$ under the function r_A. The difference is that the area under the graph of r_A is considered to be a subset of $A \times Z^+$.

Using this analogy one can associate with a given metric automorphism $\mathbf{T}$ and integer valued function h on the space of the automorphism a metric automorphism $\mathbf{T}^h$ called a primitive of $\mathbf{T}$ as follows: If $\mathbf{T}$ acts on the measure space $(X, \mathfrak{B}, \mu)$ and h is a positive integer valued function on X with $\int_X \mu(dx) h(x) = 1$, take Ω to be the set $\{(x, k) : x \in X, \ 0 < k \leqslant h(x)\}$. Using counting measure λ on the integers, Ω is a measurable subset of $X \times Z^+$ with $(\mu \times \lambda)(\Omega) = \int_X \mu(dx) h(x)$. The *primitive*, $\mathbf{T}^h$, is defined on Ω by

$$\mathbf{T}^h(x, k) = \begin{cases} (x, k+1) & \text{if} \quad 1 \leqslant k < h(x), \\ (\mathbf{T}x, 1) & \text{if} \quad k = h(x). \end{cases}$$

It is not too difficult to see that $(\mathbf{T}_A)^{r_A}$ is isomorphic to $\mathbf{T}$ for any measurable set A with positive measure. Consequently one can show that two ergodic metric automorphisms have isomorphic induced automorphisms if and only if they are both primitives of the same metric automorphism. Using this result, it is not difficult to show that the following defines an equivalence relation on the class of ergodic metric automorphisms (or dynamical systems).

DEFINITION 4.54. Ergodic metric automorphisms $\mathbf{T}$ and $\mathbf{S}$ are *Kakutani equivalent* if there exist sets A and B of positive measure such that $\mathbf{T}_A$ is isomorphic to $\mathbf{S}_B$.

Katok [62] defined an equivalence relation on metric automorphisms, called monotone equivalence, and demonstrated that automorphisms are monotonely equivalent if and only if they are isomorphic to primitives of the same automorphism. Hence Kakutani equivalence and monotone equivalence are the same.

Kakutani [60] proved that automorphisms $\mathbf{T}$ and $\mathbf{S}$ are equivalent if and only if for every function f there exists a function g such that the special flow $\{\mathbf{T}_t^f\}$ is isomorphic to $\{\mathbf{S}_t^g\}$ and, conversely, for every function g there exists a function f with the same property. It follows from this that special flows are isomorphic if and only if their base transformations are equivalent.

Kakutani conjectured that all ergodic metric automorphisms are equivalent. This conjecture was not settled until 1959, when Abramov [1] gave a formula for the entropy of an induced automorphism in terms of the entropy of the automorphism. He showed that $h(\mathbf{T}_A)=\mu(A)^{-1}h(\mathbf{T})$. Thus the Kakutani equivalence classes of ergodic metric automorphisms are decomposed into three distinct collections by entropy, and hence there are at least three distinct nonequivalent ergodic metric automorphisms.

Clearly isomorphic automorphisms are equivalent, but the converse is not true. The relationship of Kakutani equivalence does not preserve any of the usual isomorphism invariants except ergodicity, as the following theorem indicates.

THEOREM 4.55.

4.55.1. $\mathbf{T}$ *is ergodic if and only if* $\mathbf{T}_A$ *is ergodic and* $\bigcup_{n=1}^{\infty}\mathbf{T}^nA=\Omega$ *a.e.* (A proof is given in [27].)

4.55.2. *For every ergodic automorphism* $\mathbf{T}$ *there exists a function h such that* $\mathbf{T}^h$ *is weak mixing* (Chacon [29]).

4.55.3. *For every ergodic automorphism* $\mathbf{T}$ *there exists a set A such that* $\mathbf{T}_A$ *is weak mixing* (Belinskaya [16]).

4.55.4. *For every ergodic automorphism* $\mathbf{T}$ *there exists a collection of sets which is dense in the measure algebra of the space with metric given by* $\rho(A, B)=\mu(A \triangle B)$, *such that* $\mathbf{T}_A$ *is mixing for each set* A *in the class* (Friedman and Ornstein [42]).

4.55.5. *For every Bernoulli automorphism* $\mathbf{T}$ *with finite entropy and any* α *with* $0<\alpha<1$ *there exists a set* A *with* $\mu(A)=\alpha$ *such that* $\mathbf{T}_A$ *is Bernoulli* (Saleski [134]).

4.55.6. *There exist an uncountable collection on non-Bernoulli K-automorphisms with induced automorphisms that are Bernoulli* (Swanson [152]).

4.55.7. *For every ergodic metric automorphism* $\mathbf{T}$ *with positive entropy and* α *with* $0<\alpha\leqslant 1$, *there exists a set* A *with* $\mu(A)=\alpha$ *such that* $\mathbf{T}_A$ *is a K-automorphism* (Ornstein and Smorodinsky [104]).

4.55.8. *Every Bernoulli automorphism is induced by a K-automorphism which is not Bernoulli* (del Junco [32]).

Notice that statement 4.55.5, together with Abramov's formula for the entropy and the Ornstein isomorphism theorem, implies that all Bernoulli shifts with finite entropy are equivalent. This was also proven directly by Osikawa [106]. Notice also that statement 4.55.7 implies that any automorphism with positive entropy is equivalent to a *K*-automorphism.

Suppose we let $\mathcal{K}_0$ denote the collection of Kakutani equivalence classes with zero entropy, $\mathcal{K}_f$ those with finite nonzero entropy, and $\mathcal{K}_\infty$ those with infinite entropy. A major contribution to the study of these classes was made by Feldman [38] when he constructed an ergodic metric automorphism with zero entropy which is not Kakutani equivalent to an irrational rotation of the circle, which shows that $\mathcal{K}_0$ contains at least two classes. His example can also be used to obtain a *K*-automorphism which is not Kakutani equivalent to a Bernoulli automorphism. This *K*-automorphism is not isomorphic to the non-Bernoulli *K*-automorphisms of Ornstein and Shields [103], since Swanson [152] has shown that these induce Bernoulli automorphisms. By modifying Feldman's example Rudolph [129] has constructed uncountably many non-Kakutani-equivalent automorphisms in $\mathcal{K}_0$. Katok [62] has obtained the same result by another method.

In obtaining his example Feldman introduced a method of measuring distance between collections of ordered partitions which is a modification of the $\bar{d}$-metric used in defining "very weak Bernoulli" and "finitely determined" (see Section 4.7). This metric was also introduced independently by Sataev [137]. It is called the $\bar{f}$-metric and can be understood more easily in terms of an alternate definition of the $\bar{d}$-metric which we now give.

Definition 4.56. For ordered measurable partitions ξ_i and η_i, $i = 1,2,\ldots,N$, with k atoms from $(\Omega_1, \mathfrak{F}_1, P_1)$ and $(\Omega_2, \mathfrak{F}_2, P_2)$ respectively, let $\zeta_1 = \bigvee_{i=1}^{n}\xi_i$ and $\zeta_2 = \bigvee_{i=1}^{n}\eta_i$. Then

$$\bar{d}_N\left(\{\xi_i\}_{i=1}^{N}, \{\eta_i\}_{i=1}^{N}\right) = \inf \int_{\Omega_{\zeta_1}\times\Omega_{\zeta_2}} \nu(d(l_1, l_2))H_N\left(\mathbf{M}_{\zeta_1}(l_1), \mathbf{M}_{\zeta_2}(l_2)\right),$$

where the infimum is taken over all probability measures ν such that $\nu(A\times\Omega_2) = P_1(A)$, $\nu(\Omega_1\times B) = P_2(B)$, $\mathbf{M}_{\zeta_i}(l_i)$ denotes the name of l_i (Definition 4.28), and H_N is the normalized Hamming metric, i.e.,

$$H_N((x_1, x_2,\ldots, x_N),(y_1, y_2,\ldots, y_N)) = \frac{1}{N}|\{i : x_i \neq y_i\}|$$

$$= 1 - \frac{1}{N}|\{i : x_i = y_i\}|.$$

The modification needed to obtain $\bar{f}$ is to replace H_N by the following distance, which we denote by F_N, between N-tuples of integers:

$$F_N((x_1, x_2,\ldots, x_N),(y_1, y_2,\ldots, y_N)) = 1 - \frac{l}{N},$$

where l is the largest integer for which there exist sequences $i_1 < i_2 < \cdots < i_l$ and $j_1 < j_2 < \cdots < j_l$ of integers with $x_{i_1} = y_{j_1}, x_{i_2} = y_{j_2}, \ldots, x_{i_l} = y_{j_l}$. For example

$$H_6((121212),(212121)) = 1,$$

$$F_6((121212),(212121)) = \tfrac{1}{6}.$$

Definition 4.57. Let $\xi_i, \eta_i, \zeta_1, \zeta_2$ have the same meaning as in Definition 4.56. Then

$$\bar{f}_N\left(\{\xi_i\}_{i=1}^{N}, \{\eta_i\}_{i=1}^{N}\right) = \inf \int_{\Omega_{\zeta_1}\times\Omega_{\zeta_2}} \nu\left(d(l_1, l_2)F_N\left(\mathbf{M}_{\zeta_1}(l_1), \mathbf{M}_{\zeta_2}(l_2)\right)\right)$$

where the infimum is again taken over all probability measures on $\Omega_{\zeta_1}\times\Omega_{\zeta_2}$ with the correct marginals.

One can now define internal and external conditions on dynamical systems similar to "very weak Bernoulli" and "finitely determined" by using the same definitions with $\bar{d}_N$ replaced by $\bar{f}_N$.

Definition 4.58. Let $(\Omega, \mathfrak{F}, P, \mathbf{T})$ be an ergodic, invertible dynamical system and ξ a finite measurable partition of Ω. The process $(\mathbf{T}, \xi)$ or the partition ξ is *loosely Bernoulli* if for every $c>0$ there exists $N=N(c)$ such that for $n \geqslant N$ and all $m \geqslant 1$ there is a collection $\mathcal{Q}_m$ of atoms from $\bigvee_{j=-m}^{-1} \mathbf{T}^j \xi$ such that $P(\bigcup_{A \in \mathcal{Q}_m} A) > 1-c$ and

$$\bar{f}_n\left(\{\mathbf{T}^i \xi \cap A\}_{i=1}^n, \{\mathbf{T}^i \xi\}_{i=1}^n\right) < c$$

for all $A \in \mathcal{Q}_m$.

Definition 4.59. Let $(\Omega, \mathfrak{F}, P, \mathbf{T})$ and ξ be as in Definition 4.58. The process $(\mathbf{T}, \xi)$, or the partition ξ, is *finitely fixed* if for every $c>0$ there exists an integer $N>0$ and a real number $d>0$ such that for every ergodic system $(\bar{\Omega}, \bar{\mathfrak{F}}, \bar{P}, \bar{\mathbf{T}})$ whose entropy is not exceeded by $h(\mathbf{T}, \xi)$ and any partition $\bar{\xi}$ of $\bar{\Omega}$ with the same number of atoms as ξ such that

$$\left| d\left(\bigvee_{i=0}^{N-1} \mathbf{T}^i \xi \right) - d\left(\bigvee_{i=0}^{N-1} \bar{\mathbf{T}}^i \bar{\xi} \right) \right| < d$$

and

$$0 \leqslant h(\mathbf{T}, \xi) - h(\bar{\mathbf{T}}, \bar{\xi}) \leqslant d,$$

we have

$$\sup_n \bar{f}_n\left(\{\mathbf{T}^i \xi\}_{i=0}^{n-1}, \{\bar{\mathbf{T}}^i \bar{\xi}\}_{i=0}^{n-1}\right) < c.$$

It is again the case that if a system has a partition which is finitely fixed, then every partition is finitely fixed, so that one defines a dynamical system to be finitely fixed if it has a finitely fixed partition. It is also the case that a partition is loosely Bernoulli if and only if it is finitely fixed. The theorem which corresponds to the isomorphism theorem is the following.

Theorem 4.60. *If* $\mathbf{T}$ *and* $\mathbf{S}$ *are finitely fixed metric automorphisms, they are Kakutani equivalent if and only if they are in the same entropy class. Irrational rotations of the circle and Bernoulli systems are finitely fixed.*

For discussion of equivalence theory and recent results the interested reader should consult Weiss' memoir [164]. Other good discussions are given in Weiss [163] and Katok [62].

CHAPTER 5

Topological Dynamics

5.1 Introduction

Topological dynamics has its origin in the famous work of Poincaré [118] on the qualitative or geometric theory of ordinary differential equations. In Poincaré's work one finds many of the fundamental ideas and concepts of the modern theory of dynamical systems. The ideas were formalized and extended by Birkhoff [19], who undertook the systematic development of the theory of dynamical systems. The dynamical systems studied by Poincaré and Birkhoff, now called classical systems, are those that are defined from an ordinary differential equation defined on an open set or manifold contained in Euclidean n-space. In particular the second example mentioned in Section 2.8 and the example in Section 4.1 are of this type.

Specifically, a dynamical system is defined from an ordinary differential equation $\dot{x}=H(x)$, where H is any smooth vector field on a smooth manifold M contained in R^n, in the following way. The fundamental existence and uniqueness theorem implies that for each $p\in M$ there exists an open interval I_p of the reals R, which contains zero and a unique function $F_p: I_p\to M$ such that $F_p(0)=p$ and for each $t\in I_p$, $F_p'(t)=H(F_p(t))$. If M is compact, then for each $p\in M$ we may take I_p to be R and define a function $\psi: M\times R\to M$ by $\psi(p,t)=F_p(t)$. The function ψ turns out to be smooth because of theorems concerning the dependence of solutions on "initial conditions."

In particular for each $t\in R$, $\psi(\ ,t)=\mathbf{T}^t$ is a diffeomorphism of M. Since solutions of the differential equation are unique, it follows that for all $p\in M$ and for all t and s in R, $\psi(p,t+s)=\psi(\psi(p,t),s)$, or $\mathbf{T}^{t+s}(p)=\mathbf{T}^s\circ\mathbf{T}^t(p)$. The map ψ therefore defines a one parameter group

ENCYCLOPEDIA OF MATHEMATICS and Its Applications, Gian-Carlo Rota (ed.).
Vol. 12: Nathaniel F. Martin and James W. England, Mathematical Theory of Entropy.
ISBN 0-201-13511-6

$\{\mathbf{T}^t : t \in R\}$ of diffeomorphisms on M, which is called a classical dynamical system.

Two dynamical systems $\{\mathbf{T}^t : t \in R\}$ and $\{\mathbf{S}^t : t \in R\}$ are said to be *equivalent* provided there exists a homeomorphism $\mathbf{H}: M_1 \to M_2$, where $\mathbf{T}^t : M_1 \to M_1$ and $\mathbf{S}^t : M_2 \to M_2$, such that $\mathbf{H} \circ \mathbf{T}^t = \mathbf{S}^t \circ \mathbf{H}$ for all $t \in R$, that is, orbits of $\{\mathbf{T}^t\}$ are mapped onto orbits of $\{\mathbf{S}^t\}$ by a homeomorphism which preserves the orientation of the orbits. A central problem in the qualitative theory of differential equations is to determine the classes of equivalent dynamical systems. This problem was first considered by Kneser [68] and has been studied extensively by Andronov and Pontryagin [11], Lefschetz [77], Kaplan [61], and others. Smale [145] put this study in more general context by formulating the notion of structural stability. The problems in the qualitative theory of differential equations then are concerned with a study of properties of the associated dynamical system which give information about all systems in the equivalence class, as well as methods of determining the classes.

Two diffeomorphisms $\mathbf{T}_1$ and $\mathbf{T}_2$ on manifolds M_1 and M_2 respectively are *conjugate* if there exists a continuous map $\mathbf{H}$ of M_1 to M_2 such that $\mathbf{H} \circ \mathbf{T}_1 = \mathbf{T}_2 \circ \mathbf{H}$. Notice that if $\{\mathbf{T}^t : t \in R\}$ and $\{\mathbf{S}^t : t \in R\}$ are two equivalent classical dynamical systems, then for each $t \in R$, $\mathbf{T}^t$ and $\mathbf{S}^t$ are conjugate. Thus the problem of determining equivalence classes of dynamical systems includes the problem of determining the conjugacy classes of diffeomorphisms. As noted by Smale [146], this problem should be somewhat more tractable than the full problem on equivalency classes, and results obtained from work on this problem would also be applicable to classical dynamical systems.

A property of diffeomorphisms is called a *conjugacy invariant* provided that either every member of a conjugacy class possesses the property or every member of the class does not. Obviously, easily calculated conjugacy invariants are of paramount importance in determining conjugacy classes. The *topological entropy* was introduced into topological dynamics as a conjugacy invariant by Adler, Konheim, and McAndrew [7]. It was originally defined by analogy with the notion of (measure theoretic) entropy discussed in Chapter 2, and much of the work on topological entropy has been involved with clarifying its relationship with measure theoretic entropy. An alternative definition of topological entropy, arising from a study of its connection with the zeta function of a diffeomorphism [22], shows that it has some important relationships with other topological conjugacy invariants.

In this chapter we shall discuss the notion of topological entropy in the setting of a continuous function on a compact Hausdorff space. This level of generality seems most appropriate for understanding the basic properties of topological entropy and its connections with measure theoretic entropy as well as its relationship to other topological conjugacy invariants.

5.2 Definition and Basic Properties of Topological Entropy

In this section we shall give the original definition of the topological entropy of a continuous function on a compact Hausdorff space as given by Adler et al. [7] together with some examples found in their paper. An alternative definition due to Bowen [22], which generalizes their definition and makes it easier to see some relationships between entropy and other invariants, will be discussed in Section 5.4.

Throughout this section, X will denote a compact Hausdorff space. If $\mathcal{A}$ is an open cover of X, then $\mathcal{A}$ always has a finite subcover. A finite subcover of $\mathcal{A}$ is *minimal* provided no other subcover of $\mathcal{A}$ contains fewer elements. Let $N(\mathcal{A})$ denote the number of sets in a minimal subcover of $\mathcal{A}$. The *entropy* of $\mathcal{A}$, denoted by $H(\mathcal{A})$, is defined by $H(\mathcal{A})=\log N(\mathcal{A})$. The analogy with measure theoretic entropy should be clear. Since there is no measure on the compact Hausdorff space, we simply count the minimum number of sets from $\mathcal{A}$ needed to cover X and "weigh" each one equally.

For $\mathcal{A}$ and $\mathcal{B}$ open covers of X, we let $\mathcal{A}\vee\mathcal{B}$ denote the open cover of X whose elements are of the form $A\cap B$ for $A\in\mathcal{A}$ and $B\in\mathcal{B}$. We say that $\mathcal{B}$ *refines* $\mathcal{A}$, denoted $\mathcal{A}<\mathcal{B}$, if each element of $\mathcal{B}$ is a subset of some element of $\mathcal{A}$. Notice that if $\{A_1,\dots,A_N\}$ is a subcover of $\mathcal{A}$ and $\{B_1,\dots,B_M\}$ is a subcover of $\mathcal{B}$, then $\{A_i\cap B_j: i=1,2,\dots,N; j=1,2,\dots,M\}$ is a subcover of $\mathcal{A}\vee\mathcal{B}$. Therefore, $N(\mathcal{A}\vee\mathcal{B})\leqslant N(\mathcal{A})N(\mathcal{B})$ and $H(\mathcal{A}\vee\mathcal{B})\leqslant H(\mathcal{A})+H(\mathcal{B})$.

If $\mathbf{T}$ is a continuous map on X into itself and $\mathcal{A}$ is an open cover of X, then $\mathbf{T}^{-1}(\mathcal{A})=\{\mathbf{T}^{-1}(A): A\in\mathcal{A}\}$ is an open cover of X. If $\{A_1,A_2,\dots,A_{N(\mathcal{A})}\}$ is a minimal subcover of $\mathcal{A}$, then $\{\mathbf{T}^{-1}A_1,\dots,\mathbf{T}^{-1}(A_{N(\mathcal{A})})\}$ is a subcover of $\mathbf{T}^{-1}(\mathcal{A})$, possibly not minimal, and thus $N(\mathbf{T}^{-1}(\mathcal{A}))\leqslant N(\mathcal{A})$. However, if $\mathbf{T}$ is a homeomorphism, $N(\mathbf{T}^{-1}(\mathcal{A}))=N(\mathcal{A})$.

Continuing the analogy with measure theoretic entropy, for n a positive integer and $\mathbf{T}$ and $\mathcal{A}$ as above we let $\bigvee_{j=0}^{n-1}\mathbf{T}^{-1}(\mathcal{A})$ denote the open cover $\mathcal{A}\vee\mathbf{T}^{-1}(\mathcal{A})\vee\cdots\vee\mathbf{T}^{-n+1}(\mathcal{A})$, and H_n denote $H(\bigvee_{j=0}^{n-1}\mathbf{T}^{-1}(\mathcal{A}))$. If m and n are positive integers, then

$$\begin{aligned}H_{m+n}&=H\left[\bigvee_{j=0}^{m+n-1}\mathbf{T}^{-j}(\mathcal{A})\right]=H\left[\bigvee_{j=0}^{m-1}\mathbf{T}^{-j}(\mathcal{A})\vee\mathbf{T}^{-m}\left[\bigvee_{j=0}^{n-1}\mathbf{T}^{-j}(\mathcal{A})\right]\right]\\&\leqslant H\left[\bigvee_{j=0}^{m-1}\mathbf{T}^{-j}(a)\right]+H\left[\mathbf{T}^{-n}\bigvee_{j=0}^{n-1}\mathbf{T}^{-j}(\mathcal{A})\right]\\&\leqslant H\left[\bigvee_{j=0}^{m-1}\mathbf{T}^{-j}(\mathcal{A})\right]+H\left[\bigvee_{j=0}^{m-1}\mathbf{T}^{-j}(\mathcal{A})\right]=H_m+H_n.\end{aligned}$$

In addition, it is clear that for all positive integers n, $H_n\geqslant 0$. We showed in Section 2.7 that for any sequence $\{H_n\}$ of numbers satisfying these two conditions the sequence $\{(1/n)H_n\}$ has a limit.

DEFINITION 5.1. Let $\mathbf{T}$ be a continuous map on X into itself, and $\mathcal{Q}$ an open cover of X. The *entropy of* $\mathbf{T}$ *with respect to* $\mathcal{Q}$, denoted by $h(\mathbf{T},\mathcal{Q})$, is defined by the equation

$$h(\mathbf{T},\mathcal{Q})=\lim_{n\to\infty}\frac{1}{n}H\left[\bigvee_{j=0}^{n-1}\mathbf{T}^{-j}(\mathcal{Q})\right].$$

The *topological entropy* (or just entropy) of the map $\mathbf{T}$, denoted by $h(\mathbf{T})$, is defined by the equation

$$h(\mathbf{T})=\sup\{h(\mathbf{T},\mathcal{Q}):\mathcal{Q}\text{ an open cover of }X\}.$$

The definition of topological entropy given above is clearly a topological adaptation of Definitions 2.26 and 2.36. Thus we can think of topological entropy as a measure of how much a continuous map "mixes" the open sets of a topological space.

If $\mathcal{Q}$ and $\mathcal{B}$ are open covers of X, and $\mathbf{T}$ is continuous, it is easy to see that $\mathcal{Q}<\mathcal{B}$ implies $h(\mathbf{T},\mathcal{Q})\leqslant h(\mathbf{T},\mathcal{B})$ and if $\mathbf{T}$ is a homeomorphism of X onto itself then $h(\mathbf{T}^{-1},\mathcal{Q})=h(\mathbf{T},\mathcal{Q})$. These remarks provide the proof of the following basic theorem concerning topological entropy.

THEOREM 5.2. *If* $\mathbf{T}_1: X_1\to X_1$ *and* $\mathbf{T}_2: X_2\to X_2$ *are conjugate continuous maps, then* $h(\mathbf{T}_1)=h(\mathbf{T}_2)$.

Proof. Since $\mathbf{T}_1$ and $\mathbf{T}_2$ are conjugate, there exists a homeomorphism $\mathbf{H}: X_1\to X_2$ such that $\mathbf{H}\circ\mathbf{T}_1=\mathbf{T}_2\circ\mathbf{H}$ and hence $\mathbf{T}_1^{-1}(\mathbf{H}^{-1}\mathcal{Q})=\mathbf{H}^{-1}(\mathbf{T}_2^{-1}\mathcal{Q})$ for $\mathcal{Q}$ any open cover of X_2. Thus we have

$$\begin{aligned}h(\mathbf{T},\mathbf{H}^{-1}(\mathcal{Q}))&=\lim_{n\to\infty}\frac{1}{n}H\left[\bigvee_{j=0}^{n-1}\mathbf{T}_1^{-j}\mathbf{H}^{-1}(\mathcal{Q})\right]\\&=\lim_{n\to\infty}\frac{1}{n}H\left[\bigvee_{j=0}^{n-1}\mathbf{H}^{-1}\mathbf{T}_2^{-j}(\mathcal{Q})\right]\\&=\lim_{n\to\infty}\frac{1}{n}H\left[\mathbf{H}^{-1}\left[\bigvee_{j=0}^{n-1}\mathbf{T}_2^{-j}(\mathcal{Q})\right]\right].\end{aligned}$$

However, since $\mathbf{H}$ is a homeomorphism, $H(\mathbf{H}^{-1}(\mathcal{B}))=H(\mathcal{B})$ for any open cover $\mathcal{B}$ and we have

$$h(\mathbf{T}_1,\mathbf{H}^{-1}(\mathcal{Q}))=\lim_{n\to\infty}\frac{1}{n}H\left[\bigvee_{j=0}^{n-1}\mathbf{T}_2^{-j}\mathcal{Q}\right]=h(\mathbf{T}_2,\mathcal{Q})$$

for every open cover $\mathscr{A}$ of X_2. Since $\mathbf{H}$ is a homeomorphism, every open cover of X_1 is of the form $\mathbf{H}^{-1}(\mathscr{A})$ for some open cover $\mathscr{A}$ of X_2, and we have that

$$\begin{aligned} h(\mathbf{T}_1) &= \sup\{h(\mathbf{T}_1, \mathscr{B}) : \mathscr{B} \text{ open cover of } X_1\} \\ &= \sup\{h(\mathbf{T}_1, \mathbf{H}^{-1}(\mathscr{A})) : \mathscr{A} \text{ open cover of } X_1\} \\ &= h(\mathbf{T}_2), \end{aligned}$$

and the theorem is proven.

We can easily give examples of nonconjugate maps with the same topological entropy. Such examples are given by periodic functions. Recall that $\mathbf{T}$ is periodic if there exists an integer n such that $\mathbf{T}^n(x)=x$ for all x in X. The period of a periodic function is the smallest positive integer with this property. Since periodic functions are conjugate only if they have the same period, functions with different periods cannot be conjugate. On the other hand, all periodic maps have zero entropy, since $\mathbf{T}^{-k}(\mathscr{A})=\mathscr{A}$ for a map of period k, and we have that for any $n>k$, $\bigvee_{j=0}^{n-1}\mathbf{T}^{-j}(\mathscr{A})=\bigvee_{j=0}^{k-1}\mathbf{T}^{-j}(\mathscr{A})$. Thus for every open cover $\mathscr{A}$,

$$h(\mathbf{T}, \mathscr{A}) = \lim_{n\to\infty} \frac{1}{n} H\left[\bigvee_{j=0}^{k-1} \mathbf{T}^{-j}\mathscr{A}\right] = 0$$

and it follows that $h(\mathbf{T})=0$.

In order to compute the topological entropy of certain examples we use a result similar to Theorem 2.32 and Corollary 2.48. To state this result we now introduce the notion of a refining sequence of covers.

A sequence $\{\mathscr{A}_n : n=1,2,\ldots\}$ of open covers is *refining* provided that $\mathscr{A}_n < \mathscr{A}_{n+1}$ for all n, and if $\mathscr{B}$ is any open cover, then there exists an n such that $\mathscr{B} < \mathscr{A}_n$. The following is an immediate consequence of the definition of topological entropy and the remarks following that definition.

THEOREM 5.3. *If $\{\mathscr{A}_n\}$ is a refining sequence of covers of a compact Hausdorff space X and $\mathbf{T}$ is a continuous function on X, then*

$$h(\mathbf{T}) = \lim_{n\to\infty} h(\mathbf{T}, \mathscr{A}_n).$$

In case X is a metric space we can obtain a refining sequence of covers using the metric. Let d denote the metric for X, and for $\mathscr{A}$ an open cover of X let $d(\mathscr{A})=\sup\{d(A) : A \in \mathscr{A}\}$, where $d(A)$ denotes the diameter of the set A, i.e. $d(A)=\sup\{d(x,y) : x, y \in A\}$, It follows immediately from the Lebesgue covering lemma that if $\{\mathscr{A}_n\}$ is a sequence of open covers of X and if $\mathscr{A}_n < \mathscr{A}_{n+1}$ and $d(\mathscr{A}_n) \to 0$ as $n\to\infty$, then $\{\mathscr{A}_n\}$ is a refining sequence.

Thus if $\mathcal{Q}_n$ is the collection of all spheres of diameter less than $1/n$, then $\{\mathcal{Q}_n\}$ is a refining sequence. Using this particular refining sequence it is straightforward to see that if $\mathbf{T}$ is an isometry of X onto itself, i.e. $d(\mathbf{T}(x),\mathbf{T}(y))=d(x,y)$ for all $x,y\in X$, then $h(\mathbf{T})=0$.

We give one final example in this section. In Section 1.7 we defined the dynamical system $(\Sigma(S),\mathcal{F}_S,\mu,\mathbf{T}_S)$ for S a finite set of integers. We consider this example once again. This time we shall define a metric on $\Sigma(S)$ in such a way that $\Sigma(S)$ is compact and $\mathbf{T}_S$ is a homeomorphism. (For the time being we ignore $\mathcal{F}_S$ and any measure μ on $\mathcal{F}_S$.) For points $x=(\ldots,x_{-1},x_0,x_1,\ldots)$ and $y=(\ldots,y_{-1},y_0,y_1,\ldots)$ in $\Sigma(S)$, define $d(x,y)=\sum_{n=-\infty}^{+\infty}2^{-|n|}|x_n-y_n|$. It is not difficult to see that d is a metric on $\Sigma(S)$ and that the topology it induces on $\Sigma(S)$ is equivalent to the product topology obtained from the discrete topology on S. Thus $\Sigma(S)$ is compact, and since

$$\tfrac{1}{2}d(x,y)\leqslant d(\mathbf{T}_S x,\mathbf{T}_S y)\leqslant d(x,y)$$

for all $x,y\in\Sigma(S)$, we have that $\mathbf{T}_S$ is a homeomorphism. Let $\mathcal{Q}$ be the open cover of $\Sigma(S)$ consisting of the time zero cylinder sets, $\{x\in\Sigma(S): x_0=i\}$, $i\in S$. Assume that $S=\{1,2,\ldots,k\}$, so that $d(\{x\in\Sigma(S): x_0=i\})=2k$. Let $\mathcal{Q}_n=\bigvee_{i=-n}^{n}\mathbf{T}_S^i\mathcal{Q}$, so that for $A\in\mathcal{Q}_n$, $d(A)=2^{-n+1}k$. Thus $d(\mathcal{Q}_n)\to 0$ as $n\to\infty$ and $\mathcal{Q}_n<\mathcal{Q}_{n+1}$ for all n. Hence $\{\mathcal{Q}_n\}$ is a refining sequence. Next note that $N(\bigvee_{i=0}^{n-1}\mathbf{T}_S^{-i}\mathcal{Q})=k^n$, so that $h(\mathbf{T}_S,\mathcal{Q})=\log k$. The properties of entropy we have already indicated imply that

$$\begin{aligned}
h(\mathbf{T}_S,\mathcal{Q})\leqslant h(\mathbf{T}_S,\mathcal{Q}_l) &= \lim_{n\to\infty}\frac{1}{n}H\left[\bigvee_{i=0}^{n-1}\mathbf{T}_S^{-i}\left(\bigvee_{j=-l}^{l}\mathbf{T}_S^{j}\mathcal{Q}\right)\right]\\
&= \lim_{n\to\infty}\frac{1}{n}H\left[\bigvee_{i=-l}^{l+n-1}\mathbf{T}_S^{-i}\mathcal{Q}\right]\\
&= \lim_{n\to\infty}\frac{1}{n}H\left[\mathbf{T}_S^{l}\left(\bigvee_{i=0}^{2l+n-1}\mathbf{T}_A^{-i}\mathcal{Q}\right)\right]\\
&= \lim_{n\to\infty}\frac{2l+n}{n}\,\frac{1}{2l+n}H\left[\bigvee_{j=0}^{2l+n-1}\mathbf{T}_S^{-i}\mathcal{Q}\right]\\
&= h(\mathbf{T}_S,\mathcal{Q}).
\end{aligned}$$

Thus for all l, $h(\mathbf{T}_S,\mathcal{Q}_l)=\log k$, and Theorem 5.3 implies that $h(\mathbf{T}_S)=\log k$.

5.3 Connection between Topological and Measure Theoretic Entropy

In Chapter 2 we showed that the entropy of the dynamical system $(\Sigma(S), \mathfrak{F}_S, \mu, \mathbf{T}_S)$, where μ is the product measure obtained from a distribution $p_i = p(i)$ on S is given by $-\Sigma p_i \log p_i$. In particular, if S has k elements and $p_i = 1/k$ for all i, then the entropy of $\mathbf{T}_S$ is $\log k$. This is the same value we obtained for the topological entropy of $\mathbf{T}_S$ considered as a homeomorphism of $\Sigma(S)$. This and similar examples give rise to a number of conjectures concerning the relationship between topological and measure theoretic entropy (see [7], [45], [46], and [47]), which we shall now discuss.

The setting for our discussion of this relationship is that of a continuous function $\mathbf{T}$ on a compact Hausdorff space X together with a $\mathbf{T}$-invariant probability measure μ on the σ-field $\mathfrak{B}$ of Borel subsets of X. (Extensive discussions of the existence of invariant measures are given by Halmos [56] and Friedman [40].) In this setting we shall denote the topological entropy of $\mathbf{T}$ by $h(\mathbf{T})$ and the measure theoretic entropy by $h_\mu(\mathbf{T})$.

The general relationship between topological and measure theoretic entropy is contained in the following two results due to Goodwyn [46, 47].

THEOREM 5.4. *If X is a compact metric space, $\mathbf{T}$ is a continuous function, and μ is an $\mathbf{T}$-invariant probability on the Borel subsets of X, then $h_\mu(\mathbf{T}) \leqslant h(\mathbf{T})$.*

THEOREM 5.5. *If X and $\mathbf{T}$ are as above, then*

$$h(\mathbf{T}) = \sup\{h_\mu(\mathbf{T})\},$$

where the supremum is taken over all $\mathbf{T}$-invariant Borel probabilities.

The example at the end of the previous section together with its measure theoretic counterparts leads to another interesting conjecture. We know that $h_\mu(\mathbf{T}_S) = -\Sigma_{i=1}^k p_i \log p_i$, where μ is the product measure obtained from the distribution $\{p_i : i = 1, 2, \ldots, k\}$ on S. We can make $\Sigma(S)$ into a topological group by coordinatewise addition, mod k, and $\mathbf{T}_S$ is a continuous automorphism of this group. In this case it is not difficult to see that the measure μ is Haar measure in $\Sigma(S)$ if and only if the measure induced on S by $\{p_i\}$ is the Haar measure associated with S as the group of integers mod k. In order for this to be the case it is necessary and sufficient that $p_i = 1/k$ for $i = 1, 2, \ldots, k$. Thus in this case, the supremum in Theorem 5.5 is attained at Haar measure, and again we have $h_\mu(\mathbf{T}_S) = \log k$.

Another example of this phenomenon is provided by the continuous automorphisms of the torus. Recall that if T_n is the n-dimensional torus, then we can view T_n as R^n/Z^n, where Z^n denotes the integer lattice points in R^n. With this representation it is not difficult to see that if $\mathbf{T}$ is a continuous group of automorphism of T_n onto itself, then $\mathbf{T}$ is induced by an integer entry matrix A with determinant ± 1 (see Section 2.12.8). The topological entropy of such an automorphism is given in [17] as $h(\mathbf{T}) = \Sigma \log|\lambda_i|$, where the sum is over those eigenvalues λ_i of A whose absolute value is greater than one.

If $n=2$ and the eigenvalues are real, this formula is easy to deduce. Notice that in this case the eigenvalues of A are λ and λ^{-1}. If $\lambda=1$, it is easy to show that $h(\mathbf{T})=0$. Assume that $|\lambda|>1$. In this case A has two linearly independent eigenvectors. Let $\mathcal{C}_k$ be the open cover of T_n which arises from the set of all open parallelograms in R^2 with sides of length $1/k$ two of which are parallel to one eigenvector of A and the other two parallel to the other eigenvector of A. If C is a set in $\mathcal{C}_k$ and $\overline{C}$ is the parallelogram in R^2 corresponding to C, then $\mathbf{T}^{-n}(C)$ corresponds to $A^{-n}\overline{C}$, which is a parallelogram in R^2 with two sides parallel to the eigenvector associated with λ of length $|\lambda|^n/k$ and the other two sides parallel to the eigenvector associated with λ^{-1} having length $|\lambda|^{-n}/k$. It takes $|\lambda|^n$ of these parallelograms to cover one parallelogram corresponding to a set in $\mathcal{C}_k$. All of these correspond to a set in $\mathbf{T}^{-n}(\mathcal{C}_k)$. Thus

$$k^2|\lambda|^n \leqslant N\left(\bigvee_{j=0}^{n} \mathbf{T}^{-j}\mathcal{C}_k\right) \leqslant |\lambda|^n N(\mathcal{C}_k).$$

This implies that $h(\mathbf{T}, \mathcal{C}_k) = \log|\lambda|$. Since the sequence $\{\mathcal{C}_k\}$ of open covers is a refining sequence, $h(\mathbf{T}) = \log|\lambda|$.

In Section 2.12.8 we noted that using Haar measure on the torus, the entropy of an ergodic continuous automorphism is also $\Sigma \log|\lambda_i|$, where the sum is over eigenvalues of A with absolute value greater than one. Thus the topological entropy of a continuous ergodic automorphism on the torus is equal to its measure theoretic entropy with respect to Haar measure. Bowen [23] has proven the following more general result.

THEOREM 5.6. *If G is a compact metric group, $\mathbf{T}$ is an endomorphism of G into itself, and μ is normalized right Haar measure, then*

$$h(\mathbf{T}) = h_\mu(\mathbf{T}).$$

The definition of topological entropy and the techniques used by Bowen to prove this result are quite different from those we have used to this point. The alternative definition applies to a uniformly continuous map on a metric space into itself. This definition arose from work on the relationship between topological entropy and other conjugacy invariants. The next section is devoted to a discussion of this definition.

We conclude this section by discussing a class of transformations whose role in topological dynamics is analogous to the role of Bernoulli shifts in ergodic theory. These transformations are called subshifts of finite type. One reason for their importance is that a number of important classes of transformations have been shown to be measure theoretically isomorphic to subshifts of finite type. Moreover Adler and Marcus [8] introduced a weakened form of topological equivalence, which they call almost topological conjugacy, and proved that topological entropy and one other invariant form a complete set of invariants for almost topological conjugacy within the class of subshifts of finite type. A self-contained discussion of this theory may be found in [8].

Let $S=\{1,2,\dots,N\}$, and $A=(a_{ij})$ be a $N\times N$ matrix of zeros and ones with the property that it has at least one nonzero element in each row and column. A k-tuple $(x_1,x_2,\dots,x_k)$ of elements from S is said to be *admissible*, and is called an *admissible k-block*, provided that $a_{x_ix_{i+1}}=1$ for all $1\leqslant i\leqslant k-1$. Similarly, a point $x=(\dots,x_{-1},x_0,x_1,\dots)\in\Sigma(S)$ is said to be admissible provided $a_{x_ix_{i+1}}=1$ for every integer i. Let $A(S)$ denote the set of admissible points of $\Sigma(S)$. It is clear that $A(S)$ is a compact subset of $\Sigma(S)$ with the product topology.

As before, we let $\mathbf{T}_S$ denote the shift on $\Sigma(S)$. Given a matrix A as above, the set $A(S)$ is a $\mathbf{T}_S$-invariant subset of $\Sigma(S)$. The dynamical system $(A(S),\mathbf{T}_S)$ is called a subshift of finite type. Notice that if A is the matrix of all ones, then $A(S)=\Sigma(S)$; the corresponding subshift of finite type is called the full shift. Of course it is simply the example we considered at the end of section 5.2.

We let S and A be as above. As one can show, the number of admissible n-blocks which start with i and end with j is equal to the i,jth entry of A^{n-1}, which we denote by $a_{ij}^{(n-1)}$. A is said to be *irreducible* if for all i and j in S there exists a positive integer n (which may depend on i and j) such that $a_{ij}^{(n)}>0$.

The calculation of the topological entropy of $(A(S),\mathbf{T}_S)$ for irreducible A follows directly from some spectral properties of nonnegative matrices derived by Perron and Frobenius [48]. We state just the portion of those results that we need.

LEMMA 5.7. *If A is an irreducible matrix with nonnegative entries, there exists a simple eigenvalue $\lambda(A)$ which has both a left and a right eigenvector all of whose components are positive, and such that $|\mu|\leqslant\lambda(A)$ for all eigenvalues μ of A.*

This lemma makes it easy to calculate the topological entropy of $(A(S),\mathbf{T}_S)$. Let $\mathcal{Q}(A)$ be the open cover of $A(S)$ consisting of the time zero cylinder sets of $\Sigma(S)$ intersected with $A(S)$, and let $\mathcal{Q}_n(A)=\bigvee_{i=-n}^{n}\mathbf{T}_S^i(A)$. As in the example at the end of Section 5.2, $\{\mathcal{Q}_n(A)\}$ is a refining sequence, and to calculate the entropy of $\mathbf{T}_S$ restricted to $A(S)$, which we shall denote by $\mathbf{T}_S$ also, we only need to calculate $N(\bigvee_{i=0}^{n-1}\mathbf{T}_S^{-i}\mathscr{Q}(A))$. This number is equal to the number of admissible n-blocks. If we let $\alpha(n,i)$ denote the number of admissible n-blocks which end in i and $\alpha(n)=(\alpha(n,1),\alpha(n,2),\ldots,\alpha(n,N))$, then $|\alpha(n)|=\sum_{i=1}^{N}\alpha(n,i)$ is the number we need to calculate. Notice that since $\alpha(n+1,j)=\alpha(n,0)a_{0j}+\alpha(n,1)a_{1j}+\cdots+\alpha(n,N)a_{Nj}$, we have

$$\alpha(n)=(\alpha(1,1),\ldots,\alpha(1,N))A^n=\alpha(1)A^n$$

and

$$\alpha(1)=(1,1,\ldots,1).$$

Let $\beta=(\beta_1,\beta_2,\ldots,\beta_N)$ be a left eigenvector of A associated with $\lambda(A)$ such that $\beta_i>0$ for $i=1,2,\ldots,N$. Let $m=\min\{\beta_i\}$ and $M=\max\{\beta_i\}$. Now

$$\begin{aligned}\frac{\beta_j}{m}\lambda^n(A)&=\sum_{i=1}^{N}\frac{\beta_i}{m}a_{ij}^{(n)}\\&\geqslant\sum_{i=1}^{N}\alpha(1,i)a_{ij}^{(n)}\\&\geqslant\sum_{i=1}^{N}\frac{\beta_i}{M}a_{ij}^{(n)}=\frac{\beta_j}{M}\lambda^n(A).\end{aligned}$$

Thus $(1/m)(\sum_{j=1}^{N}\beta_j)\lambda^n(A)\geqslant|\alpha(n)|\geqslant(1/M)(\sum_{j=1}^{N}\beta_j)\lambda^n(A)$, so that $\lim_{n\to\infty}(1/n)\log|\alpha(n)|=\log\lambda(A)$, and it follows that $h(\mathbf{T}_S)=\log\lambda(A)$.

5.4 An Alternative Definition of Topological Entropy

Smale [145] suggested that a useful way to classify maps is according to their action on their sets of nonwandering points. [A point $x\in X$ is a *wandering point* of the map $\mathbf{T}$ provided it has a neighborhood U such that $U\cap\bigcup_{n\in Z-\{0\}}\mathbf{T}^n(U)=\varnothing$; other wise x is a *nonwandering point*.] Bowen [22] showed that if X is a compact metric space and $\mathbf{T}\colon X\to X$ is continuous, then the topological entropy fits nicely with the program suggested by Smale. In the same paper Bowen proved the following theorem, which provided one of the first connections between topological entropy and other topological invariants. The theorem has in its hypothesis the notion of an Axiom A diffeomorphism. Since this notion will not play a role in our discussion, we shall not give its definition. A hyperbolic ergodic endomorphism of the torus is an example of such a diffeomorphism. In the previous section we calculated the entropy of diffeomorphisms of this type. The reader interested in the dynamics of Axiom A diffeomorphisms should consult [22], [8], or [34].

THEOREM 5.8. *If* $\mathbf{T}$ *is a diffeomorphism of the manifold* M *onto itself which satisfies Axiom A, then*

$$h(\mathbf{T}) = \limsup_{n\to\infty} \frac{1}{n} \log N_n(\mathbf{T}),$$

where $N_n(\mathbf{T})$ *is the number of fixed points of* $\mathbf{T}^n$ *(equivalently, the number of periodic points of* $\mathbf{T}$ *of period* n*).*

The proof that $h(\mathbf{T}) \geqslant \limsup_{n\to\infty}(1/n)\log N_n(\mathbf{T})$ follows directly from a couple of lemmas. Since this argument motivates to some extent the alternative definition of topological entropy, we shall indicate how it proceeds.

First notice that all periodic points are nonwandering, and since the entropy of $\mathbf{T}$ only involves its action on the set of nonwandering points, we can restrict our attention to this set. If (M, d) is a compact metric space and $\mathbf{T}$ is a homeomorphism of M onto itself, we say that $\mathbf{T}$ is *expansive* (also unstable [160]) provided there exists an $\varepsilon > 0$ (called an expansive constant of $\mathbf{T}$) such that if $x, y \in M$ and $d(\mathbf{T}^n(x), \mathbf{T}^n(y)) \leqslant \varepsilon$ for all $n \in Z$, then $x = y$. In [22] it is shown that if $\mathbf{T}$ satisfies Axiom A, then it is expansive on its set of nonwandering points.

LEMMA 5.9. *If* $\mathbf{T}$ *is an expansive homeomorphism of a compact metric space, then*

$$h(\mathbf{T}) \geqslant \limsup_{n\to\infty} \frac{1}{n} \log N_n(\mathbf{T}).$$

Proof. Let $\varepsilon > 0$ be an expansive constant for $\mathbf{T}$. Let $\mathcal{Q}$ be an open cover of M, with the diameter of each set in $\mathcal{Q}$ being less than ε. Suppose $x, y \in M$ are periodic of period k. If for some j, $0 \leqslant j \leqslant k$, there is a set A_{i_j} in $\mathcal{Q}$ such that $\mathbf{T}^j(x)$ and $\mathbf{T}^j(y)$ are both in A_{i_j}, then for $l \equiv j \ (mod\ k)$, $\mathbf{T}^l(x)$ and $\mathbf{T}^l(y)$ are both in A_{i_j} and $d(\mathbf{T}^l(x), \mathbf{T}^l(y)) < \varepsilon$ for all $l \equiv j\ (mod k)$. Thus if x and y are periodic of period k and for each j $(0 \leqslant j \leqslant k)$ there is a set A_{i_j} in $\mathcal{Q}$ such that $\mathbf{T}^j(x)$ and $\mathbf{T}^j(y)$ are both in A_{i_j}, then $d(\mathbf{T}^n(x), \mathbf{T}^n(y)) < \varepsilon$ for all $n \in Z$, and since $\mathbf{T}$ is expansive, $x = y$. Hence if $\{A_1, A_2, \ldots, A_N\}$ is a minimal subcover of $\bigvee_{j=0}^{n-1} \mathbf{T}^{-j}\mathcal{Q}$, then each A_i can contain at most one periodic point of period $n-1$. Therefore $N_{n-1}(\mathbf{T}) \leqslant N(\bigvee_{j=0}^{n-1} \mathbf{T}^{-j}\mathcal{Q})$, and it follows that

$$\limsup_{n\to\infty} \frac{1}{n} \log N_n(\mathbf{T}) \leqslant h(\mathbf{T}, \mathcal{Q}) \leqslant h(\mathbf{T})$$

and the lemma is proven.

Actually, if $\mathcal{Q}$ is an open cover of diameter less than the expansive constant of $\mathbf{T}$, then the above argument shows that $h(\mathbf{T},\mathcal{Q})=h(\mathbf{T})$.

The lemma and its proof indicate that the topological entropy of an expansive map is related to the rate at which the map separates points. This relationship is made specific by the following definitions and theorems, introduced by Bowen [22–24].

Let (X,d) be a metric space and $\mathbf{T}: X\to X$ be a uniformly continuous function. A subset A of X is said to be (n,ε)-*separated* (with respect to $\mathbf{T}$) if for every x and y in A with $x\neq y$ there is an integer j, $0\leqslant j<n$, such that $d(\mathbf{T}^j(x),\mathbf{T}^j(y))>\varepsilon$.

For a compact subset K of X let $S_n(\varepsilon, K)$ denote the maximum cardinality of the (n,ε)-separated subsets of K. It follows immediately from the definition that if $\varepsilon_1>\varepsilon_2$, then $S_n(\varepsilon_1, K)\leqslant S_n(\varepsilon_2, K)$ for any compact subset K of X. Furthermore, since $\mathbf{T}$ is uniformly continuous on X, given $\varepsilon>0$ and n a positive integer, there exists $\delta>0$ such that if $d(x,y)<\delta$, then $d(\mathbf{T}^j(x),\mathbf{T}^j(y))\leqslant\varepsilon$. Hence there can be no more elements in an (n,ε)-separated subset of K than there are balls of radius δ which cover K. Since K is compact, this number is finite. Therefore for all $\varepsilon>0$ and K compact, $S_n(\varepsilon, K)<\infty$.

If more than one map is involved, we shall write $S_n(\varepsilon, K,\mathbf{T})$ to stress the dependence on $\mathbf{T}$ as well as ε and K. Let

$$\bar{S}(\varepsilon, K,\mathbf{T})=\limsup_{n\to\infty}\frac{1}{n}\log S_n(\varepsilon, K,\mathbf{T}).$$

Since $S_n(\varepsilon_1, K)\leqslant S_n(\varepsilon_2, K)$ if $\varepsilon_1>\varepsilon_2$, it follows that $\bar{S}(\varepsilon_1, K)\leqslant\bar{S}(\varepsilon_2, K)$ for $\varepsilon_1>\varepsilon_2$.

DEFINITION 5.10. Let $\mathbf{T}$ be a uniformly continuous function on the metric space (X,d). The *topological entropy of* $\mathbf{T}$ *with respect to a compact subset* K, $h_d(\mathbf{T},K)$, and the *topological entropy of* $\mathbf{T}$, $h_d(\mathbf{T})$, are defined respectively by

$$h_d(\mathbf{T},K)=\lim_{\varepsilon\to\infty}\bar{S}(\varepsilon, K,\mathbf{T})$$

and

$$h_d(\mathbf{T})=\sup\{h_d(\mathbf{T},K): K\text{ compact subset of }X\}.$$

This definition of topological entropy replaces the condition that X is compact with the conditions that X is a metric space and $\mathbf{T}$ is uniformly continuous.

Notice that if $K \subset K_1 \cup K_2 \cup \cdots \cup K_n$, then

$$h_d(\mathbf{T}, K) \leqslant \max\{h_d(\mathbf{T}, K_j): j=1,2,\ldots,n\}$$

so that if X is compact, $h_d(\mathbf{T}) = h_d(\mathbf{T}, X)$.

THEOREM 5.11. *If (X, d) is a compact metric space, then $h_d(\mathbf{T}) = h(\mathbf{T})$, where $h(\mathbf{T})$ denotes the topological entropy defined in Section 5.2.*

Proof. First note that in the calculation of $h(\mathbf{T})$ we can restrict our attention to finite open covers of X. Also, because X is a metric space, we can compute $h(\mathbf{T})$ using a refining sequence of covers, and hence we can restrict our attention to covers whose sets have small diameters.

Let $\delta > 0$, and $\mathcal{A} = \{A_1, A_2, \ldots, A_k\}$ be an open cover of X with $d(A_i) < \delta$ for $i = 1,2,\ldots,k$. Let ε be a Lebesgue number for $\mathcal{A}$, so that every closed ball of radius less than or equal to ε is a subset of some member of $\mathcal{A}$.

Let C be a maximal (n, ε)-separated subset of X. For $x \in C$, let $B(x) = (A_{i_0}, \ldots, A_{i_{n-1}})$, where $A_{i_j} \in \mathcal{A}$ and

$$\{y \in X: d(y, \mathbf{T}^j x) \leqslant \varepsilon\} \subset A_{i_j}$$

for all $0 \leqslant j < n$. Let $\mathcal{E}_n = \{B(x): x \in C\}$. Each element of $\mathcal{E}_n$ corresponds in a one to one manner to a set in $\bigvee_{j=0}^{n-1} \mathbf{T}^{-j}\mathcal{A}$. If $x \in X$, then there exists $y \in C$ such that $d(\mathbf{T}^j(x), \mathbf{T}^j(y)) \leqslant \varepsilon$ for all $0 \leqslant j < n$. Otherwise $C \cup \{x\}$ would be an (n, ε)-separated subset of X, violating the maximality of C. Therefore the collection of all sets in $\bigvee_{j=0}^{n-1} \mathbf{T}^{-j}\mathcal{A}$ which correspond to some element of $\mathcal{E}_n$ is a cover of X. Hence $|\mathcal{E}_n| \geqslant H(\bigvee_{j=0}^{n-1} \mathbf{T}^{-j}\mathcal{A})$, where $|\ |$ denotes cardinality. However, by construction $|\mathcal{E}_n| \leqslant |C|$, so $|C| = S_n(\varepsilon, X) \geqslant N(\bigvee_{j=0}^{n-1} \mathbf{T}^{-j}\mathcal{A})$.

Let E be a minimal subcover of $\bigvee_{j=0}^{n-1} \mathbf{T}^{-j}\mathcal{A}$, and C be an (n, δ)-separated subset of X. For $x \in C$ let $g(x) = (A_{i_0}, \ldots, A_{i_{n-1}})$, where $\mathbf{T}^j(x) \in A_{i_j}$ for all $0 \leqslant j < n$ and $\bigcap_{j=0}^{n-1} \mathbf{T}^{-j}(A_{i_j}) \in E$. If $g(x) = g(y)$ for x and y in C, then for all $0 \leqslant j < n$, $d(\mathbf{T}^j(x), \mathbf{T}^j(y)) \leqslant \delta$, which implies that $x = y$. Thus the function g is one to one on C. Thus $|C| \leqslant |E| = N(\bigvee_{j=0}^{n-1} \mathbf{T}^{-j}(\mathcal{A}))$, and we have that $\bar{S}(\delta, X) \leqslant h(\mathbf{T}, \mathcal{A})$.

We have shown that for δ a positive number and $\mathcal{A}$ a finite open cover of X with $d(\mathcal{A}) < \delta$, we have $\bar{S}(\delta, X) \leqslant h(\mathbf{T}, \mathcal{A})$ and $\bar{S}(\varepsilon, X) \geqslant h(\mathbf{T}, \mathcal{A})$, where ε is a Lebesgue number for the cover $\mathcal{A}, (\varepsilon < \delta)$. As noted above, we can compute $h(\mathbf{T})$ using only covers of small diameter, and since $h_d(\mathbf{T}) = \lim_{\varepsilon \to 0} \bar{S}(\varepsilon, X)$, we have $h_d(\mathbf{T}) = h(\mathbf{T})$, and the theorem is proven.

This form of the definition of topological entropy seems to lend itself to comparison with other topological invariants. In particular, this definition makes it clear that topological entropy is a measure of the exponential rate at which the number of orbits increases. In this context Theorem 5.8, relating the topological entropy to the exponential growth of the number of fixed points of an (Axiom A) diffeomorphism, is not so surprising. Under suitable hypothesis it has been shown that $\limsup_{n\to\infty}(1/n)\log N_n(\mathbf{T}) \geqslant \max\{\log|\lambda|\}$, where the maximum is taken over all eigenvalues of $\mathbf{T}_* : H_*(M; R) \to H(M; R)$, the induced map on real homology; (see [141]). These two results lead to the conjecture that if M is compact and $\mathbf{T}$ is a diffeomorphism on M, then $h(\mathbf{T}) \geqslant \max\{\log|\lambda|\}$, where λ is as above. This conjecture has been verified in certain cases [141, 108], but is still not settled in general.

We end this section with a brief description of an extension of the notion of topological entropy which appears to be a quite fruitful area for further investigation. The notion is that of the *pressure* of a continuous map on a compact metric space. This concept, introduced originally by Ruelle [130] and in a more general setting by Walters [162], is easily seen as a natural generalization of topological entropy as it is defined in this section. The pressure and the (measure theoretic) entropy of a map are related by a variational principle which comes from statistical mechanics. This principle gives entropy its operational significance via its relationship to other thermodynamic variables.

Let X denote a compact metric space, and $C(X, R)$ denote the Banach space of continuous real valued functions on X with the supremum norm. If $\mathbf{T}$ is a continuous map of X into itself, $g \in C(X, R)$ and n a positive integer, we let

$$P_n(\mathbf{T}, g, \varepsilon) = \sup\left\{ \sum_{x\in E} \exp\left(\sum_{i=0}^{n-1} g\circ \mathbf{T}^i(x) \right)\right\},$$

where the supremum is taken over all (n, ε)-separated sets E. Notice that when g is the identically zero map, which will be denoted by 0, then $P_n(\mathbf{T}, 0, \varepsilon)$ is $S_n(\varepsilon, X, \mathbf{T})$, the maximum cardinality of the (n, ε)-separated subsets of X.

Let

$$P(\mathbf{T}, g, \varepsilon) = \limsup_{n\to\infty} \frac{1}{n} \log P_n(\mathbf{T}, g, \varepsilon).$$

It follows, as before, from the definition of (n, ε)-separated that if $\varepsilon_1 > \varepsilon_2$, then $P_n(\mathbf{T}, g, \varepsilon_1) \leqslant P_n(\mathbf{T}, g, \varepsilon_2)$ and $P(\mathbf{T}, g, \varepsilon_1) \leqslant P(\mathbf{T}, g, \varepsilon_2)$. Thus $\lim_{\varepsilon\to 0} P(\mathbf{T}, g, \varepsilon)$ exists or is infinity.

DEFINITION 5.12. Let $\mathbf{T}$ be a continuous map of the compact metric space X into itself. The map $P(\mathbf{T},\ )$ of $C(X, R)$ to $R\cup\{\infty\}$ defined by

$$P(\mathbf{T}, g) = \lim_{\varepsilon\to 0} P(\mathbf{T}, g, \varepsilon)$$

is called the *pressure* of the map $\mathbf{T}$.

For $\mathbf{T}: X\to X$ let $M_{\mathbf{T}}(X)$ denote the subset of $C(X, R)^*$, which consists of all probability measures μ which satisfy $\int_X d\mu(g\circ \mathbf{T}) = \int_X d\mu(g)$ for all $g\in C(X, R)$. That is, $M_{\mathbf{T}}(X)$ is the set of all $\mathbf{T}$-invariant probability measures on X. The variation principle is the content of the following theorem, whose proof can be found in [162].

THEOREM 5.13. *If* $\mathbf{T}$ *is a continuous map of* X *into itself, then for any* $g\in C(X, R)$

$$P(\mathbf{T}, g) = \sup\left\{ h_\mu(\mathbf{T}) + \int_X \mu(dx) g(x) : \mu\in M_{\mathbf{T}}(X)\right\}.$$

An *equilibrium state* for $(\mathbf{T}, g)$ is any measure $\mu\in M_{\mathbf{T}}(X)$ such that

$$P(\mathbf{T}, g) = h_\mu(\mathbf{T}) + \int_X \mu(dx) g(x).$$

Noticc that if $\mathbf{T}$ is uniquely ergodic, i.e., there is only one element in $M_{\mathbf{T}}(X)$, then this element is an equilibrium state.

If μ is an equilibrium state, and we consider the continuous function g as representing potential energy, then $\int_X \mu(dx) g(x)$ is the expected value of the energy and we have

$$h_\mu(\mathbf{T}) = P(\mathbf{T}, g) - \int_X \mu(dx) g(x),$$

which is the usual relationship between pressure, energy, and entropy in statistical thermodynamics. The problem of the existence of equilibrium states is still the subject of extensive research. A comprehensive introduction to these topics can be found in the lecture notes of Bowen [25].

CHAPTER 6

Statistical Mechanics

6.1 Introduction

The task of statistical mechanics is to derive macroscopic properties of matter from the laws governing the microscopic actions and interactions of individual particles. The systems that are considered in statistical mechanics are those that consist of a large number (on the order of 10^{27} particles, say, for the molecules in one liter of air) of subsystems (the molecules). To specify such a system on a microscopic level would require the coordinates of a point in $6N$-dimensional space, where N is the number of subsystems (or particles) of the system. Recall that we considered these systems in another context in Section 2.8 and the introductions to Chapters 4 and 5.

A macroscopic description of such a system can be given in terms of relatively few quantities such as energy, volume, specific heat, etc., which are called thermodynamic variables, or functions. The entropy of a system is one such thermodynamic variable. Thermodynamics is a study of the relationships that exist between the various thermodynamic variables, and this subject, from a mathematical perspective, can be completely axiomatized [28]. In particular, the equilibrium states of a system can be described in terms of relatively few thermodynamic variables.

We shall not discuss the known relationships between the entropy of a system in an equilibrium state and the other thermodynamic variables of the state. The reader interested in this topic may consult [28] or [154]. Our objective here is to discuss that part of statistical mechanics that deals with equilibrium states and its connections with the entropy discussed in Chapter 2. Specifically, we shall introduce the notion of the (mean) entropy of an equilibrium state of a classical system and show its relationship to the entropy of dynamical systems of Chapter 2. We shall also show how

ENCYCLOPEDIA OF MATHEMATICS and Its Applications, Gian-Carlo Rota (ed.).
Vol. 12: Nathaniel F. Martin and James W. England, Mathematical Theory of Entropy.
ISBN 0-201-13511-6

equilibrium states of a system are associated with more classical descriptions of the system.

A mathematical structure which offers a convenient idealization of macroscopic equilibrium systems is one of probability measures (states) on infinite subsets (configurations) of R^n or Z^n. We shall use this model for our discussion, although it is not the one which is physically or historically the most standard. The standard description of an equilibrium system is obtained by considering the so-called thermodynamic limit of finite systems contained in phase space. These are described in terms of either microcanonical, canonical, or grand canonical Gibbs ensembles. It had been a firm belief among those working in statistical mechanics that the different ensembles gave equivalent descriptions in the thermodynamic limit. In [131] Ruelle shows that a thermodynamic variable calculated by taking the thermodynamic limit of subsystems described by any one of these ensembles is equivalent to the same thermodynamic variable when calculated using any other ensemble. In [9] it is shown that the different ensembles produce, in the thermodynamic limit, essentially equivalent measures (correlation functions) under reasonably mild additional conditions. The reason for the word "essentially" is that in the absence of a unique limit state, as would be the case at a phase transition, they show an equivalence between the sets of limit states corresponding to the different ensembles. The reader who would like to see a detailed treatment of these results should consult [131], [9], and [75].

Before proceeding with a careful formulation of equilibrium states on infinite configuration space and entropy, we shall give in the next section a brief review of the standard mathematical concepts used in statistical mechanics. This should provide some motivation for our latter discussion. Most of these results are well known, and this next section is a continuation of Section 2.8 and Section 4.1. Careful treatments of these results can be found in [154] and [66] in addition to other references indicated in this chapter.

6.2 Classical Continuous Systems

We restrict our discussion to classical systems. On a microscopic level, a classical system which contains N identical subsystems (molecules, atoms, etc.) is determined by a point $(p_{11}, p_{12}, p_{13}, \ldots, p_{N1}, p_{N2}, p_{N3}, q_{11}, q_{12}, q_{13}, \ldots, q_{N1}, q_{N2}, q_{N3})$ in $6N$-dimensional space, where for $i = 1, 2, \ldots, N$, (p_{i1}, p_{i2}, p_{i3}) denotes the momentum vector of the ith subsystem and (q_{i1}, q_{i2}, q_{i3}) the position vector. We assume that we are given a Hamiltonian of the form

$$H(p_{11}, \ldots, q_{N3}) = \sum_{i=1}^{N} \frac{p_{i1}^2 + p_{i2}^2 + p_{i3}^2}{2m} + U(q_{11}, q_{12}, \ldots, q_{N3}).$$

Here $(p_{i1}^2+p_{i2}^2+p_{i3}^2)/2m$ is the translational kinetic energy of the ith subsystem, and $U(q_{11},\ldots,q_{N3})$ is the potential energy. Since the systems generally considered are required to be contained in some bounded region Λ of R^3, i.e., $(q_{i1},q_{i2},q_{i3})\in\Lambda$ for $i=1,2,\ldots,N$, the potential U is frequently written as a sum of two terms: $V(q_{11},\ldots,q_{N3})$, which is the energy due to outside forces (such as the walls of a container forcing the system to remain in the region Λ), and a function $\phi(q_{11},\ldots,q_{N3})$, which is the energy due to interactions between the N subsystems. For example, if we were considering only pairwise isotropic interactions, ϕ would be of the form

$$\phi(q_{11},\ldots,q_{N3})=\sum_{1<i<j<N}\alpha(s_{ij}),$$

where α is a real valued function, and s_{ij} $(i\neq j)$ denotes the distance between the ith and the jth subsystems, i.e., $s_{ij}=[(q_{i1}-q_{j1})^2+(q_{i2}-q_{j2})^2+(q_{i3}-q_{j3})^2]^{1/2}$. In order for the system to exhibit thermodynamic behavior, i.e., that a thermodynamic limit exist, it is necessary to impose a number of restrictions on α. For example, a standard interaction having short range and satisfying a "hard core" condition would have an interaction function α with a graph like the one shown in Figure 6.1.

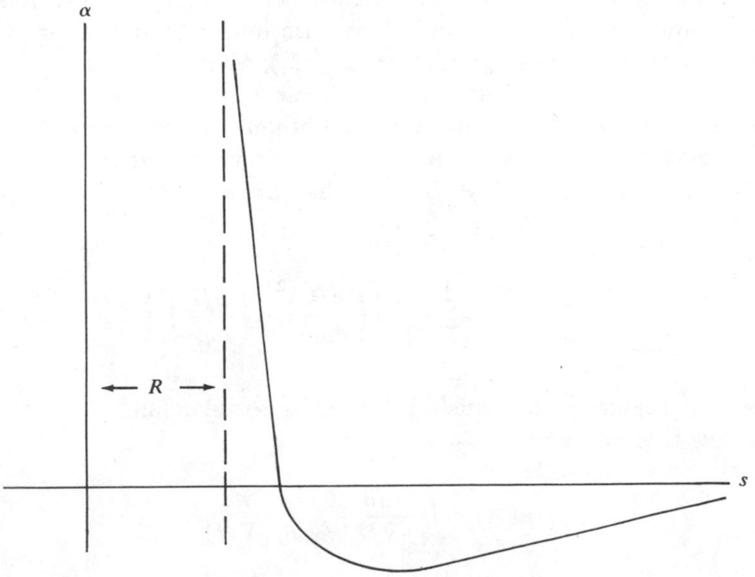

Figure 6.1

The time evolution of the system is governed by Hamilton's differential equations

$$\dot{p}_{ij} = -\frac{\partial H}{\partial q_{ij}}, \qquad \dot{q}_{ij} = \frac{\partial H}{\partial p_{ij}}, \qquad i=1,2,\ldots,N;\ j=1,2,3.$$

Given an initial point $(p^0, q^0) = (p_{11}^0, \ldots, q_{N3}^0) \in R^{3N} \times \Lambda^N$ there is a unique solution $F_{(p^0, q^0)}(t)$ to the equation passing through (p^0, q^0) at time 0, i.e.,

$$F_{(q^0, p^0)}(0) = (q^0, p^0).$$

As in Section 2.8, this solution produces a flow $\{\mathbf{T}_t : t \in R\}$ defined on $R^{3N} \times \Lambda^N$ by

$$\mathbf{T}_t(p, q) = F_{(p,q)}(t),$$

and since H is independent of time, $\mathbf{T}_t$ sends each surface of constant energy into itself. Otherwise stated, the flow lies on surfaces of constant energy. Furthermore, Liouville's theorem gives that the flow preserves Lebesgue measure in $R^{3N} \times \Lambda^N$, i.e., if $A \subset R^{3N} \times \Lambda^N$, then $\lambda(\mathbf{T}_t^{-1}(A)) = \lambda(A)$ for every $t \in R$, where λ is $6N$-dimensional Lebesgue measure.

We are not interested in the particular microscopic state of the system [the coordinates (p, q) of a point]. We are interested instead in a set of systems lying on the energy surface $H^{-1}(E)$, where E is a given constant energy, and with the distribution of these systems in time. The basic postulate due to Gibbs is that the equilibrium distribution of the macroscopic states of an isolated system is the uniform distribution on the energy surface. The energy surface $H^{-1}(E)$ has measure zero with respect to Lebesgue measure. However, if we let

$$\|\nabla H\|^2 = \sum_{j=1}^{3} \sum_{i=1}^{N} \left[\left(\frac{\partial H}{\partial p_{ij}} \right)^2 + \left(\frac{\partial H}{\partial q_{ij}} \right)^2 \right],$$

then the measure which satisfies the Gibbs postulate and is preserved by the flow is given by

$$\mu(A) = \int_A \frac{d\sigma}{\|\nabla H\|} \Big/ \int_\Omega \frac{d\sigma}{\|\nabla H\|},$$

where $\Omega = H^{-1}(E)$, $d\sigma$ is surface area measure, and A is a Borel subset of Ω. This measure is frequently called the microcanonical ensemble.

In the discussion above we assumed that the system was isolated. A different description is obtained, however, if we consider that the system is in contact with a heat reservoir. In this case the notion of temperature for a system is introduced, and a description of the system in phase space (rather than on surfaces of constant energy) called the canonical ensemble is obtained.

Assume that the system A is in contact with a heat reservoir B and the combined system $A\cup B$ is isolated. If we let $\beta=(kT)^{-1}$, where k is the Boltzmann constant and T the absolute temperature of the reservoir B, and denote the Hamiltonian of the system A by H_A, then the canonical ensemble is given by the measure

$$m(C)=\frac{\int_C \exp(-\beta H_A)\,d\lambda_A}{\int_{\Omega_A} \exp(-\beta H_A)\,d\lambda_A}$$

where Ω_A is the phase space of system A, $C\subset\Omega_A$, and λ_A is Lebesgue measure on Ω_A. In order to derive this distribution from the microcanonical distribution it is necessary to make some additional assumptions concerning the coupling of the systems A and B, i.e., assumptions about the Hamiltonian of $A\cup B$ in relationship to the the Hamiltonians of A and B. We must also assume that the Hamiltonian of B, H_B, is of some special form. For example, in [159] B is assumed to be an ideal gas. If we drop the subscripts and the normalizing factor, then the canonical ensemble is given by

$$\exp(-\beta H(p,q))\,dp\,dq=\left[\prod_{i=1}^{N}\prod_{j=1}^{3}\exp\left(\frac{-\beta p_{ij}^2}{2m}\right)dp_{ij}\right][\exp(-\beta U(q))\,dq]$$

where $p=(p_{11},p_{12},\ldots,p_{N3})$, $dp=dp_{11}dp_{12}\cdots dp_{N3}$, $q=(q_{11},q_{12},\ldots,p_{N3})$ and $dq=dq_{11}dq_{12}\cdots dq_{N3}$. This measure is defined on $R^{3N}\times\Lambda^N$, where $\Lambda\subset\mathrm{R}^3$ is the region in which the particles are contained. Notice that the momenta p in this expression can be integrated out. Hence, we can define what is frequently called a configurational canonical ensemble to be

$$\left(\frac{2\pi m}{\beta}\right)^{3N/2}\exp(-\beta U(q))\,dq.$$

In normalizing this measure the constants would, of course, be canceled out. In our future discussions we shall only consider configuration space.

The usual thermodynamic variables (in classical systems) are defined using the normalizing factor of a canonical ensemble. These normalizing factors are called *partition functions*. For example, the (configuration) canonical partition function Q is defined by

$$Q(\Lambda, N, \beta) = \frac{1}{N!}\int_{\Lambda_N} \exp(-\beta U(q))\, dq.$$

To obtain a thermodynamic variable, the logarithm of a partition function is divided by the volume of the containing region Λ, and the limit of this ratio is taken as the volume of Λ becomes infinite. The particular thermodynamic variable given by this limit depends upon which ensemble was used to obtain the partition function. For example,

$$\lim_{\Lambda\to\infty} \frac{1}{|\Lambda|} \log Q(\Lambda, N, \beta) = \text{specific free energy}.$$

Ruelle shows in [131] that the various thermodynamic variables obtained using different ensembles are related in the manner predicted by thermodynamics.

As we have indicated, we shall take the alternative route of considering equilibrium states of infinite systems directly. These states also determine the thermodynamic variables as is demonstrated in [131]. In fact, our specific objective is to show that the mean entropy per unit volume of lattice systems is exactly the entropy associated with a measure preserving transformation (or rather a group of measure preserving transformations) as discusses in Chapter 2.

6.3 Classical Lattice Systems

Classical lattice systems are mathematical models of crystals which consist of many subsystems, each of which may exist in any one of a finite number of states. Since these systems are the simplest of the classical systems to understand, we shall restrict our discussion to them. For the lattice case R^{3N} is replaced by Z^{3N} (the points in R^{3N} all of whose coordinates are integers), so that a bounded region Λ of Z^{3N} is a finite set. For each $a \in \Lambda \subseteq Z^{3N}$, the possible forms of the subsystem located at a are denoted by a finite set Ω_a. For example, in describing an alloy, Ω_a would be a list of the atomic species which could occur at a. Another example is given by taking Ω_a to be $\{0, 1\}$, where 0 might denote that site a is not occupied, and 1 that it is occupied.

Definition 6.1. The *configuration space* of a lattice system contained in $\Lambda \subseteq Z^{3N}$ is the set $\Omega_\Lambda = \times_{a\in\Lambda}\Omega_a$. A *configuration* of a lattice system in Λ is a point in Ω_Λ and a *state* of a lattice system in Λ is a probability measure on Ω_Λ.

Notice that in case Λ is a bounded subset of Z^{3N}, Ω_Λ is a finite set and each state of a lattice system in Ω_Λ can be given as a discrete probability distribution $P=\{P(\omega):\omega\in\Omega_\Lambda\}$.

Suppose we have a lattice system in a bounded region, and for each configuration ω in the configuration space of the system $U(\omega)$ denotes the (configurational) potential energy of the system. The Gibbs canonical ensemble is the state of the system given by

$$P_G(\omega)=\frac{e^{-\beta U(\omega)}}{\sum\limits_{\omega'\in\Omega_\Lambda} e^{-\beta U(\omega')}},\qquad \omega\in\Omega_\Lambda.$$

Given a state P of the system, each configuration ω occurs with probability $P(\omega)$, and the total energy of the system in the state P can be taken to be the expected value of the potential energy U, i.e., energy$=\Sigma_{\omega\in\Omega_\Lambda}P(\omega)U(\omega)$. There is an elementary mathematical result connecting the entropy $-\Sigma_\omega P(\omega)\log P(\omega)$ of the distribution P, the total energy of the system in state P, and the Gibbs canonical ensemble P_G, which can be cited as a justification for using $-\Sigma_\omega P(\omega)\log P(\omega)$ as the entropy, or equivalently, P_G as the equilibrium state. This argument is contained in the following theorem.

THEOREM 6.2. *If Ω_Λ is the configuration space of a classical lattice system in a bounded region Λ, then the function F defined on the collection of all states P on Ω_Λ by*

$$F(P)=-\sum_{\omega\in\Omega_\Lambda}P(\omega)\log P(\omega)-\beta\sum_{\omega\in\Omega_\Lambda}P(\omega)U(\omega)$$

is maximized by the Gibbs canonical ensemble P_G.

Proof. Since P is a discrete probability distribution the proof is a simple exercise in the use of Lagrange multipliers. Suppose we write $P=(x_1,x_2,\ldots,x_K)$. We wish to find the extreme values of

$$F(x_1,x_2,\ldots,x_K)=-\sum_{i=1}^{K}x_i\log x_i-\beta\sum_{i=1}^{K}x_iU_i$$

subject to the auxiliary equation

$$\sum_{i=1}^{K}x_i=1.$$

In the expression for F, U_i denotes the potential due to the ith configuration ω_i, and is independent of the state. By direct calculation one can easily show that the maximum is assumed by the distribution

$$x_i = P_G(\omega_i) = \frac{e^{-\beta U_i}}{\sum_{j=1}^{K} e^{-\beta U_j}}.$$

It is also interesting to note that the maximum value of F is given by $\log(\Sigma_{i=1}^{K} e^{-\beta U_i})$, which is the logarithm of the partition function of the Gibbs canonical ensemble.

Notice that this theorem implies that if the total energy of a system is fixed, i.e., $\Sigma_{\omega \in \Omega_\Lambda} P(\omega)U(\omega) = E$ is constant for all states, then the Gibbs canonical ensemble P_G maximizes the entropy $S(P) = -\Sigma_\omega P(\omega)\log P(\omega)$, i.e., for a classical lattice system in a finite region with constant energy the equilibrium state maximizes the entropy.

This theorem also says that the equilibrium state, i.e., Gibbs canonical ensemble, minimizes the function

$$-\frac{1}{\beta}F(P) = E(P) - \frac{1}{\beta}S(P) = E - kTS,$$

which is the Gibbs free energy of the system. Thus "nature maximizes entropy" when the energy is fixed, and "nature minimizes free energy" when the energy is not fixed.

The equation for the free energy $E - kTS$ may help explain why the constant $\beta = (kT)^{-1}$ comes into the discussion. The distributions $P(\omega)$ are dimensionless, and hence $-\Sigma P \log P$ is dimensionless. However, E has the dimensions of energy, so to combine S and E, a factor with the dimensions of energy must be applied to S. Since k has units of calories per degree Kelvin, kT is a suitable constant.

6.4 Gibbs States for Lattice Systems

In this section, we shall give the definitions and theorems leading to the definition of the mean entropy of a state. Our discussion provides an introduction to a number of the central results in [133]. Since detailed proofs are given there, we shall include no proofs and restrict the discussion to a lattice system. The statements and proofs of many of the corresponding results for a continuous system can be found in [121]. We shall use the notation of [76] and [133].

Assume that we are given a finite set Ω_0, which we will take to be $\{0, 1, 2, \ldots, K\}$ in order to simplify the discussion. For each $x \in Z^N$, let $\Omega_x = \Omega_0$.

DEFINITION 6.3. The *configuration space* is the set $\Omega = \times_{x\in Z^N}\Omega_x$. Since Ω is a Cartesian product, points $\omega\in\Omega$ are functions on Z^N. The value of $\omega\in\Omega$ at $x\in Z^N$ will be denoted by ω_x, analogously to the notation for the xth coordinate of a point. If Λ is a subset of Z^N, Ω_Λ denotes the set $\times_{x\in\Lambda}\Omega_x$. [Notice that Ω_Λ is *not* a subset of Ω, which presents notational difficulty. This can be overcome with the map p_Λ which sends Ω onto Ω_Λ and is defined by sending the function $\omega\in\Omega$ to the function ω restricted to Λ, i.e., $p_\Lambda(\omega)=\omega|_\Lambda$.] If Λ is a finite set and $\omega'\in\Omega_\Lambda$, then $p_\Lambda^{-1}(\omega')\subset\Omega$ is called a *finite cylinder set*. Let $\mathfrak{F}$ denote the σ-field generated by the finite cylinder sets. A *state* is any probability measure on the measurable space $(\Omega,\mathfrak{F})$. The collection of all states is denoted by $\mathfrak{M}$.

An alternate way to describe the states of a system is to note that Ω is a compact topological space in the product topology if we put the discrete topology on Ω_x. In this topology p_Λ is a continuous map. If $C(\Omega)$ denotes the continuous real valued functions on Ω, then $C(\Omega)$ is a Banach space with respect to the sup norm. The linear functionals on $C(\Omega)$ associated with probability measures on $\mathfrak{F}$ form a convex, compact subset of the weak dual of $C(\Omega)$ which can be identified with $\mathfrak{M}$. The positive linear functionals are then *states* of the system.

For any finite set Λ in Z^N, if $C(\Omega_\Lambda)$ denotes the Banach space of functions of the form $f\circ p_\Lambda$ for $f\in C(\Omega)$, then the Stone-Weierstrass theorem implies that $\cup_\Lambda C(\Omega_\Lambda)$ is dense in $C(\Omega)$. This fact is useful in the proof of Theorem 6.10.

DEFINITION 6.4. For $a\in Z^N$, *translation* by a is the map $\mathbf{T}_a$ which sends Ω onto Ω and is defined by

$$(\mathbf{T}_a\omega)_x=\omega_{x+a},\qquad x\in Z^N,\quad \omega\in\Omega.$$

Normally, we shall be interested only in those states of a system which are invariant under translations, i.e., those $\mu\in\mathfrak{M}$ such that $\mu(\mathbf{T}_aE)=\mu(E)$ for all $a\in\Omega$ and $E\in\mathfrak{F}$. As linear functionals these form a convex compact subset of $\mathfrak{M}$. We shall denote the collection of translational states by $\mathfrak{I}$.

DEFINITION 6.5. Let $\overline{\Omega}=\cup\{\Omega_\Lambda:\Lambda \text{ a finite subset of } Z^N\}$. An *interaction* is a bounded real valued function defined on $\overline{\Omega}$ which is translation invariant and has value zero on the empty set. Specifically, it is a function ϕ on $\overline{\Omega}$ to R such that

$$\phi|_{\Omega_\varnothing}=0, \tag{6.1}$$

$$\phi(\mathbf{T}_a\omega)=\phi(\omega),\qquad a\in Z^N,\quad \omega\in\Omega_\Lambda, \tag{6.2}$$

$$\sup|\phi(\omega)|<\infty, \tag{6.3}$$

where the sup in (6.3) is taken over all $\omega \in \Omega_\Lambda$, with Λ finite and containing the zero vector.

An interaction ϕ has *range d* if $\phi(\omega|_\Lambda)=0$ whenever $\sup\{\|x-y\| : x, y \in \Lambda\} > d$, $\omega \in \Omega$.

Notice that an interaction ϕ is a pairwise interaction such as was discussed in the previous section provided $d=2$, i.e., $\phi(\omega|_\Lambda)=0$ whenever Λ contains more than two points.

DEFINITION 6.6. For a given interaction ϕ and finite subset Λ of Z^N, an energy function U_Λ is defined on Ω_Λ by

$$U_\Lambda(\omega) = \sum_{\Lambda' \subset \Lambda} \phi(\omega|_{\Lambda'}).$$

DEFINITION 6.7. For disjoint subsets Λ_1 and Λ_2 of Z^N with Λ_1 finite, the *interaction between* Λ_1 *and* Λ_2 *determined by the interaction* ϕ is the function $W_{\Lambda_1\Lambda_2}$ defined on $\overline{\Omega}$ by

$$W_{\Lambda_1\Lambda_2}(\omega) = \sum \phi(\omega|_{\Lambda'}),$$

where the sum is over all finite sets $\Lambda' \subset \Lambda_1 \cup \Lambda_2$ with $\Lambda' \cap \Lambda_1 \neq \varnothing$ and $\Lambda' \cap \Lambda_2 \neq \varnothing$.

It may be useful to point out that if $\Omega_0 = \{0,1\}$ as in [76], then we could define an interaction to be a function defined on the finite subsets of Z^N instead of in the relatively cumbersome way we have. This is because in case $\Omega_0 = \{0,1\}$ a configuration $\omega \in \Omega_\Lambda$ can be identified with the set of all points x in Λ where $\omega_x = 1$.

DEFINITION 6.8. Given an interaction ϕ and finite subset Λ of Z^N, the *partition function* is the quantity $Z_\Lambda(\phi)$ defined by

$$Z_\Lambda(\phi) = \sum_{\omega \in \Omega_\Lambda} \exp(-U_\Lambda(\omega)).$$

The discrete probability distribution P_Λ defined on Ω_Λ by

$$P_\Lambda(\omega) = Z_\Lambda(\phi)^{-1} \exp(-U_\Lambda(\omega)).$$

is the *Gibbs ensemble* for Λ (Dobruskin [35]).

DEFINITION 6.9. A sequence $\{\Lambda_n\}$ of finite subsets of Z^N *converges to* Z^N if for each finite subset Λ of Z^N, there exists an integer K such that $\Lambda \subset \Lambda_n$ for all $n > K$.

We are now ready to give a rigorous discussion of the thermodynamic limit. To do this note that if $\Lambda_1 \subset \Lambda_2$, there is a mapping $p_{\Lambda_1\Lambda_2}: \Omega_{\Lambda_2} \to \Omega_{\Lambda_1}$ defined by restricting functions in Ω_{Λ_2} to Λ_1, i.e.,

$$p_{\Lambda_1\Lambda_2}(\omega) = \omega|_{\Lambda_1}, \qquad \omega \in \Lambda_2.$$

The natural map p_Λ defined in Definition 6.3 is one of these maps, specifically $p_\Lambda = p_{\Lambda Z^N}$.

THEOREM 6.10. *Let $\{\Lambda_n\}$ be a sequence of finite subsets of Z^N which converges to Z^N, and for each n let μ_{Λ_n} be a probability measure on Ω_{Λ_n}. Then there exists a subsequence $\{\Lambda'_n\}$ such that for each finite set $\Lambda \subset Z^N$,*

$$\lim_{n\to\infty} \mu_{\Lambda'_n}\left(p_{\Lambda\Lambda'_n}^{-1}(\omega)\right) = \rho_\Lambda(\omega)$$

exists for all $\omega \in \Omega_\Lambda$. Furthermore, there exists a unique state ρ on Ω such that for each finite set $\Lambda \subset Z^N$

$$\rho\left(p_\Lambda^{-1}(\omega)\right) = \rho_\Lambda(\omega), \qquad \omega \in \Omega_\Lambda.$$

The state ρ is called the thermodynamic limit of the finite states $\mu_{\Lambda'_n}$.

The proof of this theorem can be found in [35] and [133] and involves a simple diagonalization argument, since (as was observed before) $\cup_\Lambda C(\Omega_\Lambda)$ is dense in $C(\Omega)$.

We now want to combine the ideas of Gibbs ensembles on finite subsets of Z^N and the thermodynamic limit of such states. To do this we need the notion of a Gibbs state on Ω, the infinite configuration space, for an interaction ϕ.

Let ϕ be a given interaction and U, W respectively the corresponding energy function and interaction between subsets given in Definitions 6.6 and 6.7.

DEFINITION 6.11. A Gibbs state on Ω associated with an interaction ϕ is a *probability measure* μ on $(\Omega, \mathfrak{F})$ if for each finite set $\Lambda \subset Z^N$, each $\omega_1 \in \Omega_\Lambda$ and $\omega_2 \in \Omega_{\Lambda^c}$ where $\Lambda^c = Z^N - \Lambda$, and each $\omega \in \Omega$ such that $\omega|_\Lambda = \omega_1$ and $\omega|_{\Lambda^c} = \omega_2$ we have

$$\mu\left(p_\Lambda^{-1}(\omega_1) | p_{\Lambda^c}^{-1}(\omega_2)\right) = \frac{\exp\left(-U_\Lambda(\omega_1) - W_{\Lambda\Lambda^c}(\omega)\right)}{\sum_{\alpha \in \Omega_\Lambda} \exp\left(-U_\Lambda(\alpha) - W_{\Lambda\Lambda^c}(\alpha\omega_2)\right)},$$

where $\alpha\omega_2$ is the element η of Ω such that $\eta|_\Lambda = \alpha$ and $\eta|_{\Lambda^c} = \omega_2$. Here $\mu(\ |A)$ denotes the conditional probability given the event A. (See Section 1.5.)

Alternate definitions for Gibbs states are given in [35] and [133].

The basic result with respect to Gibbs states is that if ρ is the thermodynamic limit of Gibbs ensembles P_Λ (Definition 6.8) for the interaction ϕ, then ρ is a Gibbs state on Ω (Definition 6.11) for the interaction ϕ. See [76], [133], or [35] for proofs. A more general discussion of Gibbs states can be found in [25].

6.5 Equilibrium States and the Concepts of Entropy and Pressure

We continue to assume that we have a given interaction ϕ and for emphasis recall that all interactions are translation invariant. Furthermore, we assume that a state of our system is a translation invariant probability measure on $(\Omega, \mathfrak{F})$.

First, we consider the notion of the entropy of a state and show that it is the same as the mean entropy of the state [121, 131].

In order to define the entropy of a state we need to extend the notion of the entropy of a dynamical system given in Section 2.8, so that it will be applicable to certain groups of transformations on a probability space rather than a single transformation. The reader may recall that the definition of the entropy of a dynamical system $(\Omega, \mathfrak{F}, P, \mathbf{T})$ involved all the powers of $\mathbf{T}$, i.e., the group $\{\mathbf{T}^n : n \in Z\}$ generated by $\mathbf{T}$. It is very easy to use this analog to define the entropy of certain groups of transformations, and the facts concerning this entropy are essentially the same as those given in Chapter 2.

We give here the definition in the setting of interest to us, though more general considerations are possible. We are concerned with a measure preserving *action* of the group Z^N on the probability space $(\Omega, \mathfrak{F}, \mu)$, where $(\Omega, \mathfrak{F})$ is the measurable space of configurations described in Definition 6.3 and $\mu \in \mathcal{G}$ is a translational invariant state.

DEFINITION 6.12. A *measure preserving action* of Z^N on $(\Omega, \mathfrak{F}, \mu)$ is a group homomorphism $\mathbf{T}$ of Z^N into the group of all metric automorphisms on $(\Omega, \mathfrak{F}, \mu)$. Specifically, for each $x \in Z^N$, $\mathbf{T}(x)$ is a metric automorphism on $(\Omega, \mathfrak{F}, \mu)$, and for $x, y \in Z^N$, $\mathbf{T}(x-y) = \mathbf{T}(x) \circ \mathbf{T}^{-1}(y)$.

The particular measure preserving action of Z^N on $(\Omega, \mathfrak{F}, \mu)$ that we are interested in is given by the homomorphism $\mathbf{T}$ whose value at $a \in Z^N$ is translation by a, or in the notation of Definition 6.4, $\mathbf{T}(a) = \mathbf{T}_a$.

Notice that if $(\Omega, \mathfrak{F}, \mu, \mathbf{T}_1)$ is a dynamical system, then defining $\mathbf{T}(n) = \mathbf{T}_1^n$ gives exactly this action for $N=1$. Also, given an action $\mathbf{T}$ of Z^1 on $(\Omega, \mathfrak{F}, \mu)$, $(\Omega, \mathfrak{F}, \mu, \mathbf{T}(1))$ is a dynamical system as in Chapter 2. To carry this analogy into our notation we shall denote the values of a group action by superscripts. Thus, if $\mathbf{T}$ is a Z^N-action on $(\Omega, \mathfrak{F}, \mu)$ and $x \in Z^N$, then $\mathbf{T}^x$ will denote the metric automorphism $\mathbf{T}(x)$.

If $\mathbf{T}$ is a Z^N-action on Ω, if α is a measurable partition of Ω in the sense of Chapter 1, and if Λ is a finite subset of Z^N, then we can define the common refinement, $\bigvee_{x\in\Lambda}\mathbf{T}^x\alpha$, of the partitions $\{\mathbf{T}^x\alpha : x\in\Lambda\}$ just as was done in Section 1.3. The entropy of a finite measurable partition α is defined by the usual formula, $H(\alpha) = -\Sigma_{A\in\alpha}\mu(A)\log\mu(A)$.

Let Λ_n denote a positive "cube" in Z^N with edge length n and one vertex at 0 (i.e., $\Lambda_n = \{0,1,2,\ldots,n-1\}^N$), and let $|\Lambda_n|$ denote the cardinality of Λ_n, so that $|\Lambda_n| = n^N$. It follows as in Section 2.7 that if α is a finite partition, then the limit of the sequence $\{(1/|\Lambda_n|)H(\bigvee_{x\in\Lambda_n}\mathbf{T}^x\alpha)\}$ exists.

Definition 6.13. If $\mathbf{T}$ is a Z^N-action on $(\Omega, \mathfrak{F}, \mu)$, and α is any finite measurable partition of Ω, then the *entropy of the action* $\mathbf{T}$ *with respect to* α, $h(\mathbf{T},\alpha)$, is defined by

$$h(\mathbf{T},\alpha) = \lim_{n\to\infty}\frac{1}{|\Lambda_n|}H\left(\bigvee_{x\in\Lambda_n}\mathbf{T}^x\alpha\right).$$

The *entropy of the action* $\mathbf{T}$, $h(\mathbf{T})$, is defined by

$$h(\mathbf{T}) = \sup\{h(\mathbf{T},\alpha) : \alpha \text{ finite}\}.$$

Theorem 6.14. *If* $\mathbf{T}$ *is a* Z^N*-action on* $(\Omega, \mathfrak{F}, \mu)$ *and* $\alpha_1 \leqslant \alpha_2 \leqslant \cdots$ *is a sequence of finite measurable partitions such that* $\alpha_n \to \varepsilon$, *then*

$$\lim_{n\to\infty} h(\mathbf{T},\alpha_n) - h(\mathbf{T}).$$

The proof of this theorem follows in the same way as for Corollary 2.49.

We shall now only consider the particular Z^N-action given by translation, i.e., $(\mathbf{T}^a\omega)_x = \omega_{x+a}$ for $\omega\in\Omega$, $a, x\in Z^N$. If Λ is a finite subset of Z^N, then

$$\alpha_\Lambda = \{p_\Lambda^{-1}(\omega') : \omega' \in \Omega_\Lambda\}$$

is a finite measurable partition of Ω into finite cylinder sets.

It is easy to check that if $\Lambda_1 \subset \Lambda_2$, then $\alpha_{\Lambda_1} \leqslant \alpha_{\Lambda_2}$, and if $\{\Lambda_n\}$ is an increasing sequence of subsets of Z^N which converges to Z^N in the sense of Definition 6.9, then $\alpha_{\Lambda_n} \uparrow \varepsilon$ in the sense of Section 1.3. Finally, notice that if

Λ_0 denotes the subset of Z^N consisting of zero [i.e. $(0,0,\ldots,0)$] and $\alpha_0 = \alpha_{\Lambda_0}$, then for any finite set $\Lambda \subset Z^N$,

$$\alpha_\Lambda = \bigvee_{x\in\Lambda} \mathbf{T}^x \alpha_0.$$

The partition α_0 is analogous to the time zero partition of a shift dynamical system.

THEOREM 6.15. *If* $\mathbf{T}$ *is the* Z^N*-action on* $(\Omega, \mathfrak{F}, \mu)$ *defined by translation and* $\{\Lambda_n\}$ *are the subsets of* Z^N *used in Definition* 6.13, *then*

$$h(\mathbf{T}) = \lim_{n\to\infty} \frac{1}{|\Lambda_n|} H\Big(\bigvee_{x\in\Lambda_n} \mathbf{T}^x \alpha_0\Big)$$

$$= \lim_{n\to\infty} \frac{1}{|\Lambda_n|} H(\alpha_{\Lambda_n}).$$

Proof. Let n be a given integer and $m > n$. Then

$$H\Big(\bigvee_{x\in\Lambda_m} \mathbf{T}^x \alpha_{\Lambda_n}\Big) = H\Big(\bigvee_{x\in\Lambda_m} \mathbf{T}^x\Big(\bigvee_{y\in\Lambda_n} \mathbf{T}^y \alpha_0\Big)\Big)$$

$$= H\Big(\bigvee_{x\in\Lambda_M} \mathbf{T}^x \alpha_0\Big),$$

where $M = n + m$. Since $|\Lambda_M| = (m+n)^N$, $|\Lambda_m| = m^N$, and $|\Lambda_n| = n^N$, we have for any n

$$h(\mathbf{T}, \alpha_{\Lambda_n}) = \lim_{m\to\infty} \frac{1}{|\Lambda_m|} H\Big(\bigvee_{x\in\Lambda_m} \mathbf{T}^x \alpha_{\Lambda_n}\Big)$$

$$= \lim_{m\to\infty} \frac{(m+n)^N}{m^N} \frac{1}{|\Lambda_M|} H\Big(\bigvee_{x\in\Lambda_M} \mathbf{T}^x \alpha_0\Big)$$

$$= \lim_{M\to\infty} \frac{1}{|\Lambda_M|} H\Big(\bigvee_{x\in\Lambda_M} \mathbf{T}^x \alpha_0\Big),$$

and the result follows from Theorem 6.14.

Now to define the mean entropy of an invariant state μ on Ω, we note first of all that for each finite $\Lambda \subset Z^N$, the measure μ induces a discrete probability distribution P_Λ on Ω_Λ defined by $P_\Lambda(\omega') = \mu(p_\Lambda^{-1}(\omega'))$ for $\omega' \in \Omega_\Lambda$.

DEFINITION 6.16. If P is a discrete probability distribution on Ω_Λ, for Λ a finite subset of Z^N, the *entropy* of P is denoted by $S(P)$ and defined by the equation

$$S(P) = -\sum_{\omega \in \Omega_\Lambda} P(\omega)\log P(\omega).$$

If μ is a translation invariant state on $(\Omega, \mathcal{F})$, the *mean entropy* of μ, denoted by $S(\mu)$, is defined by

$$S(\mu) = \lim_{n\to\infty} \frac{1}{|\Lambda_n|} S(P_{\Lambda_n}), \qquad \Lambda_n = \{0,\dots,n-1\}^N.$$

THEOREM 6.17. *If μ is a translation invariant state on $(\Omega, \mathcal{F})$, the mean entropy of μ exists and is equal to the entropy $h(\mathbf{T})$ of the Z^N-action $\mathbf{T}$ on $(\Omega, \mathcal{F}, \mu)$ defined by translation. Consequently, the function S defined on the convex compact subset $\mathcal{I}$ of $\mathcal{M}$ consisting of invariant states on $(\Omega, \mathcal{F})$ is nonnegative, affine, and upper semicontinuous.*

Proof. The theorem follows immediately from Theorem 6.15 by noting that

$$S(P_{\Lambda_n}) = H(\alpha_{\Lambda_n}).$$

We conclude our discussion of statistical mechanics with the notion of an equilibrium state and how it is connected with Gibbs states and entropy. To do this, we introduce the idea of the pressure of an interaction.

DEFINITION 6.18. Let ϕ be a translation invariant interaction. The *pressure* of ϕ, denoted by $P(\phi)$, is defined by the equation

$$P(\phi) = \lim_{n\to\infty} \frac{1}{|\Lambda_n|} \log Z_{\Lambda_n}(\phi),$$

where

$$Z_{\Lambda_n}(\phi) = \sum_{\omega \in \Omega_{\Lambda_n}} \exp(-U_{\Lambda_n}(\omega))$$

is the partition function of the interaction.

The limit in this definition exists for the interactions we are considering. See [162], [131], or [133] for details.

DEFINITION 6.19. Let ϕ be a translation invariant interaction and μ a translation invariant state on $(\Omega, \mathfrak{F})$. The *energy* of the interaction for the state μ, denoted by $\mu(\phi)$, is defined by

$$\mu(\phi) = -\lim_{n\to\infty} \frac{1}{|\Lambda_n|} \sum_{\omega\in\Lambda_n} P_{\Lambda_n}(\omega)U(\omega),$$

where P_{Λ_n} is the discrete probability distribution on Ω_n induced by μ, and $\Lambda_n = \{0,1,2,\ldots,n-1\}^N$.

THEOREM 6.20. *For any translation invariant interaction* ϕ,

$$P(\phi) = \max\{S(\sigma) - \sigma(\phi) : \sigma \in \mathcal{G}\}$$

where $\mathcal{G}$ *is the set of translation invariant states on* Ω.

A proof of this theorem can be found in [35], [162], or [133]. A theorem of this form in a more general setting has been proven by Ruelle [132] and Walters [162].

DEFINITION 6.21. An equilibrium state for an interaction ϕ is any state in $\mathcal{G}$ where the maximum in Theorem 6.20 is attained.

The fundamental result in this area of statistical mechanics is that given an interaction ϕ on Ω, an invariant state is an equilibrium state for ϕ if and only if it is a Gibbs state of ϕ. See [35] and [130] for proofs. As an argument in favor of this statement notice that Theorem 6.2, in the current notation, says that for a finite set $\Lambda \subset Z^N$,

$$\log Z_\Lambda(\phi) = \max\{S(P) - P(U_\Lambda) : P \text{ a discrete probability on } \Omega_\Lambda\},$$

where $P(U_\Lambda) = \sum_{\omega\in\Omega_\Lambda} P(\omega)U_\Lambda(\omega)$, and that this maximum is attained by the Gibbs ensemble.

BIBLIOGRAPHY

1. Abramov, L. M., "On the entropy of a derived automorphism" (Russian), *Dokl. Akad. Nauk. SSSR*, **128** (1959), 647–650. Translation, *AMS Transl.*, Series 2, **49** (1966), 162–166.
2. Abramov, L. M., "On the entropy of a flow" (Russian), *Dokl. Akad. Nauk. SSSR*, **128** (1959), 873–875.
3. Abramov, L. M., and Rohlin, V. A., "Entropy of a skew product of mappings with invariant measure" (Russian), *Vestnik Leningrad Univ.*, **17** (1962), No. 7, 5–13; translation, *AMS Transl.*, Series 2, **48** (1965), 255–265.
4. Aczél, J. D., and Daróczy, Z., *On Measures of Information and their Characterizations*. Academic Press, New York, 1975.
5. Adler, R. A., "A note on the entropy of skew product transformations," *Proc. Amer. Math. Soc.*, **14** (1963), 665–669.
6. Adler, R. A., Goodyn, L. W., and Weiss, B., "Equivalence of topological Markov shifts," *Israel J. Math.*, **27** (1971), 49–63.
7. Adler, R. A., Konheim, A., and McAndrew, M., "Topological entropy," *Trans. Amer. Math. Soc.*, **114** (1965), 309–319.
8. Adler, R. A., and Marcus B., "Topological entropy and equivalence of dynamical systems," *Memoirs Amer. Math. Soc.*, 20, no. 219, (1979).
9. Aizenman, M., Goldstein, S., and Lebowitz, J. L., "Conditional equilibrium and the equivalence of microcanonical and grand canonical ensembles in the thermodynamic limit," *Comm. Math. Physics*, **62** (1978), 279–302.
10. Ambrose, W., "Representations of ergodic flows," *Annals of Math.*, **42** (1941), 723–739.
11. Andronov, A., and Pontryagin, L., "Systems grossiers," *Dokl. Akad. Nauk. SSSR*, **14** (1937), 247–251.
12. Anzai, H., "Ergodic skew product transformations on the torus," *Osaka Math. J.*, **3** (1951), 83–99.
13. Aoki, N., and Totoki, H., "Ergodic automorphisms of T^∞ are Bernoulli transformations," *Pub. Research Inst. Math. Sci. Kyoto Univ.*, **10** (1975), 535–544.
14. Ash, Richard, *Information Theory*, Interscience Publishers, Wiley, New York, 1965.
15. Ash, Richard, *Measure Integration and Functional Analysis*, Academic Press, New York, 1972.
16. Belinskaya, R. M., "Decomposition of a Lebesgue space into trajectories defined by metric automorphisms" (Russian), *Funksjonal' Analiz Ego Prilozhen.*, **2** (1968), 4–16.
17. Berg, Kenneth, "Entropy of torus automorphisms," in *Topological Dynamics* (Symposium, Colorado State University, Ft. Collins, Colorado), Benjamin, New York, 1967, pp. 67–79.
18. Berger, T., *Rate Distortion Theory*, Prentice-Hall, Englewood Cliffs, New Jersey, 1971.
19. Birkhoff, G. D., *Dynamical Systems*, Amer. Math. Soc. Colloquium Publs. Vol. 9, Amer. Math. Society, Providence, R.I., 1927.
20. Billingsley, Patrick, *Ergodic Theory and Information*, Wiley, New York, 1965.
21. Blasburg, J., and Van Blerkom, R., "Message compression," *I.R.E. Trans. Space Electronics and Telemetry* SET-8 (1962), 228–238.

22. Bowen, Rufus, "Topological entropy and Axiom A," *Global Analysis* (AMS Proc. Symposium Pure Math.), **14** (1968), 23–41.
23. Bowen, Rufus, "Entropy for group endomorphisms and homogeneous spaces," *Trans. Amer. Math. Soc.*, **153** (1970), 401–414.
24. Bowen, Rufus, "Entropy of expansive maps," *Trans. Amer. Math. Soc.*, **164** (1972), 323–331.
25. Bowen, Rufus, *Equilibrium States and the Ergodic Theory of Anosov Diffeomorphisms*, Lecture Notes in Math. No. 470, Springer-Verlag, New York, 1975.
26. Breiman, Leo, "The individual ergodic theorem of information theory," *Ann. Math. Statist.*, **28** (1957), 809–811; correction, *ibid.*, **31** (1960), 809–810.
27. Brown, J. R., *Ergodic Theory and Topological Dynamics*, Academic Press, New York, 1976.
28. Callen, H. B., *Thermodynamics*, Wiley, New York, 1960.
29. Chacon, R. V., "Change of velocity in flows," *J. Math. Mech.*, **16** (1966), 417–431.
30. Chu, H., "Some results on affine transformations of compact groups," *Inventiones Math.*, **28** (1975), 161–183.
31. Chung, K. L., "A note on the ergodic theorem of information theory," *Ann. Math. Statist.*, **32** (1961), 612–614.
32. del Junco, A., "Bernoulli shifts induced by *K*-automorphisms," *Adv. in Math.*, **25** (1977), 35–41.
33. Denker, M., "Finite generators for ergodic measure preserving transformations," *Z. Wahrscheinlichkeitstheorie Verw. Gebiete*, **29** (1974), 45–55.
34. Denker, M., Grillenberger, C., and Sigmund, K., *Ergodic Theory on Compact Spaces*, Lecture Notes in Math. No. 527, Springer-Verlag, Berlin, 1976.
35. Dobruskin, R. L., "Gibbsian random fields for lattice systems with pairwise interaction," *Funct. Anal. and Appl.*, **2** (1968), 292–301.
36. Doob, J. L., *Stochastic Processes*, Wiley, New York, 1953.
37. Feinstein, A., *Foundations of Information Theory*, McGraw-Hill, New York, 1958.
38. Feldman, J., "New *K*-automorphisms and a problem of Kakutani," *Israel J. Math.*, **24** (1976), 16–38.
39. Feldman, J., "$\bar{r}$-entropy, equipartition, and Ornstein's isomorphism theorem in R^n," *Israel J. Math.*, **36** (1980), 321–345.
40. Friedman, N. A., *Introduction to Ergodic Theory*, Van Nostrand Reinhold Mathematical Studies, No. 29, Van Nostrand Reinhold, New York, 1970.
41. Friedman, N. A., and Ornstein, D. S., "On isomorphisms of weak Bernoulli transformations," *Adv. in Math.*, **5** (1970), 365–394.
42. Friedman, N. A., and Ornstein, D. S., "Ergodic transformations induce mixing transformations," *Adv. in Math.*, **10** (1973), 147–163.
43. Gallager, R. G., *Information Theory and Reliable Communication*, Wiley, New York, 1968.
44. Gallavotti, G., and Miracle-Sole, S., "Statistical mechanics of lattice systems," *Comm. Math. Physics*, **5** (1967), 317–323.
45. Goodman, T. N. T., "Relating topological entropy and measure entropy," *Bull. London Math. Soc.*, **3** (1971), 176–180.
46. Goodwyn, L. W., "Topological entropy bounds measure-theoretic entropy," *Proc. Amer. Math. Soc.*, **23** (1969), 679–688.
47. Goodwyn, L. W., "Comparing topological entropy with measure-theoretic entropy," *Amer. J. Math.*, **94** (1972), 366–388.
48. Grantmacher, F. R., *The Theory of Matrices*, Vol. II, Chelsea, New York, 1959.
49. Gray, R. M., "Sliding-block source coding," *IEEE Trans. Information Theory*, **IT-21**, (1975), 357–368.
50. Gray, R. M., Neuhoff, D. L., and Ornstein, D. S., "Non-block source coding with a fidelity criterion," *Annals of Prob.*, **3** (1975), 478–491.

51. Gray, R. M., Neuhoff, D. L., and Ornura, J. K., "Process definition of distortion-rate functions and source coding theorems," *IEEE Trans. Information Theory*, **IT-21** (1975), 524–532.
52. Gray, R. M., Neuhoff, D. L. and Shields, P. C., "A generalization of Ornstein's $\bar{d}$-distance with applications to information theory," *Annals. of Prob.*, **3** (1975), 315–328.
53. Gray, R. M., and Ornstein, D. S., "Sliding-block joint source/noisy-channel coding theorems," *IEEE Trans. Information Theory*, **IT-22**, (1976), 682–690.
54. Hall, Marshall, *Combinatorial Theory*, Blaisdell, Waltham, Mass., 1967.
55. Halmos, P. R., *Measure Theory*, University Series in Higher Mathematics, Van Nostrand, New York, 1950.
56. Halmos, P. R., *Lectures on Ergodic Theory*, The Mathematical Society of Japan, 1956.
57. Halmos, P. R., and Von Neumann, J., "Operator methods in classical analysis, II," *Ann. of Math.*, **43** (1942), 332–350.
58. Hartman, S., "Quelques propriétés ergodiques des fractions continues," *Studia Math.*, **12** (1951), 271–278.
59. Kac, M., "On the notion of recurrence in discrete stochastic processes," *Bull. Amer. Math. Soc.*, **53** (1947), 1002–1010.
60. Kakutani, S., "Induced measure preserving transformations," *Proc. Imp. Acad. Tokyo*, **19** (1943), 635–641.
61. Kaplan, W., "Regular curve families filling the plane, I, II," *Duke. Math. J.*, **7** (1940), 154–185; **8** (1941), 11–46.
62. Katok, A. B., "Monotone equivalence in ergodic theory" (Russian), *Izv. Akad. Nauk SSSR. Ser. Mat.*, **41** (1977); translation, *Math. USSR Izvestija*, **11** (1977), 99–146.
63. Katznelson, Y., "Ergodic automorphisms of T^n are Bernoulli shifts," *Israel J. Math.*, **10** (1971), 186–195.
64. Katznelson, Y., and Weiss, B., "Commuting measure preserving transformations," *Israel J. Math.*, **12** (1972), 161–173.
65. Keane, M., and Smorodinsky, M., "A class of finitary codes," *Israel J. Math.*, **26** (1977), 352–371.
66. Khinchin, A. I., *Mathematical Foundations of Statistical Mechanics*, Dover, New York, 1949.
67. Kirilov, A. A., "Dynamical systems, factors, and group representations" (Russian), *Uspekhi Mat. Nauk.*, **22** (1967); translation, *Russian Math. Surveys*, **22**, No. 5, (1967), 63–75.
68. Kneser, H., "Kurvenscharen auf den Ringflächen," *Math. Ann.*, **91** (1924), 135–154.
69. Kolmogoroff, A. N., "Entropy per unit time as a metric invariant of automorphisms" (Russian), *Dokl. Akad. Nauk. SSSR*, **124** (1959), 754–755.
70. Koopman, B. O., "Hamiltonian systems and transformations in Hilbert space," *Proc. Nat. Acad. Sci. U.S.A.*, **17** (1931), 315–318.
71. Krieger, W., "On entropy and generators of measure preserving transformations," *Trans. Amer. Math. Soc.*, **149** (1970), 453–464.
72. Krieger, W., "On generators in ergodic theory," in *Proc. Internat. Congress of Math.* **2** (Vancouver, 1974), Canadian Mathematical Congress, 1974, pp. 303–308.
73. Kushnirenko, A. G., "On metric invariants of entropy type" (Russian), *Uspekhi Math. Nauk.*, **22** (1967), translation, *Russian Math. Surveys*, **22** No. 5, (1967), 53–61.
74. Kwiatkowski, J., and Maniakowski, F., "On the transportation problem used in the definition of Ornstein's distance $\bar{d}$," *Société Math. de France, Asterisque*, **50** (1977), 223–238.
75. Lanford, III, O. E., "Entropy and equilibrium states in classical statistical mechanics," in *Statistical Mechanics and Mathematical Problems*, Lecture Notes in Physics, No. 20, Springer-Verlag, New York, 1971.
76. Langford, III, O. E., and Ruelle, D., "Observables at infinity and states with short range correlations in statistical mechanics," *Comm. Math. Physics*, **13** (1969), 194–215.

77. Lefschetz, S., *Differential Equations*: *Geometric Theory*, 2nd edition Interscience, Wiley, New York, 1963.
78. Lind, D. A., "Ergodic automorphisms of the infinite torus are Bernoulli," *Israel J. Math*., **17** (1974), 162–168.
79. Lind, D. A., "Locally compact measure preserving flows," *Adv. in Math*., **15** (1975), 175–193.
80. Lind, D. A., "The structure of skew products with ergodic group automorphisms," *Israel J. Math*., **28** (1977), 205–248.
81. Loeve, Michael, *Probability Theory*, University Series in Higher Mathematics, Van Nostrand, Princeton, N.J., 1960.
82. Martin, N.F.G., "On the classification of some metric automorphisms defined by Standish," *J. Math. Anal. and Appl*., **62** (1978), 356–367.
83. Miles, G., and Thomas, R. K., "The breakdown of automorphisms of compact topological groups," in *Studies in Probability and Ergodic Theory*, *Adv. in Math*., *Suppl. Studies*, Vol. 2, Academic Press, 1978, pp. 207–218.
84. Miles, G., and Thomas, R. K., "On the polynomial uniformity of translations of the n-torus," in *Studies in Probability and Ergodic Theory*, *Adv. in Math. Suppl. Studies*, Vol. 2, Academic Press, 1978, pp. 219–229.
85. Miles, G., and Thomas, R. K., "Generalized torus automorphisms are Bernoullian," in *Studies in Probability and Ergodic Theory*, *Adv. in Math*., *Suppl. Studies*, Vol. 2, Academic Press, 1978, pp. 231–249.
86. McEliece, Robert J., *The Theory of Information and Coding*, Encyclopedia of Mathematics and Its Applications, Vol. 3, Addison-Wesley, Advanced Book Program, Reading, Mass., 1977.
87. McMillan, B., "The basic theorems of information theory," *Ann. Math. Statist*., **24** (1953), 196–219.
88. Newton, D., "On the entropy of certain classes of skew product transformations," *Proc. Amer. Math. Soc*., **21** (1969), 722–726.
89. Newton, D., "On sequence entropy, I," *Math. Systems Theory*, **4** (1970), 119–125.
90. Newton, D., "On sequence entropy, II," *Math Systems Theory*, **4** (1970), 126–128.
91. Neveu, J., *Mathematical Foundations of the Calculus Probabilities*, Holden-Day Series in Probability and Statistics, Holden-Day, San Francisco, 1965.
92. Neveu, J., "Sur les générateurs d'un automorphisme d'un espace de probabilité," *C.R. Acad. Sci. Paris*, **263** (1966), 83–85.
93. Ornstein, Donald, "Bernoulli shifts with the same entropy are isomorphic," *Adv. in Math*., **4** (1970), 337–352.
94. Ornstein, Donald, "Two Bernoulli shifts with infinite entropy are isomorphic," *Adv. in Math*., **5** (1970), 339–348.
95. Ornstein, Donald, "Factors of Bernoulli shifts are Bernoulli shifts," *Adv. in Math*., **5** (1970), 349–364.
96. Ornstein, Donald, "Imbedding Bernoulli shifts in flows," in *Contrib. to Ergodic Theory and Prob*. (Proc. Conference Ohio State Univ., Columbus, Ohio), Lecture Notes in Math. No. 160, Springer-Verlag, 1970, pp. 178–218.
97. Ornstein, Donald, "An example of a K-automorphism that is not a Bernoulli shift," *Adv. in Math*., **10** (1973), 49–62.
98. Ornstein, Donald, "A K-automorphism with no square root and Pinsker's conjecture," *Adv. in Math*., **10** (1973), 89–102.
99. Ornstein, Donald, "A mixing transformation for which Pinsker's conjecture fails," *Adv. in Math*., **10** (1973), 103–127.
100. Ornstein, Donald, "The isomorphism theorem for Bernoulli flows," *Adv. in Math*., **10** (1973), 124–142.
101. Ornstein, Donald, "An application of ergodic theory to probability theory," *Ann. of Prob*., **1** (1973), 43–65.

102. Ornstein, Donald, "Factors of Bernoulli shifts," *Israel J. Math.*, **21** (1975), 145–153.

103. Ornstein, Donald, and Shields, Paul C., "An uncountable family of K-automorphisms," *Adv. in Math.*, **10** (1973), 63–88.

104. Ornstein, D. S., and Smorodinsky, M., "Ergodic flows of positive entropy can be time changed to become K-flows," *Israel J. Math.*, **26** (1977), 75–83.

105. Ornstein, D. S., and Weiss, B., "Finitely determined implies very weak Bernoulli," *Israel J. Math.*, **17** (1974), 94–104.

106. Osiwaka, M., "Ergodic measure preserving transformations and equivalence in a local sense," *Mem. Fac. Sci. Kyushu Univ. A*, **26** (1972), 193–199.

107. Osteyee, D. B., and Good, I. J., *Information, Weight of Evidence, the Singularity Between Probability Measures and Signal Detection*, Lecture Notes in Mathematics No. 376, Springer-Verlag, New York, 1974.

108. Palais, J., and Pugh, C. C., "Fifty problems in dynamical systems," in *Dynamical Systems—Warwick 1974*, Lecture Notes in Math. No. 468, Springer-Verlag, New York, 1975, pp. 345–353.

109. Parathasarathy, K. R., *Probability Measures on Metric Spaces*, Academic Press, New York, 1967.

110. Parry, William, "Representations for real numbers," *Acta. Math. Acad. Sci. Hungar.*, **15** (1964), 95–105.

111. Parry, William, "On Rohlin's formula for entropy," *Acta. Math. Acad. Sci. Hungar.*, **15** (1964), 107–113.

112. Parry, William, "Generators and strong generators in ergodic theory," *Bull. Amer. Math. Soc.*, **72** (1966), 294–296.

113. Parry, William, "Principal partitions and generators," *Bull. Amer. Math. Soc.*, **73** (1967), 307–309.

114. Parry, William, "Generators for perfect partitions" (Russian), *Dokl. Akad. Nauk. SSSR*, **173** (1967), 264–266; translation, *Soviet Math. Dokl.* **8** (1967), 371–373.

115. Parry, William, "Aperiodic transformations and generators," *J. London Math. Soc.*, **43** (1968), 191–194.

116. Parry, William, *Entropy and Generators in Ergodic Theory*, Mathematical Lecture Note Series, Benjamin, New York, 1969.

117. Pinsker, M. S., "Dynamical systems with completely positive or zero entropy" (Russian), *Dokl. Akad. Nauk. SSSR*, **133** (1960), 1025–1026; translation, *Soviet Math. Dokl.*, **1** (1961), 937–938.

118. Poincaré, H., *Les Méthodes Nouvelles de la Mécanique Céleste*, 3 vols., Gauthier-Villars, Paris, 1899.

119. Posner, E. C., Rodemich, E. R., and Rumsey, Jr. H., "Epsilon entropy of stochastic processes," *Annals Math. Statist.*, **38** (1967), 1000–1020.

120. Renyi, A., "Representations for real numbers and their ergodic properties," *Acta. Math. Acad. Sci. Hungar.*, **8** (1957), 477–493.

121. Robinson, D. W., and Ruelle, D., "Mean entropy of states in classical statistical mechanics," *Comm. Math. Phys.*, **5** (1967), 288–300.

122. Rohlin, V. A., "On the fundamental ideas of measure theory" (Russian), *Math. Sbornik N.S.*, **25** (67) (1949), 107–150; translation, *Amer. Math. Soc. Transl. Ser. 1*, **10** (1962), 1–54.

123. Rohlin, V. A., "On the entropy of metric automorphisms," *Dokl. Akad. Nauk SSSR* **124** (1959), 980–983.

124. Rohlin, V. A., "Selected topics from the metric theory of dynamical system" (Russian), *Uspehi Matem. Nauk. N.S.*, **4**, No. 2 (30) (1949), 57–128; translation, *Amer. Math. Soc. Transl. Ser. 2*, **49** (1966) 171–240.

125. Rohlin, V. A., "Exact endomorphisms of a Lebesgue space" (Russian), *Izv. Akad. Nauk. SSSR Ser. Mat.*, **25** (1961), 499–530; translation, *Amer. Math. Soc. Transl. Ser. 2*, **39** (1964), 1–36.

126. Rohlin, V. A., "Generators in ergodic theory" (Russian), *Vestnik Leningrad. Univ*. Mat. Meh. Astronom., **18**, No. 1 (1963), 26–32.
127. Rohlin, V. A., "Generators in ergodic theory II" (Russian), *Vestnik Leningrad. Univ*. Mat. Meh. Astronom., **20**, No. 13 (1965), 68–72.
128. Rohlin, V. A., and Sinai, Ja., "Construction and properties of invariant measurable partitions" (Russian), *Dokl. Akad. Nauk. SSSR* **141** (1961), 1038–1041; translation, *Soviet Math. Dokl.* **2** (1961), 1611–1614.
129. Rudolph, D., "Non-equivalence of measure preserving transformations," Lecture Notes, Hebrew University, 1976.
130. Ruelle, D., "A variational formulation of equilibrium statistical mechanics and the Gibbs phase rule," *Comm. Math. Physics*, **5** (1967), 324–329.
131. Ruelle, D., *Statistical Mechanics: Rigorous Results*, Benjamin, Advanced Book Program, Reading, Mass., 1969; 3rd printing, with corrections, 1979.
132. Ruelle, D., "Statistical mechanics on a compact set with Z^ν action satisfying expansiveness and specification," *Trans. Amer. Math. Soc.*, **185** (1973), 237–251.
133. Ruelle, D., *Thermodynamic Formalism*, Advanced Book Program, Encyclopedia of Mathematics and Its Applications, Vol. 5, Addison-Wesley, Reading, Mass. (1978).
134. Saleski, A., "On induced transformations of Bernoulli shifts," *Math. Systems Theory*, **7** (1973), 83–96.
135. Saleski, A., "Sequence entropy and mixing," *J. Math. Anal. and Appl.*, **60** (1977), 58–66.
136. Saleski, A., "On mixing and entropy," *J. Math. Anal. and Appl.*, **67** (1979), 426–430.
137. Sataev, E. A., "An invariant of monotone equivalence defining quotients of automorphisms monotonely equivalent to a Bernoulli shift" (Russian), *Izv. Akad. Nauk. SSSR Ser. Math.*, **41** (1977); translation, *Math. USSR Izvestija*, **11** (1977), 147–169.
138. Shannon, C., "A mathematical theory of communication," *Bell System Tech. J.*, **27** (1948), 379–423; 623–656.
139. Shields, Paul C., *The Theory of Bernoulli Shifts*, Chicago Lectures in Mathematics, Univ. of Chicago Press, Chicago, 1973.
140. Shields, Paul C., and Neuhoff, D. L., "Block and sliding-block source coding," *IEEE Trans. in Information Theory*, **IT-23**, (1977), 211–215.
141. Shub, N., "Topological entropy and stability," in *Dynamical Systems—Warwick 1974*, Lecture Notes in Mathematics, No. 468, Springer-Verlag, New York, 1975, pp. 39–40.
142. Sinai, Ja., "On the concept of entropy for a dynamical system" (Russian), *Dokl. Akad. Nauk SSSR*, **124** (1959), 768–771.
143. Sinai, Ja., "A weak isomorphism of transformations with invariant measure" (Russian), *Dokl. Akad. Nauk SSSR*, **147** (1962), 797–800; translation, *Sov. Math. Dokl.*, **3** (1962), 1725–1729.
144. Sinai, Ja., "On a weak isomorphism of transformations with invariant measure" (Russian), *Mat. Sbornik N.S.*, **63** (105) (1964), 23–42.
145. Smale, S., "On dynamical systems," *Bol. Soc. Mat. Mexicana* **5** (1960), 195–198.
146. Smale, S., "Dynamical systems and the topological conjugacy problem for diffeomorphisms," in *Proc. Internat. Congress of Mathematicians* (Stockholm, 1962), Almquist and Wiksell, Uppsala, 1963, pp. 490–496.
147. Smorodinsky, M., "A partition on a Bernoulli shift which is not weakly Bernoulli," *Math. Systems Theory*, **5** (1971), 201–203.
148. Smorodinsky, M., *Ergodic Theory, Entropy*, Lecture Notes in Math. No. 214, Springer-Verlag, New York, 1971.
149. Standish, C., "A class of measure preserving transformations," *Pacific J. Math.*, **6** (1956), 553–564.
150. Sucheston, Louis, "On mixing and the zero-one law," *J. Math. Anal. Appl.*, **6** (1963), 447–456.

151. Sucheston, Louis, "Remarks on Kolmogorov automorphisms," in *Ergodic Theory* (Proc. Internat. Symposium, Tulane Univ., New Orleans, 1961), Academic Press, 1963, pp. 251–258.
152. Swanson, L., "Bernoulli shifts and induced automorphisms" *Advances in Math.* **33** (1979), 93–108.
153. Swanson, L., "Generators of factors of Bernoulli shifts," *Pacific J. Math.*, **71** (1977), 213–220.
154. Thompson, C. J., *Mathematical Statistical Mechanics*, Macmillan, New York, 1972.
155. Thouvenot, J. P., "Convergence en moyenne de l'information pour l'action de Z^2," *Z. Wahrscheinlichkeitstheorie und Verw. Geb.*, **24** (1972), 135–137.
156. Thouvenot, J. P., "Quelques propriétés des systèmes dynamiques qui se décomposent en un produit de deux systemes dont l'un est un schema de Bernoulli," *Israel J. Math.*, **21** (1975), 177–207.
157. Thouvenot, J. P., "Remarques sur les systèmes dynamiques donnés avec plusieurs facteurs," *Israel J. Math.*, **21** (1975), 215–232.
158. Thouvenot, J. P., "On the stability of the weak Pinsker property," *Israel J. Math.*, **27** (1977), 150–162.
159. Uhlenbeck, G. E., and Ford, G. W., *Lectures in Statistical Mechanics*, Amer. Math. Soc., Providence, R.I., 1963.
160. Utz, W. R., "Unstable homeomorphisms," *Proc. Amer. Math. Soc.*, **1** (1950), 769–774.
161. Walters, P., "Some invariant σ-algebras for measure preserving transformations," *Trans. Amer. Math. Soc.*, **163** (1972), 357–368.
162. Walters, P., "A variational principle for the pressure of a continuous transformation," *Amer. J. Math.*, **97** (1974), 937–971.
163. Weiss, B., *Equivalence of Measure Preserving Transformations*, Lecture Notes, Inst. for Adv. Studies, Hebrew Univ., Jerusalem, 1976.
164. Weiss, B., Lectures presented at Regional Conf. Ergodic Theory, SUNY, Albany, N.Y., June 1979.

Index

Index